JAMES MADISON
Secretary of State

JAMES MADISON
By Gilbert Stuart, 1804

JAMES MADISON

Secretary of State

1800-1809

BY

IRVING BRANT

AUTHOR OF

Storm over the Constitution
James Madison: The Virginia Revolutionist
James Madison: The Nationalist
James Madison: Father of the Constitution

ILLUSTRATED

THE BOBBS-MERRILL COMPANY, INC.
PUBLISHERS
INDIANAPOLIS   NEW YORK

CONTENTS

CONTENTS—*continued*

LIST OF ILLUSTRATIONS

JAMES MADISON
Secretary of State

ACKNOWLEDGMENTS

THE author is indebted to the Frick Art Reference Library of New York, and to the owners noted in the illustrations, for the portraits of James Madison, Sr., Nelly Conway Madison, George Clinton, Joseph H. Nicholson, Timothy Pickering and Charles Pinckney. The portrait of Albert Gallatin was furnished by the Metropolitan Museum of Art, New York; that of William Thornton by the National Gallery of Art, Washington, D. C.; that of General James Wilkinson by the National Park Service. All others come from the collections of the Library of Congress.

Valuable assistance in the translation of French diplomatic dispatches was rendered by John de Porry, Armand Darrigrand, Schafer Williams and Beverly H. Brown of the Library of Congress, and by members of the staffs of the French Embassy and Consulate in Washington.

American diplomatic dispatches which had been placed in the State Department files in cipher were deciphered by Hazeldean Brant, who reconstructed the lost ciphers of the Jefferson administration by a patient and skillful comparison of other ciphered letters with their decipherments.

CHAPTER I

POLITICAL REVOLUTION

IN THE presidential election of 1800, a dozen political currents converged to defeat the Federalists and put the Republican party in power. Veterans of the Revolution felt cheated by Hamilton's 1790 funding system, which enriched the speculators who had bought up army pay certificates. Mountain farmers were embittered over the whisky excise which took away their substitute for cash. Southerners and Westerners hated to be taxed to pay off government bonds owned by Eastern financiers.

To agrarians, the Federalist party was an instrument through which merchants and shipowners exploited the agricultural states. The tariff raised revenue from Southern necessities and protected Northern manufactures. Banks were suction devices to draw money into the cities. Thus, while the Federalist system was cementing men of wealth to the party of Alexander Hamilton and John Adams, the Republican party automatically drew together all who resented this way of running the country.

Hardly less potent was the political impact of Europe, in which the Napoleonic wars were dwarfing those of the French Revolution. Federalists were by instinct enemies of that revolution; Republicans were friendly to it, though not to its terrorism. Federalists called their opponents "Jacobins" or "Democrats"—terms so attenuated by overuse that they were now ineffective except in "the Jacobinical rabble" and "scoundrelly," "violent" or "filthy Democrats." The best the Republicans could hurl back was "monarchists," "aristocrats," "Anglophiles," "bloodsuckers." Toned-down passions of the American Revolution still divided men into Whigs and Tories, and the Federalists were not helped by their current alignment with England.

The country was recovering from the patriotic excitement of President Adams' naval war with France and the drummed-up frenzy over Talleyrand's bid for a bribe in the XYZ scandal. During that period of retaliation against seizures of American ships, moderate Southern Republicans became moderate Federalists. The reinforced party passed the Alien and Sedition Acts, ostensibly designed to curb the partisans of France, and went on to triumph in the 1798 elections.

The lofty Federalist edifice was like a collection of boxes and barrels tossed upward at all angles, with President Adams teetering at the top. Whatever move he made, good or bad, was sure to unsettle it. His leadership was guided by his emotional traits —passion, vanity, aggressiveness, patriotism, blunt honesty.

By insisting that the quasi war be paid for, Adams shattered the devotion of thousands of Federalists. Defying a powerful faction which cried for full-scale war, he sent a peace mission to France late in 1799. The rank and file of his party applauded, and joined the Republicans in calling for demobilization of the costly, idle army. The split in Federalist leadership widened to a chasm when Adams dismissed half of his cabinet to get rid of Hamilton's secret domination of it. "Oh mad! mad! mad!" exclaimed that deposed overlord. Far madder was the President who looked on criticisms of himself as violations of the Sedition Act, and madder still the New Englanders who transmuted their lust for power into a divine right of political domination.

James Madison watched these developments from his home facing the Blue Ridge mountains of Virginia. After eight years as the foremost member of Congress, he had left office voluntarily the day before Adams became President. Apparently he had then no desire aside from living quietly on his farm and introducing Dolley Madison to the new home she had but intermittently visited. But to combat the Sedition Act, he drafted the Virginia Resolutions of 1798 and then was drawn into the state legislature to support them with his voluminous Report of January 1800.

Madison's appearance in the summer of 1800 has been described by George Tucker, the biographer of Jefferson, in a memoir found among the papers of William C. Rives, where it was mislabeled as part of the manuscript of Rives's *Life of Madison:*

"He was then nearly fifty years of age, dressed in silk stockings and black breeches, and wore powder according to the practice that still prevailed in full dress. The first [impression] he made on me was that of sternness rather than of the mildness and suavity which I found afterwards to characterize [him]. I saw him at the home of Mr. Monroe, then recently appointed governor of Virginia, on whom I called to deliver a letter of introduction, and I know not whether it was that they were engaged in some matter of grave conference which left its impression on his features when I saw him, or such was the ordinary effect first produced on a stranger but I never perceived it afterwards."[1]

The bitter presidential campaign no doubt produced the gravity. As the Constitution stood then, each presidential elector voted for two men, the second highest becoming Vice President. Contending for a second time, President Adams and Vice President Jefferson keenly recalled that in 1796, a shift of two electoral votes would have made Jefferson President. In that contest, presidential electors were chosen by districts in six states. The fact that struck home was that the majority party got all the electors on a statewide ticket. This drove each party toward the statewide system, wherever victory was certain. Contrary to the intent of the Constitution, some state legislatures had chosen presidential electors, instead of merely fixing the method of choosing. In Pennsylvania, now assuredly Republican, the Federalist Senate at the beginning of 1800 refused to pass any election law whatever. That disfranchised the people and left the choice of electors to a legislature to be elected in October.

Madison, in the Virginia legislature, reacted instantly to this move. "It is proposed," he wrote to Jefferson on January 12, "to introduce tomorrow a bill for a general ticket in choosing the next electors." This was a novel course for Virginians and the bill passed by a majority of only five. As the avowed object was "to give Virginia *fair play,*" Madison thought a statewide election would

become popular. In March he reported that this was indeed the
case. Northerners who said it was abhorred didn't know what
they were talking about.[2]

Federalists now tried to give a congressional committee final
power to accept or reject disputed electoral votes. With Congress
once started on such licentious perversions of the Constitution,
Madison remarked, not even a veto could be counted on, for the
chief magistrate might "be bribed into the usurpations" to secure
his re-election. Indeed the recent unbridled spirit of construction
"would bid defiance to any possible parchment securities against
usurpation."[3]

The Sedition Act, which Madison had in mind, was to expire
automatically on the last day of Adams' term of office. Senator
Mason echoed the belief of Jefferson and Madison as to its purposes when he wrote to the latter in April:

"The most vigorous and undisguised efforts are making to crush
the Republican presses and stifle enquiry as it may respect the
ensuing election of President and Vice President."

Holt of the New London Bee was condemned to three months
in prison and a fine of $200 for criticizing Army influence and
morals. A printer in New York had been fined and imprisoned,
for "what I know not." Haswell, in Vermont, was indicted for
reprinting a critical letter which the discharged Secretary of
War, McHenry, had published with impunity in a leading Federalist paper. Mason described the trial and conviction of lawyer-
editor Thomas Cooper before Justice Chase of the Supreme Court
(riding circuit) and District Judge Peters:

"A more oppressive and disgusting proceeding I never saw.
Chase in his charge to the jury (in a speech of an hour) showed
all the zeal of a well fee'd lawyer and the rancor of a vindictive
and implacable enemy."

Cooper's crime consisted of saying that President Adams had
delivered up a native American seaman "to a mock trial by a

British court martial ... an interference without precedent, against law, and against mercy ... a stretch of power which the monarch of Great Britain would have shrunk from."[4]

Even the historian Hildreth, who thought that six months in prison and a $400 fine were mild punishment for saying that the President exceeded his lawful powers, admitted that the real purpose was "to punish him for his late aid to Duane in insulting the Senate." William Duane, publisher of the Philadelphia *Aurora,* had been ordered to appear before the United States Senate to defend his "false, defamatory, scandalous and malicious" assertion that the bill authorizing a congressional committee to throw out disputed electoral votes was designed (as everybody knew it was) to throw out Pennsylvania's. Duane's lawyers, A. J. Dallas and Cooper, refused to act after the Senate forbade them to discuss the constitutionality of its proceedings. Duane, refusing to appear without them, was arrested for contempt but was indicted for defaming the Senate.[5]

Madison saw some good in these vicious assaults on civic rights. However mischievous in immediate effect, he remarked to Jefferson, the spirit manifested in the Senate "cannot fail I think to aid the progress of reflection and change among the people. In this view our public malady may work its own cure." Such a demonstration of popular sentiment would be more precious, "as the late defection of France has left America the only theater on which true liberty can have a fair trial." It took Napoleon's grasp of power to shatter his faith in revolutionary France.

Madison's legislative report attacking the Sedition Act was now being circulated throughout the country. "It is an inestimable contribution to the cause of liberty," wrote John Dickinson to Jefferson, and appended his astonishment that all the measures of the stupid and selfish Stuarts were being adopted by the posterity of those who fled from their tyranny. Gabriel Duvall wrote to Madison: "The unrelenting severity with which the judiciary are daily executing the Sedition Act fills me with horror." That remark probably furnished the first impetus toward Duvall's appointment, a decade later, to the Supreme Court.[6]

If the Sedition law did not keep Jefferson from writing freely to Madison, partisan control of the post offices did. Knowing that posted letters would be rifled and misused, they agreed late in 1799 that the Vice President should write none except when private conveyance was possible. Madison had written seven times before Hore Browse Trist (grandson of Madison's Philadelphia landlady during the Revolution) stopped next March with the first reply. The Federalists, Jefferson said, were seriously alarmed about the election. In his opinion, the result would turn on Pennsylvania, New Jersey and New York. If Pennsylvania was disfranchised, New York would decide the contest. There the legislature was to name the electors, and its complexion would depend on the city election at the end of April.

Through another messenger, Jefferson sent word that Adams' peace mission had received a friendly greeting from Talleyrand. Madison welcomed the prospect that "the posture of Europe, though dreadful to humanity in general," would impel France to make an adjustment. He could not believe that the Federalist Senate would venture to thwart such a result. Still, the party bent on war had such a horror of the electoral epoch "that every stratagem ought to be suspected that may afford a chance of prolonging their ascendancy." When he was able to report on the spring elections in his part of Virginia, the results were no more striking than the language he used to describe them: "The patrons of usurpation and aristocracy will have little encouragement in this quarter."[7]

To the Federalists, the remedy for the country's troubles was more repression. "The seeds of discontent have been widely scattered," wrote future Senator Dwight Foster to the Reverend Jedidiah Morse, and some had sprouted in the Massachusetts spring election. However, the Alien Act had put one class of critics to flight (European liberals like Volney and Collot) and now the noisy naturalized foreigner Cooper was convicted of seditious libel. Be vigilant and cautious, adjured Foster, "and trust the events to a kind Providence."[8]

But where was Providence when the Republicans made a clean sweep of state assemblymen in New York City and assured the appointment of Jeffersonian electors? Commodore James Nichol-

son saw in that miracle "the intervention of a supreme power and
our friend Burr the agent. . . . His generalship, perseverance, industry and execution exceeds all description." Mat L. Davis
excluded divinity. "To Colonel Burr we are indebted for everything," he told Nicholson's son-in-law, Albert Gallatin, without
much exaggeration. A Vice President was expected from New
York; the eyes of all Republicans there were fixed on Burr.

Hearing the New York thunderclap, Federalists rushed into
secret caucus at Philadelphia. "Hamilton exhibits a figure of rage
and despair," wrote a Virginia observer. Gallatin described Hamilton's plan to salvage victory through the dual voting system.
Adams must be put forward for President in order to carry New
England. With him they would run a popular South Carolinian,
ostensibly for Vice President, who would be elected President if
his own state could be induced to vote for Jefferson and himself.
To further this plan, General Charles Cotesworth Pinckney was
put up with Adams on the Federalist ticket.

At Gallatin's request, Commodore Nicholson talked with
George Clinton and Burr about the Vice Presidency. The governor declined to run because of age and infirmities. The latter
wanted assurances that the Southern states would not desert
him as they did in 1796. On receipt of this word the Republicans
in Congress held the usual caucus (a primitive national convention) and endorsed Jefferson for President, Burr for Vice President.[9]

Before the middle of May the Adams cabinet, as Senator Mason
expressed it, was "splitting and falling to pieces in all its parts."
The ousted secretaries of State and War, Pickering and McHenry,
added their bitterness to Hamilton's hostility. The causes of
Pickering's dismissal, Roger Griswold conjectured, were such
that no man would expound them "who feels any terror from
the penalties of the Sedition law." Three days before the ouster,
Adams denounced Pickering for writing a letter, read publicly
in Boston, filled with hatred of the French peace mission, the sending of which Adams called "one of the most glorious deeds he
ever did." The peace move antagonized not only the embattled
Galliphobes, but practical idealists like Roger Griswold of Con-

necticut, who explained to his brother that by staying at war
with France while England's resources were completely tied up,
the United States might have captured the commerce of the
world. "Our wealth, strength and national character would have
increased and we could have drawn all the benefits of the war to
ourselves without partaking of its evils."[10]

Hamilton was advised to keep his election intrigue under
cover. "No direct attempt can safely be made to drop or supersede
Mr. Adams," wrote Robert G. Harper of Maryland. After electors
were chosen, "let those who think Mr. Adams unfit to be President drop him silently." Secretary of the Treasury Wolcott, still
in the Adams cabinet, stabbed his chief with an opinion to Mc-
Henry that Maryland could make Pinckney President. But John
Rutledge, Jr., after touring New England as a Pinckney scout,
gave Hamilton the saddening information that the Federalist rank
and file was devoted to Adams and "jealous and suspicious of
you in the extreme."[11]

Madison was appealed to for aid and advice. Republican Senator Charles Pinckney, cousin of C. C., besought him to tell South
Carolinians that if their electors voted for both Jefferson and
Pinckney, they might as well not vote for Jefferson at all. Duvall
asked Madison how the issue of Jefferson's unacknowledged and
garbled "letter to Mazzei" (published in 1797) should be met in
Maryland. The decision was to ignore it.[12]

By early summer the campaign of slander against Jefferson was
in full swing, with charges ranging from atheism up or down to
the robbing of widows and orphans. In Virginia, Madison was
made a joint target but his turpitude was less personal. Wrote
Thomas Mason to Norborn Nicholas in June:

"The aristocrats . . . have at last got Madison's character upon
the anvil, and into what shape they will endeavor to hammer it
is not yet exactly ascertained; it is truly melancholy that for several years past no man can support the cause of truth and virtue
but his private reputation is instantly assailed. . . . It galls me
beyond description to see men whose understanding I revere,

whose private virtues I love, and in whose intimacy and friendship I feel happy, thus weighed down."

One preposterous tale was that Madison advised Virginia to resist the collection of federal revenues till the national bank was abolished. Mason concluded that the defenders of the Sedition Act, unable to combat Madison's 1800 Report, were basely assailing his character and motives. The purpose was to create an impression that he had "long meditated a separation of the states," wherefore it must be assumed that Jefferson felt the same way.[13]

In Boston, the *Columbian Centinel* put forth a summer-long serial, "The Jeffersoniad." Atheism, cowardice in the Revolution, hostility to commerce and manufactures, limitless ambition—these furnished successive subjects, with three weeks devoted to the Mazzei letter, whose misprinted word "form" of American government (Jefferson wrote "forms" meaning formalities) was treated as a promise to destroy the Constitution. The people were warned of fearful changes in the President's cabinet: would they exchange Secretary of State Marshall for Madison, Wolcott for the "whisky patriot" Gallatin? "No—my fellow citizens, be not deceived— already are all your honors and all your emoluments appointed among these sons of darkness." Republicans countered with horrid pictures of New England's religious tyranny, lusting to expand.

Jefferson tried to avoid everything "which might drag me into the newspapers." At times, he conceded to Monroe, it was useful to help "the flame of public opinion to break out," but under existing conditions he preferred to rely "on the slow but sure progress of good sense and attachment to republicanism, and build our fabric on a basis which can never give way."

When Jefferson reached home in June, after Congress adjourned, he found that son-in-law Eppes's family had borrowed his carriage wheels, so he reversed a proposed visit by asking Madison to come down. Recent occurrences couldn't be dealt with through the spy-ridden post offices. What that led to is not recorded, but Madison carried home $50 in half dimes which Jefferson had brought for him, and they had evidence that Providence was busy with household finances if not with politics. Labels had been mixed on two packages of money addressed by Jefferson's agent, one to Madison, one to Mrs. Key. It turned out that the sum of the various items in each misdelivered package came to exactly the same amount, $270.[14]

In pamphlets, newspapers and Federalist pulpits the war of words went on. Jefferson, in September, relayed disquieting reports from North and South Carolina. But Congressman Dawson, visiting Madison, had assurance from Nathaniel Macon that the former state would divide nine to three, and Madison had learned in various ways, he told his friend at Monticello, that South Carolina was safe. ("The demagogs," a Charleston Federalist complained to Pickering, "never leave the people to a free unbiased choice.")

Next to bring news was H. B. Trist, who left Philadelphia late in September. He reported, wrote Madison to the presidential candidate, "that the prospect of a vote by Pennsylvania was rather clouded." There was increasing fear that a Federalist Senate would block all methods of choosing electors.[15]

As the intrigue for Pinckney progressed, the war of words widened from Jefferson's irreligion to the stormy passions of Adams. The latter's character, says historian Hildreth, was "hardly comprehensible by the serene and magnanimous Hamilton . . . or the crafty, secretive, dissembling Jefferson." Presumably it was Jefferson's dissembling craftiness that led him to upset his own followers by declaring that "Mr. Adams is as firm and decided a Republican as ever lived."

The serene and magnanimous Hamilton, finding that the mass of Federalists would not switch to Pinckney, wrote, signed and printed a virulent personal and political assault on Adams. This was to have been circulated at first only among Hamilton's friends, to detach electoral votes from Adams, with public distribution after Pinckney's election to justify the switch. But Aaron Burr got hold of a copy (from a dastardly printer or spy, a Federalist said) and gave it to the Philadelphia *Aurora*.

Only Hamilton and the Republicans seemed pleased. Former

Secretary of War McHenry, whose confidential letters had been drawn on by Hamilton to damn Adams, wrote to his idol: "I shall expect never to be again treated by a friend in the same manner. The truth is had you asked me I should not have consented to the publication." Not only was this condemnation omitted from Hamilton's *Works,* but in the manuscript it has been both penciled out and scratched out with blue ink over the faded brown.[16]

From the crucial state of South Carolina, to which Hamilton had rushed the pamphlet, came the moan of H. W. DeSaussure: "It is lamented as an indiscreet, ill-timed publication, likely to produce division among ourselves but utterly incapable of producing any good." Madison concluded that it wounded its author more deeply than its target, yet "has contributed not a little to overthrow the latter staggering as he before was in the public esteem."

Secretary of State John Marshall tried to salvage the South Carolina situation. "I believe," he wrote to General Pinckney, "the Senate of Pennsylvania will maintain their ground." If it did not deprive the state of its vote there might be an 8-to-6 compromise. (He meant 8 to 7.) "This will exclude Mr. Jefferson provided he gets no vote in South Carolina. But it is now reduced to an absolute certainty that any success in your state elects him."

Pennsylvania's holdover Senate lived up to Marshall's hopes by forcing an 8-to-7 division, thus in effect reducing the state to one elector. These senators, rhapsodized the *United States Gazette,* deserved the praises and blessings of all America for having "checked the mad enthusiasm of a deluded populace." Federalist newspapers were claiming victory in South Carolina, but General Pinckney sent a prediction to the contrary. Up-country Republicans were beating the Charleston banking interest.[17]

Madison was one of the Virginia presidential electors who won in a landslide vote in November. The Orange County tally was "340 odd to 7." In all states, the electors were to cast their ballots on December 4. Taking no chances on bad weather, and with Dolley accompanying him, he set out for Richmond eight or nine days ahead of time. This was the reported national standing on the day Virginia cast twenty-one votes for Jefferson and Burr:

Solidly Federalist—all New England, New Jersey, Delaware.

Solidly Republican—New York, Virginia, Georgia, Kentucky, Tennessee.

Pennsylvania, Maryland and North Carolina—Republican 21, Federalist 16.

Totals—Federalist 65; Republican 63.

Unknown—South Carolina 8.

Before Madison left for home, a messenger brought word of South Carolina's appointment of Republican electors. The victory of Jefferson and Burr over Adams and Pinckney was assured. But what of the victors? Jefferson had been *nominated* for President, Burr for Vice President, both must be *voted for* as candidates for President. A tie between them would throw the election into the House of Representatives.

CHAPTER II

BREAKING A TIE

As STATE after state showed unanimity for Jefferson and Burr, the dread of a tie increased. On the day before the Virginia electors cast their ballots, Madison received a letter from Gelston of New York assuring him that votes would be subtracted from Burr in two or three states. "But he does not name the states," Madison reported to Jefferson.

Burr had named one state, however, to Robert Livingston. "It is proposed," he wrote on September 24, "that the votes of Rhode Island be for J[efferson] and Adams," thus putting Jefferson four votes ahead of Burr. Had Madison known of that, he would have realized the significance of October letters from Burr and Gelston, making the astonishing prediction that the Republicans would carry Rhode Island. This was positively reaffirmed by the bearer of the Gelston letter, Joseph Alston of South Carolina, whose impartiality could not be questioned—except by people who knew that he was to marry Theodosia Burr in four months.[1]

Since the Republicans had no chance whatever of carrying Federalist Rhode Island, Burr was actually promising to break the tie *by the votes of Republican candidates who were sure to be defeated*. A tie would be inevitable if the South could be held in line. Gelston's first letter took care of that. Telling Madison of alarming reports from Tennessee, he appealed to him on the highest moral level:

"*Can we, may we* rely on the integrity of the Southern states? . . . We shall be faithful and honest in New York. . . . Rely upon it no exertions will be wanting, no pains will be spared . . . to secure the election of Jefferson and Burr. . . . Pray let me hear from you."[2]

In 1796, Southern electors had voted solidly for Jefferson but scattered their other votes. It was in this light that Madison read

23

the letter from Burr's agent. Gelston, he remarked to Jefferson, betrayed jealousy with respect to the integrity of the Southern states in keeping Burr "in view for the secondary station." That is, Madison construed the appeal, not as an objection to precautions against a tie, but as a move to prevent Burr's defeat for *Vice President*. Accordingly he urged Monroe to guard against "a division of the Republican votes, by which one of the Republican candidates may be lost," and sent assurances to Gelston.

"I hope," he wrote to Jefferson, "the event will screen all the parties, particularly Virginia, from any imputation on this subject; though I am not without fears that the requisite concert may not sufficiently pervade the several states."

Early in November Madison had another visitor, George W. Erving of Boston, introduced by Monroe as a young Republican who wished to discuss the danger of getting "in the first station a friend we did not intend to place there." For some unexplained reason, Erving departed without mentioning the subject. He came back later and did so, but bore a letter from Congressman Nicholas begging Madison not to rekindle the old jealousy and distrust. The latter, in the meantime, had written to Monroe:

"You know my sentiments. . . . I cannot apprehend any danger of a *surprise* that would throw Mr. J. out of the primary station. I cannot believe that any such is intended, or that a single *republican* vote will abandon him. The worst, therefore, that could possibly happen, would be a tie, that would appeal to the H. of R., where the candidates would certainly, I think, be arranged properly, even on the recommendation of the secondary one."

Madison expressed the same confidence when visited by Congressman George Jackson of Virginia. Should there be a tie, "Congress would not hesitate to decide and Mr. Burr would give way." Reminding Madison of these words a few weeks later, Jackson said he was informed that Duvall of Maryland, an elector, would have dropped Burr except for assurances from Madison that the vice-presidential candidate would lose two or three votes in Virginia.[3]

It is clear from this that Madison trusted Burr, also that he went to Richmond intending to forestall a tie. There, just before the voting, he received Gelston's second letter. Burr's lieutenant had just helped choose twelve electors who would vote unequivocally "for our Jefferson." Madison's letter of October 24 had removed many fears and jealousies and Gelston would not resume the subject but for a report from John Taylor of a calculation that "one, two or more votes must be taken from Colonel Burr in order to insure Mr. Jefferson's election as President." He could not believe that such measures were contemplated:

"Integrity and honor we rely upon in Virginia. We shall be faithful and honest in New York. We know that the honor of the gentlemen of Virginia and New York was pledged at the adjournment of Congress. We in this state have our attachments for Colonel Burr. We will not however *even think* of taking a vote from Mr. J. We should consider it as sacrilege."

Then came the decisive part of the letter:

"We are well aware from good information that three states, two at least, will give Mr. J. three or more votes more than Mr. B. will have, but I trust that it never will be said that either Virginia or New York could be guilty of such a subterfuge."

If this statement was true, it not only insured Jefferson's election, but made it impossible to subtract additional votes from Burr without the likelihood of defeating him. Madison appended a footnote to Gelston's statement:

"A confidence that this would be the case induced Virginia to give an unanimous tho reluctant vote for B. as well as J."[4]

Madison had no suspicion, at the time he held the Virginia electors in line for Burr, that he had been deliberately deceived. This charge he put in writing twenty-three years later in a letter to Jefferson which has been buried in the Rives Papers for the last century:

"It is a fact within my own knowledge that the equality of votes which threatened such mischief in 1801 was the result of false assurances dispatched at the critical moment to the electors of one state, that the votes of another would be different from what they proved to be."

To the draft of this letter, which is in Dolley's hand, Madison penciled this footnote: "See letter of David Gelston to J. M."

The conviction of treachery must have been heightened when, in December 1801, Madison heard the story of the New York elector Anthony Lespinard, who refused to give a pledge to vote for Jefferson and was held in line by a last-minute resolution requiring all twelve electors to show their ballots to one another. "We shall be faithful and honest in New York," Gelston had written. Had that brand of honesty worked as planned, Burr would have won the Presidency in the electoral college.[5]

Returns came slowly to Washington, the new capital to which the federal government had just moved. On December 14, having received an incorrect report from Editor Peter Freneau that the tie was broken in South Carolina,[6] Jefferson invited Chancellor Robert R. Livingston to be Secretary of the Navy. The next day the *National Intelligencer* (a new Republican newspaper) published the stunning correction—a tie vote in South Carolina, making one in the nation almost sure.

Alexander Hamilton's son and biographer, erroneously asserting that the tie vote was known in Washington on December 13,[7] accused Jefferson of making the offer to Livingston in order to gain the support of his brother, Congressman Edward Livingston, in the coming contest with Burr in the House of Representatives. The historian McMaster embellished this with the word "bribe." Even if these writers had been right about the dates, their charge would still be false.

Jefferson let Madison know of his letter to Livingston in these words: "I wrote to R. R. L. by a confidential hand three days ago. The person proposed for the T[reasury] has not come yet." Madison knew, without being told, what was in the letter to Livingston and who was to head the Treasury. Since this was Jefferson's first letter from Washington, it indicates that the cabinet appointments were discussed when he stopped at Madison's home on November 24. The offer to Livingston was a gentle way of telling the country's first foreign secretary that he could not be Secretary of State. His refusal apparently was anticipated and his ultimate assignment agreed on, for without a further exchange with Madison, Jefferson offered Livingston the post he accepted—minister to France—his experience outweighing his deafness. That step never would have been taken without Madison's approval.[8]

From Congressman Dawson, late in December, Madison learned that the Federalists were planning to support Burr, "not from a wish to elect him but to prevent a choice by withholding a majority." If they succeeded, who would be President? "In short, what is to become of our government?"

Madison's reply is known from accounts of it by Federalists—"a strong and angry letter" was the description sent from New York to London. Senator Gunn saw it and wrote to Hamilton that "revolutionary opinions are gaining ground." Madison had declared that if the present House did not choose Jefferson President, the next House would have a right to choose between the two highest on the list. He had asserted moreover that the nature of the case and the support of the great body of the people would justify Jefferson and Burr jointly in calling the new House into special session for the express purpose of choosing a President. Gunn continued:

"In other parts of his letter he speaks of America being degraded by the *attempt* to elect Burr President. What say you, my friend?—the little Virginian must have been a little ferocious."

If Madison's physique could be disparaged, not so the effect of his advice. The Jacobins, Gunn believed, had reached a decision to resist the election of Burr at every hazard, and would succeed, for they would "destroy the government sooner than yield their point."[9]

In January, Madison heard from Jefferson that the Federalists

were talking of a "stretch of the Constitution," by which they
would pass a law putting the Presidency into the hands of a President *pro tem* of the Senate. Madison rejected this likelihood:

"Desperate as some of the adverse party there may be, I can scarcely allow myself to believe that enough will not be found to frustrate
the attempt to strangle the election of the people and smuggle
into the chief magistracy the creature of a faction. It would seem
that every individual member who has any standing or stake in
society, or any portion of virtue or sober understanding, must revolt at the tendency of such a maneuver."

Was it possible that President Adams would countenance such
intrigues? Uncertain of the answer, Madison warned against a
project Jefferson had in mind, to seek "a candid understanding"
with Adams as soon as the state of the election was perfectly
ascertained. Friendly attentions were all right, but Adams was
"infinitely sunk in the estimation of all parties." Repeating the
advice he had given Dawson, Madison suggested that in the event
of an interregnum or the intrusion of a President *pro tem,* the
new House be summoned after March 4 "by a joint proclamation
or recommendation of the two characters having a majority of
votes for President." One or the other of these must have the
power to issue the call, so the requisite authority would be included if they concurred. If this was not strictly regular, it was a
defect of constitutional form, not of substance. All the other
remedies proposed were "substantial violations of the will of the
people, of the scope of the Constitution, and of the public order
and interest."

The House, by this time, was in the center of a nationwide orgy
of speculation and intrigue. The Federalists let the *"pro tem"*
idea drop and proceeded, in the words of Senator Gunn, "to
choose among rotten apples." Congressman Harrison G. Otis
saw a chance, by electing Burr, to sow "the seeds of a mortal division" among the Republicans. But, he asked Hamilton, would
Burr act with his new friends and not try to redeem himself with
the old by violent measures? Put no trust in Burr, Hamilton

warned—"a profligate, a bankrupt, a man who laughing at democracy has played the whole game of Jacobinism." Jefferson was far less dangerous and had pretensions to character. But Griswold of Connecticut chose Burr because "it is much safer to trust a knave than a fool," while the Reverend Jedidiah Morse told himself and his father:

"Burr is descended from New England and very pious ancestors. . . . Who knows but that as he is the son of many prayers, he may turn about and become a good man."[10]

Democratic leaders, not yet distrusting Burr, took the emphatic stand that it was the will of the people that Jefferson should be President. A week passed, ten days, and not a word from Burr, while Federalist newspapers dripped with forecasts of his election. "The Democrats are in agonies," wrote Griswold.

Then, on the last day of the year, Congressman Samuel Smith of Maryland published a letter written to him by Burr on December 16. Making Smith his "public proxy," he disclaimed all thought of competing with Jefferson in the "highly improbable" event of a tie.

"As to my friends [wrote Burr] they would dishonor my views and insult my feelings by a suspicion that I would submit to be instrumental in counteracting the wishes and expectations of the United States."

A wave of relief swept over the Republicans. Jefferson called Burr's conduct "honorable and fair." He deserves immortal honor, cried Caesar Rodney of Delaware.[11]

But what did Burr know about the election when he wrote to Smith on December 16? On the seventeenth, the New York *Daily Advertiser* stated that a gentleman who left Washington on December 12 and "arrived here yesterday," brought news of the Republican victory in South Carolina. Whether or not this man carried Freneau's letter (and there are positive indications that he did), nobody who left Washington on December 12 could have failed to hear the report that jumped from house to house the evening before—Jefferson 8, Burr 7. Reaching New York on the sixteenth, that news would have gone instantly to Burr.[12]

So, when he made General Smith his "public proxy" to disclaim presidential ambitions, Burr thought Jefferson had already won by a single vote. What was his attitude after he discovered his error? The suggestion was made to him that he end the controversy by stating publicly that he would not serve if elected. This inspired him to write once more to Samuel Smith: "The suggestion was unreasonable, unnecessary and impertinent, and I therefore made no reply." If he had replied, he would have rejected the request: made a candidate against his will, he now was "insulted by those who use my name for suffering it to be used."[13]

Burr was easily insulted. In his first letter, written when he thought Jefferson had won, he was insulted at the suspicion that he would usurp Jefferson's place. In the second, unpublished letter, written after he knew there was a tie, he was insulted at the request that he refuse to usurp it. In the first, he was a nominee for *Vice President*. In the second, he was a candidate for *President*—made so by people (Republicans) who now insulted him for suffering his name to be so used (by Federalists). Here was an admission that he did permit its use. The only question left was one of tactics. On that point he had sound advice from R. G. Harper:

"Keep the game perfectly in your own hands, but do not answer this letter, or any other that may be written to you by a Federalist man, nor write to any of that party."[14]

Alarmed at Burr's second letter, General Smith met him in Philadelphia on January 4, and gave an account of the interview to Congressmen Christie and Dent of Maryland. He asked Burr what was to be done if the Federal members refused to yield. To his great surprise, Burr answered that "the House could and ought to make a choice, meaning if they could not get Mr. Jefferson they could take him." Smith "came away much mortified."

THE CAPITOL IN 1800
Watercolor by Birch

GEORGETOWN AND FEDERAL CITY
After a painting by G. Beck

Burr and Smith, it happened, were not wholly by themselves at this meeting. Colonel B. Hichborn of Massachusetts talked with both of them in the hotel and wrote immediately to Jefferson:

"Colonel Burr is in the house with me and General Smith from Baltimore has been here. I am convinced that some of our friends as they call themselves are willing to join the other party in case they should unite in favor of Colonel Burr."

Three years later he told Jefferson what Burr said to him: "Our friends must join the Federalists, and give the President." At breakfast next morning Hichborn asked who would be Vice President. "Colonel Burr answered, 'Mr. Jefferson.'"

On his return to Washington Smith wrote quickly to Burr. During his absence, "a Mr. Ogden" of New York had been there, claiming to be in Burr's confidence, and boldly attempted to swing the New York and New Jersey delegations to him. Rely on it, said Smith, eight states would vote to the end for Jefferson. Burr replied that he had said nothing to Ogden, nor anything to contravene his letter of December 16, "but to enter into details would take reams of paper and years of time." It would have taken little of either to get out of the race.[15]

Although the Federalists (thanks to the sweep of 1798) had a majority in the House, each state delegation had one vote in this election and nine were needed to elect. Democratic hopes were pinned on four Federalists: Linn of New Jersey, butt of a standing joke that his delegation had two and one-half in each party; Baer or Craik of Maryland, both of whom had opposed war with France, and Delaware's lone congressman, Bayard. Unknown, then, was Bayard's reply to Hamilton that he was inclined to support Burr, whose friends "distinctly stated that he is willing to consider the Federalists as his friends, and to accept the office of President as their gift." Linn settled his state's position on January 31, by attending a secret caucus in which New York and New Jersey Republicans gave mutual pledges to stand by Jefferson.

Jefferson now needed one state, Burr three, but the Federalists could say: Take Burr or nobody. Congressman Jackson told Madison of the Republican reply: Produce an interregnum if you dare, but look to your banks and your bonds and see if your small states will get so much power in a new Constitution.[16]

So they began to vote on February 11, with Nicholson of Maryland carried in on his sickbed, a snowstorm raging outside, and the result exactly as foretold—eight to six, with two states divided. All night they stayed in session—seventeen ballots up to ten o'clock, twenty-nine by the following noon, and all the same. "We are resolved never to yield," wrote Dawson to Madison. "I have not closed my eyes for thirty-six hours."[17]

With hope for Burr fading, it became "anybody but Jefferson" with the Federalists. Wilson C. Nicholas had just entered the Senate to fill a vacancy. During the balloting, a senator told Congressman John Nicholas that the Senate would elect his brother President *pro tem* and help pass a law making him President of the country. This offer to violate the Constitution fell flat.

The Federalists knew they were beaten. An interregnum would crush public securities. Usurpation meant civil war. "Any attempt to give us a President by law," wrote Dallas of Philadelphia, "will irritate and inflame the calmest and coolest among us. The Federalists of property and character here are terrified and disgusted."[18]

On February 14, after three more fruitless ballots, Bayard notified fellow Federalists that he intended to end the conflict by voting for Jefferson. "You cannot well imagine the clamor and vehement invective to which I was subjected for some days," he told Hamilton. (Bayard's nerves, lamented Griswold, were not strung in a Northern climate.) He did not mention what he claimed five years later: that General Smith gave him assurances as to Jefferson's views on the Navy, commerce, the public debt and the non-firing of well-behaved public officials. But he did write to Collector Allan McLane that his job was safe.[19]

Two ballots on February 17, and an express galloped south for Richmond. At Fredericksburg he dropped a handbill which Storekeeper Fontaine Maury copied for Madison:

"This moment the election is decided. Morris from Vermont absented himself so that Vermont was for Jefferson. The four members that had voted for Burr from Maryland put in blank tickets. The result was then ten for Jefferson. I hope you will have the cannon out to announce the news."[20]

From Jefferson, in Washington, Madison received an account of the final shift. Seeing the impossibility of electing Burr, the certainty that legislative usurpation would be resisted by arms, the Federalists held a consultation. Should they go over *en masse,* or yield only a bare majority and remain as a phalanx of future opposition? The vote revealed their decision. Besides the changes in Vermont and Maryland which raised Jefferson's votes to ten, Delaware and South Carolina put in blanks, leaving Burr four New England states. We consider this, said Jefferson, "as a declaration of war on the part of this band." But Bayard reported that one stubborn man from Connecticut (Griswold no doubt) prevented the Northern Federalists from going over with the others.[21]

In this record there is nothing to support the common opinion that Hamilton brought about the final shift to Jefferson. Creditable as his stand was, it seemingly had no effect. Bayard, callous to Hamilton's portrayal of Burr's character, remarked that Burr could have won "by deceiving one man (a great blockhead), and tempting two (not incorruptible)." His failure to use this chance "gives me but a humble opinion of the talents of an unscrupulous man."

Such an appraisal was absurd. How could the greatest Republican blockhead have been won by *concealing* the commitment demanded by the Federalists, when the *absence* of it failed to win him? As for bribery, Matthew Lyon said that these words were used in seeking his vote for Burr: "What is it you want, Colonel Lyon? Is it office, is it money? Only say what you want, and you shall have it!"

The outcome of the contest, Madison observed to the President-elect, created no surprise in his quarter. It was not thought that the Federalist phalanx would hold out against the revolt of its partisans outside of Congress, "and without any military force to abet usurpation." How fortunate that Congress refused to create such a force, "and what a lesson to America and the world, is given by the efficacy of the public will when there is no army to be turned against it."[22]

From first to last, the work of Burr and his agents supports the charge Madison made against him, that he deliberately produced the tie which threw the election into the House of Representatives. That accomplished, he did all in his power to take advantage of it.

It has been said many times that Burr, though willing to accept the Presidency from the Federalists, lost it by refusing to commit himself to their policies. On the contrary, he followed the only course that could conceivably have given him the place. Every Federalist who wanted a commitment from him was voting for him without one. To get three more states he must have Republican support. As long as he kept still, and avoided overt injury to his party standing, some of the Jeffersonian members might come over. By committing himself to the Federalists, he could have prolonged their support, but would have cut off every chance of getting the Republican votes needed to create a majority.

Had Burr been sincere in his professions, he could have settled the contest at either of two decisive points:

1. He could have arranged for one elector in his own state of New York—someone devoted to Jefferson—to throw away his second vote. Public announcement of that would have assured him the vote of every other Republican elector in the country.

2. He could have stated that he would not accept an office which the voters did not intend him to have.

Had Burr been a man of principle, or had he been shrewd enough to employ the better parts of human nature, he would have taken the lead in forcing the House to elect Jefferson. If he had done that, the future road to the Presidency would have had two figures on it, his own as well as Madison's. But history is not recorded in rejected alternatives.

CHAPTER III

First Minister

Nobody was surprised when President Jefferson nominated James Madison for Secretary of State on March 5, 1801. The offer had been tentatively accepted long before the election, and only extreme partisans questioned its fitness. Federalist William Vans Murray, minister to Holland, predicted his own recall, yet observed that "if Madison be Secretary of State there will be more justice and liberality of opinions on party men. He is the best of them all." For John Dickinson, Quaker pamphleteer of the Revolution, the changes in government opened "a cheerful prospect to those who love their country; and one of the most pleasing circumstances is thy holding thy present station."[1]

Madison had been initiated into diplomacy as a youth of twenty-nine, in the Continental Congress. There, his activity in committees gave him the functions of a foreign secretary before one existed. In his 1780 instructions for a treaty with Spain, in his attitude toward the peace negotiations at Versailles and his later resistance to the soft Spanish policy of Foreign Secretary Jay, he became known as a determined champion of American claims to Western territory and navigation of the Mississippi. In the new Congress of the United States, from 1789 to 1797, he was an aggressive supporter of American rights at sea and in foreign trade, a friend of revolutionary France, and an implacable opponent of British mercantilism.

Jefferson besought Madison to come to Washington in advance of the change of administration. Such a forecast of his entry into the cabinet would assuage the Federalist minority "and inspire in the majority confidence and joy unbounded." Congressman Dawson wanted both him and Monroe there, to restrain the policy of conciliating Federalists. Jefferson needed "the aid of men of decision."[2]

35

Madison did not go, but offered some thoughts on the newly arrived peace convention with France. In the Senate, the Federalist war party was fighting ratification because, to obtain peace, the commissioners violated their instructions by throwing the question of indemnities for commercial losses into the future. Also, senators objected to the surrender of captured warships and privateers, of which the United States held eighty-nine, France none. "As the stipulation is mutual," Madison observed, "it certainly spares our pride," allowing ratification on the score of self-interest. The public mind, he remarked, was already sore and jealous of the Senate because of Jay's British treaty of 1794. It would abhor an unjust or unnecessary war. If there was anything inadmissible in the convention, better give it a qualified ratification "than rush into a provoking rejection."

Justice and prudence, he thought, could steer the United States peacefully through its difficult situation. France was showing friendliness. Great Britain, "however intoxicated with her maritime ascendancy," must look to this country for bread for herself and supplies for her West Indian islands. The prospect of a neutral confederacy in North Europe should inspire caution toward the United States—the only other source of naval stores.[3]

Here was an indication both of the policies Madison wished to follow, and the way in which he would approach them. Justice and prudence, devoted to peaceful achievement of national aims— these were to be his guides and his objectives, and even now he was seeking to penetrate the thinking of his adversaries.

In this same letter, Madison told why he could not go to Washington at once and might not be able to go at all:

"My health still suffers from several complaints, and I am much afraid that any changes that may take place are not likely to be for the better. The age and very declining state of my father are making also daily claims on my attention, and from appearances it may not be very long before these claims may acquire their full force."

Madison's illness had started at Richmond in December—an attack of rheumatism which increased after his return in spite of "temperance and flannels." Although these considerations jeopardized their contemplated arrangement, it was not his purpose "to retract what has passed in conversation between us on that head." Apart from this, it would be awkward to appear on the political theater before he was regularly called to it, and he doubted the utility of doing so.

Following his victory over Burr, Jefferson sent a new and urgent appeal to Madison to come immediately after March 4. The latter made ready to go, as the health of his father seemed to revive. "A few days past, however," wrote James, Jr., on February 28, "he became sensibly worse, and yesterday morning rather suddenly, though very gently, the flame of life went out."

James Madison, Sr., lacked one month of being seventy-eight when he died. Fatherless after the age of nine, he had lived from early childhood on the Orange County estate, enlarging it through the years by land purchases and the increase of slave families which he refused to break up or send to their deaths in Southern swamps. Only the old people could remember when he was not the foremost "squire" of the region. Justice of the peace, vestryman and sheriff, he had been county lieutenant in the Revolution, committeeman, army recruiter and wagon builder. The brilliance and fame of his eldest son never impaired the father's primacy in community affairs.

Shortly before his death the senior Madison settled his long-standing open account with Thomas Barbour. Everything had been put down—salt, wagon wheels, a pound of Jesuit's bark in 1778, beef and brandy for the army, debts collected or paid as agent, including thousands of pounds in continental currency still to be translated into a few score hard dollars. In 1779, he noted, "you had my old mill gudgeon and steps . . . say what you think they were worth." On May 9 and June 4, 1787, "I lent you four gallons of brandy, for which you promised to return me good rum." Please send it. And how much was due to Madison "on the profits of the sheriff's place for the two years you acted in my stead?" Running through it all was the note of trust in a neighbor's word, and the statement closed with a hint of what was to come: he was fatigued by making out the account.[4]

When the will was opened, Madison found himself executor, with plenty of work ahead. The testament had been written thirteen years before, with both specific and residuary bequests to his wife and children. Since then, Ambrose and Francis Madison had died intestate, the latter leaving many minor heirs. Since a division of the land called for "amicable negotiations, concessions and adjustments," the new Secretary of State hoped that the other heirs would allow for "the political lien" to which he had subjected himself.

To determine, among other things, whether a residuary bequest of slaves included or excluded the heirs of the two children who had died, it was decided that James as executor should bring a friendly suit against all the other heirs and let the court decide. The list of defendants was a family roster: Nelly Madison, the widow; William, son and acting executor; three daughters and their husbands: Isaac Hite and Nelly his wife, Thomas Macon and Sarah his wife, Robert H. Rose and Frances his wife; also Nelly Conway Madison, only child and heiress of Ambrose, and the nine children and one son-in-law of the late Francis Madison. The court limited the residuary shares to the children still living. Dr. Rose and Frances, dissatisfied on some other point, brought a suit of their own, which included "a great scope of demand."[5]

James Madison, to whom the family home had been left, proceeded to make trades with the other heirs. The jointly owned mill on the Rapidan was sold, and Madison acquired the older one—half a mile down the road to Gordon's—by deeding more than a thousand acres to the three other owners. Dr. Rose and wife were pacified with 551 acres for their mill share and certain claims to lands in Kentucky and Virginia. James was left with three farms of about 5,000 acres, running compactly from the top of the Southwest Mountains to the Rapidan.[6]

Had the Madison heirs been inclined to quarrel, there was plenty of opportunity in a heavy bag found in the house. In 1835, when General William Madison found it necessary to establish a reputation for financial disinterestedness, he appealed to Dolley's memory of an incident in 1801. She wrote:

"I recollect that soon after the death of Father Madison a bag of gold said to have been left in his desk was a subject of frequent conversation in the family, all of which left me under the impression that it was presented as a gift by common consent of his children to their mother. I remember also hearing Mrs. Rose mention her brother William Madison's having placed the bag in the hands of his mother."[7]

"Mother Madison," sixty-eight years old when her husband died, was given separate quarters to the right of the central hall, and lived independently for the next twenty-eight years.

During March, Madison received brief accounts of the cabinet. Attorney General Levi Lincoln, called by Jefferson the ablest Republican in New England, was acting as Secretary of State. General Henry Dearborn had taken over the War Department. Gallatin was not yet nominated for the Treasury—to prevent immediate rejection by the Federalist Senate, he would receive a recess appointment. Livingston, General Smith and John Langdon all had refused the Navy post. Samuel Dexter and Ben Stoddert, mild Federalists, were staying on for a time in these two places. What a misfortune, the President observed, that Robert Morris was in debtor's prison! He would be a most valuable man for the Navy.

President Adams had found that the government would run itself during his long stays in Quincy. Jefferson seemed to think it would do as well now. He wrote to Lincoln from Monticello on April 10:

"I reached this place on the 4th having passed an evening with Mr. Madison who is in as good health as for some time past, but that is very indifferent. He will set out for the seat of government about the time I shall."

During that evening, Jefferson no doubt heard praise of his inaugural address, with its call for freedom of speech and press, for wisdom and frugality in the conduct of affairs. In the declaration against entangling alliances Madison saw a rewording of his own doctrine, indorsed by Congress eighteen years before and repeated in Washington's Farewell Address. But what of that seductive remark: "We are all Republicans: we are all Federalists"? The motive of it Madison must have approved—to bring moderate Federalists into the Republican party—but his own superaccurate pen would have excepted the Essex Junto.

Related to this was the question of retaining or discharging the Federalists who for six years had monopolized federal offices. In Washington Jefferson had outlined a system—to oust anybody guilty of official misconduct, but not to discharge men for political reasons, except to break the Federalist judicial monopoly by appointing Republican attorneys and marshals. This was tentative, the President wrote to William B. Giles: "Madison and Gallatin being still absent, we have not yet decided on our rule of conduct."

The judiciary issue had been dramatized by President Adams' appointment of twenty-three "midnight judges," following a last-minute enlargement of the judiciary designed to make it a Federalist bastion through the Democratic storm. Jefferson was able to tell Madison that some of the commissions had not been delivered, and he had ordered them withheld. He could not foretell that this would put the Secretary of State's name into one of the most famous lawsuits in American history, *Marbury* v. *Madison,* with the facts of which he had only a tenuous connection.

The outgoing President, Madison had commented in February, did not manifest "a very squeamish regard to the Constitution." Some of the appointments he considered void, since Adams had shifted public officials to the courts and filled their old offices before they were vacated.[8]

Jefferson's visit with Madison on April 3 apparently brought two major decisions. Following it, the President wrote that Congress would be asked to repeal the law creating the new circuit judgeships—a course which would eliminate the holders of them. Also, seeking suitable nominees for district attorney and marshal in Virginia, he required that they be most respectable, and Republicans, for that is "the only shield for our republican citizens against the federalism of the courts."

Madison's departure for Washington, with Dolley and her sister Anna, was delayed by an intensified illness which kept him in bed for three or four days. Jefferson spent the night of April 26 with him and sent back highway advice. To avoid being tipped over on the Ravensworth Road, he should go by way of Fairfax Courthouse. Farmers were engaged to haul his carriage over Bull Run Hill, the worst ever seen on a public road, though not so bad as the mudholes of the Centerville route. Dinner would be held for him until four o'clock. The ride must have served as a tonic, for after his arrival on May 1, Madison was reported "better than when he left home." The oath of office was administered next day by a "midnight judge" who escaped the purge—William Cranch, brother-in-law of Abigail Adams.[9]

Four years had passed since Madison last saw the raw city emerging from the Maryland forest. Two white edifices dominated the sylvan scene—the new Capitol, with one wing completed, and the President's sandstone "palace." The latter was flanked by the square brick Treasury building and the combined offices of State and War, both replacing buildings recently destroyed by fire. The two main centers of government were connected by a mile-and-a-half stone footway bordering Pennsylvania Avenue—a streak of mud newly cut through woods and alder swamps.

Along that avenue, wrote Gallatin to his wife, "not a single house intervenes or can intervene without devoting its wretched tenant to perpetual fevers." Of all the radiating avenues and intersecting streets which were to surround the Capitol, most were invisible. Some were rows of stumps, and only New Jersey Avenue toward the south gave a suggestion of metropolitan development. It had houses on each side, but fell away so steeply toward the Eastern Branch (the Anacostia) that wood and coal carters could barely climb it with their loads.[10]

Shacks and houses and magnificent estates were scattered through the woods, but the principal built-up section of Washington followed a single highway that pierced the wilderness between the President's house and Georgetown. At what is now Washington Circle (Pennsylvania Avenue and Twenty-second

Street) stood the Six Buildings, temporarily housing the Department of State. The square between Nineteenth and Twentieth streets, north of the avenue, contained the Seven Buildings and half a score of lesser habitations. East of the President's house, five or six houses had been built in a single block, with others scattering. Grouping was useful, for there were robbers in the city, but no police.

While Federalists moaned over living conditions which they could not ascribe to Jacobin misconduct, the new President found the environment more satisfactory. The Madisons, he wrote to his son-in-law in June, had been living with him since their arrival, but went to housekeeping toward the end of May. "We find this a very agreeable country residence, good society and enough of it, and free from the noise, the heat, the stench and the bustle of a close built town." Federalists accused him of collecting rent from his guests.[11]

Before he left Virginia, Madison was invited by Dr. William Thornton, designer of the Capitol, to live with him on F Street east of Fourteenth. On his arrival, Thomas Law attempted an eastward pull. Law, an Englishman who made a fortune in India, had outdone George Washington by building nine houses on Capitol Hill. (Washington built two.) But, he complained, most were empty because all executive officers and diplomats lived west of the President's house, and congressmen who could afford hackney coaches were gravitating in that direction. If, wrote Law, Madison's health would permit him to live in one of these for a few months, "a great change must soon take place and the General's spirit (if terrestrial concerns ever claim attention) will with joy look down and see his favorite object fulfilled."

Madison's convenience, if not his health, persuaded him to stay close to his own offices, which were being slowly transferred (it took months) from the Six Buildings to the new structure. In that square brick building, a diplomat wrote, he "received foreign ministers in a very indifferent little room into which they were ushered by his clerk."

Temporarily, it seemed, Madison lived in one of the Six Buildings. His health, Jefferson noticed, sensibly improved and he hoped it was due to "the application of his mind to things more congenial to it than the vexatory details of a farm." Madison's own prognosis, after a severe setback with bilious fever, was that if he could get quickly into the pure air he breathed at home, he would "have a more flattering prospect than . . . for nearly two years past."[12]

Leaving for Virginia, Madison gave instructions to Thornton, who was to look for a new house. He should promise no advance rent, because the Secretary had borrowed $1,000 for household equipment—only $250 less than his quarter's salary. Nicholas Voss, a contractor, was building next to Thornton's house—an ideal location—but needed the whole first year's rent ($600) in advance. Dr. Thornton borrowed the money, first deducting the interest, and put Voss under bond to complete the house by October 1. He ordered the third floor divided into four dormered bedrooms and the cellar into wine and coal rooms, with a cupola on the roof "for security against fire." Still to be constructed were a coach house and stables for four horses. The whole ménage was on a lot measuring 27 feet 8 inches by 113 feet 8½ inches at what is now 1333 F Street, Northwest.[13]

Thanks to Dolley Madison's genius for hospitality and her husband's conversational gifts, their house quickly became a social center. The President, living alone, was aided at dinner parties and receptions by the wives of cabinet members, and the main part of this congenial duty fell on Dolley. The Madisons' location, two blocks east of "the palace," reduced the social pull of Georgetown, and when the Spanish minister took one of Law's houses near the Capitol, his lavish dinners helped to bring hungry congressmen back to the Hill.[14]

Remaining on his farm from July until October 1801, Madison established a pattern which he followed for sixteen years. Like Jefferson, he wished to be away from Washington during the season of malaria and bilious fevers. With continuous contact needed between these two, the affairs of government went more smoothly when they were thirty miles apart in Virginia than when one of them was in the capital. Special mail routes were set up and couriers brought important dispatches. A constant stream of notes passed between them and personal visits were frequent.

Visitors too flowed in, including diplomats, foreign travelers, scientists, public men, youths out to see the country. Dr. Thornton's French wife entered in her diary on September 5, 1802: "Arrived at Mr. Madison's country seat about 110 miles from the city of Washington." It was in a wild romantic country covered with flourishing timber. The house was "upwards of eighty feet in length" (proving that the wings had not yet been added) of a "plain but grand appearance rendered more pleasing by displaying a taste for the arts which is rarely to be found in such retired and remote situations." From the house they could see the Blue Ridge, sometimes obscure and far away, sometimes sharp and distinct and often like rolling waves. The grounds were then being developed, and when this work was completed, the approach would rival the most beautiful to be found in Sandby's views of English country seats.

After a fortnight Bishop Madison and his son arrived and on the following morning the two Madison families and the Thorntons set out for Monticello. They reached the foot of the mountain after dark, and, wrote Mrs. Thornton, "had it not been for the lightning was played almost incessantly we should not have been able to have seen the road at all." At last it became so dangerous that "all but mama" (Mrs. Brodeau) walked the remaining three quarters of a mile, arriving just ahead of a deluge of rain.

Monticello, as usual, was in a litter with rebuilding. It had been "so frequently pulled down and rebuilt" that it looked like a house going to decay. The outlook was beautiful, yet, as Mrs. Thornton saw it, there was "something grand and awful in the situation but far from convenient or in my opinion agreeable—it is a place you would rather look at now and then than live at."

During their week's stay another Thornton arrived—Edward, the British chargé d'affaires, who had been at the Natural Bridge and Sweet Springs. Jefferson took this occasion to unlock his library and show some of his fine prints. A southeast storm held Madison and his guests for an extra day. They stopped overnight at John Walker's on their return, where "Mr. Madison had to

borrow two of Col. W's horses, three of his having gone off." After
dining with the manager of Madison's Black Meadow farm, they
reached home at sunset.[15]

Madison was more inclined to receive guests than to be one.
Thanking General Gates for an invitation to his "hospitable mansion," he said he must deny himself the benefit ("pleasure" truthfully crossed out) because, "In my relaxations from this place
[Washington] I am obliged to keep in mind that I am a farmer
and am willing to flatter myself that my farm will be the better
for my presence." To some observers, these farm activities did
not look like relaxation. In August 1803, Dr. Thornton wrote to
him:

"I hope for the character of Orange and particularly of Montpelier you will not expose yourself to the fatigues that your industry may prompt you to call pleasures as you traverse your extensive domains."

That may be the first written reference to the name of Madison's estate. Dolley wrote of going "to Montpellier" in 1804, and
Madison began three years later to date his letters from that place
instead of Orange. Montpellier, France, not Montpelier, Vermont, was in his mind, and he never liked what he called the
"Yankee trick" played on the French spelling. But virtually nobody else doubled the "l" and even he forgot to do so during the
War of 1812.

Madison's interest in scientific farming made him a member
of the Farmers' Society of Sandy Springs, Maryland, and in 1803
he became the first president of the American Board of Agriculture. This was an association of farm groups, initiated by the
Quaker farmer-engineer Isaac Briggs, and organized at a meeting
called by Madison in the Capitol. Blessed by Jefferson, it had the
active support of Dr. Samuel L. Mitchill, Dr. George Logan (the
pacifist plowmaker, now a senator) and members of Congress
from all over the Union. In soliciting Madison's help, Briggs referred to their agreement on the need for an Agricultural Experi-
mental Garden. Briggs felt sure "of the coincidence of thy opin-

ion with mine that agriculture, scientifically understood and judiciously and industriously followed, is the surest basis of our national happiness, dignity and independence."[16]

The difficulty of mixing statecraft and farming was described by Edward Thornton's successor, Legation Secretary Augustus J. Foster. About to return home, he journeyed through Virginia in August 1807 (the trip greatly raising his opinion of America) and spent some time with Madison, of whom he wrote in his "Notes on the United States":

"No man had a higher reputation among his acquaintance for probity and a good honorable feeling, while he was allowed on all sides to be a gentleman in his manners as well as a man of public virtue."

Directly at Montpelier, Foster found, Madison had a farm of about 1,200 acres. During his long absences he was obliged to trust a great deal to his overseer, who received £60 Virginia currency per annum and all living expenses. Madison assured him "that after providing for this overseer; clothing his Negroes and deducting the expenses for repairs," the profits did not exceed the overseer's pay. He had however two other farms from which the income was larger though very fluctuating. Tobacco and corn were the principal produce.

"The expense of a Negro he estimated at $25 or $30 a year according to the situation, and you can only calculate, on an average, upon half the number of slaves being fit for service at any given time. . . . The Negro habitations are separate from the dwelling house both here and all over Virginia, and they form a kind of village as each Negro family would like if they were allowed it, to live in a house by themselves. . . . They appeared to me to be a happy thoughtless race of people when under a kind master as was the Secretary of State."

Great depredations, Madison told Foster, were committed in the depths of his forests when he was long away. The owners of village tanyards employed people to bark his trees and for several years a neighboring overseer had been breaking off the branches and tops of his pines in order to make and sell lampblack. There were wild turkeys in great numbers on Madison's place "and I very much regretted not having brought my fowling piece as the Secretary of State had none to lend me."

Foster went through the workshops, finding "a forge, a turner's shop, a carpenter and wheelwright; all articles too that were wanted for farming or the use of the house were made on the spot and I saw a very well constructed wagon that had just been completed." Women slaves, preferring field work to spinning, were unwilling to make their own clothes, "yet the cloth they did make was superior to the coarser English cloth because they threw the wool of best quality into the stuff in which the English use the worst."

In retrospect, Foster described Jefferson as more of a statesman and man of the world than Madison, who was "too much the disputacious pleader." Yet the latter "was better informed, and, moreover, was a social, jovial and good humored companion full of anecdote, and sometimes matter of a loose description relating to old times, but oftener of a political and historical interest." These traits seem to have impressed all associates. George Tucker wrote of Madison:

"Though mild and gentle in his manners and conversation he had an unfailing good humor and a lively relish for the ludicrous which imprinted everything comic on his memory and thus enabled him to vary and enliven his conversation with an exhaustless fund of anecdote."

J. K. Paulding described him after a thirty-years' acquaintance:

"He was a man of wit, relished wit in others and his small bright blue eyes would twinkle most wickedly when lighted up by some whimsical conception or association."

The personal traits thus indicated were not evident to the eminent historian who wrote an article in 1938 entitled, "If James Madison had had a Sense of Humor." Yet that does no more violence to fact than diplomatic histories which do not even mention that Jefferson had a Secretary of State.[17]

CHAPTER IV

To the Victor Belongs One Half

Entering upon his State Department duties in May 1801, Madison found work piled up because diplomatic notes were unanswered: the President "did not wish anything important done without receiving his advice." It was a situation in "little accord with my unsettled health," and forced a complete discontinuance of private correspondence. Sixteen years passed before the old free flow of letters was resumed.[1]

American diplomats consisted of ministers, Barbary consuls (salaried), other consuls (paid in fees), Jay Treaty commissioners, and agents for American seamen. Seven clerks were inherited from Secretaries Timothy Pickering and John Marshall. Publisher William Duane, who barely knew Madison, sent a man-by-man description of the staff to Gallatin. The top three, headed by Chief Clerk Jacob Wagner, were "complete picaroons" (not thieves, but disciples of Pickering). The others consisted of a Hamiltonian, a nothingarian, a nincompoop and one modest man. Madison cut off one picaroon to save money. The nincompoop, Daniel Brent, still held his job in 1837, when he told President Van Buren that his message to Congress "reminded him of Mr. Madison who he thought understood the use and value of words better than any other man."

The chief clerk was in effect an undersecretary. Wagner had intended to resign (he wrote to Pickering) but was "dissuaded on public grounds" by Marshall. Instead he asked Madison whether his resignation was desired. The answer: he seemed qualified for the work, and honor and delicacy could take the place of political conformity. Mr. Madison, Wagner commented, was certainly an amiable and moderate man, from whom he expected nothing but justice. He intended, however, to make no concession beyond "a neutrality of conduct between the belligerent parties. My opinions shall never be sacrificed." A year later,

48

seriously ill and laboring under "heavy oppression and gloom," Wagner sent the Secretary a shakily written letter of resignation in which he expressed "gratitude and thanks for your uniform kindness." Madison kept him on salary for three months (until he refused it), held the place open as long again, and then invited him to come back, which he did. It was a bit hard on the Secretary himself and on the other clerks, who complained that four men were doing the work that eight men did in the Adams administration.[2]

United States consuls, who were also merchants, furnished the Madison and Jefferson tables with French, Italian, Spanish and Portuguese wines, in heavy demand for official and semiofficial dinners. This was but a shift of agents. James Yard of Norfolk wrote in 1800 that he was sending Madison twenty cases of Madeira, partially paid for long before. No doubt, he commented, "you must long since have given over every hope of seeing one drop of this deposit—our friend Monroe is in the same situation with this difference that he has got angry with me." He would have been more attentive had he thought the triumph of republicanism was so near, but "my fear that this precious liquor would be prematurely consumed . . . induced me to keep it back till I thought it fit for use, which it will now be in one year." Madison soothed Monroe's feelings with a reference to Yard's "usual pleasantry."

As American consuls lived by exporting European goods, filling wine orders was normal business. It sometimes seemed, however, that insecure officials were the most zealous in adding personal touches. After Consul William Lee at Bordeaux assured Madison of the falsity of the charge (emanating from Pickering circles) that he had attempted to collect an illegal commission, he put on board the brig *Lyon* "two small boxes for yourself and the President of the United States containing each a *paté de Perigueux* composed of partridges and truffles. These pies are in great estimation in Europe and . . . are eaten of sparingly." Merchant Thomas Newton, port surveyor at Norfolk, furnished Madison with wine from Brazil and "made many efforts to procure you some crab cider." Some traffic was in the opposite direction, as when United States Consul Wichelhausen of Bremen, a Prussian, offered hearty thanks for two boxes of Montpelier peach brandy carried to him by his brother.[3]

Applications for office poured in on Madison. Tench Coxe, who yearned to be Secretary of the Treasury, would take less. Cousin Hubbard Taylor wanted to be United States marshal for Kentucky. Pierce Butler asked that "any little place in the post office" be given Philip Freneau, now indigent. "Oh, in pity be so kind," supplicated the French dancing master who drilled Madison's nieces and nephews at Orange Courthouse. But if no office was available he would "kiss the hand which chastises me and say *delende est Gaullier."* Charles Peale Polk had a logical argument: the Federalists, who had all the money, wouldn't employ a democratic portrait painter.

One application furnished Madison with an oft-told dinner-table story. A newspaper writer whose coarse attacks on Federalists injured his own party came for his reward. He wished to be governor of a Western territory. There were competitors with superior claims, the Secretary replied. A collectorship would do. Or a post office. The man came down and down until he reached his final request. Did Madison have any old clothes he could spare?[4]

Harder to deal with was Publicist James Thompson Callender, one of Judge Chase's Sedition Act victims. Convicted in a barbarously misconducted trial, Callender spent nine months in the Richmond jail for his criticisms of the Adams administration. One of Jefferson's first actions was to pardon him and remit all penalties, but this took place just after he had paid a $200 fine. Jefferson ordered the fine returned, but the marshal refused to accept the legal opinion of the Attorney General. Callender waited several weeks, while past sufferings, poverty and alcohol worked upon his mind. Then he complained to Madison—the only man in the new administration "whom I could without hypocrisy profess to feel an attachment for." Does the President reflect, he asked, on what might happen if a small piece of history should be delivered to his enemies? He never had trusted Jefferson, and if he received anything from the new administration he would be "much disposed to ascribe it entirely to you." What he wanted was to be postmaster at Richmond. Think it over, he advised, and meanwhile let Mr. Jefferson reflect that "it is not proper for him to create a quarrel with me." Governor Monroe wrote to Madison that Callender had called on him twice, bitter, unstrung and weeping, trying to borrow money for a trip to Washington. Then Callender showed up in Madison's office.

"It has been my lot [the latter reported to Monroe] to bear the burden of receiving and repelling his claims. What feelings may have been excited by my plain dealing with him I cannot say, but am inclined to think he has been brought by it to some reflections which will be useful to him. It is impossible however to reason concerning a man, whose imagination and passions have been so fermented. Do you know too, that besides his other passions, he is under the tyranny of that of *love*."

The presumably young and beautiful object of his flame, Madison wrote, was in Richmond, and in a sphere above him. He had flattered himself "that the emoluments and reputation of a post office would obtain her in marriage. Of these recommendations however he is sent back in despair."

Callender received his $200, but went forward into besotted drunkenness and publication of the foulest calumnies of Jefferson. Without reviling Madison, he blamed him in part for the delay, leading Gallatin to point out that Madison had nothing to do with the refunding. Callender stopped his slanders when he stumbled drunkenly into the James River and was drowned in three feet of water.[5]

In July, by direction of the President, Madison issued orders dropping the long-delayed trial of William Duane in federal court for libeling the Senate. But, the Senate's instruction to prosecute being still in force, the district attorney should either proceed under some state law that did not violate the Constitution, or give an official opinion against such action. That ended the case. The Senate was slapped on the cheek instead of the teeth, and seditious libel slumped into a well-earned grave.[6]

Jefferson's emphasis was on economy. "We are hunting out and abolishing multitudes of useless offices, striking off jobs, and never were such scenes of favoritism, dissipation of treasure and disregard of legal appropriation seen," he wrote. The President gladly enforced an act signed by Adams, ordering much of the Navy sold. Thomas Paine told him of an idea he had given Napoleon, of building a vast armada of small, cheap gunboats for invasion of England. Conceiving that these would do equally well for harbor defense, Jefferson made them the basis of his naval policy, with not the happiest results.[7]

By midsummer of 1801, patronage policies were taking shape. Senator Nicholas urged Madison to oppose wholesale removals, which would invite corruption and antagonize Federalists who might otherwise be won over. But if (though he hoped not) Postmaster General Habersham was slated for removal, Nicholas would be willing to take his place. Since Jefferson, without consulting Congress, had decided "to consider the post office as within the Department of State," Madison replied without consulting the President. If a change were to be made, he doubted whether a Virginian would be selected, although "the individual spoken of by you" would be perfectly desired, except for robbing another important station (the Senate) of his services.

Removals and appointments, Madison remarked, were embarrassing the Executive and producing discord among their friends. In Connecticut "the fever and murmur of discontent" over one removal (the jerking out of a last-minute Adams appointee) had produced a remonstrance to the President "in the strongest terms that decorum would tolerate." The spirit in that state "must be rectified by a peculiar mixture of energy and delicacy."[8]

Federalist decorum was typified by the assertion of President Dwight of Yale that democratic victory had given us "a country governed by blockheads and knaves." Two days after Madison's comment came Jefferson's reply to the New Haven remonstrance. It informed the Federalists that they would lose 50% of the offices they now monopolized, and that the rate of change must be faster than that produced by slow deaths and no resignations. By implication, this told the Republicans to expect only half of what they were so loudly calling for. The effect, however, was to increase their clamor for that half and make them hope for the remainder.

Gallatin brought the issue to a head by sending the President a proposed circular to collectors. He wished to tell them that in filling minor positions they should be guided solely by integrity and capacity; also that they ought to enjoy full freedom of opinion and suffrage, but "any exercise of official influence to restrain or control the same rights in others" was destructive of republican government. Madison happened to be with Jefferson when he opened the draft. Agreeing thoroughly in principle with the proposal, they "both thought it better to be kept back till the New Haven remonstrance and answer have got into possession of the public." Also, they both thought an equilibrium should "be first produced by exchanging one half of their subordinates," after which merit alone should rule. Whenever the reaction to the New Haven papers indicated a proper state of the public mind, Gallatin might send out a circular either with or without consulting the President.

Three years later, during the campaign of 1804, Jefferson complained to Gallatin that federal officers were meddling too much with public elections. Shouldn't that be stopped? The Treasury chief reminded him of his original proposal "which you, as well as Mr. Madison, thought premature." They all hated to admit that they were dealing with uncontrollable pressures from hungry partisans.[9]

The heaviest of these came from New York, magnified by the competitive ambitions of the Burr, Clinton and Livingston factions. The first three New York appointments, in April, brought Madison an alarmed protest from Samuel Osgood, his ancient antagonist in the Continental Congress. The men named were entirely devoted to Burr and had it been in their power "Mr. Jefferson would not have been President." The Vice President was now telling everybody that he had not been consulted. Then by whose influence, a Federalist commented, did the United States marshal's job go to John Swartwout, "notoriously the runner and tool of Burr on all occasions?"[10]

Burr's two chief henchmen, Matthew L. Davis and David Gelston, were yet to be taken care of. For them, he demanded the posts of naval (customs) officer and collector of the port of New York. At an interfactional conclave, Gelston was agreed to by all, and Burr was told that Davis was slated for the customs job. However, the list sent to Jefferson named Congressman Theodorus Bailey for naval officer and Davis for a lesser post. Burr protested to Gallatin that Bailey was "utterly incompetent." He then assailed the fitness of Congressman Linn of New Jersey for an appointive office. It was Linn who swung the New Jersey delegation to Jefferson and paved the way to his election.

Gallatin brought this revealing document to Washington in mid-May, by which time Madison had received Osgood's warning and the advice to consult Governor Clinton. He and his nephew DeWitt Clinton were then sweeping local offices from governor to lamplighter and had little interest in federal posts, but were quick to resist Burr's use of them to control the state and gain national ascendancy. The solution proved simple. The Federalist naval officer was not removed. Burr raged to Gallatin about "secret machinations" against his man: "Davis is too important to be trifled with."[11]

The final act of the melodrama took place in Virginia. One day in September, Mat Davis came riding up to Madison's house. Goaded (wrote Burr) "by the instances of an hundred friends," he was en route to Monticello for a showdown with the President. Davis carried a letter from Gallatin to Jefferson which glowingly indorsed his fitness for the naval office but described the creation of a vacancy for him as "yielding to that general spirit of persecution, which, in that state particularly, disgraces our cause and sinks us on a level with our predecessors." Madison asked Davis to take with him, to Monticello, a packet of letters from the State Department. As he was writing the covering note, more letters arrived, and he concluded: "The inclosed very confidential letter from DeW. Clinton was brought by Mr. G. [John Graham] very apropos to be forwarded to you." The nature of that letter may be judged by one which Clinton wrote a few weeks later to James Cheetham, naming the men who worked with Burr in 1800 to capture the Presidency, and were now endeavoring to bring the administration into disrepute and thereby place Burr in the presidential chair.[12]

Carrying his death warrant with him, Davis rode to Monticello. He arrived about the same time as a fast-traveling private letter from Gallatin which completed his destruction. The first necessity, said the Pennsylvanian, was for Republicans to decide who was to succeed Jefferson when he should think fit to retire.

"Where is the man we could support with any reasonable prospect of success? Mr. Madison is the only one, and his being a Virginian would be a considerable objection."

The Constitution, Gallatin pointed out, would bar a Jefferson-Madison ticket in 1804, both men being from the same state. So the party must either support Burr for Vice President once more, or arrange to scatter the second electoral votes. In the first instance, they would be giving Burr a pledge of eventual support for the Presidency, if the Federalists didn't put him in at once by intrigue. Had he realized in advance, said Gallatin, the total want of confidence felt by Republicans toward Burr, he never would have consented to his nomination for Vice President. However, in New York he still had the backing of a majority, and if Mat Davis was refused the office he wanted, the refusal "will by Burr be considered as a declaration of war." That was enough. Without waiting to hear what his visitor had to say, the President wrote to Madison and Gallatin that he would tell Davis nothing could be decided until the cabinet reassembled in Washington.

Davis rode back to New York, where he became "exceedingly clamorous and loquacious" against the administration. The Federalist whose place he wanted remained in office for two years, and the post then went to Osgood, whose letter to Madison first sounded the warning against a future rival for the Presidency.[13]

In contrast, Federalist Postmaster General Habersham was finding it hard to say yes or no. Resigning in the summer of 1801, he asked Madison for a judicial appointment and then refused it. Madison received the refusal on September 3, while at Monticello. The same post brought Jefferson the resignation of United States Treasurer Meredith. The place was offered to Habersham, who asked for time and then refused it or any other office. The sequence completely disproves the assertion of Habersham's Federalist biographers that he resigned because he construed the Treasury offer as a request to do so.[14]

During the summer Jefferson completed his cabinet. John Langdon refused the Navy post a second time. It would be the delight of his heart, he wrote to Madison, to take part in the administration if the decline of life (he was sixty) did not forbid, but nothing could give more general satisfaction than Madison's presence in it. Representative Samuel Smith had been looking after the Navy, and the President finally handed the portfolio to Robert Smith, his vain, half-competent, ambitious brother.

Ability and personal ties put Madison in the top cabinet position. Ability alone made Gallatin head of the Treasury. Geographic selections furthered the two political imperatives—to break the Federalist hold on New England and offset Northern jealousy of Virginia and the South. Hence the naming of two Massachusetts men, Lincoln and Dearborn, while not a solitary place went to the five Republican states of the Southern and Western perimeter.

Jefferson, like Washington, submitted policy questions to a vote of the cabinet, but not in the same self-abnegating way. Surer of principles than of methods, he wanted the chastening effect of advice on his own impulsive judgment, yet pride made him reluctant to change a declared position. The result was constant informal consultation with those he most relied on, commonly followed by cabinet ratification. But what would be the relative position of the two men whom everybody recognized as the cabinet leaders? The British chargé d'affaires, Edward Thornton, gave his opinion to Lord Hawkesbury less than a month after they took office:

"It is to this gentleman [Gallatin] and to Mr. Madison that I would turn your lordship's attention as the ministers likely to enjoy the whole of the President's confidence and to influence the most powerfully all his actions: they may hereafter be rivals for his favor and in the event of a contest there is room to think that notwithstanding the ties of friendship by which the latter is united to the President, the talents for business, the great application, the superior art, and above all the greater force and decision of Mr. Gallatin's character would finally triumph."

Thornton did not overrate Gallatin's qualities. But like all diplomats on first contact, and like the public in general, he underrated Madison's. It was as true then as when French Chargé Otto said it in 1787, that "one must study for a long time in order to make a fair appraisal of him." The Federalists, instead of waiting for a Madison-Gallatin contest to develop, invented a topsy-turvy one. Judge Walter Jones, after a visit at Madison's home, sent him an extract from a friend's letter: "I hear that Mr. Madison is to resign, Mr. Levi Lincoln to succeed him and Mr. John Nicholas to be appointed attorney general." Jones elaborated:

"I suppose you have heard how the directors of the federal party have labored to impress the opinion generally that a very serious schism has taken place in the administration—that the President has given himself up to the direction of Mr. Gallatin and the violent Jacobins of the East, and that the most merciless persecution of their opponents is to follow, that you and some others viewed these measures with extreme disgust and much more such stuff, as is calculated to shake the attachment, the hopes, or the confidence of the weak and lukewarm. The above report is a portion of this plan."[15]

This rumor was at once a reflex of prejudice and fear, and an appeal to those emotions. For years the Federalists had been using Gallatin as a whipping boy because of his foreign birth, his French accent and his defense of the "whisky rebels" of western Pennsylvania. When, in Congress, he gave evidence of great financial talents, this only made him appear more dangerous. The Swiss-born Treasury head seemed more of an extremist than Madison because he dove head-on into obstacles which the latter went around. Jefferson felt the prod of his driving energy, but had there been rivalry for the President's favor, Gallatin would have been hopelessly outclassed. He was forgiven a bluntness which, had Madison employed it, would have torn Jefferson's soul asunder and broken a great friendship.

In preparing his first annual message to Congress in the fall of 1801, Jefferson sent the draft to Madison, asking for an immediate revisal both of matter and diction. Two days later he sent it to Gallatin, with the observation that several paragraphs were "to be altered or omitted according to further information." In the final draft he struck out a long paragraph declaring that the Sedition Act was unconstitutional and he was treating it as a nullity. "It was thought better," he noted on his fair copy, to omit this "as capable of being chicaned and furnishing something to the opposition to make a handle of." Since nothing was said to Madison on the subject, it is obvious that the advice to omit came from him.

"What belongs to the departments of State and War," Jefferson wrote Gallatin, are "in unison with the ideas of those gentlemen." He had not consulted the Treasury or Navy heads, presumably because he wanted to shape his own policies of economy and tax reduction. Gallatin offered many criticisms which strengthened the President's position and they were readily accepted.[16]

Jefferson, Madison and Gallatin formed one of the greatest administrative teams in American history. They supplemented one another, and were bound together by basic unity and friendliness. Jefferson symbolized the love of liberty, the hopes and aspirations of the plain people, and could evoke their support, almost their worship, in all sections not dominated by the Federalist clergy. He and Gallatin held an identical belief that the best government was one that taxed little and spent less.

Fundamentally a philosopher, Jefferson was also a man of action, but somebody had to keep his speculations from running away with his policies. That help he had from Madison's analytical mind, working with strategic skill in the broad field of international and domestic policy. These two set the course and held the steering oar together.

CHAPTER V

First Look at Europe

On the evening of May 1, 1801, Chargé d'Affaires Louis Pichon went eagerly to salute the President, who had returned from Monticello two days before. With him he found Madison, who arrived that afternoon, and other department heads. Pichon himself had reached America only seven weeks before, but this thirty-one-year-old diplomat was no stranger, having been legation secretary under Ministers Genet and Fauchet. To Talleyrand, that same night, he wrote of the friendly treatment he received, and made some comments on American policy. Federalists greatly feared that Jefferson would join the Northern powers (Russia, Sweden, Denmark and Prussia) in the armed neutrality against England, but the truth was that if the President was for the compact, he would do no more than rejoice at its success.

"He will be, like his predecessors, very pacific, and will be as much so toward England as toward us; toward us, with the greatest sincerity."

Courage and insight were needed to produce that prediction, for Pichon was instructed to work for American entrance into the armed neutrality. But such traits won him this assignment. Sent to Holland in 1798 to persuade Minister Murray that France's desire for peace was not to be measured by the XYZ scandal, he first converted Talleyrand to a new policy by sending evidence that President Adams was more pacific than his emissaries. Then "good Mr. Pichon," as the American minister called him, made such effective use of Talleyrand's response that Murray reversed his position and advised Adams to send the mission that ended the quasi war.[1]

England, too, lacked a minister, but Chargé Thornton knew the country from long experience. In Spanish affairs, Madison would deal with Don Carlos Martinez d'Yrujo, son-in-law of Governor McKean of Pennsylvania. President Adams had demanded his recall, but Jefferson, knowing "the integrity, sincerity and reasonableness of his conduct," requested his continuance. Yrujo hoped that Madison could end the uncertainty which "keeps us yet wandering like a Gipsy family from place to place." Mme. d'Yrujo (Sarah McKean) needed only this assurance, her husband wrote, in order "to embrace again her old friends and take the proper measures to fix our winter quarters, which we hope will not be distant from yours." They arrived in February.[2]

To cut expenses, all American legations were ordered closed except in England, France and Spain. Rufus King was left in his London post. Robert Livingston was held back to await Bonaparte's reaction to the Senate's emasculated ratification of the French treaty. An appointment to Madrid rewarded Charles Pinckney for his political services.

Madison began his work just as the flames of war were dulling to embers on the continent of Europe. Bonaparte, dictatorial First Consul, had smashed the Second Coalition and dismembered the Holy Roman Empire. Unknown, as yet, was England's surprise attack of April 2 on the Danish fleet, which ended Napoleon's scheme of an armed confederacy of neutrals. The United States, barely out of its naval war with France, was about to enter another.

Following European practice, the Washington and Adams administrations had paid annual tribute to the beys and deys of Northern Africa, for protection of commerce from piracy. Payments to Algiers were three years in arrears. Tripoli was demanding more money. Jefferson's cabinet voted unanimously, on May 15, to send four warships to the Mediterranean to protect commerce, but the promises to Algiers must be fulfilled. Madison had a list of presents made up, including loaf sugar, coffee, pepper, china dishes and tea sets, India and Irish linen, five redbirds, two squirrels and four mahogany logs. It was hoped, he wrote to Consul Eaton, that Tunis and Algiers would not follow Tripoli's perfidious example, but should they do so, "their corsairs will be equally repelled and punished." The frigates had not yet sailed when the Bey of Tripoli cut down the flagpole of the American consulate—his method of declaring war.[3]

A few days after taking office, Madison notified Thornton that belligerent warships could not lurk in American seaports and pounce on near-by enemy merchantmen. He cited a 1794 order limiting hostile vessels to twenty-four hours in port. The British diplomat complained in turn that a Spanish armed ship had brought a British prize up the Delaware, and newspapers suppressed the story to cover the landing of the cargo. This, he alleged, not only violated the treaty of 1794, but conflicted with a 1793 ruling made by Jefferson as Secretary of State. Madison disagreed on the first point. The treaty forbade the entry only of national privateers—not of private vessels carrying letters of marque. But he and the President agreed the prize must leave.[4]

In conveying decisions, Madison always used the language, "The President has decided." This not only encouraged historians to ignore the Secretary of State but led to some peculiar results at the time. Thus, in the summer of 1801, Thornton protested that French prisoners had overpowered their guards and brought the English snow *Windsor* to Boston. He wished it to be declared a prize taken by France, and ordered away under the treaty of 1794. Madison, at Montpelier, referred the question to Jefferson, in Monticello, suggesting a reply "that the case is not considered as within the purview of the treaty." The vessel could then be sent away under the rule invoked against the Spanish prize at Philadelphia.

Jefferson thought the vessel must be considered as a prize "to which no shelter or refuge is to be given in our ports according to our treaty." He favored expulsion both in this and the Spanish case, but, "wishing you to revise this opinion of mine I refer it back to yourself to give the order for departure or any other answer you think best." Madison wrote at once to Gallatin: "It was readily decided that the treaty of '94 is inapplicable to the case." The President "has thought, as I do," that the ship should be sent away under the Spanish precedent. When Thornton received his answer he declared himself "entirely at a loss to comprehend the grounds on which the President is pleased to regard the cases . . . as in no manner falling within the provisions of the treaty of 1794." Madison used the President's name even in reversing him.

This action involved no reversal of policy. Thornton was contending that a clause in Jay's treaty became applicable to France on suspension of the Franco-American treaty of 1778. Jefferson did not realize that admission of this claim would make it harder to place the prizes of the two countries on a parity. It proved easier to convert the President than to persuade federal officials to obey orders. Visiting Madison's estate a year later, Thornton complained that the *Windsor* had been illegally condemned and remained in Boston until European peace made recapture impossible. "Perfectly irregular and illegal," Madison termed this conduct, but the only remedy lay in court action. Thornton dropped the case because the customs officers were Federalists and he didn't want them fired.[5]

Of the diplomatic issues in 1801, none was more difficult than that presented by the French colony of St. Domingue, universally called St. Domingo by Americans. There the revolted General Toussaint Louverture ruled half a million Negroes who had thrown off slavery and dominated fifty thousand whites and as many mulattoes. Holding a commission in the French army, he considered himself as good a Frenchman as Napoleon Bonaparte, who rose to power in much the same way. First establishing his primacy in the French part of the island (Haiti), Toussaint had driven out his mulatto rival, General Rigaud, and occupied the larger Spanish portion (Santo Domingo) which had been ceded to France in 1795 but never transferred.[6]

During the naval war with France, the Adams administration sent Dr. Edward Stevens (Hamilton's boyhood friend in the West Indies) to the island with the title of consul general. He became Toussaint's trusted adviser, and helped engineer an agreement between the black chief and British General Maitland by which Toussaint agreed not to engage in ocean commerce or privateering, provided the sea lanes were kept open for supplies from America. Stevens resigned in January 1801, but remained at his post until summer.

In March, Pichon sounded President Jefferson and was told that the United States could not act contrary to French rights in

St. Domingo without helping to throw the island into the hands of the English. This seemed to reverse the Adams policy.[7]

There was no hint of a change, however, when Dr. Stevens was succeeded in June by Tobias Lear, onetime private secretary to President Washington. Lear was instructed that the only restrictions legally possible were such as could be drawn from the law of nations, from treaties, or from regulations within St. Domingo. Consequently the United States "expect no interruption or vexation will be given to their commerce whilst pursuing its legitimate course"—no British seizures.

To spare the feelings of First Consul Bonaparte, Lear was called a commercial agent instead of consul, and was given credentials to a locality, Cap Français, not to the rebel general. But he and others were sent in disregard of French regulations which excluded commercial agents from colonies. As to Toussaint, Lear was told:

"You will conform to the intention of the President by an amicable and conciliatory line of conduct, regulated by the principle of neutrality, towards all powers, internally or externally connected with the island."[8]

These instructions harmonized with the momentary (and unknown) policy of Napoleon, who, unable to send an army to overcome Toussaint, had just declared him captain general of St. Domingo. But they contradicted the assurances the President had given to Pichon, who repeatedly questioned Madison and found him "very reserved on this matter." Late in July, knowing that the Secretary had talked with returning agents, Pichon undertook "to discover the opinions of the government either by his absolute silence or by nonequivocal clarifications."

Madison readily gave the names of Lear and other new agents. Informed that it would be a fitting mark of confidence in the First Consul to communicate their instructions, he replied that *the United States took things in this colony as they found them, without presuming to judge,* and desired only to continue their commerce." It was important to them, to be sure, that France should recover the colony, but the administration could not risk getting embroiled with Toussaint. As for news brought by the old agents, Pichon "ought to know what was not any secret at St. Domingo, that all is ready for a coming declaration of independence," and in the Secretary's opinion, England did not favor it any more than the United States. "This," said Pichon, "was all I could get out of Mr. Madison."

The dismayed diplomat hastened to Jefferson. "I told him," he reported to Talleyrand, "that from the equivocal and reserved language of Mr. Madison, I did not know but that the United States favored Toussaint's project." Jefferson denied this. But as France could not act, the United States could do nothing. Commerce with the island was important, and suspension of it would bring on a needless row with Toussaint and gravely compromise the government in public opinion. Pichon remarked that suspension of commerce would drive Toussaint into the arms of England, but if France herself were to act against the rebels, would not joint action with the United States be possible? "Without difficulty," replied the President, and electrified Pichon with his next words:

"But for this joint action to be complete and effective it would be necessary that you make peace with England. Then nothing would be easier than to supply everything for your army and navy, and to starve out Toussaint."

Jefferson assured Pichon that American public opinion did not back the Negro rebel. His example represented the greatest danger to two thirds of the states. England herself shared this fear, and no doubt would join in stamping out the rebellion. Piracy was another danger, and England had no more desire than the United States to see "St. Domingo become an Algiers in American waters."[9]

Jefferson's statement made a profound impression on Napoleon. St. Domingo was the military keystone of French power in the Western hemisphere—the base from which France, once free of

PRESIDENT THOMAS JEFFERSON
After a painting by Gilbert Stuart

DOLLEY MADISON
By Gilbert Stuart, 1804

British naval restraints, might establish and protect a new empire on the North American continent. Secretly, in the yet undisclosed Treaty of San Ildefonso, Bonaparte had begun this process. The old French province of Louisiana, lost by France in the Seven Years War, had been retroceded by Spain in 1800. It was to be delivered after Napoleon should give a yet nonexistent kingdom (Etruria) to the son-in-law of the King of Spain. Without St. Domingo, Napoleon could not hold and organize this vast territory. With the Caribbean island firmly in his grasp, he might build Louisiana into a populous colony and absorb other Spanish provinces as he chose—the Floridas, Cuba, Mexico—with a possibility of taking over the American West.

On this basic issue, Jefferson and Madison thought alike. The former, however, hearing of Toussaint's declaration of independence, reacted to his fear of a servile insurrection. Madison, after a returning consul told him of the coming event, remarked that it presented "many important aspects to the United States, as well as to other nations," and proceeded in total disregard of its example to American slaves.

To the reports of the retrocession of Louisiana, which had been coming since May, the two men had identical reactions. Unwise and very ominous, the President called it. Madison thought it fitted the shift of France from revolution to conquest and dictatorship. If it went through, French policy would be "conciliatory to the minds of the western people"—a soft term for seduction to disunion. He did not know that a South Carolinian in Paris had warned Joseph Bonaparte that French proximity to the West would sow the seeds of inevitable war by reviving the spirit of insubordination there.[10]

American measures in Europe would have to await the arrival of Ministers Livingston and Pinckney. Outlining the Executive's views to the latter, in June, Madison emphasized the probability that France was taking Louisiana out of fear that Britain would do so. This, he asserted, was unlikely without American co-operation, which the clearest policy forbade. Livingston was to lead France to see and shun the danger of collisions growing out of contiguity of territory.

Meanwhile, Madison made this a task for himself in the conference on St. Domingo which so alarmed Pichon. Turning to Louisiana, the Secretary said that the reported transfer was announced by London in terms that did not permit doubt. Then (Pichon reported) "summoning up the most circumspect and studied expression he could," he added that if this measure had been projected during the late naval war, it was to be hoped that France would abandon the idea now that peace was re-established. The French monarchy, in the treaty of 1778, had renounced the expectation of possessing anything in North America. The French revolutionary government turned once toward that idea, but sacrificed the project when the United States objected. With France holding Louisiana, the navigation of the Mississippi would cause daily collisions, which would be made dangerous by the remoteness of the two governments.

The United States, Madison assured the French envoy, did not feel any concern for its own safety. With the growth that was taking place in the West, any forces France could have in Louisiana need cause no worry. He was thinking solely of a good understanding. The Americans were accustomed to the Spaniards, and regarded them as peaceable, though absurd in their prohibitions.

Pichon replied that he knew nothing concerning the truth of the rumors. But several times since the Revolution, France had sought to reacquire Louisiana. Did the United States wish to go beyond the Mississippi? "Madison regarded this idea as a chimera." As for navigation, Pichon resumed, didn't Europe have common waters, heavily used? "It is different here," replied Madison. "There is no means of avoiding quarrels."

Surely, said Pichon, the United States would not make it a crime for France to recover lost territory. Her principles were more enlightened than those of Spain. What if the Republic offered an agreement covering all points that could cause dispute? Madison repeated that if the transfer took place, it would almost certainly bring on a collision.

Pichon apologized to his superior for venturing into this debate without instructions. But the conversation "was too categorical, the circumstances too urgent," for him to remain passive. The transfer of Louisiana, he warned, would carry the germ of a future conflict if the choice of men was not made with most scrupulous attention, and if, from the outset, France herself did not know how to act on all points that concerned American security and commerce. Adopting Madison's argument, he pointed out that Kentucky had increased in fifteen years from 60,000 to 250,000 souls, and was shipping millions of dollars of produce through New Orleans.[11]

But what about St. Domingo, the key to Louisiana? In spite of all that Jefferson had said, the policy Pichon suspected Madison of following seemed to remain in effect. The *National Intelligencer,* official organ of the government, had greeted the proclamation of Dominican independence with "prodigious eulogies of General Toussaint, his qualities, his genius, his nobleness." Since the President and Secretary of State were by this time in Virginia, Pichon could not suppose that they inspired these articles. Nevertheless, he declared to his foreign secretary, "I am not far from thinking that they reflect the principles of regard and extreme reserve which have been adopted and are being followed toward Toussaint." Pichon was convinced that the instructions to Lear were conceived in that spirit, for he had delivered an address to American merchants at Cap Français which was precisely of the sentiments expressed in Washington, Lear pledging his best efforts to maintain good relations between the United States and the colonial government "under which we reside."[12]

During the summer, American policy toward the European war began to take shape. Livingston, conferring with Jefferson and Madison, was told that the United States would stand aloof from the armed neutrality. But it saw the value of a general treaty, open to all nations, supported by commercial penalties against *future* belligerents who interfered with the commerce of neutrals. The new minister to France, hungry for authority, asked Madison for credentials to the Russian, Scandinavian, Dutch and Italian courts to work on such a project. Instead, he received an unofficial letter from the President ostensibly explaining his position, but actually reversing the stand he had taken in 1793, when he got rid of clamorous demands from Minister Genet by agreeing with the British doctrine that enemy-owned goods, even if noncontraband, could be searched for and seized in the ships of neutral nations.

Pichon, for some months, refrained from speaking of American entry into the armed neutrality, "even to the Secretary of State." Passive neutrality, he concluded, was fixed on the country by the President's genuine devotion to it, and by hunger for riches drawn from war trade. But in the enthusiasm of his July talk with Jefferson about General Toussaint, he hinted at American membership and remarked that Russia's defense of ocean commerce had made England more deferential to the United States. England also knew, the President replied, that the United States government "is in the hands of persons who are not disposed to suffer as much as those who preceded it. If every time they arrested one of our sailors, the government had seized an English merchant here, you would have seen this power conducting itself very differently."[13]

As sailors were still being impressed, the contrast with Adams was not wholly realistic. But a stiffening policy was also evident in what Madison was writing to Rufus King, who was endeavoring to revise Jay's treaty. Duty to public rights and sensibility forbade the government "to pass lightly over the spoliations and impressments which the British government has so long authorized or tolerated." Property unlawfully seized ran into the millions. Impressed seamen now numbered near 2,000, four fifths of them native Americans, and only one third of them had been set at liberty. Mariners were being taken under the menace of pistols and cutlasses, without the least respect for the legal protections they carried. They were then threatened or maltreated into enlistment and exposed to the hazards of war as regular members of British crews. Hope was not altogether lost of a return to right and reason, but if no change of conduct became apparent, American policy could hardly fail to take a more remedial shape. The United States was fully disposed to cultivate good will, but cordiality could be restored only if Great Britain returned the justice and respect offered by the United States.

He had written thus far to King when pleasing dispatches arrived from that minister. The new cabinet (in which Hawkesbury succeeded Grenville in foreign affairs) had issued orders to check depredations on American commerce in the West Indies. The American squadron in the Mediterranean would receive a welcome and supplies at British bases.

Britain, Hawkesbury added, had no wish to see the outcome of the Seven Years War reversed, and Canada and the West Indies menaced, by a transfer of Louisiana and the Floridas to France. There was self-interest, Madison suspected, in this sudden liberality, but he welcomed it. King not only should continue to press for a reform of the obnoxious practices at sea, but, now that the West Indian depredations were disavowed, he should ask for complete redress for the individuals injured by them. The United States would use peace and persuasion to work against the territorial transfer, but it should be kept in mind that the worst possible change would be to have Great Britain frustrate French ambition by taking these provinces herself.[14]

This was no new apprehension. In 1797, Madison had interpreted the Blount conspiracy for detachment of the West as a British move to forestall a cession of Louisiana to France. Only Bonaparte's staggering victories in Italy, he then thought, prevented the landing of a British army in Pensacola. He did not know that Talleyrand, in April of that year, had written that France in possession of Louisiana and Florida would form a "wall of brass forever impenetrable to the combined efforts of England and America." He did not know that the British, in 1795, had intercepted a letter from Minister Fauchet saying that if France or any other strong country gained control of Louisiana, it would establish its sovereignty over the whole Mississippi basin. But his interpretations of French and British policy were the same as if he had possessed these facts.[15]

Where Spain was concerned, Madison's attitude was unchanged from that day, in 1780, when he wrote the demand of Congress for a free port at the mouth of a free Mississippi. Four years later he declared to Jefferson that Spain must either yield peacefully, or be overwhelmed in time by an irresistible combination of passion and power. In the declining days of the friendly French monarchy, he would have welcomed the sway of France over the great river. Its liberal policies, he remarked to Lafayette, would make New Orleans "the Grand Cairo of the new world." This feeling vanished when the postrevolutionary aggressions of France were added to the chronic ambitions of England. Spain was the temporary, pestiferous custodian of American destiny: the two great powers were menaces to its fulfillment.

As a current raider of American ships, Spain was by no means impotent. It had been hoped, Madison wrote to Pinckney in the fall of 1801, that these attacks would cease with the ending of hostilities between the United States and France. Instead, predatory Spanish cruisers were sallying out of Algeciras and seizing vessels and cargoes which had to pass near Gibraltar. Even the pretense for seizure was fraudulent, for "the state of Gibralter is not and never can be admitted by the United States to be that of a real blockade." Those words foreshadowed the rejection of vastly larger "paper blockades" declared by England.[16]

Madison was at Monticello, early in September 1801, when a report came that France had postponed action on the peace treaty (actually ratified on July 31). Livingston, it was decided, should wait no longer. Madison went home to prepare his instructions, which Jefferson approved on his way to Washington. The minister was to inform France that Lear, when he went to St. Domingo, carried no letter to the island chief. "A strict and honorable neutrality has guided the President in this case" as it would continue to do in all transactions relating to foreign nations.

Neutrality, of course, would leave American merchants free to trade with Toussaint at their own risk. The promise to help France starve the rebels was out the window.

On the subject of Louisiana and Florida, Livingston was to make every effort "to dissuade the parties from adhering to their object." He should stress the anxiety of the United States to maintain harmony with the French Republic, the danger of collisions resulting from territorial contact, and the security France ought to feel from American unwillingness to see this territory transferred, either voluntarily or compulsively, from Spain to Great Britain.[17] He might also remark on the danger of the Western states being embroiled in future conflicts between Canada and Louisiana (by-products of Anglo-French wars) and on the disquiet of Southern states whose slaves had been taught that France was the patron of their freedom. Under such conditions, it could be suggested, the presence of France might turn American thoughts toward a closer connection with Great Britain. It could possibly produce a crisis in which French possessions "would be exposed to the joint operation of a naval and territorial power."

Should the cession be irrevocable, sound policy would require that nothing be done to irritate our future neighbors, or check the disposition to a liberal trade and navigation system.

"In the next place, it will deserve to be tried whether France cannot be induced to make over to the United States the Floridas, if included in the cession to her from Spain, or at least West Florida, through which several of our rivers, particularly the important river Mobile, empty themselves into the sea."

Such a proof of good will, said Madison, would help to reconcile the United States to a disrelished arrangement, and would afford a fund for indemnifying Americans holding claims against France. If the Floridas were not included, France might be disposed to help the United States obtain a cession from her ally Spain.[18]

These instructions, though conciliatory in wording, had a stern and sweeping content. They discarded historical relations with France and offered that country a choice. She could leave Louisiana and Florida with Spain, relying on the United States to keep England from taking them, or she could go ahead, and risk the loss of the country *through a union of American land power and British sea power*. This penalty might be escaped by putting the United States in possession of all or part of the Floridas.

There was no thought at this time that France would sell the whole territory of Louisiana or its great entrepôt, New Orleans. West Florida was sought in order to open a new commercial route through its network of rivers and to give the United States a strong base on the Gulf of Mexico. Controlling Mobile Bay, the United States could dominate the Mississippi delta and bottle up the entire colony. The corollary to this was that Napoleon never would let the United States acquire West Florida unless he was ready to abandon Louisiana. To seek part was the same as seeking all.

CHAPTER VI

STORM IN THE WEST INDIES

PICHON's reports to his government, after Livingston's departure, reinforced his original warnings. American merchants were violently wrought up by Spanish seizures of ships off Gibraltar and Spanish America. Back of the popular clamor was the appetite for Spanish booty. "I am afraid they may strike at Louisiana before we take it over." He sent new census figures showing a tremendous growth of population. Immense regions above the Ohio would soon be states, and the march of population was toward New Orleans. Keeled ships were descending the Muskingum, the Ohio, the Mississippi, and sailing to the West Indies. Smaller boats covered these rivers, carrying surplus produce to the sea. The growth of population would continue as long as the prospect of riches was held out to the poor. And population was power.[1]

On November 24, 1801, word reached Washington that France and England were at peace. The *National Intelligencer* published next day the lament of the London *Gazette:* "We gain nothing in the Mediterranean or in Europe, while France gains all Holland and the Netherlands, a large part of Germany, Switzerland and two thirds of Italy." Britain remained supreme at sea, and got Trinidad, but France was free to move in the Western hemisphere.

Pichon kept plying Madison with questions about Tobias Lear, and learned nothing. Although the government had disapproved Lear's felicitations to General Toussaint, the consul was plainly "an authority of great weight in the colony." Peace in Europe did not prevent Jefferson from talking stiffly about Louisiana. If France took possession, he told Pichon, the next war in Europe would produce an American alliance with England. The French would remain there "no longer than it pleases the United States."

Within a few days, London newspapers brought false rumors

that Britain would aid the transport of a French army to St. Domingo. Madison sent new orders to Lear. He should take no steps that would either controvert French authority or irritate the people. He and other unrecognized commercial agents were not to leave until it became dangerous to stay.

Guadaloupe was now in revolt, with the black General Pelage eagerly inviting American commerce—one more proof, commented Pichon, that West Indian colonies were dependent on the United States. "They need only say the word to detach them from us without return." He protested to Talleyrand against the conduct of expelled governors, retiring to a foreign island, launching impotent manifestoes against American commerce, and expecting him to make them effective. However, hearing that Pelage's rebel agent had landed in South Carolina, he went at once to see Madison and obtained "explicit assurance" that they would ignore him: American policy acknowledged the complete sovereignty of France over her colonies. But when Pichon disclosed an order of the Guadaloupe prefect for seizure of all ships that failed to touch at certain ports, Madison told him that no direct measures could be taken to stop commerce. Would the government publish Pichon's letter giving notice of the order? No. But the *droit public* forbade trade with rebels. Public law, Madison replied, had nothing to do with it. Trade was forbidden by a French regulation, which foreigners ought to respect, but which the United States could not help to enforce. "Mr. Madison and I understood each other very well," Pichon wrote. "In these arguments as in my replies, it was really St. Domingo that was at issue."

Madison finally said that the United States did not intend to excite the population of these colonies and throw into them germs of enmity which could finally be brought to birth in the states. In other words, the slaveholding Southern states had more to dread from the unfriendliness of ex-slave populations than from their independence. Pichon had an answer:

"I recalled to Mr. Madison that the President, last summer, made me hope for more in saying positively that the United States would join in starving Toussaint."

Again the French diplomat went to Jefferson to obtain a reversal of Madison's St. Domingo policy. Times had changed: "I found him very reserved and cold, while he talked to me, though less explicitly, in the same sense as Mr. Madison."[2]

On March 3, 1802, an American schooner arrived in Baltimore with a story of drama and horrors. General Leclerc, with a large fleet and 20,000 French soldiers, had arrived off Cap Français one month before. The black General Christophe burned the city before retreating to the mountains, and wholesale slaughter of civilians accompanied the fires. Captain John Rodgers brought a letter from Lear to Madison, confirming the captain's account, but there was far more alarm over another letter he brought. This was from a former Kentuckian, Captain Fulton of Leclerc's mounted police, stating in confidence that part of the expeditionary force was *ultimately destined for Louisiana*. He did not mention that he alone was the part so destined, on his own application to Leclerc, with Talleyrand's ex post facto approval.[3]

Madison advised Lear to cultivate the good will of the new commanders, who, unluckily, expected that, but had none to offer in return. When Napoleon asked Britain for supplies from Jamaica for his St. Domingo army, he paraphrased Jefferson, saying: "the interest of civilization being to destroy the new Algiers which is being organized in the middle of America." The English rejection roused him to defiance: "We have never let any one lay down the law to us."

Leclerc was instructed to make use of American trade until all the blacks were disarmed, then to re-establish the prewar French monopoly. Supplies could be obtained in the United States: "Jefferson has promised that the instant the French army arrives, all measures will be taken to starve Toussaint and to aid the army."[4]

Sent with almost no money, entering a destroyed city, and finding all provisions held at exorbitant prices in American vessels or warehouses, the French commander sent an agent to New York to sell drafts for a million francs. All such bills had been dishonored for years. Even the French houses in Philadelphia (Du Pont de Nemours and Sadeu) refused them now at 30 per cent discount. Leclerc was Napoleon's brother-in-law, and knew it.

He seized American cargoes at his own price and forced French bills on the hapless owners. Objectors were browbeaten and insulted. Voyages were canceled. Denunciations filled the American press. With French soldiers instead of Toussaint's starving, Leclerc and the Paris ministry threw the problem into Pichon's lap. The humble chargé d'affaires was told to feed the army.

Pichon had been sending a stream of letters to Leclerc, pointing out the errors and dangers of his proceedings. He begged his government to intervene, declaring that the expedition could succeed only with the friendly support of the United States. The order for him to supply the army, he boldly declared to Talleyrand, seemed to be a confession of incompetence in France. He would do what he could, however, to achieve the impossible.

Following Leclerc's arrival, Madison and the President both told Pichon that they desired France to win quick success, but there could be no aid in enforcing French regulations. Pichon tried to play once more on Jefferson's fear of a slave insurrection. The black chiefs, he wrote to Madison, were refusing to submit to the white race. All civilized nations, but especially those in which slavery existed, should be interested in re-establishing the upset order. Trade with St. Domingo, he gave notice, was now restricted to ports controlled by the French, and France expected that the United States would not permit its citizens to trade with the rebels. Pichon asked whether he or the American government should publish this letter and the Secretary's expected reply.

Madison promised an answer conforming to duty. He could not place a stigma on his own government by making Pichon's letter public, but would suggest a better means of achieving his end. The national spirit (said Pichon's summary to Paris) longed for extension of commerce. The war opened St. Domingo to trade and the revolt assured it. Peace and the reduction of the colony threatened to wipe it out. The South might fear the Negroes, but the North cared little for the slave states and wouldn't hesitate to support Toussaint so that he could buy its products. Pichon, catching the point, shifted to a simple proclamation of the trade restriction, avoiding the points touched on with Madison, or any which could "stir up party men and enthusiasts."[5]

The chargé took up the supply problem under a barrage of questions from the Secretary of State. What was the purpose of so large an expedition? Why was not the United States told of it in advance? Was it true that part of the squadron was to take possession of Louisiana? Pichon got past that, aided by a friendly letter from Admiral Villaret to the President, and at length obtained $150,000 due to France under the new treaty. He then asked for a loan.

Don't even speak of it, was Madison's reply. Imagine what outcries there would be if Congress advanced money to France after refusing to indemnify American merchants with claims against that country. Pichon went over Madison's head and reported the results to Talleyrand:

"The President spoke to me with the language of sincerity and marked interest, and even gave me some hope, saying he expected to have some members of Congress at his house to consider what could be done. Mr. Madison on the contrary spoke a language entirely discouraging."

Two weeks later, Pichon sadly recorded that only anti-French congressmen were encouraging him—their object, to create prejudice by maneuvering the administration into a pro-French appearance.[6]

Tension over Louisiana mounted steadily in 1802. From Livingston, who reached Paris in the previous December, came Talleyrand's unconvincing denial that anything had been concluded. Madison put a quick veto on a suggestion, made by Livingston to King, that Great Britain be induced to throw obstacles in the way of a cession. Such an overture might be used to sow jealousies between the United States and France and frustrate the American objective. King, after a guarded inquiry, assured Madison that Britain would do nothing about Louisiana, for fear of upsetting the new balance of Europe.[7]

From King, Madison received a year-old treaty between France and Spain, setting up the kingdom of Etruria and referring unmistakably to the cession of Louisiana by a previous treaty. The effect was seen in a dramatically worded letter from the President to Livingston. From the moment that France takes possession of New Orleans, said Jefferson, "we must marry ourselves to the British fleet and nation." The striking metaphor was built on Madison's earlier warning about the joint operation of British naval and American territorial power. But Jefferson's trenchant language made this, for many historians, the beginning and climax of American policy. Pierre du Pont, who carried the letter, warned the President that Bonaparte would be more offended than moved by menaces. Far more could be accomplished by a liberal offer to buy what was wanted east of the river.[8]

Madison saw dark prospects at this time. "No hope remains," he wrote to Livingston on May 1, "but from the accumulating difficulties of going through with the undertaking," and its destructive effect on Franco-American relations. Spare no efforts to lead France to abandon her purpose, he ordered, and then duplicated Du Pont's advice before it was received. Livingston should ask for a definite price on the Floridas and New Orleans, if they were included in the cession. It would be a precious acquisition, and if applied on the claims of American citizens, "great liberality would doubtless be indulged by this government."

Chief among the accumulating difficulties was the position of France in St. Domingo. On May 6, Lear showed up in Washington. He had been expelled from the island after protesting the imprisonment, without trial, of two American sea captains—one of them the same John Rodgers who risked death to save French lives at the burning of Cap Français. For Jefferson, in Monticello, Madison summarized Lear's political report: "The idea in the army is that republicanism is exploded," that monarchy must be forced on an unwilling nation "and that Bonaparte is the proper successor to the cashiered dynasty." Lear's military report inspired him to call for stronger efforts by Livingston to obtain a reversal of the Louisiana cession:

"The prospect of a protracted and expensive war in St. Domingo must form a very powerful obstacle to the execution of the project."[9]

Imprisonment of the sea captains produced an immediate request for Pichon's intervention. These men, Madison wrote, had been "treated as the vilest of malefactors." Pichon hastened to Madison's house and found Lear there. The latter handed Madison a letter which the Secretary read aloud. It was from Leclerc, heatedly charging that Rodgers had spread calumnies about the French army while in the United States. Captain Davidson was arrested because his ship's name, *St. Domingo Packet,* created a suspicion that Toussaint owned it. Pichon wrote to Leclerc with maddening logic:

"In law, General, a citizen of a foreign nation does not have to answer before the authorities of another country for acts he may have committed outside the boundaries of the country exercising the authority. . . . As for Mr. Davidson, allow me, General, to observe that the name of a ship and suspicions do not constitute a misdemeanor."[10]

On the very day this was written, Leclerc was complaining to Napoleon about *le citoyen* Pichon. He was devoted to the American government, believed all the calumnies about the French army and wrote improper letters. More dangerous was Leclerc's advice to the Minister of Marine:

"The role of minister from the Republic to the United States should not at the present moment be filled by a mediocre man. It will be difficult to make them relish the occupation of Louisiana. It is necessary to send a minister plenipotentiary to the United States, one who has a good personal reputation, who is truly French, and who receives a salary sufficient to keep him from living in misery."

When Leclerc received Pichon's protest over the sea captains he exploded completely. This man is a *fripon,* he wrote to the First Consul—*c'est un miserable,* a rascal who takes money on the side while buying supplies, a wretch whose indecent letters he would no longer answer. *"Je demande son changement."* He notified Pichon of his action.[11]

During the fortnight before Leclerc's first denunciation reached Paris, Napoleon ordered the immediate occupation of Louisiana and appointed Louis Otto minister to the United States. Once chargé at Washington, he was now ambassador to England. When Madison heard of it he wrote to Jefferson: "I am glad to find that Otto is to share in the negotiations concerning Louisiana because it is probable he may retain the original policy of France on that subject"—renunciation of territorial ambitions. At the first rumor of this appointment, in August 1801, Jefferson had written to Livingston, from Monticello, that Otto was personally objectionable to him. Madison may have had something to do with the withdrawal of that objection six months later, when the souring policies of Napoleon made Otto's friendship for the United States more important than his onetime affinity for Hamiltonians. (Neither of them knew that Otto, in 1788, had called Madison a more profound statesman than Hamilton.) All this was rendered moot by one little detail. Otto never received sailing orders and Pichon held his position for another two-and-one-half years.[12]

Following the arrival of Leclerc's charges (all of which were later withdrawn), Napoleon ordered Talleyrand to send a stinging rebuke to the chargé d'affaires. What Bonaparte wrote revealed his reaction to Madison's brand of diplomacy.

Tell Pichon, the First Consul ordered, that if the Minister of Marine has not sent funds to him for St. Domingo, they were provided for in another manner, but that a credit of two million francs has been set up for him in London. (Napoleon no longer hoped that the United States would supply his army in order to suppress slave insurrections.)

Tell him, Bonaparte went on, that he should engage in business talks only, not in political conversations which belittle the government; his excessive zeal has subjected him to disagreeable remarks by American ministers, such as no French agent ought to listen to. (Napoleon did not relish the dissection of his policies by Madison's analytical mind.)

Tell him, said the First Consul, that the proceedings of the army at St. Domingo were blamable, but he had no business to

judge the motives of General Leclerc in arresting the sea captains, Leclerc having undisputed police power. (Napoleon could
not tolerate the correction of a general by a civilian, even when
the civilian was saving his country from the disastrous results of
the general's errors.)

Tell him, continued Bonaparte, that if Leclerc was irritated
against the United States, he had nevertheless been very moderate
toward American ships found with munitions in their holds. It
might be true that the French used hard words against the Americans, but American newspapers were filled with the most indecent calumnies of France and her army, and it was most extraordinary if the Americans attached more importance to the one
than the French government did to the other.

Here Napoleon completely missed the point made by Pichon
to Leclerc, that French army officers, dependent for their survival
on American supplies, were antagonizing both people and government by vilification of the United States and menacing language in connection with Louisiana. He missed the point about
to be made by Madison, who instructed Livingston to tell France
"that our presses are not under the regulation of the government,
which is itself constantly experiencing more or less of their abuse."
The French ruler could not understand that the press campaign
stirred up by Leclerc made it virtually impossible for the American government to aid France even if it wanted to.

Here was the conflict in methods between a personal autocrat
and the servants of a democratic republic—one responsible to
himself, the other to the people and to public opinion. The contrast went farther. Pichon, criticized by Talleyrand for having
talked to members of Congress about a loan to France, sent back
this enduring commentary:

"I give full weight and justice to your observations on this subject. But by the nature of this government, all is known to the
members of the legislature, and it is impossible to avoid the in-
convenience of publicity."

Among the encouraging reports Madison heard was a rumor
that Spain had disowned the treaty which ceded Louisiana.

Godoy, Prince of Peace, had in truth been seeking to annul the cession, but drew this order from Napoleon to his ambassador in Madrid: "If this system is continued, say boldly to the queen and the Prince of Peace [the queen's ex-paramour] that it will terminate in a thunder-bolt." To his Minister of Marine the First Consul wrote:

"My intention, Citizen Minister, is that we take possession of Louisiana with the least possible delay; that this expedition be made in the greatest secrecy; that it have the air of being directed to St. Domingo."

As if to foster this ambition, Toussaint surrendered—betrayed by lesser chiefs and deceived by Napoleon's promise of universal liberty and personal honors. The news found Washington incredulous. Jefferson suspected that it "was in reality a surrender of Leclerc to Toussaint"—a device to cover the giving up of seaports.[13]

Bonaparte sent Toussaint to die in a French dungeon and ordered slavery re-established in St. Domingo. Ship me the rest of the black generals by September, he adjured Leclerc. "Without this, we shall have accomplished nothing. . . . Defeat these gilded Africans, and there will remain nothing more to desire." Their capture would open the way to Louisiana and a new field of empire.

Leclerc did not send the gilded generals. Where Toussaint left off, yellow fever and guerrillas carried on. In June, the French commander wrote that half of his officers were dead; if the frightful malady kept up until October he would have but 4,000 men left alive. What Jefferson suspected about Toussaint proved true of his betrayers, Christophe and Dessalines. Leclerc made them the commanders of regions he could not control. As his army shrank, their commands expanded. Then came the news that slavery had been publicly proclaimed in Guadeloupe, and open rebellion flared over every hill and valley of the larger island.[14]

Four obstacles stood between Bonaparte and the North American empire so nearly in his grasp. Three were actual: American diplomacy, combining warnings with financial offers; France's desperate need of money; a disaster in St. Domingo, destroying the Western fulcrum of French power. The fourth was prospective: a new war in Europe, closing the seas to France and leaving Louisiana open to seizure.

American diplomacy, taken by itself, might be ignored. But it could not be separated from the other obstacles.

CHAPTER VII

FRANCE'S WALL OF BRASS

PRESIDENT JEFFERSON was well satisfied with the session of Congress which came to an end on May 3, 1802. "They have carried into execution steadily almost all the propositions submitted to them in my [opening] message," he wrote to Joel Barlow in Paris. Congress had repealed the Judiciary Act of February 1801, getting rid of circuit courts and most of the "midnight judges." Internal taxes were abolished and steps taken to reduce the public debt. The liberal naturalization law of 1795, written by Madison, was restored. Statehood for Ohio was authorized. Among important measures, only the reorganization of the militia was held over. Several New England states were showing Republican majorities. But Jefferson's hope of unifying the people had been dashed by "the grossest lies and misrepresentations" of Federalist leaders made furious by despair.

The Federalists were in truth cruelly shocked. The ignorant Jacobin scoundrels in Congress were so unequal to their task, wrote Griswold early in the session, that they did nothing but "stare at us and at each other." Federalist members, "in consequence of their superior skill," would have a decided influence on legislation. In a few weeks Senator Hillhouse was crying that never was a set of men more blindly devoted to the will of a prime minister than these Republicans to that of the President.[1]

In a Congress dominated by men who lived close to the soil, Jefferson was not hurt by the rough sheep fence he put up around the presidential mansion—"not fit for the yard of a barn," wrote Federalist William Plumer. Nor was there any political handicap in the personal appearance described by Plumer in December 1802:

"In a few minutes a tall highboned man came into the room; he was dressed, or rather undressed, with an old brown coat, red waistcoat, old corduroy small clothes much soiled, woolen hose and slippers without heels. I thought this man was a servant, but General Varnum surprised me by announcing that it was the President."

Pichon wrote to Talleyrand of "the lack of dignity which makes Mr. Jefferson go on foot, on horse, without servants, and makes him receive . . . in an unseemly negligé, very often in slippers." However, "the whole administration is not on this footing. Mr. Madison lacks nothing of dignity, but Mr. Gallatin prides himself also on an absolute lack of it." British Chargé Thornton saw another trait in the President:

"A jealous sense of praise and of censure is among the most striking features of Mr. Jefferson's character and his gratitude for the former is in exact proportion to his implacable resentment against the latter."[2]

Fisher Ames desponded. Jefferson, he conceded, probably believed in the wisdom of extreme democratic principles. "Madison certainly knows better and yet there ever was a strange vein of absurdity in his head." These men were the Roland and Condorcet of America's French Revolution. Whether it would go on to a Robespierre depended on accident and Federalist energy. Senator Uriah Tracy was even less hopeful. Unprincipled and visionary men were in the directories, and "we are all going the downhill road to democracy, naturally and with our whole might."[3]

In the House, John Randolph of Virginia was rising fast to leadership. This "pale, meager, ghostly man" of shrill voice and dreaded invective became chairman of the Ways and Means Committee in his second term. He was the Republicans' most effective orator, though some were "unwilling to own a leader who has the appearance of a beardless boy." At the time of Jefferson's election, Randolph decried the "spirit of personal attachment" to him by men whose republicanism was open to doubt. A year later, he classified the parties:

1. "The old Federalists courting popularity."

2. "The *gens gris* who are mostly old Federalists republicanized and are army- and navy-wise. These expect to hold the balance."

3. "The real Republicans whose principles are unchanged by situations and who I trust will prove too hard for both."

Pichon, reporting this same division, saw Jefferson losing votes. In trying to democratize the government and strengthen the states, he was exalting Virginia and antagonizing the rest of the country. Strong-minded men were uniting to form a middle party of Federalists and split-off Republicans, through whom "Mr. Burr will certainly reach the Presidency." He cited a toast by Burr at a Federalist dinner, "To the union of all honest men," but later reported a reaction, with Burr "irretrievably lost."[4]

Robert Troup, of the Hamiltonian wing of Federalism, saw the Vice President losing ground rapidly with Jefferson's supporters. He would probably be dropped at the next election, and if the Federalists should take him up "Hamilton and many of us will secede from the Federal party and remain passive spectators." Troup told of Hamilton's utter despair of a government already fallen by predestination into the hands of demagogues, and continued:

"Giles and Randolph of Virginia are the leaders of the House. . . . Madison is in a deep decline and it is thought will soon quit his office. . . . Jefferson is the idol to whom all devotion is paid."

But Joel Early, a radical who had bitterly fought Madison's entry into Congress, wrote to him about "the monstrous mistake under which I then lay as to the tendency of your politics. . . . Believe me all doubts are vanished and not even a shadow remains."[5]

Federalists could not accept the fact that a man of Madison's honesty, intelligence and mental balance could be a Democrat; or, being one, that he should not be on the point of quitting such a party or being thrown out of it. They were misled by the way he buried his light under Jefferson's bushel, and by the courtesy he showed to opponents. He himself complained that civility to of-

fice seekers was often interpreted as a promise of support. When
Federalist William Vans Murray returned from his abolished
diplomatic post, he found Madison "greatly more cordial than
any one else." Yet neither the Secretary of State nor the President,
when he dined at their houses, asked him a single question about
affairs in Holland.[6]

Theodore Sedgwick thought that Rufus King was kept in London because Republican leaders, "a certain little great man excepted," viewed nothing with more horror than a rupture with
Great Britain. If Madison was less pacific, he was no less anxious
to make use of the Amiens interlude to establish American rights
at sea. In 1791, British ships trading between the two countries
had outnumbered American ships by 27 per cent. Two years
later, due largely to Madison's system of retaliatory duties, American ships outnumbered British by 58 per cent. Jay's 1794 treaty
gave Great Britain the right to lay countervailing duties, but the
effect of doing so was offset by British war insurance with the result that sixty-two British and five hundred thirty American ships
engaged in this trade in 1801. French law gave a strong preference
to French ships, but the British navy cancelled that. Then, late
in 1801, the war ended.[7]

Peace, Madison wrote to King, would give a great shock to
American navigation. (The mere news of it, a banker said, "operated almost like the hand of death upon all business.") There
were three methods of dealing with this, the Secretary said. Bur-
dens of a new kind could be laid on foreign ships, but that would
violate the spirit of the treaty. The United States and Great Britain both could repeal their discriminatory laws, but that would
be too slow. The third remedy was immediate removal of in-
justices by executive action.

Britain's countervailing duties, Madison observed, were intended to balance ten per cent of the American duties. Instead,
ten per cent had been added to British duties, which were many
times higher than the American level. Thus the discrimination
had been "made infinitely greater in favor of the other side."
Moreover, American exports, coming from farm and forest, were
ten times as bulky as British exports of the same value. Conse-

quently, discriminating duties operated ten times as strongly in
favor of British ships, which could come over in ballast to pick
up American cargoes. To remedy this simply and conveniently,
Congress and Parliament each could pass a repeal law, effective
when the other country acted. The President wished King to
work to that end. France would either fall into line or face new
penalties.[8]

Ten days after King took the subject up in London, he sent
word that the British government would agree to reciprocal abolition. This complaisance was encouraged by Chargé Thornton's
report that the United States might not be the chief beneficiary.
British capital, colonial monopoly and cheaper shipbuilding
would assure equal competition.

Panic and politics governed the New England reaction to Britain's surprising offer. Congressmen whose states had most to
gain, said Madison, so perverted the issue that action was postponed for a year. Instructing King to work for unconditional
removal of British duties, he declared that nothing else except
renewal of the war could save American shipping from lasting
injury. King replied that the congressional postponement made
it impossible even to mention the subject.[9]

By midsummer of 1802, Madison was taking note of an act of
Parliament laying heavier duties on exports to America than to
other places. The good sense and good faith of the British government, he hoped, would repair this breach of the treaty of 1794. A
little reflection should make them see that they had in effect
granted a bounty to American manufactures. By the end of
1802, American merchants and shipowners were crying even
more loudly to retain the discriminations that threatened to ruin
them. The President told Thornton that his party would bring
the repeal bill forward, but, to avoid accusations against the South,
they would let the navigating states decide its fate. Show no
eagerness, the British diplomat advised his government; let the
New Englanders feel the full disadvantage of their system.

More cheering was the Senate's quick ratification of a convention, signed by King, wiping out $20,000,000 in pre-Revolutionary
British debt claims by a lump payment of 600,000 pounds ster-

ling—a figure agreed to in advance by the Jefferson cabinet. The British government was now interested in cutting the claims down, instead of swelling them, and thankfully accepted Madison's offer of evidence that a full half of them were fraudulent.[10]

Peace sharply altered the trouble over seamen. Americans were no longer being impressed by British warships, but lenient magistrates gave deserting foreign seamen the protection of American law. Under a new Virginia statute, any judge who delivered up a deserter was subject to punishment himself. As a result, Thornton reported, every British ship entering a Virginia port was immediately abandoned by her crew, to whom the American ships afforded secure asylum. Madison, the chargé said, "lamented with great appearance of sincerity and candor that the law gave him no authority to surrender any deserter." But he also pointed out that the British admiralty had in no instance lent their aid in delivery of any American seamen, whether impressed or not, and suggested reciprocal laws on the subject.

Thornton was puzzled by Madison's attitude. He should have recalled a phrase in his own private note to the Secretary, a few weeks earlier: "With your passion for chess." That makes it easy to understand why Madison worked slowly, studied every possible motive for the moves of his adversaries, and looked to the future consequences of his own. In this instance his conciliatory attitude may have reflected the need for friendlier relations with Britain in the face of French ambitions in Louisiana, over which Lord Hawkesbury had expressed concern in the debate over the Treaty of Amiens.[11]

At this period, in June 1802, Louisiana was thrown violently into the American political arena by an article in the semiofficial *Gazette de France*. The United States, it charged, furnished the contraband guns, cannon and powder found at Cap Français. By its rapid increase of population, industry, trade and wealth, that power was plainly destined "to rule over the new world, and to place under its yoke all the West-India colonies." Europe should postpone that epoch by opposing an impenetrable barrier to the spreading torrent. Louisiana was to be "a counterpoise to the domination of the United States."[12]

Here was Pichon's description of America, underpinning Talleyrand's "wall of brass." Was it surprising that Livingston was meeting with neglect, denials and rebuffs in his negotiations for New Orleans and the Floridas?

Pichon described the effect of the article. Federalist writers blamed the administration for being played with and deceived at Paris and Madrid. They charged the government with feebleness, with imprudence in cutting military strength when faced with a turbulent neighbor of boundless ambition. Both parties condemned the French course, and were further envenomed by the hate-filled epithets of French officers at St. Domingo, boasting that the expedition to Louisiana "would bring the United States to its senses."

Madison, Pichon continued, had entered into a very serious discussion with him. The Louisiana retrocession, disquieting in itself, was made more so by the silence and denials of France. It appeared from the *Gazette de France,* said Madison, that French policy aimed at weakening the United States by splitting them apart. It was an error to think that the separation of the Western states would weaken the Atlantic states very much, and a still greater error to think that the former wished to withdraw. Custom and language drew the Americans together; geography unified them, and so did the West's need of security. With all America united, "it should be admitted that France cannot long preserve Louisiana against the United States, and nothing would do more to unite the whole continent than having France in the neighborhood."

As to Louisiana being a safeguard to more distant colonies, Madison went on, the contrary was true. An American alliance with Great Britain, in the next war, would throw them into British hands. Even without a war, the United States by placing itself in the balance with England "could without difficulty divide with her, in ten years, not the [South American] colonies—the United States could never desire any possession there—but all the export and import trade of these colonies."

It was thus, said the French diplomat, that Madison talked, "with much coolness, much method, and as if he had been prepared." The President said less, he added, but what he said was very significant. For ten years, France had been taking a stand against the United States "and you will end by making a union with Great Britain universally popular." If that country consents to French possession of Louisiana, said Jefferson, "it will be on account of what she well knows will result from it." (A Franco-American war, he told Thornton.) Holding the administration back, Pichon thought, was the embarrassment of a reversal of policy toward England and unwillingness to try the country's strength before it had made a ten-year gain in population and riches.

Though despondent over Leclerc's charges against him, the chargé wrote, he would make some observations on these reflections of the President and Secretary of State. He then calmly tore Talleyrand's basic policy to ribbons. France distrusted the future power of the United States and their ambition. This development was foreseen and weighed when the decision was made to aid American independence. France preferred, and he thought wisely, a strong and independent country, rather than one equally strong but serving the power and plans of England.

"Today the same question returns when one speaks of repressing their growth by force. Force will throw them inevitably under the hand of England, and it is only by a continuation of good dealings that this reunion can be prevented."

Pichon called attention to the almost daily reports he had sent of American growth, but said he reached a very different conclusion from that arrived at by the advocates of repression. It was necessary "to be resigned to their future power, to conciliate them, and acquire the merit, useful in other respects, of acceding to that which the force of events will give them in spite of us."

Here, relayed from Madison and Jefferson, were the most persuasive arguments against French retention of Louisiana that reached Napoleon from any source, and they were supported with irrefutable logic and astonishing courage by a French diplomat who knew that the dictator's powerful brother-in-law was seeking his dismissal. Some days after this interview, Pichon received a long outline of the position Talleyrand had taken in talks with Livingston on St. Domingo and other matters. He was to present this to Madison as the definitive position of the French government. He did so, and sent back the Secretary's oral answer, point by point.

Madison agreed with Talleyrand (overruling Livingston) that no indemnities should be paid when prizes were restored, but took note that the French interpretation of the 1800 treaty tended to exclude the return of prizes taken in the colonies. All not finally condemned, he insisted, were to be returned. He denied responsibility for the arming of St. Domingo rebels by President Adams. If the Jefferson administration was accountable for what was done during the naval war, so must the First Consulate be responsible for the acts of the Directory. The present government, he said, had broken completely away from the Toussaint-Maitland agreement, but if all trade had been stopped, would it not have turned the island over to the British? By what right could the United States break communication with Toussaint, a French general, when France had not condemned his conduct? Would not that occasion commotions in the colony? Although he knew that Talleyrand alone might stand between him and dismissal, Pichon interjected his opinion of Madison's argument:

"These conclusions, Citizen Minister, are irresistible."

Continuing, he said that Madison granted the general right of European powers to regulate colonial commerce as they pleased. But when colonies were opened to foreigners, the United States claimed a right of its own, "to place national dignity and the safety of commerce out of reach of all arbitrary action and injury." This, he declared, required the admission of American consuls, also that American citizens be guaranteed the same liberty of trade and personal immunities accorded them in Europe. Secondly, the United States would no longer submit to "the despotism and caprice to which their carrying trade was subjected by the European states." If France did not follow England's example in removing discriminatory duties against American goods, especially tobacco, "the United States would be infallibly forced to make reprisals." Britain still required that American goods be carried to British colonies in British ships. The true rule was that commerce and ships be admitted together, and today "we have the means to compel a more just treatment of our rights."[13]

Pichon believed that the American government, though somewhat swayed by self-interest, wished for French sovereignty and order in St. Domingo. This was abstractly true of Jefferson, but Madison was so immersed in strategy that his abstract views were invisible. The conclusions Pichon found irresistible were designed to bulwark an American policy which might promote a far-off reconciliation, but could only fortify the rebels against the speedy subjugation desired by Napoleon and the extermination[14] advocated by Leclerc. In yielding to the self-interest of New England traders, the administration served its own object of delaying and discouraging the occupation of Louisiana by France.

Had Leclerc and his aides exploited the South's fear of servile insurrections, they might have made a great asset of their West Indian campaign. Instead, they allowed stories to spread of a plan to exile rebellious Negroes to Louisiana, and gave color to it by bringing shiploads of them into American harbors. Pichon wanted to ship the prisoners to France, but lacked the means, and Madison was loath to urge him for fear it might lead to applications for financial aid. Wild stories spread over the country. "The infernal French at this moment are vomiting all their wretched blacks upon our coast," screamed a South Carolina letter published in Washington. It proved to be a political canard to affect South Carolina's 1802 election, and reached New England just in time to affect the choice of congressmen there.[15]

Late in the summer, Livingston undertook to break through the wall of silence Talleyrand had built around him. He presented two memoirs. The first, dealing with sea power, contended that France could become invulnerable at sea only by dividing the empire of it with such a natural maritime power as the United States. Given a proper commercial treaty, he predicted, Americans would have such an interest in the prosperity of France that they would unite with her in hostile operations.

Thus he wrote, in violation of his country's policy, against history, against reason, for the shrewd eyes of Talleyrand and Napoleon, who knew that the United States had entered a naval war against France while formally allied with her.[16]

The second memoir, of six thousand words, was designed to prove that Louisiana would disappoint all French hopes, either commercial or military. French goods could be introduced into the Western states only by putting New Orleans under American sovereignty, thus encouraging American merchants to invest there. It should remain forever a free port of entry to French ships and fabrics. Livingston's reasoning was sound, but was marred by his rasping dogmatism. Why tell twenty sensitive Frenchmen (for he made that many copies) that their ideas were based on "the most perfect ignorance" of Mississippi River navigation? What could he gain by informing them that French wines were ill-suited to Western palates and that American peach brandy was superior to the best in France? Livingston then undertook to make national policy with a statement so improper that to protect him it was stricken from the memorial when published in *American State Papers* in 1832:

"This commerce is useful to both nations; this union of sentiments and interest rests upon principles which ought to form the maritime code, and deliver the world from the tyranny founded by Great Britain which she maintains, and which never will be combated with success, until the other powers by uniting will abridge her means, by transferring to nations more moderate a part of her commerce."

It must be a strong inducement, he went on, that compelled France to "convert a natural and warm ally into a jealous and suspicious neighbor, and perhaps, in the progress of events, into an open enemy." He then made a strong exposition of Madison's thesis that when two nations border each other along a great artery of commerce, at a vast distance from their governments, local rivalries will produce uncontrollable collisions and lead to war.[17]

After sending this paper to Talleyrand, Livingston on August 19 resubmitted his unanswered note of February 20, which asked whether the Floridas were included in the cession. Such prolonged silence, he said, created serious distrust. He asked for assurance that France would respect the rights of commerce and navigation to which the United States was entitled by treaty with Spain.

On the last day of the month, Livingston offered Talleyrand some propositions and was told they were premature. He did not tell Madison what these were, but the legation secretary, Thomas Sumter, wrote a memorandum on the subject a year later, after he had resigned. During the summer of 1802, he said, Livingston held a series of meetings with Daniel Parker, expatriated Boston speculator. Sumter entered the room while they were going over a Florida map. Parker put the total ungranted West Florida land at 30,000,000 acres and Livingston placed the possession value at $20,000,000—an estimate, Sumter said, based on impressions obtained from Collot and Adet (agents of France in the 1797 conspiracy to take the Southwest from Spain), and from James Swan, another Boston speculator and former French purchasing agent. (Among his purchases was Senator S. T. Mason, to whom he paid $2,333 for a copy of Jay's treaty, desired by Adet before it was ratified.)[18]

Sumter told Parker and Livingston that nearly all the good lands had been granted while England held Florida, and the remainder was not worth more than one fifth of Livingston's figure. Begging Parker, out of the minister's hearing, not to encourage this excessive valuation, Sumter was told that the acquisition would be of great value to the United States and "a man might make his own fortune too." Talleyrand, Parker stated, could accomplish this. The United States could save much, and whoever brought it about could make something handsome by getting land grants in advance of the cession. On August 31, Sumter continued, Livingston submitted an offer with the price left blank, but Talleyrand "blew up the bubble" by saying that nothing could be done before possession was taken.

Sumter's account is inferentially supported by Livingston's dispatches to Madison. France, he said at the end of July, was very anxious to obtain Pensacola and St. Augustine, to prevent American control of the Gulf of Mexico. "If they would be content with these, and give us West Florida and New Orleans, even at a *large price* [italics his], we should not hesitate." A few days later he wrote that they would be "a cheap purchase at twenty millions of dollars." The sentence was cut off at the word "purchase" when the letter was published in 1832.

Judging by the target of Livingston's disgust, it was Napoleon who upset his hopes. Never, he wrote to the Secretary of State, was there a government where less could be done by negotiation. Bonaparte was everything, seldom asked advice and never heard it unasked. His extreme hauteur was making England sour and peace was not likely to last long.[19]

Late in October, finding himself still ignored, the American minister turned to Joseph Bonaparte. The latter offered to carry unsigned communications to his brother, by-passing Talleyrand. In line with his May 1 instructions, Livingston suggested that all differences be wiped out by the return of Louisiana to Spain and the delivery of New Orleans and the Floridas to the United States in payment of American war claims.

To his astonishment, Joseph asked whether the United States preferred Florida to Louisiana. There was no comparison in value, Livingston answered, but the United States was only seeking security and had no wish to extend its boundary beyond the Mississippi.[20]

Joseph Bonaparte did not act for his brother when he suggested an American bid for Louisiana. Napoleon, with far different purposes, had just written to the puppet King of Tuscany (Etruria) offering him his ancestral duchy of Parma. By adding it to Etruria, it would be easy to induce the King of Spain to "reunite Florida to Louisiana." He meant that just as the Queen of Spain had induced the king to cede Louisiana in order to make their daughter Queen of Etruria, so now she would force him to cede Florida in order to enlarge that synthetic kingdom.

This bad news reached Livingston a few days after the subject of buying Louisiana came up. "France has cut the knot," the

CHARLES MAURICE TALLEYRAND

ROBERT R. LIVINGSTON
By John Vanderlyn, Paris, 1804

ANTHONY MERRY

GENERAL LOUIS MARIE TURREAU
without His Whiskers

EDWARD THORNTON

GEORGE CANNING

minister wrote to Madison. Napoleon had sent troops into Parma and ordered General Victor's Holland army to embark for Louisiana in twenty days. The government would "say nothing of their limits or of ours under the Spanish treaty." General Victor had referred to the Spanish-American treaty as waste paper, as far as the American right of entrepôt was concerned. An attack on Natchez was probable. From his talk with Joseph Bonaparte, Livingston had drawn "some small hopes, but they are of no avail now that the expedition is determined upon."[21]

After writing thus despondingly, Livingston asked Talleyrand for a positive answer to his notes. The First Consul, that minister replied, had ordered him to give the most positive assurances that American treaty rights in Louisiana would be strictly observed. Asked to put that in writing, Talleyrand said it could easily be done when the absent Bonaparte returned. Livingston joyfully penned the news to Madison.

The latter, meanwhile, was taking comfort from the earlier report that the transfer of Louisiana to France was in suspense. Spare no means for diverting the French from that unwise project, he urged. If, in doing so, the United States could gain New Orleans and Florida, "the happiest of issues will be given to one of the most perplexing of occurrences."[22]

Livingston's two letters, dated the same day, went by different ships. As usually happened, the bad news traveled fast, the good news slowly—too slowly, in this instance, to undo the good which the bad news wrought. This paradox was a by-product of blunders made by Spain.

CHAPTER VIII

Bidding for New Orleans

Startling information reached Washington in November 1802. At New Orleans, using the pacification of Europe as a pretext, Spanish Intendant Morales had closed the port to all except Spanish vessels and prohibited the deposit of American goods. This, Madison wrote to Pinckney in Madrid, was so direct a violation of the treaty of 1795 that he could not believe it was authorized by the Spanish government. The treaty permitted closure after three years, provided another port was opened. None had been.

Spanish Minister Yrujo sent a special messenger to New Orleans with protests from himself and Madison. This was expected to produce results, but Pinckney should ask for an immediate revocation. To our Western citizens, said Madison, the Mississippi is everything. "It is the Hudson, the Delaware, the Potomac and all the navigable rivers of the Atlantic states formed into one stream." Kentucky alone had half a million in goods afloat and exposed to loss. If the intendant proved to be as obstinate as he had been ignorant or wicked, nothing but energetic action by the American government could temper the indignation of the Western people.[1]

The intendant's action followed lesser treaty violations at New Orleans and aggressions elsewhere. New England and Philadelphia shipowners were angry over seizures of their vessels by the Spanish viceroy at Buenos Aires. They wanted the United States to negotiate directly with the colony by sending a special mission on a warship—a proposal, Madison commented to the President, which "seems to have no rational object and to be of an injurious tendency." An effort to protect "smuggling adventures," Jefferson called it. All of these developments were part of the transition from war to peace, from open trade back to colonial monopoly, with a painful dislocation of the American economy.[2]

Madison outlined American policy to Chargé Thornton. The United States must obtain absolute sovereignty over some position near the mouth of the Mississippi, with an unrestricted right of navigation. Growth of the West put it beyond doubt that if this was not granted peaceably, New Orleans would fall into their hands by force. The Secretary was thinking more of France than of Spain. In a belligerent warning sent to Livingston, he predicted that the New Orleans proclamation would be rescinded:

"The excitement however which it has produced ought to admonish the holders whoever they may be of the mouth of the Mississippi that justice, ample justice, to the Western citizens of the United States is the only tenure of peace with this country. There are now or in less than two years will be not less than 200,000 militia on the waters of the Mississippi, every man of whom would march at a moment's warning to remove obstructions from that outlet to the sea, every man of whom regards the free use of that river as a natural and indefeasible right and is conscious of the physical force that can at any time give effect to it. This consideration ought not to be overlooked by France and would be alone sufficient if allowed its due weight to cure the frenzy which covets Louisiana."

Other considerations, he continued, seemed likely to co-operate for the same purpose. St. Domingo and other islands must be lost to France without large and speedy reinforcements to offset new disasters. Renewal of the war in Europe was not improbable and would be the more critical to Bonaparte as he had "at once provoked it by his external measures and made no provision for it by measures of credit or economy at home. We are anxious to learn how far the project of Louisiana may be shaken by any of these or other causes."[3]

Americans did not miss the significance of France's annexation of Piedmont and Elba, England's retention of Malta, the failure to remove French troops from Holland, all in violation of the

Treaty of Amiens. Bonaparte's expanding ambition in the old world was making him more vulnerable in the new.

A few days before Madison dispatched this warning, Livingston sent a remarkable proposal to Napoleon through Joseph Bonaparte. It was that France keep East Florida and sell to the United States West Florida, New Orleans, and the portion of Louisiana north of the Arkansas River. This, he said, would give France command of the Gulf of Mexico, and furnish a sufficient outlet for her population and trade. Any other plan would throw the whole country into the hands of England, who could attack Louisiana by sea and from Canada, expel Spain from Florida and command the West Indies. All this, it seems, with the help of the United States, for as Livingston summed it up:

"France, by grasping at a desert and an insignificant town, and thereby throwing the weight of the United States into the scale of Britain, will render her mistress of the new world."

This plan, Livingston argued a few weeks later, would place a French buffer between the United States and Mexico, and an American buffer between French Louisiana and Canada, thus preventing both American and British aggression. The treaty he was proposing, he told Joseph, could form the basis for immediate discharge of debts due to American citizens, provided secrecy was observed. Secrecy was needed to "prevent the debts being the object of speculation *other than such as the First Consul shall authorize.*" This letter was not sent to Congress. When published in *American State Papers* in 1832, with the Secretary of State deciding what should go in, the words here italicized were omitted, thus converting a bribery proposal into a sermon on financial morality. The Secretary of State who made this and similar expurgations was Edward Livingston, Robert's brother.[4]

Livingston's plan would have robbed *uninformed* American claimants for the benefit of Joseph Bonaparte and Talleyrand. It would not have hurt informed insiders like James Swan, who had claims against France of about 2,500,000 livres, nor John R.

and Peter Livingston, whose claims ran up to 1,500,000 livres. These would be considered on their merits, and the more easily if the Livingston claims agent, Major Mountflorence, were given official status. A move in that direction drew the following from Legation Secretary Sumter:

"Should you determine to perform what you threatened on the 22nd [of October], viz. to make Major Mountflorence your secretary, you must employ him in some other place than in my office, for while I have the honor to hold the commission of secretary of the legation—which I thank God, will not be long—I shall continue to refuse and resist the employment of a person in it who has not the confidence of our government."

Sumter, a high-strung South Carolinian, already had resigned, telling Madison that he refused to be Livingston's personal servant. But to the minister himself he specified another reason—unwillingness to mix "the public and private agency of claims."[5]

Authorized speculation, Livingston soon concluded, was not a direct enough inducement. He expressed fear to Madison that his efforts to collect the debt would remain unsuccessful until "some motive more efficacious than that of justice, or national faith or credit," was held out:

"To enter into the financial arrangements of people in power here would lead me into a very delicate discussion, which would not tend to any advantage proportioned to the risk it might subject me to. I still think that if anything is done to satisfy our citizens, it must be by some advantageous offer on the part of our government. You will find some of my ideas on that subject sketched in my former letters."

That is, the necessities of French officials could be taken care of without risk to himself if the United States would adopt his August 10 suggestion of paying $20,000,000 for the Floridas.[6]

Livingston's December memoir to Joseph Bonaparte was sent to Talleyrand on January 18, 1803, as part of a note forcefully protesting the closing of New Orleans by Spain.[7] This complicated memorial had useful features. It continued the depreciation of Louisiana as a French asset and spelled out the inability of France to keep the colony out of British hands. But Livingston damaged his country's position by picturing the United States as both an abettor and victim of British imperialism. Instructed to persuade France that American self-interest forbade either a "voluntary or compulsive transfer" of Louisiana from *Spain* to Great Britain, he was portraying the United States as indifferent to a compulsive transfer from *France* to Britain. His memorial ran counter to Madison's warning to Pichon that if the United States were forced to join England, it could take these territories for itself. It fortified French colonial ambition by sanctioning French control of the Gulf of Mexico. And what would an American buffer line against England be worth to France if the United States were weak and subservient?

The logical conclusion from this memoir was that France must protect the colony herself, either by defeating England or by postponing a European war until St. Domingo was reconquered. The true American threat lay in emphasis on growing population and the unruly ambition and commercial necessities of 200,000 armed Westerners.

From Madison, through Pichon, Napoleon heard of an America so strong and determined that France had no choice but "of acceding to that which the force of events will give them in spite of us." Livingston pictured a people who would stand idly by while their most dreaded enemy surrounded their country on three sides by land and the fourth by sea—a people who out of pique against France would help make Britain the mistress of the Western world.

Livingston waited six weeks before dispatching this December 11 memoir to Madison. But twelve days after his original delivery of it, he wrote a cryptic note saying that he had "in a private memoir under the Consul's eye, touched a string that has alarmed them." (At that time, as shown by his correspondence with Joseph Bonaparte, he had heard nothing whatever of the reaction to it.) He continued to Madison:

"The minister [Talleyrand] knows nothing of this. Set on foot a negotiation fixing our bound with Britain, but by no means conclude until you hear from me that all hope here is lost."

Madison described this message as an enigma, suggesting "some hazardous finesse or some unwarrantable project rather than a hope of successful negotiation." And what possessed Livingston to put such a confidential letter, "not even in cipher, into the hands of a British minister" (who carried it for him to London) when he could have sent the whole memoir in cipher through the French mails, safely and more quickly? Jefferson replied that if the American minister was "contending by stratagem against those exercised in it from their cradle," he would undoubtedly be outwitted.[8]

A week after Livingston delivered his December memoir, Napoleon learned that Leclerc's army was virtually blotted out. He instantly (but too late) ordered General Victor to sail for Louisiana before the Dutch harbors froze up, and gave him sealed orders to divert all but 2,000 of his men to St. Domingo. Victor already was instructed to take possession of New Orleans and everything west of the Mississippi, supplant American commerce with the French West Indies, and fortify the colony against American or British attack by alliances with Indians east of the river.[9]

On the last day of the year, Napoleon chose the No. 2 man of France, General Bernadotte, for minister to the United States. Livingston argued against a shift of negotiations to Washington: it would delay a treaty. The foreign minister replied that it was necessary to gather information on the right of deposit for a final decision in Paris, but Livingston "must consider the purchase of the country as out of the question."

Bernadotte had no power of negotiation. He was instructed, in effect, to employ his military and personal prestige to make the Americans swallow the French occupation of Louisiana. As to the right of deposit, France saw with pleasure (he was told) that Spain had established its treaty right of granting or refusing it at will. France could maintain freedom of choice more easily than Spain established it.[10]

Thus, in the opening weeks of 1803, the French foreign minister showed hostility to every major American objective. Napoleon gave no sign of abandoning his colonial ambitions. Another stunning blow in St. Domingo—Leclerc's death by fever—produced an order to send 15,000 men to his incompetent successor. Livingston, unremittingly active, had made no visible progress. For the sake of a finesse on French fear of Britain he had thrown away the concept of American strength and determination needed to back his much bolder utterances about New Orleans.

To overset these conditions a conjuncture was needed: new pressures from the United States and a heightened prospect of war in Europe. The First Consul, who usually chose war, had freedom of choice. He could maintain temporary peace in Europe and concentrate on St. Domingo and Louisiana. He could abandon those colonies temporarily and hope to get them back by defeating England. Or he could use war in Europe to cover the failure of his American undertakings. The second and third choices overlapped and were being pushed on him by the steady deterioration in St. Domingo after Leclerc's death. To bring about permanent abandonment of North America one thing more was needed—a conclusion, the admission of which could not have been dragged from Napoleon by artillery horses, that the United States would join England in the next war and take Louisiana away from him.

This final pressure began to come. On December 22, the French foreign office received a political analysis from Pichon, written prior to the New Orleans news. Madison had spoken to him of unfriendly articles in the controlled French press. The administration wanted better relations, while the Federalist party, seeking to ride into power, "sounds the tocsin against our supposed ambition, our tendency to universal empire, and our principles." The tendency of French coldness, said this shrewd diplomat, "is to alienate one party from us irrevocably without the slightest chance of winning the one which hopes to profit from it." The Federalists were systematically hostile to France, friendly to England. Should they win, the counterpoise of the opposing party would be destroyed and the feeling of danger would push the United States and England into an alliance. France should prepare for the consequences, the chargé warned, "if we have sufficient motives for following a system which seems likely to bring on this combination."

On January 4 Pichon wrote that he had visited Madison at his home the day before and learned from him "how uneasy and estranged they were" in regard to France. "I furnish you, Citizen Minister, word for word and without comment the conversation of Mr. Madison." The Secretary said:

"Is it not singular, Mr. Pichon, that Mr. Livingston had not been able to obtain, at the date of his last letter from Paris, a word of response to the inquiries he has made on the subject of our interests and our rights upon the Mississippi? Certainly if people behaved thus toward you, you would regard this silence as a sort of declaration of war. It is absolutely necessary that our position with respect to you be clarified, or it will soon become more serious. We wish to live in peace with all the world, but I fear that in France they may not be willing to let us follow our inclinations in this regard."

Pichon enclosed a Philadelphia newspaper article quoting Jefferson as saying at dinner that it might become the policy of the United States to make an alliance with Great Britain to resist Bonaparte's passion to dominate the world. Whether the President actually said this he didn't know, but it conformed to the sentiments published in Republican newspapers.[11]

With Western commerce still blocked, the Jefferson administration was under tremendous pressure to make war on Spain. Forcible possession of New Orleans, Chargé Thornton wrote on January 3, would be the most popular action the President could take. The war cry of the Westerners was spontaneous. Federalist editors and politicians, for partisan advantage, goaded them on and denounced the government for weakness. Congress, in which passions ran high, obtained executive papers on the treaty violation, together with the President's pledge to maintain the rights of the nation by just and honorable means.

By early January, Madison had received Livingston's desponding note of November 11, forecasting his own failure and a probable French attack on Natchez. Advice had come from Du Pont to offer $6,000,000 for the Floridas—a suggestion which actually was his own idea, but which was taken to mean that he had sounded the French government.[12]

Partly to attack the diplomatic stalemate, partly to reduce the Western war fever, President Jefferson decided to appoint a special envoy. Retiring Governor James Monroe, former minister to France, was united in separate missions with Livingston in Paris and Pinckney in Madrid. Acting secretly on a committee report "which it's well known was drawn up by Mr. Madison," Congress voted $2,000,000 for unspecified diplomatic purposes. "The Floridas and New Orleans," wrote Madison for the committee, "command the only outlets to the sea" for the American West, and "must become a part of the United States, either by purchase or conquest." Knowing that some congressmen were advocating conquest, he prefaced the request for the appropriation by asking whether we should lay the foundation for future peace or the hazards and horrors of war, "the great scourge of the human race."[13]

Advice leading to the Monroe mission came first from John Graham, secretary of the Madrid legation—"a sensible and steady young man" who spent two days at Montpelier in 1801 and furnished ideas which went into the instructions to his own superior.[14] From him, late in November 1802, Madison received a far more accurate account of the Spanish attitude toward the Mississippi and war claims than he read in Pinckney's cheerful forecasts. Following the signing of a limited claims convention, Graham felt it his duty to state that:

"In my opinion nothing will be done here advantageous to the United States unless another minister is sent out pointedly charged to speak boldly . . . a man of talents and address."

Graham reported that Spain's cession to France followed ancient boundaries. Frenchmen in Madrid were saying "they get
back Louisiana as of right belonging to them," meaning, he
thought, a boundary on the Mobile River. With this uncertainty
prevailing, Monroe was instructed to go first to Paris, then to
Madrid "should the whole or any part of the cession be found to
depend . . . on the Spanish government." As far as personal
factors entered into it, he was sent because of Pinckney's weakness,
not from distrust of Livingston. His function was to add weight
to the efforts in France, or furnish competence to those in Spain.[15]

But that was only part of the story. Appealing to Monroe to
accept, President Jefferson said he must go in order to calm the
West and to thwart the Federalists, whose object was to return
to power by winning the fevered Westerners. "Their confidence
in Monroe will tranquillize them," he wrote to his son-in-law.[16]
Thus Jefferson was swayed by aversion to war and federalism,
while Madison used Western unrest as a weapon to promote the
cession which both desired. The instructions to Livingston and
Monroe, written by Madison and heartily indorsed by the President, directed them

"to treat with the Government of the French Republic on the
subject of the Mississippi, and the territories eastward thereof,
and without the limits of the United States. The object in view
is to procure, by just and satisfactory arrangements, a cession to
the United States of New Orleans and of West and East Florida,
or as much thereof as the actual proprietor can be prevailed on
to part with."[17]

Purchase of territory beyond the Mississippi was outside of the
object but not beyond their implied powers. They were to negotiate and sign a treaty, their "full power" set forth, "concerning
the enlargement and more effective security of the rights and
interests of the United States in the River Mississippi and in the
territories eastward thereof." The most effective security to rights
in a river lay in the ownership of its banks, and this applied as
much to the headwaters of the Missouri and the Arkansas as to

the Mississippi delta. France's claim to the northwestern plains and mountains was based on the doctrine that discovery and occupation of a river mouth gave title to the entire watershed. The thought of ultimate American possession lay behind Jefferson's decision to send his private secretary, Captain Meriwether Lewis, on an exploring trip to the Pacific Northwest. When that project was laid before Congress, just after Monroe's appointment, Senator Plumer recorded the President's remark on Christmas Eve that "we might through those agents purchase land of the Indians or think of conquest."[18]

Madison's instructions took French acquisition of Louisiana as a certainty and assumed that France did not mean to court or force war. The French could hardly fail to see that hostile measures against the United States would "connect their councils and their colossal growth with the great and formidable rival of France." Prudence alone ought to warn that country against assuming the hazards of proximity revealed by the collisions at New Orleans. The unanimity of the nation should convince France that friendship and peace "must be precarious until the Mississippi shall be made the boundary between the United States and Louisiana."

Madison refuted the reasons related to the United States, which led France to desire Louisiana and the Floridas. First was the fear that the Atlantic states, leaning toward a coalition with Great Britain, would enable that power to acquire New Orleans and thereby either extend its influence over all the states or seduce the West into a separate government allied with her. This, he asserted, mistook both the disposition of the East and the temper of the West. Nor could France split the nation. The Atlantic states were disposed to amity and impartiality toward both France and England, except as they met with injustice from one or the other. As for the rest of the country:

"The Western people believe, as do their Atlantic brethren, that they have a natural and indefeasible right to trade freely through the Mississippi. They are conscious of their power to enforce this right against any nation whatever."

This contrasted sharply with Livingston's memorials, which held that New Orleans and part of the Floridas should be transferred to the United States to prevent British conquest of them with American support. Madison emphasized that as a source of supplies, Louisiana would be useless to the West Indian colonies when most needed, in time of war. The envoys were to promise France the right of deposit at New Orleans for ten years, by which time a French port could be built on the opposite shore, and special tax and commercial privileges. Annexed inhabitants should be pledged full rights of citizenship, by law.

The price was left flexible, but the President was willing to go up to fifty million livres ($9,375,000),[19] including $2,000,000 already authorized. The remainder was to be applied by the United States to the claims of American citizens against France. Should that country refuse any territorial cession whatever, the envoys were to seek an enlargement of the right of deposit at New Orleans, by ownership of real estate, maintaining consuls, etc., and were to try to obtain similar depots at the mouths of other navigable streams.

In a private letter, Madison pledged a spirit of justice and peace as long as the conduct of other nations allowed it. But, he told Monroe, France and Spain would have to revise their relations to the United States if they wished to retain American friendship or avoid a more formidable state of affairs than either of them had yet experienced.[20]

Explaining the Monroe mission to Thornton, Madison was so fluent that the latter suspected a bid for an alliance. The Secretary, he commented, "has from his natural temper been less frank with me than the President," yet he opened the subject without waiting for leading questions. The closing of New Orleans, Madison said, "had excited so many new impressions that they should be very poorly satisfied indeed with restoring things to the footing on which they stood by the treaty with Spain." Their object, with France, was to extend their rights by absolute jurisdiction over all the territory they could acquire "by purchase or any other inducement" on one side of the river.[21]

Here was the reason for the diminishing alternatives in the

Monroe instructions. Without war or the coercive threat of it, the United States could not go beyond its treaty rights with Spain unless France was willing. At this time nothing was known of Livingston's overtures for the Arkansas country. When his memorials and arguments are compared with Madison's instructions and talks with Pichon, it appears that Livingston asked for more than his reasoning warranted, while Madison put sustaining logic behind more than he asked for. The effect was to put Madison's reasoning behind the combined projects, with the force of it coming from the temper of the American people.

CHAPTER IX

Pressure through Pichon

Confirmed on January 12, 1803, Monroe sailed with his family for France on March 9 and landed April 8. Madison financed the private costs by buying more than two hundred pieces of solid silver tableware, including "one soup spoon, the other in Albemarle to be had of Hannah," and other articles which Monroe had brought from France when he retired as minister. Dolley Madison rejoiced over three dozen Sèvres porcelain plates and a set of white and gold tea china. To finance the deal, Monroe borrowed several thousand dollars at various banks and £40 from his overseer, which Madison was to pay off. It was a good bargain for the envoy, who needed one. By replacing these compact articles at a lower price, he could recoup some of the $4,000 he had paid to French pirates for packing and freighting his furniture at his previous return.[1]

Livingston, meeting with steady rebuffs, was made more despondent by news that a colleague was coming. He sincerely wished, he wrote to Madison, that this would be attended with the desired effect: "It will, however, cut off one resource on which I greatly relied; because I had established a confidence which it will take Mr. Monroe some time to inspire on what regards 540.1675.1460.1541. and had made arrangements for satisfying them which I must now relinquish." Madison did not interline the ciphered passage. When published in 1832 the sentence was cut off at the word "inspire." The words in cipher were "personal interest."[2]

It would indeed take a long time to inspire Talleyrand with confidence that Monroe would join in giving him what he failed to obtain in the XYZ affair. Writing to Gouverneur Morris, who would understand such things, Livingston was more specific:

"I had prepared everything, first by creating a personal interest, next by showing the inutility of Louisiana to France. . . . I had advanced so far as to have been upon the point of concluding when the appointment of Mr. Monroe stopped my operations."[3]

It was untrue that he was on the point of concluding anything, but if he stated the sequence correctly, the arrangement to satisfy Talleyrand preceded delivery of his memoir of August 1802. That was the period of his bribery discussions with Daniel Parker and of his suggestion to Madison that the United States pay $20,000,000 for the Floridas. Over and over he revealed himself as a would-be briber of the French ministry, and the evidence of it was stricken out of his published dispatches.

Madison rendered these overtures abortive by ignoring them, but his opinion was evident in a comment to Monroe. Remarking that King George's March message made war certain between England and France, he wrote: "I hope we shall be wise enough to shun their follies and fortunate enough to turn them by honest means to our just interests. You will probably have arrived very critically for the purpose." American prospects looked bright to him:

"Excepting the case of Louisiana, there is scarcely a cloud in them. Remove that, and the possibility of our being embarrassed by the war of others, and our country will be what has been so often applied to another, the admiration and envy of the world."[4]

Late in February, Livingston with Talleyrand's permission wrote directly to the First Consul. The result was a rebuke for mixing delicate territorial questions with war claims. "With respect to Louisiana," Livingston wrote to Jefferson, "I think nothing will be effected here." And telling Madison that France was fixedly determined to treat only in America (though Talleyrand in this same note had stated the contrary), he said he had "nothing more to do on this subject than to endeavor to get the right of depot" restored at New Orleans. If Monroe could suggest anything better, he would heartily concur with him. However, one statement in Talleyrand's harsh note was cheering:

"As to the American debts . . . it is entirely new to us that they can be raised, by any valuation whatever, to the sum of twenty millions [of livres]. The First Consul charges me to request of you an exact, full, certain, and verified statement of these debts. . . . You may rest assured, sir, that upon being furnished with such a statement, every claim will be promptly and fully discharged."[5]

Although this promise was full of loopholes, it was the first positive pledge that Livingston had been able to extort and he made the most of it. "You will find in it," he wrote to Madison, "such strong and such satisfactory assurances on the subject of the debt, as I think gives us the firmest prospects of its speedy payment." To prevent creditors from suffering "by the speculations of those who were in the secret," he said, he had notified those who were then in Paris and directed a friend to make it public in America.

This solicitude was touching, coming from a man who had just tried to finance the bribery of French officials by taking advantage of the ignorance of these same claimants. Why did not Livingston prevent speculation by the simpler method of *saying nothing* about Talleyrand's letter? His obvious desire was to obtain publicity. In Paris he obtained it by calling a public meeting of the resident American claimants, who numbered about thirty and centered in a group led by James Swan. To them he read portions of the Talleyrand note, thus *creating the need* to protect several hundred claimants in America by similar publicity.

When a New York politician acts thus in Paris, *cherchez le candidat*. The day after he told of these maneuvers Livingston wrote once more to Madison. He was sick of courts and of expenses beyond his salary. He hoped that Monroe was empowered to take his place, as he had in no event intended to remain beyond the spring of 1804 and would like to return by September 1803. To restate this politically, he was planning to run for Vice President, with the American creditors as his expected backers and James Swan his Paris campaign manager.[6]

During March, Livingston handed Talleyrand the most powerful note he ever penned, on the American determination to keep the Mississippi open and the likelihood of armed action if farm produce rotted for lack of transport. It was in the spirit of Madison's instructions of December 16, toned down to suit the amenities of diplomacy. A few days later (so he informed the Secretary of State) Talleyrand told him that a reply had been prepared and everything would be arranged about American rights in New Orleans. "Unfortunately," Livingston continued, "dispatches arrived at that moment from Mr. Pichon, informing them that the appointment of Mr. Monroe had tranquillized everything." Talleyrand decided to wait for the storm to blow over and sent a different note "which contains nothing."[7]

Talleyrand's apparent devotion to French interest conflicts with Livingston's assertion that he had arranged to satisfy personal interest. However, something else was happening just then. On March 21, the day before Pichon's dispatches arrived, British Ambassador Whitworth sent a message to his government. *In a day or two* he would sound out Talleyrand on the acceptance of a £100,000 bribe, to be divided with Joseph Bonaparte and others, on condition that they persuade Napoleon to preserve the peace of Amiens and leave Malta in British hands in exchange for a free hand on the continent. On the twenty-fourth, he wrote that Talleyrand and Joseph were both willing, but others had to be brought in and it would take at least double that sum.[8]

The recoil on American affairs was instantaneous. Whitworth's offer of cash wiped out Livingston's less metallic arrangements and produced an abrupt reversal by Talleyrand and Joseph Bonaparte. The British concessions meant little to a conqueror aiming at Egypt through Malta. The strongest inducement to a sacrifice of that island was the argument that by remaining at peace he could retain Louisiana, resist American demands at New Orleans and gain the Floridas.

Senator Fouché, Whitworth reported, was the only bribetaker who dared oppose Napoleon's war plans to his face. Retention of Louisiana, with European peace as the way to it, was dinned into his ears by Talleyrand and Napoleon's brothers. Talleyrand begged him not to dismember the French Empire, but admitted, when Napoleon raised the point, that France would not be dis-

membered by sale of Spanish territory. Joseph and Lucien Bonaparte invaded their brother's bath and defended Louisiana so violently that they were deluged with perfumed water, the valet
fainted, and historians grew ecstatic over their patriotic devotion
to France.[9]

Pichon's report of a tranquillized West was the pretext, not the
reason, for Talleyrand's about-face. Nevertheless, the conspiratorial pressure on the French ruler enormously increased the importance of events and attitudes in America. Judged solely by conditions in Europe, the advice thrust upon Napoleon by his bribed
counselors was sound. With his brothers and his foreign minister
urging him to hold Louisiana and keep the British out of the
province by remaining at peace, any indication of American weakness or indecision might tip the balance. On the opposite side was
Napoleon's lust for conquest in Europe and Africa. It would be
most likely to prevail if fortified by evidence that Louisiana would
sooner or later be taken by the United States. Into the scales, at
this point, were thrown the Monroe mission and the crucial dispatches of Pichon.

The chargé d'affaires told of a conflict between the peaceful disposition of the Jefferson administration and the high spirit and
energetic intentions of the people. He said that if France had
hostile aims in Louisiana, conditions in St. Domingo and Europe
were expected to delay French action and give time for negotiations. If these failed, the United States could make alliances and
act with greater vigor after ten years' growth. Back of this was
awareness that the costs of war would hurt the administration's
popularity. So Monroe was sent to appease and control the fer-
ments of the West.

Six days later (March 28) the French government received a
further account from Pichon which first documented and then
radically changed his earlier story. Dining with the President on
January 12, he had been told "that Mr. Monroe was so well known
to be a friend of the Western people that his mission would con-
tribute more than anything else to tranquillize them and prevent
unfortunate incidents." The administration "would try peaceful

means to the last moment and they hoped that France would be disposed to concur in their views for the preservation of harmony."

On the fourteenth, Madison invited Pichon to his office and gave him a very different story. Events at New Orleans proved that navigation of the Mississippi would never be surely guaranteed until the boundary marked by nature separated the Americans from their neighbors and freed them from foreign caprice. If France should obtain Louisiana and the Floridas, all difficulty could be prevented by ceding the territory east of the Mississippi to the United States. The treaty could assure France all of the commercial advantages she expected from the acquisition of Louisiana, and Monroe would be authorized to offer perhaps two or three million dollars, which the situation of St. Domingo might render especially useful.

Using a map, Madison showed that the Floridas were useless to France but increasingly important to the United States as cotton growing expanded on the upper reaches of the Mobile and other rivers. "The free navigation of these rivers was inseparable from the very existence of the United States." On the other hand, New Orleans was of no interest to France, which could quickly build a better located city on the opposite shore.

Madison then offered an argument that was destined to make a deep impression on Napoleon. He warned France, in well-veiled terms, not to provoke a forcible expansion of the United States beyond the Mississippi. It was not to the interest of his country to have circumstances arise (that is, a war) which would carry its population to the western bank. Said the Secretary:

"Was it not evident in fact that, since these emigrations tended to weaken the state and slacken the concentration of its forces, it was not sound policy to encourage them? In spite of the affinities of custom and language, a colony beyond the river could not exist under the same government. It would give birth infallibly to a separate state, having in its bosom the germs of collision with the East, all the more ready to develop because there would be more connections between the two empires."

It might happen, Madison continued, that the conduct of France would "determine the political combinations" (that is, produce the American alliance with England) that would lead to these eventualities. No doubt these would be unpleasant for the United States, but the alliances would be still more so for France. These were the considerations that led to the sending of Monroe, and "public opinion and the interests of the United States imperatively required that this mission should have a prompt conclusion."

As it related to expansion beyond the Mississippi, Madison could have picked his own argument to pieces more readily than anybody else. He was describing what would result from holding Louisiana as an American *colony* open to uncontrolled immigration. Settled slowly and admitted state by state, it would (and later did) fit perfectly into the doctrine which guided him in the making of the Constitution—that in a self-governing republic, stability and freedom increase in proportion to the country's size, provided it is federally organized. The argument, however, served perfectly to carry a threat of war, so worded that it could not be treated as such.

Pichon realized at once that the motive of "tranquillizing the West" was out of the window. "The implicit language of Mr. Madison, which I have taken care to convey faithfully to you," he wrote to Talleyrand, "brings to light ideas too general to be neglected." Long ago, he said, he had displayed the germ of these ideas to his government, in the contrast between the growth and progress of the United States and the jealousy and inattention shown toward them in Europe. French policy, the diplomat asserted, must be founded on these (among other) incontestable conclusions:

1. French colonies, as experience proved, could not exist at any time without the friendship of the United States.

2. In Louisiana, "we are dependent on them in time of peace: at their mercy in the first war with England."

"The crisis, [Pichon declared] grows greater every day, and we cannot push it into the distant future. . . . I should fail in my duty if I did not tell you that these feelings of concern which Mr.

Madison expressed to me are generally felt and that public opinion in the latest circumstances expresses itself at least as strongly and
energetically as the government."[10]

Napoleon and Talleyrand now had before them two contra-
dictory descriptions of American policy—from Jefferson an assurance of devotion to peace and harmony to the last moment,
from Madison a warning that war could be averted only if France
speedily changed her ways. The two men were not in actual dis-
agreement. Jefferson gave voice to his pacifism and made a domestic political utterance, both in the wrong place. Madison made
effective use of an American war spirit which he did not share.
The President corrected himself a fortnight later in a letter to
Pierre du Pont: "Our circumstances are so imperious as to admit
of no delay. . . . Whatever power, other than ourselves, holds the
country east of the Mississippi becomes our natural enemy." Like
his 1802 remark about marrying the British fleet and nation (also
paraphrased from Madison) this had a brilliance which swept it
to fame as a supposed determinant of policy. In reality it did not
even reach its destination. Livingston and Monroe withheld it
because, the former said, Du Pont's warm imagination made him
a risky ally. However, the full weight of Pichon's dispatches supported these vigorous sentiments as Madison had expressed them
earlier, and a supplemental note testified to the shift in Jefferson's
position:

"Necessity is forcing Mr. Jefferson to give up his pretensions
and scruples against an English alliance. I have observed at table
that he redoubles his kindnesses and attention to the British
chargé d'affaires."[11]

Talleyrand could not believe that this was the same country
to which he fled from the revolutionary terror. "Have conditions
changed so greatly today that the United States have a different
interest?" he asked Pichon. Explanations, he felt sure, would end
the distrust and he awaited eagerly the arrival of Monroe. Talleyrand now did a surprising thing. He praised the modest diplo-

mat who for two years had been blowing holes through his policies. With Pichon's duties as chargé d'affaires drawing to an end

"I wish to testify to you how well satisfied I have been at the manner in which you have fulfilled them. You have more often had to be an observer of events than to direct them, . . . but I have nonetheless examined with great attention the different objects with which you have been occupied, and I shall continue to pay the same attention to those you continue to deal with."[12]

This was a small fraction of the recognition Pichon deserved. He was the keenest observer, the clearest analyst, the sanest counselor and the most courageous critic of his own superiors that the French Republic had ever sent to America. He had been rebuked for exceeding his powers but never for failures of interpretation. Through him, not through Livingston, came the impressive, persuasive statements of American policy. Nothing he reported could swerve Talleyrand from his new zeal for Louisiana, inspired by Whitworth's £100,000, but all that he wrote reached Napoleon, whose mind was inscrutable and whose policies were fluid. What would Napoleon, who had publicly told the British ambassador "I must either have Malta or war," think of a colony which would be at the mercy of the United States, if not of England, the moment hostilities started? What would he think of a union between this newborn giant and his direst enemy? And what of the hint that Louisiana, if seized by the United States, would ultimately break the American colossus in two and neutralize its power?

In Washington, Madison continued to press Pichon, who reported to Talleyrand in February that people and government were growing more suspicious every day. Public opinion, stirred by the unbroken blockade at New Orleans, was making a remarkable swing toward England, and the Federalist party "moves heaven and earth for war." Senator Ross of Pennsylvania, seeking to convict the administration of weakness, had moved to give the President authority to raise 50,000 men and take New Orleans by force. His violent speech urging seizure of Louisiana before the

French arrived was delivered behind closed doors, but, senatorlike, he repeated it to Pichon himself in the Capitol lobby.

As Madison saw them, Ross's propositions "drove at war through a delegation of unconstitutional power to the Executive." Yet partisan as the senator's action was, it reflected the genuine feeling of others. Only after weeks of violent debate were the administration forces able to pass a milder substitute. Madison, during the agitation, warned the governors of Pennsylvania, Kentucky and Tennessee against a lawless plan to send armed forces into Louisiana. The report of an invasion troop gathering at Pittsburgh, he told Pichon, was without foundation. But, speaking so loudly in a social circle that many heard him, he made all possible use of this war spirit.

"He told me [reported the French diplomat] that it was true the nation was in a ferment, especially in the West; that it felt its strength, and that it needed all the confidence it had in the government to prevent it from acting. That this circumstance had made the United States itself examine the national disposition, and to conclude that it held the balance in the new world and could decide it at any moment: there was one power which realized this perfectly, and it was to be hoped that all would realize it."

Madison then laid down a policy which not only anticipated the Monroe Doctrine, but foreshadowed the extension given it by President Cleveland in the Anglo-Venezuelan dispute of 1895:

"That the United States had no inclination to make a trial of their strength, but if they were obliged to do so, it was easy to see what the outcome would be: that in truth their interest was that the new world remain at peace; that the wars of Europe should not prolong their ravages there, and that it would depend in great part on them, one day, to guarantee it this tranquillity."[13]

Tension eased just then on receipt of a long-delayed November letter from Livingston containing Talleyrand's oral pledge to respect American treaty rights derived from Spain. Had this promise been in writing, Madison remarked to Pichon, the present ferment would be dissipated. He hoped that all the past would be buried in the results of the Monroe mission, but gave notice that if the European war was renewed, as seemed likely, "the United States would be obliged to take a higher tone than he had used." Their moderation had been taken in Europe as proof that they would not go beyond it.

Pichon and Yrujo were now working with Madison to reduce the war spirit by putting pressure on the stubborn intendant at New Orleans. Both of these ministers, the Secretary reported to Jefferson, "are deeply alarmed at the apparent tendency of things and seem willing to risk themselves for the purpose of checking it." Relying on Livingston's letter, Pichon published a letter to the Spanish governor saying that France disapproved of the closing of the port. Though otherwise futile, Madison remarked, his action rescued France "from the odium thrown on her suspected agency." Underneath all this, according to British Chargé Thornton, was a deep-seated belief that the intendant never would have taken so important a step without positive orders from home. That was indeed the truth, though more than a hundred years elapsed before the proof of it came to light.[14]

Monroe himself carried Pichon's February dispatches, helpful to his cause, but he had been two weeks in Paris before they were recorded as received by the Foreign Office.[15]

On February 20, Napoleon sent a message to the French parliament on the glory and soundness of France and the need of more troops and taxes. He swept the world in microscopic detail, naming more than fifty countries, colonies, cities and rivers— everything on earth that came within the orbit of French interest except the following: he did not mention Spain, the United States, Louisiana, New Orleans or the Mississippi. Such omissions could indicate only embarrassment, uncertainty or secret purposes. The First Consul countermanded the order for General Victor to sail to New Orleans, but that was a natural precaution against war hazards.

As war and Monroe's ship both drew closer, Livingston was inspired with new hope and an overwhelming desire to present

his colleague with a *fait accompli*. His old instructions authorized him to "ascertain the price" at which New Orleans and the
Floridas could be bought. He had complained several times about
his lack of power to make a definite offer, but short of that his
powers were adequate. Instead of waiting for reinforcements
and fresh instructions, he addressed a new memorial to Talleyrand. "The critical moment is arrived," he averred, "which rivets
the connection of the United States to France, or binds a young
and growing people for ages hereafter to her mortal and inveter-
ate enemy." He told how highly he esteemed the old Franco-
American alliance and repeated his proposal that France cede
New Orleans and Louisiana above the Arkansas. The alternative
was British conquest of the whole territory and encirclement and
possible domination of the United States.[16]

Both of Livingston's alternatives made his country the tail of
a European kite. The first violated government policy by suggesting a renewed alliance with France. The second ignored all
that Madison had written about preventing a transfer of Louisiana
to Great Britain and pictured his country as too weak to prevent
it. Both of them conflicted with admonitions Monroe was bringing that the United States wished to act with friendly impartiality
toward both France and England, but would uphold its rights
against any nation whatsoever.

As late as April 1, Napoleon still seemed to retain hope of holding Louisiana. Bernadotte's prolonged stay in Paris, he wrote to
Talleyrand, was very harmful. "The necessity of his presence in
America does not admit another hour's delay." His departure
was urgent only if Napoleon had thoughts of holding Louisiana
through a war, with American aid.

A week passed and the French ruler had news. Livingston, on
April 8, sent Talleyrand a clipping from the New York *Chronicle*,
giving the text of Senator Ross's motion to appropriate $5,000,000
and raise 50,000 troops for the seizure of New Orleans. But instead of using this to enlarge his demands and backing them with
the imminence of Monroe's arrival, the minister's only thought
was to get ahead of his colleague. To open the way for separate
negotiation he said there were reports that Monroe's departure

might be postponed—a probably fatal fact, if true. Nothing would be more grateful to his own feelings "than to be indebted solely to the friendship of the First Consul for the restoration of our rights" at New Orleans. Saying not a word about a land cession, he used the powerful weapon of the Ross resolution to support a microscopic concession to his own prestige.

A continent, not the American right of deposit, was in Napoleon's thoughts. And here, in this newspaper clipping, was menacing corroboration of the warnings which had been pouring in from Pichon. Louisiana was lost, either to the British or the Americans, and one thing more was plain: if the Americans stood ready to take this country from Spain, to forestall France, they would never let it pass from themselves to England.

On that same day Monroe landed at Le Havre. The hour of decision was at hand.[17]

CHAPTER X

NAPOLEON SELLS AN EMPIRE

LIVINGSTON had scant hope when he sent a greeting to Monroe on Easter Sunday, April 10. "War may do something for us," he wrote. "Nothing else would. I have paved the way for you, and if you could add to my memoirs an assurance that we were now in possession of New Orleans we should do well." No such assurance could be given, but knowledge of Monroe's coming fortified the threat contained in the Ross resolution. "I have apprised the minister of your arrival," Livingston went on, "and told him you would be here on Tuesday or Wednesday."

Napoleon said nothing of his purposes when notified of the envoy's landing. With Talleyrand it was now or never. Louisiana must be held if he was to deter Napoleon from war and win Lord Whitworth's £100,000. To paralyze the mission, he drafted a reply to Livingston's ignored memorials, the last of which had been given to him a week or two before. The First Consul would willingly remove misunderstandings, but Louisiana was ruled by an independent foreign power. The silence of the friendly French government could mean only that some uncompleted negotiation existed between Spain and France. The United States would surely be the first to whom the result would be officially communicated.

Perhaps Napoleon saw this letter; perhaps not. It lies in the French archives, marked *"Nulle."*[1]

On that same Sunday, the First Consul summoned Marbois and Decrès to St. Cloud. What took place is known chiefly from Marbois' *Histoire de la Louisiane,* written a quarter of a century later—an account dressed up for his own glory but generally sustained by contemporary records. Napoleon, Marbois wrote, told his ministers that he knew the value of Louisiana and had wished to repair the diplomatic blunder by which it was lost in

1763. England was steadily stripping France of colonies and had both the desire and the power to take this one. Said the First Consul:

"I have not a moment to lose to put it beyond her reach. . . . I am thinking of ceding it to the United States. . . . They ask me only for one city of Louisiana, but I regard the entire colony as already lost, and it seems to me that in the hands of this new-born power, it will be more useful to the policy and even to the commerce of France, than if I should try to retain it. Tell me, each of you, what you think."

Finance Minister Marbois realized that the decision was already made, but to agree imposed no strain. He had spent years in the United States and St. Domingo. His wife was an American. "We should not hesitate," he replied, "to sacrifice what is going to slip away from us." How could Louisiana be defended against British naval power? The Americans could conquer it still more easily. Reaching the Mississippi by a number of navigable rivers, "they need but enter the country to be its masters." Even if it could be held by France, the ancient French commercial monopoly could not be restored, and prosperity would carry the germ of independence.

Admiral Decrès (who at twenty-one served under De Grasse at Yorktown) told his chief that France could have no Navy without such colonies. Even if the British took Louisiana, a French conquest of Hanover, whose royal family ruled England, would be the pledge of its restoration. Napoleon kept the two ministers in the palace that night. At daybreak he summoned Marbois and said:

"I renounce Louisiana. It is not only New Orleans that I mean to cede; it is the whole colony, reserving none of it."

The finance minister was to conduct the negotiations. Nobody else but Talleyrand was to know of it. Marbois should see Livingston that day, not waiting for Monroe's arrival. The price?

Fifty million francs would be acceptable. (Napoleon's draft of a treaty specified one hundred millions, plus American assumption of war claims, and that was what Marbois asked for.) But the sale must produce real money to help finance the coming war with England.[2]

So much from the *Histoire*. Telling Livingston about this meeting, Marbois remarked that he had spoken of the story, published in England, about Congress raising 50,000 men to take New Orleans. "The Consul said he had seen it too, and had also seen that something was said about two millions of dollars being disposed among the people about him, to bribe them." Livingston, whose own plans for taking care of Talleyrand had come to naught, told Madison how this senatorial canard affected Napoleon. He distrusted the foreign minister "and meant to put the negotiations into the hands of Marbois, whose character for integrity is established."[3]

Napoleon had later news than Livingston about the American war threats. "The London cabinet," he remarked to Marbois during their Easter conference, "is informed of the resolutions taken at Washington." This meant that he had received the London newspapers of April 7. He renounced Louisiana after reading of the Senate's vote for fifteen gunboats to cruise in the Mississippi, of the impending call for 80,000 militia, of Senator Smith's statement that he considered the country "as on the eve of a war." In the *Times,* which came to him daily by diplomatic pouch, he read the following:

"Whether Spain continues in possession of Louisiana, or possession is taken by France, it is no longer doubtful that the deliberations of Congress are in unison with the feelings of the people. . . . The government and people seem to be aware that a decisive blow must be struck before the arrival of the expedition now waiting in the ports of Holland."

Except for price and boundaries, the Louisiana negotiations were over before they began. Talleyrand took up the subject with Livingston before Marbois did. Livingston responded with an effort to get something on paper before Monroe reached Paris. He told Madison that as he was pressing Talleyrand that day (April 11) on the danger of British conquest, the foreign minister asked "whether we wished to have the whole of Louisiana. I told him no, that our wishes extended only to New Orleans and the Floridas," but that it was sound French policy to give the country above the Arkansas. Talleyrand, pretending that he was acting without authority, said that without New Orleans the rest would have little value, and asked what the United States would give for the whole. Livingston supposed they would not object to twenty million francs, which the foreign minister thought too low. "I told him that, as Mr. Monroe would be in town in two days, I would delay my further offer."

The decision to sell Louisiana, Livingston reported, resulted from his persuasion of Talleyrand, and from the probability of European war. The New Orleans affair gave him "two very important strings to touch." The United States was likely to take the Floridas from Spain, while Great Britain assuredly would seize them, and open the way to conquest of Louisiana, the instant they were transferred from Spain to France. The decision was precipitated, he believed, by his sending of the Ross resolution to Talleyrand, with "an informal note expressive of my fears that it would be carried into effect, and requesting that General Bernadotte might not go till something effectual was done."[4]

In dealing with Livingston, one always has to compare what he says with what he did. Talleyrand was overruled by Napoleon, not converted by Livingston, and the latter's belief that the Ross motion would pass was expressed in these words: "What the effect of these resolutions were was not known." His note of April 8 said not a word about Bernadotte, but on April 12—the day after he wrote in this fashion to Madison—he made a decidedly different request of Talleyrand. Not that Bernadotte be held, but that he be speeded on his way bearing dispatches from Livingston alone. "Before Mr. Monroe arrives, before he has been formally received," wrote his distressed colleague, "there will be a lapse of time too valuable to be lost." He pleaded with Talleyrand to "answer my last note with something positive," or even send "an unofficial piece which I could transmit by General Bernadotte as forming the basis of negotiations which have been opened," and for which Livingston could anticipate an agreeable ending.

No paltry financial arrangements (impossible to make without Monroe's participation) should cloud this noble gesture. Livingston knew just what he wanted:

"Something in the form of a note or letter on your part . . . couched in generous terms. You could express the friendship of the First Consul for the United States, his desire to give them striking indication of it in ceding the whole of Louisiana to them. . . . That in reply to my various notes you are charged to ask me to present some particular proposition . . . and that the First Consul is disposed to listen to such a proposition with the generosity and moderation that mark his high character. . . . After this note we could work to mature the treaty even before the formal reception of Mr. Monroe. I will profit by his advice and he will appear as a contracting party before the treaty is concluded."[5]

Livingston had one rational moment while writing this incredible appeal. "Please, Sir," he concluded, "regard this as unofficial." That enabled him to conceal it from his own government. Monroe reached Paris on the day this was written. Marbois took over from Talleyrand and the financial talks began, the first of them a dramatic and decisive midnight meeting with Livingston, who excluded Monroe because he had not yet been presented at the Foreign Office.

In Washington, the continued closure of New Orleans spread pessimism and intensified the war spirit. On April 8 (the same day that Ross's resolutions reached Napoleon) Jefferson asked his cabinet to vote on terms of an alliance with England, should one prove necessary. Madison, Gallatin and Smith, outvoting Dearborn and Lincoln, approved a mutual pledge of no separate peace. All voted not to let England take Louisiana, and against an offer of commercial privileges to her.

Madison embodied these decisions (except the last) in new instructions to Livingston and Monroe. If France had formed proj-

ects which must be forcibly opposed, they were to invite Britain
to join in a war against her. Should France deny free navigation
of the Mississippi, they were to assume that war was inevitable.
But if the river was left open, and only the right of deposit refused, Congress might not regard this as calling for an instant resort to arms. Great Britain could be offered a ten-year commercial
equality with American citizens in conquered territory, but any
British pretensions to conquest west of the Mississippi "must be
resisted as altogether repugnant" to American policy.

In effect, this would give the United States the option of taking
Louisiana at once from France, or leaving it with Spain until fu-
ture events determined its fate. There was little in this for Great
Britain except the general value (stressed by Madison) of having
the United States in the scale against France, and of upsetting
French ambitions in North America.

The next day word came that Spain had ordered the right of
deposit restored at New Orleans—an event, the Secretary wrote
to Monroe, which "will be a heavy blow to the clamorous for
war" and soothing to Westerners. The wording of the Spanish
order, he thought, cast doubt on the cession to France, but they
should not slacken their efforts.

Madison's inference was incorrect. Faced with the bitter truth
that Louisiana was lost to Spain, Godoy apparently restored American rights to make sure that France would derive no benefit from
his prior decision to violate them.[6]

Cordiality toward Spain vanished when dispatches arrived from
Pinckney. Had he known in time, Madison remarked to Pichon,
that the reopening was exhibited as proof of the king's condescension, his own reply to Yrujo would have been couched in very
different language. A few weeks later, when Yrujo gave him an
opening, Madison expressed satisfaction at Spain's "upright and
friendly" action, but observed that it "was ascribed inadvertently
it is presumed to the condescencion and generosity of His Catholic Majesty instead of that justice and good faith . . . to which
alone the appeal had been made."[7]

In early June Madison's hopeful feeling about France was
dashed by a false report that Bernadotte had left for America at

the very moment of Monroe's arrival. He could not believe it, he told Pichon. Such a delaying tactic made him wonder whether all that had happened at New Orleans was not concerted between France and Spain. "He despairs," the chargé reported, "that we will be prepared for the radical remedy, which is the cession of New Orleans, and thinks that nothing but the momentary pressure of England and the certainty of a rupture [with America] could dispose us to it."

In case of war, Madison predicted, England would seize New Orleans but would relinquish it to the United States, receiving in return the same commercial advantages that the United States was willing to give France. Pichon strongly advised his government to make the cession. Otherwise the United States would join England and take the colony away from France. That would further jeopardize the Spanish establishments beyond Louisiana, which were already in great danger because of the provocative nature of the Spanish administration. "Mr. Madison this morning combed out this prospect in great detail and it was impossible to answer him."

There was no basis, Talleyrand was told, for his hope that the United States would support France against England in Louisiana in the event of war. "Madison said this morning that the intervention of England in the Louisiana affair was a political blow that we would feel." American moderation, said the Secretary, "has been too much relied on."

Madison's aggressive language reflected near-war news from Europe and a change of tone in England. Jefferson's cabinet, by unanimous vote, had just decided that, if war broke out, American neutrality was something to be paid for. France could pay by giving New Orleans, England by just conduct. Madison saw a favorable omen in Britain's blocking of the French expedition to Louisiana. Prime Minister Addington, he informed Livingston and Monroe, had told Rufus King that England would probably occupy New Orleans in the event of war, but only to keep it out of French hands, "which in his [Addington's] opinion would be best effected by its belonging to the United States." This offer and the war crisis, Madison told the ministers, should cause them to press for better terms from France. There must, at the very least, be American jurisdiction over a port of entry.[8]

Privately, in a letter which remained undeciphered until 1952, Madison said the British could not serve themselves better than by helping the United States get New Orleans. Even if their advances were insidious, they could be made to serve the American interest. Their proposal about New Orleans was "calculated to decoy us into the war," to hamper the negotiation with France by swelling American claims and to furnish a ground for comparison and censure in case France should give too little or charge too much. By shrewd management this could be made to stimulate "the yielding dispositions of France." But if the United States armed too heavily, France might be more ready to remain at peace with England.

"In case of an adjustment between them, without one between us and France, we might be on the worst of terms. To avoid this danger from a reconciliation, and at the same time to make the most of agreement between the parties, will call for all that sound discretion in which we confide. . . . Whatever turn the present posture of things between France and England may take, a war can not be distant. This consideration must have great weight with all parties and will no doubt be properly touched in your appeals to the prudence of the French cabinet."

The Spaniards, Madison added, were proving the necessity of using a stronger tone with them. That country "must fear us more without being less our friend. . . . Should France hold a like language you will know how to answer it."

This was a real assignment: to swell American pretensions and use the threat of armed power, up to the limit of their coercive effect on France, but not to the point which would cause her to remain at peace. Unknown to him, England and France had been two weeks at war when he wrote this.

Ten days later Madison received the amazing news that Louisiana had been offered and nothing remained but to agree on the price. The Secretary's reply to Monroe, likewise undeciphered for a century and a half, swept away all thought of limiting American aspirations:

"The dawn of your negotiations has given much pleasure and much expectation. . . . The purchase of the country beyond the Mississippi was not contemplated in your powers because it was not deemed at this time within the frame of probability. . . . It is presumed that the defect will not be permitted either by yourself or by the French government to embarrass, much less suspend, your negotiations on the enlarged scale."

France, he added, "can feel no real doubt that your engagements for western Louisiana, though not expressly authorized, would be confirmed." Any hesitations on that ground would be evidence of evasive or dilatory purposes and should be so treated. Completion of the purchase would exhaust the Florida fund but there was no need to worry about that.

"The President concurs in the opinion that it will be best to take time for deciding this question. The Floridas can easily be acquired, especially in case of a war, and perhaps by arrangements involving little or no money."

That is, the Floridas might be ceded in payment of American claims for damages to commerce in the last war. The Senate had failed to approve Pinckney's convention covering part of them, so the whole settlement still lay ahead.[9]

Livingston and Monroe told how Marbois presented Napoleon's high figure but said he would try to cut it to 80,000,000 francs, of which 20,000,000 would be used to pay American war claims. The two envoys offered 50,000,000 including war claims. The last word, written by Monroe on April 19, was that Marbois had warned him, when he adhered to the lower American figure, that the temperamental First Consul "might dismiss the subject from his mind." It looked, Madison told Pichon, as if the United States would get all it could hope for, but nothing would be said publicly of the favorable augury.[10]

Livingston and Monroe finally accepted Marbois' price. Sixty

million francs ($11,250,000) were to be paid in stock irredeemable
for fifteen years. France was to receive 20,000,000 francs in American treasury notes with which to satisfy American creditors. The
stock was already sold to Baring Bros. of London and Hope of
Amsterdam. These bankers were to pay France $9,750,000, but
accrued interest, paid by the United States, would cut their invest-
ment to $8,830,000, giving them a profit of close to $2,500,000.
Gallatin (who figured this out) had advised Monroe, through
Madison, that he preferred to pay everything in bills on the Treasury, but that presumed a much smaller payment for much less
land. Rufus King afterward hinted to Gallatin that better terms
could have been obtained from other London bankers (equally
ready to finance their country's enemy), and seemed inclined to
think that Talleyrand's financier, Cazanove, devised this stock
system. Monroe's journal shows that it came from Livingston
and himself.[11]

Completed on May 1, the treaty was signed next day (though
dated April 30) but the text and dispatches did not reach Washington until July 14. Rufus King, landing in New York a fortnight earlier and assuming that the news was known, made no
mention of it in a letter to Madison but casually inclosed a letter
from the envoys to himself, telling about it. A hallelujah chorus
resounded through the nation. Amid the din, Federalists who
had been shouting for a war of conquest began to cry that the
administration was bankrupting the Treasury to buy a desert.

The two envoys seemed worried over their deviation from instructions. Livingston wrote to Madison on the day Louisiana
was offered: "I would rather have confined our views to smaller
objects; and I think that, if we succeed, it would be good policy
to exchange the west bank of the Mississippi with Spain for the
Floridas, reserving New Orleans." Monroe wrote after the signing: "The decision of the consul was to sell the whole, and we
could not obtain any change in his mind on the subject."[12]

Madison's reaction was enthusiastic. "A truly noble acquisition," he called it—one which under prudent management would
do much good and prevent much evil. His pleasure makes it clear
that he had tongue in cheek when he told Pichon how bad it

would be for the United States if French intransigence forced the nation to conquer the country west of the Mississippi. The dangers then cited—scattering of military strength and East-West disunion—were to be avoided through the prudent control of emigration.

Probably Madison never learned of the effect that remark had on Napoleon. Marbois in his *Histoire* quotes the dictator as saying to him that "we must expect rivalries in the bosom of the Union. Confederations which are called perpetual last only until one of the contracting parties finds it to its interest to break them." Talleyrand, reminding Napoleon in 1806 of the reasons he gave for selling Louisiana, named three results which were expected from the enlargement of the United States: it would enfeeble England in America, breed Anglo-American rivalry in military power and commerce, and check American political development by "separating the interests of the eastern and the western states and perhaps prepare the moment when they would divide into two powers."

This final thought was deliberately planted by Madison in the mind of an autocrat who was incapable of refuting it through the concept of a democratic federal republic. With Napoleon, it probably was more of a rationalization than a reason. It helped him to avoid the two admissions which pride forbade him to make— that St. Domingo Negroes had made Louisiana impossible to defend, and that the uncontrollable growth and ambition of the United States insured the ultimate loss of the province.[13]

Among the letters accompanying the treaty was one complaining of Livingston's conduct. "The most difficult, vexatious and embarrassing part of my labor," wrote Monroe, "has been with my associate." Instead of waiting to act under their joint powers, he made effort after effort "to conclude something before I got here." This incessant agitation and teasing, Madison was told, produced only a refusal by Talleyrand (on March 22) to act before Monroe's arrival. Seeing Livingston's mortification and not wishing to embarrass the negotiations, "I observed the most cautious and circumspect conduct." Monroe added:

"It is a justice however which I owe to my colleague to observe that he has manifested an invariable zeal to promote the object of the cession, and to extend our rights on the Mississippi. . . . By any errors, if such were admitted, no real harm is done."[14]

Livingston's letters, Madison replied, "have fully betrayed the feelings excited by your mission." He was "precipitating the business even after your arrival" without respect to the measures of the government or to the advantage of co-operation with an envoy freshly informed of them.

"It is highly probable that if the appeal to the French government had been less hackneyed by the ordinary minister, and been made under the solemnity of a joint and extraordinary embassy, the impression would have been greater and the bargain better."

Madison's diagnosis was sounder than his deduction. Heightened solemnity would not aid a mission whose success depended on factors outside itself. In speaking of a better bargain, Madison had reference to objections by Gallatin. The $11,250,000 of stock being irredeemable for fifteen years made discount purchases impossible and forced the paying of $10,125,000 interest. Chiefly Gallatin protested that the $2,000,000 cash voted by Congress had been used to promote the interests of American war claimants instead of to reduce the price. Also, the treaty barred a priority among claimants. Ordinary creditors, who took a gambler's chance in selling supplies to revolutionary France, had been put on a par with merchants whose ships and cargoes had been unlawfully seized by armed force.

The origin of these last two errors, Madison commented, was easily understood (a reference, presumably, to the claims of John R. and Peter Livingston and James Swan). He told Monroe what transpired a few days before the treaty arrived:

"You will find in the gazettes a letter from Paris understood to be from Swan inclosing a copy of his [Livingston's] memorial representing it as the primary cause of the cession, praising the patriotism which undertook so great a service without authority, and throwing your agency out of any real merit while by good fortune it snatched the ostensible merit."

Both the letter and memorial, Madison went on, had been printed in all the newspapers along with another letter from Paris, "which makes him Magnus Apollo." He found it hard to believe that the minister was responsible for publicizing his suggestion of a Franco-American alliance:

"The publication of the memorial is so improper and in reference to the writer invites such strictures that a sanction from him is not to be presumed. The passages against England have not escaped the lash [of Federalist editors]. It would not be very wonderful if they were to be noticed formally or informally by the British legation here."[15]

Madison's direct rebuke of Livingston was a mild suggestion that he "trace the indiscretion to its author." In reply, the minister expressed regret that "a bad translation" of the memoir had found its way into the papers. It was due, he supposed, to the zeal of friends who were endeavoring "to do me the justice they know I was entitled to." His next informed Madison that he had authorized the French government to publish this same memoir, unofficially, as one "attributed to me." A French minister requested this because they looked on it "as containing the reasons which influence the government [of France] and which they think will convince the nation."

The absurdity of a statement that the French people were agitated over Louisiana, while locked in a death grip with England, caused Madison to suspect that Livingston's vanity was being played on to foster British distrust of the United States. He directed the minister to ask for a withdrawal of the request. Publication by the French government would have "all the authenticity and effect of a direct publication by yourself," as well as the appearance of collusion with France against England. Already, Madison said, he had been compelled to answer British protests against the memorial and further explanations would be even more disagreeable because more difficult. Livingston's reply left no doubt that the whole story was a fiction to reinforce Swan's eulogy of him. "Reflecting more fully" on the effect of publication by France, he wrote nearly half a year later, "I had some time since taken measures to suppress it."[16]

When Monroe heard of the Livingston-Swan maneuver his anger flared but his perceptions grew keener. Calling the memoir "long-winded and empty," he pointed to evidence of collusion with Swan, whom he first called, then decided not to call, "the greatest scoundrel in Europe." From whom but Livingston could he have learned that the envoys exceeded their instructions? And Swan had made the same erroneous statement that Livingston attempted to place in a joint letter to Pinckney—that Napoleon's decision to sell was made on April 8, before Monroe's arrival was known. "Such a concurrence in an error could not well happen by accident."[17]

Livingston in fact went much farther along that line. The correct date of the decision to sell, Sunday April 10, was reported by him to Madison at once. A month later he wrote that the decision was made "as I informed you, on the 8th of April." To Congressman Mitchill and General Gates he sent a whole series of fictitious dates. Events of April 10, 11 and 12, correctly dated in his official dispatches, were moved back to the eighth, ninth and tenth.[18]

Monroe met the attempt to obliterate him by exhibiting Livingston's desponding letter of welcome. To fit this unlucky epistle into the new chronology, Livingston reminded Madison of the offer, "previous to the arrival of Mr. Monroe," of the whole of Louisiana, and of Talleyrand's denial that what he said was authorized. Receiving, just then, a note from Monroe telling of his arrival at Le Havre, "I wrote to him a hasty answer under the influence of these ideas excited by these prevarications of the minister."

Only one thing was wrong with this: The hasty note to Monroe was written on April 10, the day before Talleyrand made the offer and denied his authority to do so.

All dates had been "corrected" now except that of the telltale note to Talleyrand, begging for a written statement, after Monroe's arrival was known, that negotiations were already in progress. Dated April 12 in the French Archives, it appears as April 10 in the minister's diplomatic letter book, with the figure "2" peeping out from under the "0."[19]

Both Livingston's misstatements and his incorrect dates reappear in the eulogy of him sent by Swan for publication in America. Even the language is similar. Apparently he not only gave Swan the memoir but wrote the praise of himself and attack on Monroe which accompanied it.

The minister furnished Gates and Mitchill with fairy-tale versions of his December-to-March effort to procure part of West Florida and the country above the Arkansas. Napoleon, he told the former, "sent me word that he was pleased with my idea, and that he would in part accede to it, but that he would not sell." If Napoleon ever made any response whatever, Livingston failed to mention it in his official dispatches. There he reported only that Talleyrand promised to show the memoirs to the First Consul and said the purchase was "out of the question."

Quite different, but no more accurate, was the account given Congressman Mitchill. First, Livingston asserted, he "procured an assurance" from Napoleon that a satisfactory arrangement on Louisiana would be made in America by General Bernadotte. (In reality, hearing a false report that Bernadotte was to negotiate, he protested to Joseph Bonaparte against such a course.) Then, "though wholly without powers," he made an explicit offer for this country and received "a verbal assurance . . . that the next day should bring me a full and satisfactory answer . . . when unfortunately letters from Pichon"—that was a fatal detail. The negotiations affected by Pichon's dispatches related to American commercial rights. Dr. Mitchill, not suspecting that Livingston's letter was a tissue of falsehoods, allowed it to be copied and circulated among Federalists throughout the country.[20]

Writing to Madison, Livingston did not claim that his memoirs converted Napoleon. They merely reduced his ardor. What drove him to sell Louisiana "was the promise which the First Consul had hastily made me to pay our debt fully and promptly; and which he found himself in no situation to fulfill, and yet knew not how to elude, as I pressed it at every turn." The notion that Napoleon ceded half a continent because he could not violate a promise would seem to require a drastic rewriting of history and biography, especially as he had given a written pledge to the king of Spain that the province would never be alienated.[21]

In his public letter felicitating the two envoys, Madison proceeded (as he explained privately to Monroe) to "touch the policy of Mr. Livingston" in complaining that their commission was limited to purchases east of the Mississippi. He congratulated them on the acquisitions beyond the river and conveyed the President's "entire approbation" of their conduct—an approbation "in no respect precluded by the silence of your commission and instructions." When these were made out, the hopes of the most sanguine did not extend beyond the river, nor could more have been sought without creating the suspicion of a greedy ambition. In addition, the ample views of the subject carried by Monroe, and the confidence felt in both of them, lessened the necessity of providing for every turn the negotiations might take. Livingston's whole correspondence with the French manifested such a repugnance on their part that no extensive cession seemed possible, unless advantage could be taken of some favorable crisis. Such a crisis, Madison averred, gave birth to the extraordinary mission:

"It consisted of the state of things produced by the breach of our deposit at New Orleans, the situation of the French islands, particularly the important island of St. Domingo; the distress of the French finances, the unsettled posture of Europe, the increasing jealousy between Great Britain and France, and the known aversion of the former to see the mouth of the Mississippi in the hands of the latter."

These considerations, it was hoped, might "open the eyes of France to her real interest and her ears to the monitory truths which were conveyed to her through different channels"—open them far enough, at least, to reconcile her to making the Mississippi a natural boundary, or to some other concession which would justify the United States in waiting for a better opportunity to accomplish its wishes.[22]

The reasons Madison gave for *pressing the sale* were also given by Napoleon and Marbois *for selling,* in the latter's account of their conference. Talleyrand put it more simply to Pichon: "We can only base a durable peace on the cession of this colony." But Madison did not mention to the two American envoys competing for glory that the "monitory truths" which drove the arguments home had been uttered chiefly by himself, or that he had shaped American policy to give maximum value to the influence of St. Domingo. Like nearly everything else relating to him that leads in the direction of pre-eminence, this has to be dug out of the records.

CHAPTER XI

Louisiana "As It Was and Is"

President Jefferson put the Louisiana treaty before his cabinet on July 16. Ratifications had to be exchanged by October 30 and Congress was recessed until November. The cabinet voted for a special session beginning October 17. That left two weeks for action—time enough with a quick-acting body like the United States Senate.

The cabinet decided that Monroe should try to purchase the Floridas from Spain, at prices already agreed on. He might go to Madrid, stay in Paris, or go to London at once as Rufus King's successor. Jefferson commented in his cabinet notes: "We are more indifferent about pressing the purchase of the Floridas, because of the money we have to provide for Louisiana, and because we think they cannot fail to fall into our hands." Madison had used almost the same words to Monroe, privately, three weeks before.

There was one little difficulty. Jefferson considered the purchase unconstitutional. This was a reversal of his position in January, when he wrote to Gallatin: "You are right, in my opinion . . . there is no constitutional difficulty as to the acquisition of territory, and whether, when acquired, it may be taken into the Union by the Constitution as it now stands, will become a question of expediency." However, he continued, "I think it will be safer not to permit the enlargement of the Union but by amendment of the Constitution." Since he could not ask for an amendment on the ground that it was unsafe to use an existing power, the President was automatically pushed into a denial of its existence. As he expressed it to Senator Breckinridge of Kentucky:

"The Constitution has made no provision for our holding foreign territory, still less for incorporating foreign nations into our

Union. The Executive in seizing the fugitive occurrence which so much advances the good of their country, have done an act beyond the Constitution."[1]

Concluding that Congress should ratify first and amend afterward, Jefferson drafted an amendment and submitted it to the cabinet members individually. Decreeing that Louisiana "is incorporated with the United States and made a part thereof," it specified various powers which Congress could or could not exercise in the territory. The design was to maintain the northern portion as a reserve for Indians of the entire country.

Madison, like Gallatin, thought Congress had power to acquire foreign territory, but felt able to admit (he said later) that the Constitution had not provided for its incorporation into the Union. What disturbed him most was that the amendment implied lack of power to acquire Florida. He drafted two corrective measures. The first, to be a part of Jefferson's amendment, provided that southerly territories east of the Mississippi "which may be acquired by the United States" should be incorporated into it and be subject to the same authority of the general government as could now be exercised under like circumstances within the Union. This assumed a pre-existing power of territorial expansion, and gave an example, in the Florida clause, of the way to avoid a specification of powers. Madison's other proposal, a substitute for the entire amendment, also implied that none was needed for the acquisition of territory:

"Louisiana as ceded by France is made part of the United States. Congress may make part of the United States other adjacent territories which shall be justly acquired. Congress may sever from the United States territory not heretofore within the United States, with the consent of a majority of the free males above twenty-one years, inhabiting such territory."[2]

Jefferson had these proposals before him at Monticello in August, when letters arrived from Livingston including one whose contents "must be known only to yourself and Mr. Madison." It was largely in cipher, and the key was in Washington, but enough was written out to reveal a French desire to alter the Louisiana financial arrangements and a threat to void the whole agreement if it was not complied with in the time prescribed. Thoroughly alarmed, Jefferson sent the letters to Madison and remarked:

"I infer that the less we say about constitutional difficulties respecting Louisiana the better, and that what is necessary for surmounting them must be done *sub-silentio.*"

He still wanted an amendment, but didn't want France to hear of it. Madison saw no wish by France to get out of the bargain. Rather, there was "an anxiety to secure its execution against the intrusions of Great Britain" and to find out whether the United States had an understanding with the British on the subject.[3]

That is, by connivance, the British might conquer Louisiana, and deliver it to the United States without any payment to France. Jointly, the envoys verified this interpretation, writing later that the French were "fearful that the British may take the territory." Individually, Livingston continued to pile up his warnings. France, feeling that "we obtained an immense advantage," was "sick of the bargain"; Spain much dissatisfied; the slightest excuse would end the treaty.

This was self-portraiture, to show how Livingston had outsmarted the French. It also was nonsense. Napoleon sold the province because it was "already lost." A repudiation of the treaty would lose him the purchase price too. Had he been sick of the bargain he could have ended it instantly by advising Spain not to deliver the territory to France. Instead, he responded to Spanish foot dragging with a thunderous note to Charles IV, telling him that if Godoy was the real king of Spain, he would be "forced to make war on this new king."[4]

Following up his *"sub-silentio"* remark, Jefferson rewrote his amendment. He opened with the first sentence of Madison's substitute, accepted his idea of general authority instead of specific powers, and revised the Indian provisos by advice of Secretary Smith. Madison's crucial point—the implication of existing power to acquire territory—was put in, but his incorporation clause was narrowed: "Florida also, whenever it may be rightfully obtained, shall become a part of the United States." Sending this to Attorney General Lincoln, Jefferson said nothing about the modification of constitutional views and treated the other changes as his own:

"On further consideration as to the amendment to our Constitution respecting Louisiana, I have thought it better, instead of enumerating the powers which Congress may exercise, to give them the same powers they have as to other portions of the Union generally, and to enumerate the special exceptions."[5]

Jefferson, Madison and Gallatin were now in agreement that the Constitution authorized the acquisition of foreign territory. Jefferson still saw the necessity or expediency of an amendment authorizing citizenship and statehood. If this really was necessary, it meant that Congress had implied power to acquire colonies but no power to treat their inhabitants as free and equal human beings. How was Jefferson led into this position? After performing a service which only a broad construction of the Constitution could justify, he wished to preserve the blessings of a narrow construction. To Senator Nicholas, who pointed out that the expressly stated power of Congress to admit new states was not limited to territory already possessed, Jefferson replied on September 7:

"When an instrument admits two constructions, the one safe, the other dangerous, the one precise, the other indefinite, I prefer that which is safe and precise. I had rather ask an enlargement of power from the nation, where it is found necessary, than to assume it by a construction which would make our power boundless."

That statement was outdated before it was written. Napoleon's uneasiness twisted the factors. The course Jefferson wished to follow had become precise and dangerous; the other was indefinite and safe. Citing Livingston's alarmist statements, the President said he still wished Congress would quietly submit an amendment, but if his friends thought differently, he would "acquiesce with satisfaction." That ended the matter.[6]

A more difficult issue remained. The United States was buying from France exactly what France was acquiring from Spain, but what was that? Did it take in all or part of West Florida?

When Livingston, Monroe and Marbois sat down together, no American knew what was in the secret treaty of San Ildefonso, by which Louisiana was ceded to France on October 1, 1800. All reports represented guesswork. As Marbois recalled matters in his *Histoire,* the American envoys insisted at first on a definition of the extent of Louisiana. They yielded reluctantly to his warning that "the mere name of Florida" would produce difficulties with Spain, and agreed to a cession of Louisiana as acquired in the treaty of San Ildefonso. This tended to support the contention of Henry Adams and other historians that the American claim to West Florida was a fortuitous by-product of that wording, never thought of until after the treaty was signed.

In reality, Livingston and Monroe wrote to Marbois on April 22 that the treaty draft which he had submitted to them was too indefinite. The first article should *recite and affirm* the treaty of San Ildefonso and then transfer and guarantee "the whole of the country ceded by the treaty in the very words by which it is so ceded." The thought behind this was recorded by Monroe in a note to Livingston dated "April 1803." It mattered not, he said, whether the San Ildefonso treaty was inserted in the new treaty or appended to it—the effect would be the same if that wording gave "a claim, or the sanction of France to such claim, to West Florida, which without it we should not have." Here is irrefutable proof that Livingston and Monroe were trying to include West Florida, and relied on the San Ildefonso wording to achieve it.[7]

Marbois rejected the guaranty but agreed to the definition. So it was written into the agreement that Spain had retroceded to France, and France now ceded to the United States, "the province of Louisiana, with the same extent that it now has in the hands of Spain, and that it had when France possessed it, and such as it should be after the treaties subsequently entered into between Spain and other states."[8]

The "such as it should be" clause confirmed the 1795 boundary treaty between the United States and Spain and thus excluded ancient claims to *Louisiane Orientale* north of the Floridas. But, barring this, what was the extent of Louisiana "when France possessed it"? What was the extent "it now has in the hands of Spain"?

Livingston had given his opinion long before. "I find," he wrote to Madison in the summer of 1802, "all the old French maps mark the river Perdido as the boundary between Florida and Louisiana." On the day the treaty was signed, Livingston wrote to Jefferson:

"We have mentioned that this is the construction we put on it, so that there will be no deception should we claim it in treating with Spain."[9]

After the two envoys had taken this joint stand, Livingston proposed that they advise their government to take possession of this country, by force if necessary. Monroe was unwilling to recommend such drastic action until, by thoroughly probing old treaties, charters and maps, they could prove "that it was founded in principles of justice." He suggested that they study the subject separately before writing an official letter.

That gave Livingston a fine opening. He wrote at once to Madison, saying that he would miss a conveyance of this important letter if he waited even a day. He had no doubt "that Mr. Monroe will concur with me in opinion after we have discussed the subject," but until their joint letter should be received, he wished this to be considered as a private communication. He then told what he (no longer "we") had said to Marbois about the Perdido boundary and recommended "in the strongest terms" that the United States take possession of the country.[10]

Three days later Livingston addressed a letter to his associate. Since Monroe had not "sufficient leisure" for a full investigation, "I with pleasure undertake the task and I trust I shall leave no doubt upon your mind." He then went into a discussion of early settlements, maps and treaties, but saw no need "to probe this business to the bottom" because "the only object of this is to induce you to agree with me" that the United States should demand and take the country as far as Mobile. Monroe kept on probing and found evidence which remedied a possibly fatal flaw in Livingston's position.[11]

Monroe wrote their joint letter on West Florida, and it comprehended his findings, but Livingston won the battle for credit. His private-public letter to Madison was officially published, making him sole sponsor of a claim to West Florida which they had jointly prepared and asserted to Marbois.

In main outline the American claim as Livingston stated it was simple and convincing. If Spain retroceded Louisiana as it was when France possessed it, and the Perdido then divided Louisiana from Florida, that river must be the eastward limit of the cession. But there were complications.

On November 3, 1762, France secretly ceded to Spain the Island of New Orleans[12] and all of Louisiana west of the Mississippi. In the peace treaty of February 10, 1763, Spain ceded Florida to England, and France ceded to England the portion of Louisiana lying between the Island of New Orleans and the Perdido River. England divided her acquisition at the Appalachicola River, into East and West Florida, and ceded these provinces to Spain twenty years later. Thus, from two sources, Spain acquired all of Louisiana as it was when France possessed it. That, said Livingston, was what she retroceded to France in 1800.

This case had a hole in it. If the cession to Spain preceded that to England, Louisiana as it was "when France possessed it" was undefinable. The cession would be governed by the extent it "now has in the hands of Spain." Spain could say (as she did) that the territory acquired from England had never been reincorporated in Louisiana and the word "retrocede" did not apply to it.

Monroe discovered that the preliminary articles of the peace treaty were signed on November 3, 1762, and included the territorial cessions. Thus the transfers to Spain and to England took place on the same day. Louisiana as it was "when France possessed it" remained a definite territory, all of which finally passed to Spain and was "retroceded" by the 1800 treaty.[13]

This conclusion was offset by the fact that two years after Spain retroceded Louisiana, Napoleon sought a separate cession of the Floridas. Spain refused, and the November instructions to General Victor, for taking possession of Louisiana, stated that everything east of the Mississippi, except the Island of New Orleans, remained the property of Spain.

That would settle the matter except for important offsets to the offset. France's negotiator at San Ildefonso in 1800 took with him a treaty *projet* calling on Charles IV "to retrocede to the French Republic the colony of Louisiana, with the same extent it now has in the hands of Spain," in exchange for creating the Etrurian throne for his daughter. As soon as Charles consented he received a demand for ten warships and both the Floridas. The king agreed to furnish six vessels and to retrocede Louisiana "as it was delivered by the treaty of 1763." He absolutely refused, *"pour le moment,"* to cede any part of the Floridas, but, said Foreign Secretary Urquijo to Special Envoy Berthier, "at the general peace the king might cede the part of West Florida between the left bank of the Mississippi and the River Mobile."

Berthier insisted that the cession of both Floridas was indispensable. The king again refused, citing the shock to his people if traditionally Spanish territory were given up. However, he allowed Urquijo to submit a draft which dropped the conformity to the 1763 cession and included the definition of Louisiana with the same extent "that it had when France possessed it." Berthier wanted something more definite:

"I asked that the territory included between the Mississippi and Mobile Bay, and which was part of Louisiana before the treaty of peace of 1763, and which we ceded to England, be returned to us. The minister replied that upon a special request being made for it by the First Consul at the time of the general peace, he was persuaded that His Majesty would grant it."[14]

After the peace of Amiens, Napoleon could have demanded the remainder of Louisiana under the 1800 treaty. Such restraint did not appeal to a man who paid for Spanish territory by giving Italian duchies to his puppets. So in 1802 he demanded both of the Floridas in exchange for adding Parma to Etruria. It will be easy, he wrote to the Etrurian king, to make a treaty by which Spain "will *reunite* Florida to Louisiana." His treaty draft provided that Spain *"retrocedes* to France the river and port of Mobile and the territory which belonged to her before 1763 to the west of this river. . . . In addition she *cedes* to France the other parts of West Florida and all of East Florida."

Talleyrand advised him to ask only for West Florida. "It completes the *retrocession* of the French colony, as it was given to Spain," with Pensacola added.

Spain's unwillingness and the sale to the United States aborted all this, but the full record makes it plain enough that the Treaty of San Ildefonso deliberately laid the ground for a French claim to the country west of the Perdido or the Mobile. In addition, the language employed in 1802—*"réunirait"* by Napoleon, *"rétrocession"* by Talleyrand, *"rétrocède"* and *"cède"* contrastingly used in the treaty draft—completely destroys the contention that the verb *"rétrocéder"* in the San Ildefonso treaty excludes West Florida because Spain received it from England. The treaty fulfilled Talleyrand's instruction to Berthier that he demand the cession of Louisiana "actuelle et totale"—at once and entire.[15]

Inheriting France's claim to West Florida, the United States had the same choice of methods for obtaining it. The province could be demanded from Spain as part of the cession, with force used if necessary. Spain could be asked to sell what seemed to have been bought from France. Or the claim could be used as a lever to aid a purchase of both Floridas. Napoleon, as policy dictated, could interpret the treaty to aid either country, or keep silent and let them come to grips. The choice was visible in Talleyrand's reply to a question from Livingston:

"What were the east bounds . . . ? He said he did not know;

we must take it as they had received it. . . . But what did you mean to take [from Spain]? I do not know. Then you mean that we shall construe it in our own way? I can give you no direction; you have made a noble bargain for yourselves, and I suppose you will make the most of it."

A remark by Napoleon during the American negotiations leaves little doubt that Marbois and Talleyrand were under orders to be ignorant: if there were no obscurity about boundaries in the treaty, "it would perhaps be good policy to put it there." The effect was to make both the United States and Spain seek the support of France.[16]

Madison knew of the Livingston-Monroe claim to the Perdido, but not the supporting arguments, when he wrote to Pinckney on July 29: "The Floridas are not included in the treaty being it appears still held by Spain." This was no rejection: it was to prevent the distrusted minister from raising the boundary issue before Monroe joined him. On the same day Madison instructed Livingston and Monroe, separately, to look into the question "whether any and how much of what passes for West Florida" was fairly included in the cession. "The proofs countenancing our claim to a part of West Florida" might be of immediate use at Madrid. By the time the evidence of these two ministers arrived, late in August, Jefferson had reached similar conclusions from study in his library. Madison, acknowledging maps sent by Tench Coxe, said it seemed "pretty certain" that the treaty conveyed title to the area in dispute.[17]

American strategy was to claim as far as the Perdido, but to merge the claim in an offer to buy all of Florida. Arguments were outlined in Madison's July 29 instructions to Monroe. Separated from her other colonies, the Floridas "must ever be a dead expense in time of peace, indefensible in time of war, and always an obstacle to peaceful relations with the United States."

With Spain likely to be involved in the current war, powerful use could be made of Great Britain's recent intention to seize New Orleans and turn it over to the United States. Better for Spain, the Secretary said, to have the Floridas in American than in Brit-

ish hands; better to cede them with benefit to herself than to have
the United States receive them from Great Britain.

As for a price, Madison went on, the acquisition of Louisiana
lessened the anxiety to buy a territory "which now more certainly
than ever, must drop into our hands." However, the President
would permit him to offer the sum already allocated, $2,500,000.
Spain might propose to exchange the Floridas for the country
beyond the Mississippi. "Such an exchange is inadmissible." By
gaining the western bank, the United States had been given the
entire control of the river, and "we are the less disposed also to
make sacrifices to obtain the Floridas, because their position and
the manifest course of events guarantee an early and reasonable
acquisition of them." Jefferson wrote in the same vein to Senator
Breckinridge a fortnight later. The United States would get the
Floridas without an exchange and he would "not give one inch
of the waters of the Mississippi to any nation."

Among the Federalists, Hamilton supported the purchase.
Wolcott termed it a Pandora's box pregnant with evils. King said
the party shared his view that "we do not want territory over the
river." Josiah Quincy cried out that the extent of the country was
already a national misfortune. It was bad enough to have Kentuckians in the national legislature, but should this new treaty go
into operation "other like thick-skinned beasts will crowd Congress Hall—buffaloes from the head of the Missouri and alligators
from the Red River."[18]

Reports spread that England was opposed to the cession. Madison authorized the *National Intelligencer* to affirm the contrary,
then was asked by powerful and jealous William Duane for a
more specific statement for his Philadelphia *Aurora*. It was improper, Madison felt, to have more than one outlet for communications from the government. So he refused, with "tenderness in
the refusal," he wrote in asking Jefferson's approval of the letter.
Duane entered the incident in a growing catalogue of grievances.[19]

Madison intended to leave for Montpelier late in July, as soon
as a pair of horses should arrive from there. The ciphering of
dispatches held him several days and the delay was doubled by

the breakdown of his carriage en route. It was August 8 before his party reached home. Delivered just after he left, and locked in his Washington coach house, was a chariot of "neat plain elegance," and silver-plated harness. The body was glassed all around, with complete Venetian blinds, light-colored cloth and handsome lace, "coachman's seat in a circular form, wheels boxed." The lamps held candles instead of oil. Each door carried a silver "M." Dolley Madison soon became a familiar figure in this striking outfit (built in Philadelphia at a cost of $594) and no senator or representative was displeased when she gave him a lift to or from Capitol Hill.[20]

At Montpelier, on September 11, Madison received a notice from Yrujo that Spain regarded the sale of Louisiana as "a manifest violation" of French obligations. The sharp wording denoted a drastic change in that minister's attitude. France, he asserted, lacked power to alienate Louisiana without the consent of Spain. He quoted what Ambassador St. Cyr wrote to the Spanish Secretary of State on July 22, 1802, about the ceded province:

"I am authorized to declare to you in the name of the First Consul that France will never alienate it."

This caveat against the purchase would be very serious, Madison observed to Jefferson, if French or even British collusion could be suspected. But that being highly improbable, he saw it as a device to obtain a price for Spain's consent, and to resist the American boundary claim. If she stood alone, there would be no difficulty in going through with American purposes.[21]

Reaching Washington late in September, Madison found the French chargé ready to help. Following a confidential talk, Pichon asked Yrujo, still in Philadelphia, to certify certain papers needed for the delivery of Louisiana to the French representative. His purpose was to "put him to the test" and forestall counterorders which might be sent to New Orleans by the Court of Madrid. Yrujo refused to sign, avoided explanations and sent another protest to Madison without informing the French legation.

This second protest set forth that Louisiana was ceded to France on condition that France cause the King of Tuscany (Etruria) to be recognized by other European powers. Great Britain and Russia had withheld recognition, so the deal was incomplete. The United States had no right to acquire the territory and ought not to meddle with Spanish rights.

Pichon ascribed Yrujo's bitterness to the humiliating collapse of his Louisiana policy. The Spanish minister, he reported, had promoted the cession of the colony to France in order to create an impassable barrier to American expansion toward Mexico. He credited himself with the great results expected from that transfer, among them "the prospect, according to his phrase, of strangling Hercules in the cradle. His excessive vanity could hardly endure our change of plan." Certain it is that Yrujo was unhappy. "I wish," he wrote to his father-in-law, "Louisiana was at the bottom of the sea." Three crises in his career "all originated from that devoted province."[22]

Spain, Madison saw, was in no humor for bargaining about Florida. At the same time, word came that Monroe had gone to London instead of Madrid. Consuls Cambacérès and Lebrun, both friendly, urged him not to ask for Florida while Spain was balking over the delivery of Louisiana. Bonaparte used similar language in their farewell interview. So Monroe slapped down Livingston, who was making a surreptitious attempt to open Florida negotiations with the Spanish ambassador, and departed. Livingston explained his intervention to Madison. He had merely made some half-jesting remarks to Ambassador D'Azura about a sale. The Spaniard, taking it in earnest, wrote to Madrid for power to treat and informed Monroe that he had done so. Thereupon Livingston told Monroe that he knew he had no powers; he had merely tried to enable Monroe to treat with Spain in Paris rather than Madrid. A bit different was the account he sent to Edward Livingston. He had started negotiations with Spain "with some flattering hopes of success but Mr. Monroe took my interference amiss . . . and I having no power I was obliged at his request . . . to revoke what I had done."

Madison notified Monroe that in the absence of other orders, he should stay in London until a change of circumstances offered "a clear invitation to Madrid." Delay was made the more desirable by mounting evidence that the most important part of the territory desired was comprehended in the conveyance from France.[23]

Turning next to Yrujo, Madison informed the marquis that his objections to the sale of Louisiana were of no avail. To prove the right of France to sell, he need only quote the written statement of Secretary Cevallos to Minister Pinckney in declining to discuss a sale. France had recovered Louisiana and "the United States can address themselves to the French government to negotiate the acquisition of territory which may suit their interest." Yrujo replied that the Cevallos statement was merely a deferential transfer to France of the duty of making a decisive refusal. Madison's failure to be impressed with this subtle explanation gave Yrujo a very poor opinion of him. Accusing him of having twisted Cevallos' words from their natural meaning, he remarked to that minister:

"This conduct is as suited to the present political conditions and claims of this government, as it is analogous to the personal character of this secretary of state. . . . For his replies are as full of subterfuges, evasions and subtleties, as they are destitute of logic, solid reasoning, and devoid of that good faith which he always puts on display when speaking and writing, and which squares so little with his political conduct."

Madison found the Spanish objections "too futile to weigh." Expecting Spain to press them in Paris, he directed Livingston to point out that the ambassador's promise not to alienate formed no part of the treaty of retrocession to France (made fifteen months earlier) "and, if it had, could have no effect on the purchase by the United States, which was made in good faith, without notice from Spain of any such condition." The argument from the failure of England and Russia to recognize the king of Etruria was equally groundless. He was to be recognized by unnamed powers—but surely not by England, an enemy country—*before taking possession* of the throne. By taking overt possession, he had notified the world that the conditions on which this action depended had been fulfilled or waived.

As to Spain's belated contention that France's title to Louisiana was faulty, the orders signed by the King of Spain for putting France into possession "are an answer which admits of no reply." In the meantime, the United States would proceed with arrangements to take possession. Congressional action would suffice to deal with the discontents of Spain.

"The rightful limits of Louisiana [he added] are under investigation. It seems undeniable, from the present state of the evidence, that it extends eastwardly as far, at least, as the River Perdido; and there is little doubt that we shall make good both a western and northern extent highly satisfactory to us."[24]

This reflected the tone of the cabinet meeting on October 4. With Madison, Gallatin and Dearborn present, Jefferson asked: "Will it be advisable for forcible possession of New Orleans to be taken, if refused?" The answer was unanimous: "It will." All agreed that a military force should be prepared at once, to be ready if Congress authorized action.

The President's message, on the seventeenth, explained the territorial cession in detail. Sent to Madison late in September for revision, it was altered to avoid laying the treaty before the whole Congress, for legislative purposes, before it had been ratified by the Senate. At his suggestion, Jefferson struck out a statement that a proviso for observance of Spanish-Indian treaties would require the government to maintain a Roman Catholic pastor. It was inadvisable, Madison thought, to call attention to that deviation from principle. In the Indian treaty itself "it will be less noticed than in a President's message."

The draft contained a threat to cut off commercial intercourse with any belligerent who should violate American rights at sea. Madison preferred to submit this to "the wisdom of Congress." Gallatin objected to raising the issue prematurely, and it was omitted entirely. Once more, however, basic policy had been foreshadowed.[25]

Federalists were now echoing Yrujo's public charges that France had no power to cede Louisiana. Pichon, in a powerful letter to Madison, ripped these contentions to pieces and pledged delivery as soon as the ratifications were exchanged.

On this point, unknown to the public, a more serious hazard existed. Napoleon had ratified the treaty in May. Now, fearful of Anglo-American collusion, he was insisting on a reservation in the *exchange* of documents. French ratification would be declared void in case the funds were not transferred within the time prescribed.[26]

The Senate, overwhelmingly Republican, ratified the treaty after two days' debate, 22 to 7. Congress quickly authorized possession and payment, then proceeded more slowly to set up a territorial government. John Quincy Adams, who favored the treaty but was late in arriving, did not believe that Congress had power to bring the annexed inhabitants into the Union. Calling upon Madison, he asked whether the Executive had arranged for an amendment on that point. Madison replied that he knew of no universal agreement that it was necessary. Had he been on the floor of Congress, "he should have seen no difficulty in acknowledging that the Constitution had not provided for such a case as this," but the matter ought to be judged by the magnitude of the object. He agreed with Adams that the question should be cleared up—probably it would be, after the pressing objects were gone through. *If he should have any agency* in it (the italics are Adams') he would ask the senator in charge to consult the Massachusetts member. The next time they talked about it, Madison said that nothing would be done. Adams raised the issue in the Senate and met defeat. Describing the incident thirty years afterward, he said that the administration had determined to exercise power without asking questions about authority. To Gouverneur Morris, this was the one pleasing feature of a westward expansion which jeopardized the political supremacy of Atlantic commercial interests. "The Democrats," he wrote to moaning Roger Griswold, "have as I expected done more to strengthen the Executive than Federalists dared think of even in Washington's day."[27]

On October 21, the day after the ratification, Madison and Pichon did some shadowboxing. Pichon said all he could in favor of Napoleon's insulting demand and repeated his arguments to the President. The latter "held a language similar to that of the Secretary of State" about the impropriety of the reservation. The Secretary of State then handed Pichon a counterreservation providing that if Louisiana was not delivered as stipulated, the United States would be free to declare the treaty null. France could choose—take both or omit both. Their omission, Madison suggested, would be more conducive to mutual confidence.

Pichon now did what few French diplomats would have dared to venture. He dropped Napoleon's mandatory reservation. Yrujo's conduct, he explained to Talleyrand, made it dangerous to create any uncertainty about the transfer. Madison's counter-reservation was to pave the way for seizure of the colony if Spain delayed a peaceable relinquishment. In such a case, the United States could make difficulty over the payment. So Pichon consented to a simple exchange of ratifications, governing himself, he wrote to Madison, "by the constant desire of the First Consul to see ... the treaty executed on both sides with equal promptness and fairness."[28]

During this critical period Madison and Jefferson were sitting on a piece of news which, had it been known, might have raised the pitch of Federalist voices in the Senate. On Monroe's insistence, he and Livingston had authorized an advance of $2,000,-000 to France by Hope and Baring, to serve as a guaranty of American good faith. Monroe's letter telling of it was handed to Madison late in September by Alexander Baring, who crossed the ocean to see that there was no slip in delivery of the Louisiana stock.

By his imprudence, Monroe removed any danger of a damaging reaction by Napoleon to the omission of his reservation. That it was Monroe's imprudence, nobody conceded more willingly than Livingston, who wished their action to be "buried in eternal oblivion." Livingston himself had offered Marbois the $2,000,000 guaranty on April 13, when it was not wanted. But when Monroe renewed the proposal as a cure for Napoleon's reputed summer madness, Livingston built up a written record of opposition before agreeing. "The old soldier," Monroe wrote sarcastically to Madison, " ... endeavors to throw the whole responsibility on me. . . . I shall . . . fix the cause on him, in great good humor however." All of Livingston's official letters, he warned, were written with an idea of publication if his political pretensions were not realized. Certain Americans in London were saying "that the Federalists have an eye to him [for President] in case they cannot succeed themselves." Monroe then sketched a possible message to Congress on Louisiana in terms which might have been construed as a "Monroe for President" announcement.[29]

Under the Baring-Hope contract with France, one third of the Louisiana stock was to be delivered directly to the bankers. Pichon tried to speed this up, thereby hastening the day when British gold would be available for French use in the war against England. Immediate delivery, he argued to Madison, would be a fitting response to the new evidence (supplied by himself in violation of orders) of French good faith. There was force to this argument, the Secretary conceded, but the constitutional division of power required him and the President to conduct themselves with very great prudence.

Pichon pushed his point in a memoir. Taking note of the threats of Spanish military action which Yrujo was planting in the newspapers, he said that the Spanish minister admitted privately that he expected no resistance. It was unreasonable to say that the formal Spanish protests made the French title too doubtful to allow immediate payments, yet did not impair the right of France to deliver the country to the purchaser.

Madison replied that the President could and would deliver the stock as soon as New Orleans was put in American possession, without waiting three months as the treaty allowed. On the same day he sent congratulatory letters to Talleyrand and Marbois on the return of France and the United States to their ancient friendship. Spain's embarrassing conduct, he ventured to predict, would only produce a fuller demonstration of French honor and good faith.[30]

All was ready now for the double transfer of possession, from Spain to France, from France to the United States. American regulars and militia under General Wilkinson moved down the Mississippi, while 500 mounted Tennesseeans rode to Natchez as a reserve. Should Spain resist delivery, Madison wrote to Livingston, Governor Claiborne and Wilkinson would decide on the practicability of a *coup de main*. Yrujo by this time was telling everybody that France would back Spain in refusing to yield the country. He was completely discomfited when Pichon informed him that France had already accepted part of the purchase price.

On Christmas Day, a courier from New Orleans brought word that French Commissioner Laussat was in full possession. Pichon again urged Madison to deliver the stocks, but was told that the interest date could not be fixed until it was known when the American commissioners arrived. The next courier, on New Year's Day, reported those officials floating down the river from Fort Adams. A week later, no news. On January 15, 1804, a horseman rode in from New Orleans. Louisiana had been peaceably delivered to the United States on December 20.

Congress gave a great dinner, with the President and cabinet as honor guests, to celebrate the acquisition of this empire. Informing his government of the climactic event, Pichon remarked:

"The acquisition of Louisiana and the peaceful manner of possession have raised Jefferson and his friends to a high point of popularity and regard. His re-election must be considered as assured."[31]

CHAPTER XII

Toujours Gai

WITH the Louisiana crisis surmounted, diplomatic tensions shifted. American diplomacy had won richer fruits from the new Anglo-French war, before it started in May 1803, than either belligerent could hope for. Now the United States faced the difficulties of neutrality, with British naval power and American mercantile ambition defining the encounter.

The war's outbreak was still unknown when Madison protested the boarding of a French ship in Hampton Roads for seizure of a British deserter. The talk broadening, Chargé Thornton ventured the opinion that Great Britain suffered more from the seduction of her seamen onto American ships than the United States did through impressment of Americans. He cited the unwillingness of the United States to agree to mutual return of deserters. Madison's position was outlined to Mayor DeWitt Clinton of New York. The United States was not bound by law or treaty to return deserting seamen. It rested with the individual states, therefore, to return them or not. Some did and some didn't.

With Madison's approval, Rufus King was then making a last effort to secure the mutual agreement against impressment on the high seas which he asked for during the Adams administration. When King returned to the United States in July, he reported that the First Lord of the Admiralty agreed, but sent a note next day excepting "the narrow seas" between Britain and the continent, which he called territorial waters. As impressments were heaviest here, King dropped the negotiation.[1]

Madison had barely read this unpleasant report when Thornton protested the arming of American merchantmen. The Secretary's abrupt reply impressed the Briton as "written with a little degree of humor." The United States would remain strictly neu-

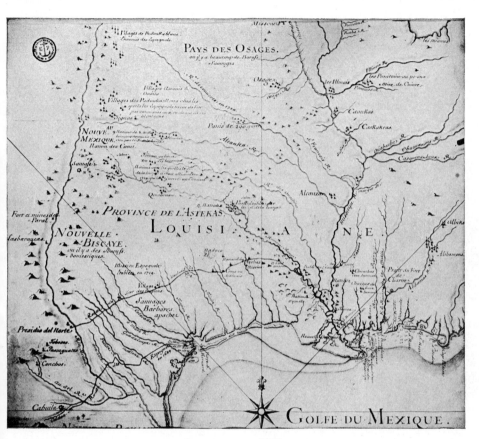

LOUISIANA IN 1720

"New map" of part of the province, by Beauvilliers, after the observations of Bénard de La Harpe. From Bibliothecque Service Hydrographique, Paris. The Perdido River, east of the Mobile, is shown within Louisiana.

Invoice of Sundries Shipped on account and Risk of James Madison Esqr. Secretary of State, by his orders, in the Schr. Three Friends of Baltimore Edwd. Harvey Master bound for Baltimore to be Consd. to the Collector of the Customs there & forwarded by him to the said Secretary of State, being for his table's use. Viz.

with direction No.328.	1 Chest Contg. 50 Botles white hermitage Wine demi paille year 1803 @ F.5.50. p btle	F.275.—		
329.330.	2 do. each 50 btls in all 100 do. white virgin Wine Jendan 1803 @ F.4. p btle	400.—		
331.	1 do. 25 do. white virgin Wine, Sealed with black Wax Jendan 1802 @ F.4.	100.—		
	25 do. white Cotillon Wine Sealed with yellow Wax, 1802 @ 3	75.—		
	4 Chests 200 btls F. 850.—			
	Abatement @ 3 p Ct 25.50.			
	Waggons from Tains F.54.— 824.50.			
	Permit and duties 6.50.			
	Priserage & Craftage 3.— 63.50	F. 888.—	
	1 Box Contg. 24 large botles Superf. Aix Olive Oil @ F. 30. p Doz.	60.—	
	1 Box 12 double Boxes Superf. Capres @ 2.50. p btle F 30.—		
	1 do. 12 do. anchovies 2.25. do. 27.—		
	1 do. 12 do. olives Amelan 1.50. do. 18.—		
	1 do. 12 do. ditto verdales 1.— do. 12.—		
	4 Boxes 5.—	92.—	
	1 Box Packed in Canvas Cords &c. Containing		
	15. Sweet Shelled Almonds @ 80 cents p lb F.12.—		
	4 Bitter Ditto 90. 3.60		
	30 Sweet Soft unshelled Almonds, à la princesse 90. 27.—		
	12 Boxes of 29 Superfine Marseille Figs 40.— 11.60		
	24 do. Black prunaux, Fleuris 48½ lb 40.— 19.40.		
	Box, Canvas & package 7.30.	80.90.	
	1 Jar Containing Viz.		
	18 Boxes Glazed preserved Dry Fruits, assorted @ F 1.60 p box F. 28.80.		
	24 Pots Preserved Fruits in Syrup & Gelées 1.80 43.20.		
	8 lb. Dragies, à la Grose 2.50 20.—		
	Jar, Cork, Glacier &c. 8.—	100.—	
	Permit & Duties F. 7. 10.	F. 1220.90	
	Priserage & Craftage 4.—	11.10.	
	Errors Excepd. Marseilles the 31 octob. 1806	F. 1232	
	Stephen Cathalan, Junr.		

INVOICE
Goods shipped to Madison by United States Consul at Marseilles.

tral but hoped not to suffer in this war the irregularities practiced
in the last.

That hope was vain. Early in August Madison sent Thornton
the deposition of a native American seaman who swam ashore
from a British frigate which impressed him and three others off
Norfolk. "The United States," the Secretary of State asserted,
"can never acknowledge a right in any other nation to take from
their vessels on the high sea any persons whatever," other than
military personnel of an enemy. It violated the neutral flag, tres-
passed on the law of nations, and was "no less impolitic than it is
unjust." The three remaining seamen could be speedily set at
liberty because Captain Douglas had brought his frigate back at
once to the port "whose kindness and commerce it had insulted."
To this he added a sharp protest against the conversion of American ports into supply bases and centers for operations against
American commerce. Thornton was sorry, he wrote home, to
see in Madison "a bitterness of tone and of insinuation" like that
in the newspapers, and a doctrine "destructive of the well-being
of every civilized state."

"I cannot but persuade myself, my lord, that the President, if
he had been previously consulted on this occasion, would not have
acquiesced in either the language or the doctrine of Mr. Madison's
letter."

Thornton's rejoinder to Madison asserted the right of his sovereign to control the actions of all his subjects, wherever found.
British warships, he averred, had used American ports only to
protect British merchant ships from French cruisers which enjoyed too friendly treatment in those harbors.

These "very exceptionable remarks," Madison wrote to the
President, were in the spirit, but beyond the degree that he expected, and he considered it best to give no answer. Jefferson
thought them too serious to be ignored. Better return "an answer
bien motivé," and ask Great Britain to act on the King-Hawkes-
bury stipulations as if they had been signed. Madison reminded
him of the reservation about the narrow seas. The British, in his

opinion, would not retreat from this because its purpose was to frustrate any arrangement that would end impressments. The Secretary repeated his feeling that Thornton's letter should not be answered, especially as a British minister was expected. However, as he was coming over to Monticello within a few days, he would do nothing until he had "the pleasure of being able to take your directions in person."[2]

Here was an example of the working relations of these two men and the ease of being misled concerning them. Madison's apparent wish was to govern his course by the President's directions given in person. But he already had them in writing. The personal discussion was to insure adoption of his own contrary course, and that is what followed.

For a year and a half before he sailed in September 1803, Anthony Merry had been slated for the vacant diplomatic post in Washington. A plain, unassuming and sensible man, Rufus King called him. A worthy candid man was Monroe's description. He was not the sort whom Thornton advised sending in the spring of 1803. His Majesty's minister should be of a social rank so high that he need not fear debasing himself by condescension, in a country where he would find few men of education and fewer still with the manners of gentlemen, or he should be surrounded with all the advantages which opulence could supply. Thornton spoke out of his own experience, in a post which paid so little that "I have not had it in my power to show the slightest hospitality to a passing Englishman."[3]

Merry had neither title nor wealth, and there was ironic unfitness in the punning nickname, *Toujours Gai,* which he bore in the Foreign Office. Augustus J. Foster, who joined him a year later as secretary of legation, described him as slow, indefatigable, clear-sighted and vigilant—a clockwork minister with no imagination. The splendor was furnished by Mrs. Merry, a large, bejeweled woman who scolded the servants and kept house and husband in good order. Foster described her as "a fine woman accustomed to adulation," who suffered horribly from association with the degenerate sons and daughters of British ancestors. Wrote twenty-four-year-old Augustus to his mother:

"The women here are in general a spying, inquisitive, vulgar and most ignorant race. They are many of them daughters of tavernkeepers, boarding housekeepers and clerks' wives and yet as ceremonious as ambassadresses. Even you with all your resources and powers of self amusement would absolutely be puzzled here."

Lady Elizabeth Foster, widow of Sir John, was indeed a woman of great resources. Living at the time with the Duke and Duchess of Devonshire, she had borne the Duke two children. Her legitimate son, after his American apprenticeship, was made minister to Sweden because, wrote Foreign Minister Canning, Swedish "Baron d'Armfeldt conceives himself to be father of Augustus Foster."[4]

The Merrys had dark portents—their ship held back for months by Atlantic storms. Merry's first shock came when he went in full dress to see the President, and found him in old clothes and slippers. Told by Madison that the Danish minister had been similarly received, he protested that the Dane was a diplomat of the third rank, he himself of the second. It pleased Merry that both Jefferson and Madison expressed concern over the dangerous ascendancy Napoleon was gaining in Europe. But that was small offset to his feelings when he learned that he was expected to call first on other cabinet members, not they on him. Madison pointed out that the rule laid down for him prevailed in England.

Merry had learned from former Minister Liston that President Adams always conducted Mrs. Liston to the table. But when the Merrys were entertained on December 2, the President gave his arm to Mrs. Madison. Madame Yrujo took the chair at his left, and Mrs. Merry was placed by Mr. Madison below the Spanish minister. Merry himself was pushed aside by a congressman when he started to take the chair next to Madame Yrujo. And among the *selected* guests was M. Pichon, from a nation with which England was at war. When Madison heard of this objection, he told Merry that "a liberal oblivion of all hostile relations ought to take place" at the President's table.[5]

Jefferson despised protocol. Madame Yrujo had failed to re-

ceive precedence at dinner and for a time her angered husband
went alone to presidential parties. The President thought no
more about his discourtesy to newly arrived guests than about
its possible diplomatic effect. Madison had no option except to
support Jefferson's course or sabotage it. Pichon described the
result:

"All these intrigues and displays of Mr. Merry had the effect
some days later of causing an incident at the home of Mr. Madison, where Messrs. Yrujo and Merry were dining, and I chanced
to be present. All the colleagues of Mr. Madison, and their wives,
were there. Mr. Madison gave his hand to Mrs. Gallatin. This
opening step caused a sort of derangement in the salon. Mrs.
Merry found herself alone, all the other men in place having
chosen a lady, and Mr. Merry, astonished, had to give her his
hand."

This procedure struck Pichon as new, for he had seen his own
wife and Madame Yrujo given precedence at Madison's dinners.
It was evident that the Secretary wished "to make Mr. Merry feel
more strongly the embarrassment of the scandal he had created.
But this incident increased it." Genuinely anxious not to offend
the Merrys, Madison invited them to a social dinner after the
formal one. "Mr. Merry indeed came," he related, "but with an
excuse from his lady although the day had been arranged with
her."

Merry already had assured his government that design, not ignorance and awkwardness, "though God knows a great deal of
both . . . is to be seen," was responsible for these slights. He felt
the second offense in greater degree because of "the subordinacy
of Mr. Madison's situation" compared with the President's and
because of the preference given to the wives of cabinet members,
"a set of beings as little without [sic] the manners as without the
appearance of gentlewomen. . . . Everything else in the federal
city is equally as perfectly savage." This butchery of the king's
(though not King George's) English obscured neither his meaning nor his temper.

The blaze would have died down, Pichon thought, except that Yrujo, "who is vanity personified, blew the fire more strongly than ever." Merry and Yrujo agreed that first place at presidential dinners must go alternately to their wives, thus shutting out Dolley Madison and other cabinet peeresses. Meanwhile the two ladies would avoid the President's house, and would take precedence over cabinet wives at legation dinners. Both this and the presidential boycott were carried out.

Yrujo seemed to expect Pichon to imitate his course, though he had made the arrangement "without asking my advice, and even insinuating . . . that I was not of a rank to enter into these questions." Instead, Pichon reported, he continued to conduct himself with respect and deference for the President, and gave precedence in his own house "to Mrs. Madison over the other women and to Mr. Madison over the other men." Merry was now telling his ministry that Jefferson and Madison were guided by a studied design "to degrade the character of a foreign minister" by placing him "on a level with the lowest American citizen."[6]

Apprehensive that Merry would charge unfriendliness toward England, Madison was forced to deal soberly and at length with what he called "a foolish circumstance of etiquet," "diplomatic superstition," "nauseous," "frivolous," "a farce." Falling in with Senator Pickering, he asked the former Secretary of State about social practices in his day. Pickering knew that Jefferson and his "democratic scullions" were moved by "a malicious pleasure in overturning whatever bears the stamp of Washington." So, opening with the remark, "You know, sir, that General Washington was remembered for his correctness in all such cases," he proceeded to uphold Merry and Yrujo.

Replied Madison: "Do you think that at London Mr. Pitt (if he had a wife) or Lord Grenville would have given to Mrs. King the precedency of their own ladies?"

The person to answer such questions was Rufus King, whom Madison now addressed on a subject "unworthy the attention of either of us." King replied that foreign ministers never were invited to royal parties, and in the queen's drawing room there was no precedence, just confusion. But "Mrs. King reminds me" that at social affairs the women usually trooped into the dining room ahead of the men, "the highest title taking the lead." At the farewell dinner given for Mr. and Mrs. King by Lord Hawkesbury, the host led Lady Melville to the table.[7]

Here was little to cheer *"Toujours Gai."* Had the English system been transplanted, Mrs. Merry would have been permanently subordinated to the former Sally McKean, whose husband had lately become Marquès de Casa-Yrujo. But worse was to come.

Jerome Bonaparte, Napoleon's nineteen-year-old brother, while looking at the natural beauties of America in the fall of 1803, espied Elizabeth Patterson, niece of Samuel and Robert Smith, and promptly married her, or *vice versa.* At a presidential dinner for the bridal pair, Jefferson gave his hand to the glamorous Madame Bonaparte. When the Merrys heard of this, their indignation rose anew. Precedence had been given to Napoleon's sister-in-law instead of to the wife of the Secretary of the Navy. The purpose? To exalt France and humiliate Mrs. Merry.

More than that lay behind the outburst. Mrs. Merry, as described by Margaret Bayard Smith, was large and rather masculine, so entirely the talker "that her good husband passes quite unnoticed." As long as the competition lay only with Dolley Madison, who also was more conspicuous than her husband, Mrs. Merry could resort to her unmatchable jewels and satins. In the putting on of clothes, she was supreme. But Madame Bonaparte's talents lay in exactly the opposite direction.

At a grand ball given by the Robert Smiths, the British minister's wife wore dark blue crepe over white satin extending into a long train, with white crepe drapery silver-spangled to her knees: her head and bosom ablaze with diamonds. But the wife of Jerome Bonaparte wore such a gown that "no one dared look at her but by stealth," and her aunt joined the other ladies in an ultimatum to the "beautiful little creature." Either she would wear more clothes at the Pichons' next evening, or they would not be there. At the Pichon dinner, Yrujo took great offense when the host led Mrs. Madison to the table, but nobody sensed a diplomatic plot when Aaron Burr gave his hand to Madame Bonaparte.

"I realize," Pichon remarked in describing these events, "that with tact on the part of Mr. Jefferson, he could have avoided all these uproars." But the indiscretion of the ministers did not conform to the respect they owed to the head of state, and with the best intention on Jefferson's part of repairing what had been done, "they have closed all the avenues of doing it."

Jefferson rejoiced that his daughters were not with him. The brunt of the battle, he wrote to Martha, was falling on Mrs. Madison and her sister, "who are dragged in the dirt of every Federalist paper. You would have been the victims had you been here, and butchered the more bloodily as they would hope it would be more felt by myself."[8]

With Madison keeping silent, Yrujo at length asked him for a presidential decision on the momentous issue. Hereditary monarchs, he argued, had greater dignity than elected ones and the disparity extended to their ministers. Following a discussion in the cabinet, Yrujo and Merry were informed that there would be complete *pêle-mêle*—no precedence for anybody. This led Merry and Madison into their first talk on the former's social grievances. The Secretary remarked that at his own house in private life, Mrs. Merry as a stranger probably would have received the first attention, but as an official he had "thought it most proper not to deviate from the established course."

Usage, Madison observed, was so different in different countries as to leave all free. In Russia military rank predominated, at Rome ecclesiastical, at Berlin domestic rank over foreign, in England hereditary over all. When he spoke of the subordination of Mrs. King at Hawkesbury's dinner, Merry replied that he had been there—it was an unofficial party and the host was subject to no rule. That, rejoined Madison, should settle the matter, "since the dinner given to Mr. and Mrs. King was as much official as mine to Mr. and Mrs. Merry."

Reporting all this to Monroe, Madison said he protected Thornton by refusing to discuss Merry's protest that *pêle-mêle* would subject him to the humiliating possibility of sitting below his own secretary of legation. Distinctions among diplomats, Madison replied, were a labyrinth he declined to enter. "I blush at having put so much trash on paper," he remarked to Monroe, but there might be a need to guard against serious inferences in England from all this nonsense. Also, he wanted Monroe to get Merry "on a footing that will keep him among us, for I really think favorably of him as a medium of conciliatory and useful communication with his government."

An invitation to dine familiarly with the President—no wives present—brought the reply that, while awaiting his government's instructions, Merry had no power to accept unless the Secretary formally assured him that former "usages of distinction" would be observed. Yrujo and Thornton likewise sent refusals. "I need not comment," Madison wrote to Monroe, "on this display of diplomatic superstition, truly extraordinary in this age and country." Since Merry blamed his self-inflicted mortifications on American hostility toward England, "To apply an antidote to this poison will require your vigilant and prudent attention."[9]

Pichon found himself next to Madison at the President's table, the day after the aborted dinner. "They couldn't be more hurt at the conduct of these two ministers," he told Talleyrand. Jefferson regarded their concerted refusal to dine alone with him as an insult.

"It is unheard of, he told me, that a foreign minister has need of the permission of his court to sit down at the table of the head of a state: I shall be highly honored when the king of England is good enough to let Mr. Merry come and eat my soup."

Madison told Pichon of his answer to Yrujo's contention that foreign ministers had a right to require continuation of the usages of former Presidents until changes were officially announced to them. "Things of that sort announce themselves." To claim the contrary was to place in doubt the right of a government to regulate its own affairs.

"Mr. Madison told me that the President would never tolerate the idea of assigning places at his table, and that it would be vain indeed to measure the importance of one's mission by the side or end of the table he occupied. This is aimed at M. d'Yrujo, who invariably seizes the first place, wherever he is."

Jefferson remarked to Pichon that Yrujo's singular intimacy with Merry indicated an expectation of war between Spain and

France. Such a conclusion transmuted one diplomat's vanity and the other's uxoriousness into world politics. But it truly revealed the effect of their folly. Few turns in diplomacy could damage Spain more than a working alliance between Yrujo and Merry, directed against the American government. By creating the illusion of an Anglo-Hispanic bond, it was bound to increase the American determination to gain possession of the Floridas.[10]

The Merrys continued to suffer. Their imported white servants left to become landowners and citizens. A fellow named Suttle, "nothing more than an inferior clerk," sent constables to arrest his Negro slave who had hired himself to the British minister. Madison abetted these "uncivil and lawless proceedings" by refusing to override the law of the District of Columbia and bring him back. And Suttle himself, who somehow or other had learned to read and write, addressed a letter to Merry almost as if they were social equals: "I regret very much that any conduct of mine should have given displeasure to a gentleman with whom I have not the pleasure of an acquaintance," etc. The crowning blow came when Mrs. Merry, beginning to relent, accepted an evening invitation to the Madisons' and found "her haberdasher and his wife to be among the company invited to meet her."

Augustus Foster, chronicling this and prior grievances, wrote to his mother: "Were you so placed, how would your feelings have been shattered! It is indeed a country not fit for a dog."[11]

There was nothing in the horoscope to foretell that an English princess, about to ascend the throne, would one day be the guest of a former haberdasher in the White House.

As far as Monroe could discover, Merry's complaints produced no effect whatever in London. They arrived just ahead of the overthrow of the Addington ministry by Pitt. A government too well-disposed to be moved by such nonsense was giving way to one which had more important matters to be unfriendly about. Monroe told of some earlier slights to himself and his wife, which he dismissed as not intended to be disrespectful. But he missed the significance of the most striking incident. Referring, at a Hawkesbury dinner, to flower festivals in South Carolina, he said that they brought out a great concourse of people with gay equipages. What kind of equipages had they? asked Lord Castlereagh. Why, said Monroe, the same as in London.

"Sir William Scott then remarked that he had lately read an account of a grand *fête* at the Cape of Good Hope, which concluded with that all 'the beauty taste and fashion of Africa were assembled there.'"

Monroe was pleased that the foreign minister did not join in the burst of laughter. But Hawkesbury was on his way out and Sir William Scott was not. As highest judge of the British Admiralty, he could set the current toward peace or war by his decisions in prize cases. And it was to come to pass that when he had helped to bring the two countries to the verge of conflict, the final decision would depend on Lord Castlereagh, who was surprised that there were carriages in Charleston.[12]

During all these social troubles, Madison and Merry discussed Anglo-American affairs without reserve. The Secretary disavowed both the contents and publication of Livingston's Louisiana memorial, which Merry found "so hostile and offensive" that it could not be ignored.

The minister asked why the United States had not ratified the convention signed by Rufus King in 1803, to settle the northern boundary of the United States. Madison explained that the Senate was apprehensive lest one of its articles should interfere with the territory acquired from France. The 1783 peace treaty called for a line running *due west* from the Lake of the Woods to the Mississippi. Madison corrected this geographical blunder in 1802 by suggesting a line from the lake to the nearest source of the river, but the convention embodying it was not signed until ten days after the signing of the Louisiana treaty.

Former Minister King assured Madison that the action in Paris was unknown in London, therefore the convention did not modify the treaty. But Merry remarked that the object of the clause was to give Great Britain access to the Mississippi River. The treaties couldn't clash because Spanish territory (Louisiana after 1763) never extended eastward of the proposed line. That was the same as saying that Great Britain intended, now, to claim the territory west of the line from lake to river, and to assert a navigational right in the Mississippi by virtue of contiguity to its headwaters. Such a right had been conceded at the close of the Revolutionary War because it was supposed that the river rose in Canada. Madison's revised lake-to-river boundary, suggested before the purchase of Louisiana, was to be an actual one only if Great Britain had a valid claim against France or Spain to the territory westward of it. Merry, however, was using it after the purchase to create such a claim against the United States.

The minister didn't realize what he had done. He complained that Madison suddenly became so negative and elusive that one sensed a design of "encroachment on His Majesty's just rights." The Senate in February 1804 ratified the boundary convention without Article V, and Madison directed Monroe to uphold the excision on the ground that the United States owned the territory on both sides of the line.

Merry thought of a drastic counterstroke. Other articles of the convention, he reported to his government, were very important to the Eastern states. Congressmen from those states had told him they were holding secret meetings to plan secession. Rejection of the treaty by Great Britain, with the exclusion of Article V given as the reason, would cause the New Englanders "to go forward rapidly in the steps which they have already commenced towards a separation from the Southern part of the Union." Great Britain rejected the convention and it died.[13]

Impressment held first place in Madison's early talks with the British minister. Silence was impossible, the Secretary told him, until a remedy was applied. At the same time he renewed his objections to Great Britain's "pretended blockade" of Martinique and Guadeloupe. Madison's language, the Briton reported, was temperate and conciliatory, but cloaked a strong design to obtain greater respect for the American flag and more favorable neutral navigation than British interests had hitherto found tolerable.

That intention was clear enough in a policy outline which the Secretary sent to Monroe. The purpose was to get rid of impressments, to define blockades and contraband as in the last Anglo-Russian treaty, to regulate visits and searches at sea by the Anglo-French treaty of 1786, and "to put aside the doctrine that a colonial trade not allowed in time of peace is unlawful in time of war." In return the United States would agree to a mutual surrender of deserters and to a legislative ban on exportation of contraband to enemy ports.

Presenting these objectives to Merry, Madison told him of the rising feeling in Congress and among the people over the mistreatment of ships and seamen. The United States would never desist from their claim "that the American flag should give complete protection to whatever persons might be under it," military enemies of Great Britain alone excepted. But as part of a general agreement, British deserters would be returned.

Merry replied that if Americans carried goods owned by themselves between France and her colonies, the trade could be fraudulently expanded to cover all French colonial commerce. Nor did he see anything serious in a summary of impressments Madison had reported to the Senate—only seventy in twelve months. That report, the Secretary answered, was toned down to discourage legislation. New complaints were producing such a sensation that the government had to work for a remedy. Great Britain could settle the matter by including the "narrow seas" in the King agreement. As to American-owned goods in French colonies, they already were carried circuitously to France. All that was wanted was direct conveyance, for which an equivalent was offered—security against contraband.[14]

Madison felt some hope (he told Monroe) that Merry saw the business as he did. That was not the case, although the minister was more moderate than Thornton. The latter had been willing to see impressment at sea *tacitly* abandoned, but should the *right* to repress be formally renounced, he warned his government, British desertions would multiply. Now, alarmed at Merry's attitude, he sent a private note to Undersecretary Hammond. Be firm, indifferent and just, he advised.

"If we yield an iota without a real and perfect equivalent (not such imaginary equivalents as Mr. Madison mentions to Mr. Merry) we are lost. Every concession will be, as it has always been, ascribed to our fears; and this country is rising fast, if it be not checked very speedily and effectually, to an importance which will most sensibly annoy us."

Merry moved in this direction too when he observed the progress of bills in Congress for the protection of seamen against impressment. Madison "endeavored to persuade me of his total ignorance" of these bills, saying they were spontaneous reactions against the conduct of British naval officers. But "I found Mr. Madison prepared to defend the bills on every point"—including punishment of foreign naval officers for offenses committed in American waters. He even heard the Secretary say that privileges granted foreign warships in American ports were a matter of courtesy and not of right.

The bills, Merry now believed, were provoked solely by the unfriendly disposition of the Executive. They were postponed near the end of the cession, after serving as an outlet for congressional eloquence and adding weight to Madison's instructions on impressments, blockades and captures.[15]

The Secretary drafted a convention of thirteen articles supported by ten thousand words of argument. The essential objects, he advised Monroe, were suppression of impressments and the definition of blockades. Next in importance were reduction of the list of contraband and the enlargement of America's neutral trade with hostile colonies. The last two were "highly important," the first two "absolutely indispensable."

Neither nation was to take any person whatever, unless in the military service of an enemy, out of the other's ships at sea. Any citizen or subject serving the other nation compulsively was to be forthwith released. Warships searching merchant vessels were to remain out of cannonshot and send no more than two or three men on board. Military and maritime deserters would be returned.

Contraband was limited to specified military items. Each party would forbid contraband trade, but all other goods were to pass freely unless owned by an enemy. No port was to be considered blockaded unless investing warships created "an evident danger of entering." Madison contrasted two opposing views of impressment. Except for military personnel, "we consider a neutral flag on the high seas as a safeguard to those sailing under it. Great Britain on the contrary asserts a right to search for and seize her own subjects." Under that cover, American citizens and other neutrals were seized and taken off.

Great Britain, Madison said, did not deny the general rule that the high seas were free, with such exceptions as the law of nations recognized. But "in what usage except her own" was there a sanction to the taking of any but military enemies from a neutral ship?

If neither international law, usage nor treaties authorized this practice, what did? Could it be pretended that national sovereignty extended beyond a country's dominions and ships? If the law of allegiance could be enforced on foreign ships at sea, so could any other municipal law, in peace as well as war. Impressment deprived men of their dearest rights. Ships and cargoes seized in war had to be carried before a regular tribunal, where the captor himself was subject to damages for abuse of power. But seamen were taken without a trial, their destiny determined by the will of a naval officer, "sometimes cruel, often ignorant," and generally (for want of mariners) interested in his own decisions.

Taking note of the claim that similarities of features and language made arbitrary authority necessary, the Secretary said that this indefensible principle led to evils of a deeper dye in practice. Men were forced into an abhorrent service, cut off from their most tender connections, exposed to humiliating discipline and the danger of death, not on proof of British allegiance, but by a reversal of the just and ordinary procedure. Every seaman on board an American ship, though "sailing under the American flag, and sometimes even speaking an idiom proving him not to be a British subject, is presumed to be such, unless shown to be an American citizen." Apparently Madison was not thinking of those fair-minded naval officers he often talked about who never impressed an English-speaking seaman unless, on being asked to pronounce "p-e-a-s," he answered "paze."

It may safely be affirmed, he went on, that Great Britain would be among the last nations in the world to suffer such an outrage and indignity. Yet this was being done to Americans, not only against the presumption of their citizenship, but often in defiance of the most positive proof of it.

In defense of impressment at sea, Madison said, Great Britain probably would cite the great number of British seamen serving in the American trade, and claim dominion of the narrow seas. The number of such seamen was less than generally supposed, and a wrongful remedy was not made right by expediency. In 2,059 impressment cases complained of by the United States between 1797 and 1801, only 102 seamen were finally found to be British subjects, 1,142 were discharged as non-British. Eight hundred five cases awaited further proof, with the strongest presumption that nearly all were Americans. For every British seaman gained by violence, ten or even twenty innocent victims suffered, and the whole advantage was swallowed up in ill will and the threat of redress. Sending a copy of one of the pending bills, he said it was proposed with reluctance and probably would not be pressed if there was hope of an amicable settlement.

"But such is the feeling through this country, produced by the reiterated and atrocious cases of impressment and other insults on our flag, that a remedy of some kind will ere long be called for in a tone not to be disregarded."

As to the narrow seas, the claim of dominion over them was so indefensible that he could scarcely credit the making of it. There was a time, he granted, when Great Britain not only claimed but exercised control akin to sovereignty over all the seas from Spain to Norway. But that was when power alone decided questions of right, and ignorance of the law abetted usurpation. In these seas her pretensions were now as out-of-date as the title "King of France," which British monarchs sacrificed at last "to the lessons of a magnanimous wisdom." Should the right to impress in the narrow seas be maintained, Monroe was told, "your negotiation will be at an end."

Madison's article forbidding seizure of neutral goods was copied from a Russo-British treaty, with the added words "in any case or on any pretext." This was to cut off the British doctrine that a colonial trade, not allowed by the mother country in time of peace, could not be opened to neutrals in time of war. All nations including England, he said, changed their colonial trade regulations in wartime. British practice conceded the right of neutrals to trade directly with the colonies of her enemies, and this sufficed to set up an indirect trade with all countries. Restriction of it produced only expense and vexation. Monroe could compromise on this issue only by remaining silent on what he could not get.

During the previous war, Madison asserted, Britain's "fictitious blockade" formed one of the greatest abuses ever committed on the high seas. Ports were proclaimed in blockade before the arrival of a blockading force and held to be so after its departure. Every vessel bound to such ports was seized, at any distance from them, and condemned in British prize courts. "The whole scene was a perfect mockery, in which fact was sacrificed to forms, and right to power and plunder."

He had hoped that the current war would witness no more of these "mockeries and mischiefs." It was found, however, that Martinique, Guadeloupe and St. Domingo had been proclaimed in blockade by a small and distant naval force. Merry, Madison said, did not pretend to justify the measures. Still, the fact that a naval officer took such action proved that no contrary orders had been issued. All that was needed was to carry the wording of the Anglo-Russian treaty into a convention with the United States, and live up to that definition of a blockade.[16]

In his impressment instructions, Madison strengthened the position taken by President Adams in 1799. Adams denied England's right to take any nonenemy seamen from American ships on the high seas, but in presenting this contention, Minister King relied chiefly on analogy—the British flag protected all seamen sailing under it. Madison gave the same doctrine a basis in international law, and his statement became the classic defense of the rights of seamen.[17]

CHAPTER XIII

Trading with Dusky Rebels

ALTHOUGH the blockade of St. Domingo was ineffective against American ships, British control of the sea lanes cut off military supplies from France. As Rochambeau's weakening army gave up one seaport after another, American trade with the Negro rebels expanded. In October 1803 the main French forces held only four ports and two of these were ready to call in the English to prevent starvation. The people of Cap Français lived on what Pichon sent them, and those of Port au Prince saw bargeloads of blacks sweep the waters and seize arriving ships. Total evacuation of the colony seemed inevitable.

Going to see Madison, Pichon asked what would be done about a letter which the Negro commander, Dessalines, had sent to President Jefferson. Madison hadn't heard about it, but next day it was in his hands—forwarded to Jefferson from Monticello. Written in European style, the ex-slave's letter promised to shake off the yoke of the tyrants and expel their hangmen. It invited the United States to establish formal trade relations and promised protection to American commerce. Pichon read the letter and waited in silence.

The American government, Madison remarked, found the situation very embarrassing. Recognizing that France was sole sovereign of St. Domingo, they wished to omit nothing required by duty and respect. Dessalines would receive no answer. The full rigor of French law could be exerted against American trade in the evacuated ports. However, suppose France evacuated the entire colony. How far would French regulations be maintained after that? Pichon replied that only his superiors could answer.

Future possibilities, Madison rejoined, could be reduced to three: either (1) England would occupy the island, or (2) she would establish her commerce there under informal treaties, or (3) the country would be recognized as independent. All probabilities

177

pointed to the second system, especially to a British trade monopoly such as was sought from Toussaint Louverture.

Now, Madison added, it surely was not sound French policy to promote a British monopoly by stopping neutral trade. If American commerce continued, the products of the soil and industry of France would continue to reach the island, perpetuating interests and habits favorable to the mother country. This happened under Toussaint. Finally, since France could not conquer the rebels during a European war, was it to her interest to starve the colony and hamper its internal progress? Would not such a course embitter the blacks and lead them to new excesses, perpetuating "the passions which will close forever the door to a settlement, when peace permits the government to occupy the colony again?"

Pichon repeated that he was not authorized to deal with the subject, adding that the trade was illegal and he would denounce it to his government. The truth was, he wrote to Talleyrand, that an extensive two-way commerce was already being carried on in the evacuated ports. He knew what the answer would be if he asked that the American government forbid the trade, instead of merely leaving the traders to punishment by the French. Madison would reply, as he had done a year before, by quoting France's *memoir justicatif* of 1778, which defended her refusal to cut off contraband trade with Britain's revolted American colonies.[1]

While this was going on, Pichon heard with disgust that General Rochambeau had written to Madison, asking a $100,000 loan to save *"le plus belle possession des Français."* To make rejection more certain, he referred to the United States as "an allied nation" which ought to reunite with France. Madison just then was feeling less chilly than usual toward Rochambeau, whose military and diplomatic blundering matched his butcheries of the black population of St. Domingo. The Secretary had just cordially thanked Pichon for the general's release of three American merchants who had been thrown into jail when they objected to being impressed into the French army. But how could the Secretary be told that the men were set free when their sentences expired, and that Rochambeau, who knew neither of their arrest nor release, acknowledged Madison's indignant protest by threatening to put the Americans to death if he found they had been selling arms to the rebels? "It will surely appear to you," Pichon commented to Talleyrand, "that this was hardly a paper which I could communicate to the Secretary of State." Both incidents, it seemed to him, showed an unthinking readiness to cut off American help and create apprehension as to France.[2]

A few days after this was penned, Rochambeau signed an armistice with the rebels, and surrendered his army to the British navy. Only the French garrison in the old Spanish city of Santo Domingo remained on the island. The United States now heard the old tune from new players. General in Chief Dessalines wrote to his agent, Bunel: "I need 100,000 dollars." General Christophe asked for guns and powder, and hinted at the wiping out of French cities. The carrier of these letters died suddenly at Norfolk and they were sent to Pichon. He concluded that Bunel and the island chiefs were communicating with Madison through Dr. Stevens, former adviser of Toussaint, but in a way not hurtful to France. Stevens, he reported, had come to Washington in December 1803, after a trip to St. Domingo. (Actually, he came to collect back pay.) The ex-consul told Pichon that the Negroes could be won back, if assured of their liberty. From hints dropped by Jefferson, it seemed possible that the American government would play the role of mediator. A system of this sort, the chargé was told, would assure France "all the advantages of the trade of St. Domingo, with a nominal independence."[3]

By the end of winter American trade with the island was burgeoning. It was carried on, Pichon protested, not only with great publicity, but with government sanction at customhouses. Suppose, he wrote to Madison, that the black population of the Southern states had revolted and a similar commerce were tolerated by the government of France. "Imagine what feelings would be excited." He asked the Secretary to recollect his unequivocal admissions that this commerce was illegal under the law of nations, and that the United States would leave those engaged in it to the police measures of France. How could these declarations attain their end if traders were protected by American law and even allowed to arm their ships against French cruisers?

Madison reaffirmed his 1802 position—that contraband trade with a revolting colony was no different from the same trade with an independent warring nation. Both were subject to capture but the United States was no more obligated to repress one than the other. Pichon contended that they were sharply different, even apart from the quality of persons (ex-slaves) engaged in this revolt. Trade with rebels was a sort of war directed against the state itself, whereas contraband trade with an independent nation clashed only with loosely defined and temporary rights.[4]

It soon appeared to Madison that under the guise of combating contraband of war, French and Spanish colonial authorities were combining in a piratical assault on American commerce. Officials expelled from St. Domingo issued vast numbers of privateering commissions without regard to French law. The vessels were fitted out in Cuban ports and manned chiefly by Spaniards. American ships were seized regardless of destination and brought before illegal French prize courts in Spanish islands. Cargoes of all kinds were unloaded and sold and the ships scuttled and sunk. Profits were commonly divided among the privateersmen, the judge and the colonial agent who issued the commissions, the last two sometimes being the same person.[5]

Madison notified Yrujo that Spain would be held responsible for this misconduct, and asked him to intervene with the colonial governors. The minister countered rhetorically. The United States was handing poignards to assassins and torches to incendiaries in a French colony. Spain, authorized by the sacred right of self-defense, required "the most decisive measures" to end this trade. If the United States ignored the demand it would find some of the foremost nations of Europe supporting His Catholic Majesty. After consulting the President, Madison asked whether they were to understand that France had asked for this intervention of a third power. Yrujo had to admit that he spoke for Spain alone.

Having opened his opponent's guard, Madison informed him that his peremptory and menacing intervention in Franco-American affairs could no more be reconciled with the respect due to France than with that due to the United States. He had acted without the privity of the one in an effort to overawe the other. His demand was not addressed to the friendship of the United States, but asserted an absolute right on the part of Spain. That country was declaring that the United States must not only abandon to Spanish authority their citizens trading to a French territory, but "co-operate with Spain against them by positive and compulsive acts." That, asserted the Secretary, was a demand which Spain could not make even if she were at war with France. "Not being at war she has no right on the subject."

Spain, Madison observed, talked about arming assassins but demanded the cutting off of food supplies "which by no figure of rhetoric can be called either torches or poignards." She did not seem to consider herself a neutral nation. "I must repeat," the Secretary concluded, "that Spain cannot be regarded as having at the same time both neutral and belligerent rights." Still less could she be permitted, as a neutral, to go farther than a belligerent could in capturing and condemning the trade of American citizens.[6]

Now that he was fighting France's battles, Yrujo decided to resume diplomatic relations with Pichon, whom he had treated "as an enemy minister" (the latter said) since their break over the etiquette issue. If Pichon would come to Yrujo's house at a certain hour, he would receive valuable information. Pichon sent word that he would be available at his own house at that hour. He heard no more from the marquis. This harmful Spanish intervention was most singular, Pichon commented, coming from a power which lighted the fire at St. Domingo. Spain still paid pensions in Europe to the black chiefs it had employed to massacre the French at Fort Dauphin. It still allowed Spanish ships to engage in the trade it wished the United States to stop.

As depredations increased in the West Indies, so did private armaments. Many American ships carried twenty cannon. Pichon, a gentle person who feared nobody, assailed the United States and French colonials with equal zest. The American government, he wrote to Madison in May, was allowing its nationals to carry on a private and piratical war, conveying munitions to rebels under its very eyes. Continued inattention could only be construed as an encouragement "to all the excesses which cupidity may attempt."

But to Talleyrand, Pichon wrote that "Mr. Madison's complaints on this subject are well founded. You will hardly conceive the conduct pursued by the many cruisers flying the French flag with which the seas are covered." He drew his information not merely from American newspapers, but directly from French officials in the West Indies. These privateers seized American ships on the mere pretext that they were trading to St. Domingo.

"Most often they are pillaged and sunk at sea. In all other cases, they are taken to some obscure point in Cuba or Porto Rico and there sold without form of trial . . . by the agent of the colony from which the letter of marque emanated. . . . I am told by French officers, and Mr. Madison himself has asserted to me, that these agents are interested in these armaments and in their captures . . . the agent of Guadeloupe sells commissions openly."

Often, said the diplomat, there were scandalous quarrels between agents competing for the plunder. Commenting on one French "judge" in Cuba, brother of the St. Domingo paymaster, Pichon wrote:

"I leave you to judge, Citizen Minister, how things stand when an agent without public status . . . sets himself up, contrary to all law and all custom, as sole judge in the matter of prizes in a foreign island: when he is himself interested in the armaments, when finally he gives orders on his own private authority to privateer against a nation with which we are at peace."

In the matter of armed ships, Madison was on the defensive. To escape, he blamed the arming on Cuban irregularities. Pichon replied that his protests had preceded the unlawful privateering. Madison pointed out that it could not be stopped without legislation, and Congress had adjourned. That, said Pichon, was why he had made his first protest before the adjournment. It was common practice, Madison argued, to arm private ships in time of peace, to defend property. This was indeed common in certain seas, the chargé retorted, but they could not use that argument against France "unless they likened us to the Barbary States and the Malays." It was an effective rejoinder, although, since Pichon's own report placed French corsairs on the level of pirates, the argument drew more strength from national pride than from logic.

Madison told him, finally, that some of the most distinguished lawyers in America had advised the shipowners that they had a right to arm for defense, but could be tried in American courts for murder if they fired on a properly commissioned French cruiser and killed anybody. Once more he admitted the government's embarrassment. Far from taking an interest in this trade, he regarded it as injurious to the United States.

At this, Pichon recalled the protests he had made against the trade at its inception. The Secretary "seemed always to elude these appeals on my part." Instead of leaving all island traders to their fate, he was now drawing a distinction between contraband and provisions. The former could be seized on the high seas, the latter only within the limits of municipal laws. The chargé, in rebuttal, denied that rebelling Negroes could be accorded the same legal rights as other people.

"I did not pretend [he wrote to Talleyrand] to justify this difference of principle, but argued it as a fact admitted by the nations, and one on which the United States itself established part of its social edifice, not only in what relates to the blacks but also in what concerns the aborigines of America."

The only trouble with that keen thrust was that Madison, no less than Pichon, regarded this part of the American social edifice as a denial of inherent human rights. The chargé disclosed his suspicion that the State Department was in secret communication with the black chiefs. The Secretary flatly denied it. Pichon called attention to the renewed massacre of Frenchmen in St. Domingo—a war to the death during which Americans traded peaceably with the assassins for the spoils of the victims. If the United States regarded this trade as legitimate, why didn't they protect it by convoy? Everybody knew, Madison replied, that convoys would cost more than the protection was worth. However, he was not ready to say that these goods could be given naval escort, since France had a right to seize them within French jurisdiction. He could have added that the owners of armed ships wanted no convoy system. They say, Senator Smith wrote to Madison from Baltimore, "we know our risk . . . the profit is tempting—the loss we can insure against." Their fear was that France might construe government protection to be a breach of neutrality.

Pichon called attention to the American government's changing language. At first, under Toussaint, they justified trade only by saying that he was recognized by France. When the new insurrection started, they abandoned traders to French law. Now they were defending commerce in provisions as long as the ships were on the high seas. He hoped for a categorical explanation of these ambiguities.

The food shipments to the rebels, Madison replied noncategorically, could be regarded as a benefit to France, which surely had no wish to see an English monopoly on the island. If clearances were denied, ships would sail under false papers. (They were already doing so, according to Senator Smith.) Perhaps France would agree to a trade in provisions on condition that the United States cut off the flow of munitions. Pichon answered that his chief concern at the moment was not so much the trade itself, as the arming of ships to protect it, which "seemed an injury to peace as well as to the rights and dignity of France."

Madison could have met the charge of inconsistency by quoting his own writings on the causes of faction in government. The vigor of the American justification of St. Domingo trade varied inversely with the military fortunes of the French in the West Indies, but was influenced at all times, and most strongly in the year of a presidential election, by the political power of American merchants. There was a hint of this in the concluding statement to Pichon—that on account of the domestic issues involved, the government wished to stir the question as little as possible.

Reflecting on Madison's state of mind at the close of this "very lively conference," Pichon decided to ask the captain general of

Cuba to forbid French agents to mix in prize affairs on Spanish soil. That would forestall the Secretary's promised stroke in Paris and take away all pretexts for armaments. Within a few weeks he had an anguished letter from one of the piratical judges protesting the closing of his Cuban court.[7]

On May 26, the President recorded a cabinet decision: "D[earborn]. Whether we shall prohibit our merchant vessels from arming to force a trade in St. Domingo as requested by Pichon? Unanimously not." This ratified what Jefferson and Madison had long since agreed on, the more readily since they saw no power of interference in the Executive. However, in his next talk with Pichon, Madison presented the matter more affirmatively. The cabinet, he said, was seriously occupied with finding a means of repressing the armaments. It was hoped, through the courts, either to prevent the armed trade, or at least compel the participants to give bond not to use their arms contrary to the law of nations. Apparently Madison believed international law to be enforceable in the courts, without a specific supporting statute.

The Secretary apologized for not answering the chargé's notes, saying he was most anxious to avoid a dispute "in which the United States would have disagreeable recriminations to produce." What recriminations could there be, asked Pichon, in a dispute where the first injuries came from the United States? Pichon cited new aggravations, especially a boastful newspaper story of the armed schooner *Union's* attack on three French privateers. The conference having led "to a moment of ill-humor on Mr. Madison's part," the chargé was led to reflect (to his government) that since France had no effective means of checking the commerce with the rebels, it would be a grave error to antagonize the United States without repairing the injuries to the island.

Informing Madison of the closing of the illegal prize courts, Pichon drew a contrasting picture of the armed ships in the New York and Philadelphia harbors. Filled with Negroes (exiles for whose return Dessalines was paying $40 a head), they produced "all the appearance of a state of war declared between France and the United States." But Pichon stood his ground when the aide-de-camp of Commander in Chief Ferrand came to the United

States to insist that he withdraw what he had written to the governor of Cuba. The sale of American ships, this army officer told him, had become the sole resource of the beleaguered French garrison. "I will not yield at all to these demands," Pichon informed Talleyrand. Until given orders to the contrary, he would persist in holding the restraint of American commerce "within the limits of the law of nations, our own laws and those of justice and policy."

While waiting for news from Paris, Madison tried to keep the angered shipowners quiet. The Executive, he assured Philadelphia merchants, was seeking a relaxation of restrictions on the "profitable trade with St. Domingo." Meanwhile those who violated the regulations must assume all the risks legally incident to their action. All others would receive the patronage of the government against the "gross irregularities" of insular officials.[8]

This was written three days after Talleyrand, following two months of studied silence, finally stated the French position. Livingston's protests and Talleyrand's reply virtually duplicated the less conciliatory portions of the talks between Madison and Pichon. The foreign minister spurned Madison's distinction between food and guns. When brigands were deluging a country with blood, did any peaceable and honorable nation have an interest in helping such people to live? He hoped this would end all thought of claiming damages on account of the blockade. On the other hand, if colonial governors had been provoked to misconduct by the unlawful actions of American shipowners, their regulations would not receive "the imperial sanction."[9]

That phrase reflected the march of history. On May 18, 1804, Napoleon Bonaparte made himself emperor of the French. The Republic, five years dying and two years dead, was buried. When news of this aggrandizement reached America, Madison treated it with cold reserve. Replying to an official notice from Pichon, he merely acknowledged the right of every nation to change its government, and expressed pleasure that his Imperial Majesty temporarily recognized old letters of credence. "I have thought it best," the Secretary wrote in asking Jefferson's approval, "to decline any expressions which might enter in the smallest degree into the character of the revolution in the French government or even be personal to the emperor; although something of the latter sort may probably be looked for." If any such civility should be thought consistent with American principles and neutrality, it could be furnished through the legation in Paris.[10]

Madison had greeted Napoleon's original seizure of power as a death blow to French liberty, leaving the United States as the only remaining theater of true freedom. This new step concerned him more directly. The moment the dictator reached for a crown, French diplomacy became imperial in style and imperious in tone. There was a whiff of diplomatic grapeshot in the phrase "imperial sanction." Henceforth, the American government would have to cope with a selfmade monarch aiming to rule the world by arms and edicts.

CHAPTER XIV

THE WATERS OF MOBILE

ALL through 1804 relations with Spain grew more tense. In the preceding December, President Jefferson asked the Senate to ratify the 1802 claims convention which had fallen two votes short when first submitted. If, he said, Spain did not withdraw her own ratification after this long delay, the limited indemnities agreed to could be accepted, and the remainder be taken up in the boundary negotiations made necessary by the purchase of Louisiana.

This advice reflected the failure of an effort to enlarge the convention. During the recess of Congress, Pinckney had once more demanded indemnities for American ships seized by private French cruisers and condemned in Spanish ports, during a war in which France and Spain were allies. Spain replied that a royal order denied prize-court powers to French consuls on Spanish soil. That, Madison averred, was a confession of liability, since the order had never been enforced.

The Senate promptly ratified the convention. Even though Spain, bitter over Louisiana, should withdraw her own consent to it, American ratification would be useful. The entire mass of spoliation claims was now in shape to be used as pressure and as payment for a cession of the Floridas.[1]

Among the papers sent to the Senate were the replies of five American lawyers to a query from the Spanish minister. Using the letters A, B and C in place of the names of countries, Yrujo asked whether the United States could claim damages from Spain, for injuries inflicted within Spanish territory by France, Spain being unable to prevent it and the United States having previously relinquished its claim on France. They answered unanimously, No.

When Madison read this trickily worded query, he so far forgot

the special privileges of lawyers as to exclaim that Edward Livingston, Jared Ingersoll, William Rawle, J. B. McKean and P. S.
Du Ponceau ought to be prosecuted under the Logan Act. This
1799 law of dubious constitutionality and terroristic purpose, enacted in resentment against the private peace mission of Dr.
George Logan to France, made it a crime for any American to
communicate with a foreign government for the purpose of obstructing the policies of the United States. A senatorial committee
thought the lawyers should be prosecuted. Dr. Logan himself,
who had been punished by being sent to the Senate, helped to
put the whole matter in limbo through a motion (not voted on)
declaring that such a recommendation was not within the Senate's duties.[2]

The five-lawyer opinion was weakened by the presumption
that it was paid for; also by the fact that McKean was a brother-
in-law of the Spanish minister, Du Ponceau was attorney for foreign legations, Livingston had recently been ousted as United
States District Attorney because of a $43,000 shortage in his ac-
counts.[3] And Ingersoll was an aggressive Federalist. If the United
States chose to use similar tactics, Madison observed, it would be
easy to line up more lawyers on the other side, including Spanish
jurists.

The Secretary indirectly answered this legal opinion when he
notified Pinckney of the Senate's approval of the Spanish convention. It was true, he said, that in the ratification of the 1800 convention with France, the Senate gave up spoliation claims in exchange for release from the alliance of 1778. But no claim had
ever been made by the United States, against France, on account
of depredations committed by French citizens under Spanish jurisdiction. These damages, therefore, were not included in the
release. No claim lay against France for such actions. When
French consuls condemned American ships in Spanish ports, they
either did so under the authority of Spain, or without lawful authority. In that case their actions were nonconsular and private.
"As well might Spain say that a theft or robbery, committed in
the streets of Madrid by a Frenchman or an American, is to be
redressed by France, and not by her, as pretend that redress is to

be so sought for spoliations committed by cruisers from, or condemnations within, Spanish ports."

There could be no escape from this responsibility, Madison asserted, unless Spain "not only pleads a duress, suspending her free agency and prostrating her national honor, but proves the reality of this duress." Meanwhile, depredations of the same sort were being repeated in Spanish ports of the West Indies and would be made a ground for claiming additional reparation. Pinckney should bear in mind that all of these claims, probably exceeding what they were to offer for Florida, were to be brought into their negotiations for purchase of that colony.[4]

Although Madison proved Spain's technical responsibility for French depredations in Spanish jurisdiction, he probably would have argued the other way had France been the weaker country. As it was, the real problem was to make Spain give up a province she intended to keep, in exchange for cancellation of a debt she did not intend to pay.

From the moment Louisiana was transferred, American thoughts centered on the portion of West Florida regarded as part of it. French Commissioner Laussat said nothing publicly about boundaries, either in receiving the province from Spain or in passing it on. But in a private conference, as Madison reported to Livingston in January 1804, he stated that no part of the Floridas was included. With respect to the West he "held a language more satisfactory," placing the boundary at the Rio Bravo (Rio Grande).

Livingston was to assure France that a parental interest was being taken in the people of Louisiana. The bill to set up government would not suddenly give them the full powers dictated by republican theory, but "it may fairly be expected that every blessing of liberty will be extended to them as fast as they shall be prepared and disposed to receive it."

This assurance reflected but did not fully adopt the opinion of Governor Claiborne that the ignorance and credulity of these well-disposed, pleasure-loving people unfitted them for self-government. Within a few weeks, Americans, Creoles and transient foreigners were enjoying a series of riots at the public balls in New

Orleans. French army officers drew their swords in protest against American insistence on the barbarous, pro-British *"Contra Danse Anglaise"* instead of delightful French quadrilles and waltzes. It was not quite clear whether General Wilkinson restored order by going around the room saying "we are all brothers" (as Madison was told) or by a bayonet charge into the dance hall, as Laussat reported to Paris. Claiborne was grieved to find his own lenity blamed for the disorders. There were Americans in New Orleans, he told Madison, who wished him "to suppress by the force of terror even a tumultuous thought. . . . That fearful and sullen calm which despotism produces has no charms for me."[5]

The twenty-eight-year-old governor sent a wave of bitterness through the people by ordering the use of English in the courts. He had to do so, he explained to Madison, because the judge spoke nothing else: the loudest complaints against American jurisprudence came from debtors who had escaped judgment in the dilatory Spanish courts. Laussat, however, wrote that it would be hard to find two men less suited than Claiborne and Wilkinson to win the hearts of the people—the former a man of charming private qualities but awkward in action, the latter full of silly inconsistencies and often drunk. "They have thoroughly and heedlessly run counter to the habits, prejudices and character of the people of the country."

One thing Claiborne did know: American, French and Spanish speculators were uniting to hold onto huge land grants made by Intendant Morales after he learned of Spain's cession of Louisiana to France. These men, to injure him, would "resort to every expedient short of assassination." He rejoiced at word from Madison that the President would be pleased to have Morales induced, without violence, to move to some part of the United States where he would be harmless and "his wealth could be engaged with more advantage." Claiborne was hardly less anxious for Laussat to depart, finding him intemperate, opinionated and an interferer in government.[6]

A day or two after the February cabinet action on Morales, Yrujo complained to Madison about a reported decision to send five or six hundred more troops to lower Louisiana. The Secretary of State had not heard of it, but thought it probable, as there were many slaves in the territory and the attitude of the white population was uncertain. After talking with the President, he informed the marquis that three extra companies were to be sent. Reporting this to Madrid, Yrujo admitted that the reason was valid but doubted that it excluded the idea of taking West Florida by force. All that restrained the United States was the continuance of peace between Spain and England, and Merry had told him that Jefferson and Madison were eagerly asking whether a British declaration of war was imminent.[7]

Madison's dispatches to Livingston disclosed a different reason for this eagerness—the effect of such a war on French and British policy. Monroe was to go to Madrid as soon as he had dealt with impressment in London. Livingston should gather evidence to support the American claim to the Mobile region and to the 49th parallel (accepted fourteen years later) as the proper boundary line with Canada. He must do all in his power to keep the French government "in our scale, against that of Spain." France should welcome a transfer of the Floridas to the United States "as the only effectual security against their falling into the hands of Great Britain" in case of war between Britain and Spain.

Madison explained the failure to demand West Florida when Louisiana was taken over. A refusal would produce "a premature dilemma" between overt submission and a resort to force. Also, silence would be no bar to a later plea that delivery of the seat of government was in effect delivery of the whole. In the meantime an amicable settlement with Spain could be sought.[8]

The United States was ready to buy all of Florida while negotiating for possession of what was believed to be already purchased. Even as this plan was being defined it was promoted or set askew—it was hard to say which—by passage of the "Mobile Act" in Congress. Introduced by Majority Leader John Randolph in November 1803, and signed on February 24, it extended the revenue laws to all territory ceded by France, and impinged uncertainly upon the portion in dispute with Spain.

Section 4 added to the Mississippi customs district "all the navi-

NAPOLEON BONAPARTE AS FIRST CONSUL
Etched by Jacque Reich after painting by Jean-Baptiste Greuze

JOHN RANDOLPH
After a painting by J. Wood

ALBERT GALLATIN   JOSEPH H. NICHOLSON
By James Sharples   By St. Memin

gable waters, rivers, creeks, bays and inlets lying within the
United States, which empty into the Gulf of Mexico east of the
River Mississippi." That seemed to make Spanish-held land as
far as the Perdido a part of an American customs district.

Section 11 gave the President discretionary power to create a
separate customs district embracing "the shores, waters, and inlets of the bay and river of Mobile" and other waterways east of
the Mobile and westward to the Pascagoula. It did not contain
the words "lying within the United States."

These two sections produced no recorded debate. Randolph
had said in the Louisiana treaty discussion that the United States
had "not only obtained the command of the mouth of the Mississippi, but of the Mobile." In that light, Section 11 appeared to
invite the President to take possession of the Mobile area. But
Randolph was the usual introducer of administration bills. If this
one came from Jefferson, the prior utterances of its congressional
sponsor were no guide to its meaning.

Two or three weeks after the bill became law, Madison told
Pichon that the sole reason for inserting Section 11 was to ward
off the inconveniences that would take place if Spain should
agree to the Perdido boundary during the ensuing recess of Congress. That is enough to show that the bill came from the President and his cabinet, and their view of it was already on record.

On February 18, while the bill was awaiting the President's
signature, the cabinet approved three alternative territorial offers
to Spain. For recognition of the Perdido boundary, the United
States would give up its claim to Texas. For a boundary on the
Appalachicola, a pledge would be added to keep a broad western
belt empty of settlers for a certain number of years. For both the
Floridas, cash would be added. The cabinet then voted to make
Fort Stoddert the port of entry for the Mobile district to be set
up under Section 11 of the new law. That fort lay on the Mobile
River, a few miles north of the 1795 Spanish-American boundary.[9]

Putting these things together it is evident that the Mobile Act
was a cabinet measure; it was not an instrument of force, and
there had been a decision, before the bill was signed, not to exert
the President's discretionary power in the disputed territory. No-

where did the bill define the eastward boundary—an omission which fitted the flexibility of the intended territorial negotiation.

This pacific intent was put into words three days after the signing, when Secretary Gallatin sent instructions to the collector of the new District of Mississippi, Hore Browse Trist.[10] It was the President's intention to negotiate for this part of West Florida, not to occupy it by force "and you are therefore to exercise no act of territorial jurisdiction within the said limits, though part of your district." He should check smuggling and abstain from acts dangerous to the peace.

Madison, a month later, enumerated similar purposes to Livingston. In providing for collection of revenue and "guarding against the new danger of smuggling," Congress included a provision for West Florida "by vesting in the President a power which his discretion might accommodate to events." Instead of being an afterthought produced by Spanish protests, as some historians have assumed, Madison's explanation was a restatement of purposes put on record before those protests were made.[11]

The storm broke on March 5. Yrujo, as Madison described the scene, "called at the Office of State, with the gazette in his hand, and entered into a very angry comment on the 11th section." The Spanish minister had said not a word about the bill during the many weeks it lay before Congress, though two printed copies were sent to him, so Madison was inclined to discount his belated anger. He tried to assuage it, by showing that the law was not so drastic as was supposed, although (and this was all that Yrujo seemed to hear) West Florida was "clearly ours." Two days later, with "a rudeness which no government can tolerate," the minister addressed a letter to Madison which drew this comment from him to Pinckney in Madrid:

"To speak of an act of Congress as an 'atrocious libel'[12] . . . as an insulting usurpation on the unquestionable rights of his sovereign; and as a direct contradiction to the assurances given to him from the President, would have justified an answer less mitigated than was given."

The President, Madison continued, did not ask for the recall of the Spanish envoy. Remembering his laudable deportment on other occasions, he was willing to make allowance for fervid zeal. But the "intemperance and disrespect" of this minister had put him on a footing unfriendly to cordial communication, and it would remain with the Spanish government to provide a remedy. In other words, Spain should recall or censure him without being asked to do so.

In addition to using invectives, Yrujo vigorously defended Spain's title to West Florida, chiefly on the ground that the treaty of San Ildefonso was one of *retrocession,* and Spain had "restored to France all the territory *which she had received from her."* Nothing but vague conjectures, he asserted, could be cited to support the action of Congress. Even if the treaty had given ground for such pretensions, justice, delicacy and the mutual decorum and respect of nations should have induced the United States to clear up doubts by negotiation before proceeding to a legislative decision. He demanded that Section 11 be annulled and revoked.[13]

While this conflict was developing, Yrujo sought out the British minister and told him there was great dissatisfaction among the Spanish and French in New Orleans. The governor was a low fellow, speculators and wild adventurers were flocking in, and American troops were being sent to prevent an explosion. The marquis was the more open, Merry reported to Lord Hawkesbury, because he believed that Great Britain might wish to help check American expansion. Spain's policy would block an outlet for Georgia's produce and deny the United States a commanding position over British islands in the West Indies. The British minister saw even greater advantages in confining the West to the single port of New Orleans. A well-informed American had just told him that the West was riper for secession than New England, and that the movement would be aided if British agents were sent to the port of entry to build up trade relations. Merry grew enthusiastic. By purchasing all supplies for the West Indies in New Orleans, he advised his government, and flooding the Mississippi Valley with manufactured goods via Canadian waterways, Great Britain could build an intimacy with the West, break its commercial ties with the East and promote complete independence. This need never be feared because the new nation, having only one seaport, could never become a maritime power. He didn't explain how such a bottled-up country, after it became populous, could be prevented from blowing out the stopper and overflowing the whole Gulf Coast.[14]

Instead of discussing boundaries with Yrujo, who had no powers, Madison answered his arguments in new instructions to the American ministers in Europe. On other points there was ground to clear. On March 15 Secretary Gallatin wrote to Jefferson:

"Conversing with Mr. Madison on the subject of Mobile and our regulations respecting the Mississippi, he seemed to apprehend some difficulty in justifying our conduct or rather instructions to impartial men. If upon a full consideration of the subject that difficulty shall be obvious, it would follow that we have not taken solid ground."

Madison's objection was to orders, designed to curb smuggling, which would exclude Spanish ships from Baton Rouge and the Amite River. Should the President wish to change this, Gallatin wrote, it could be made to appear that the Treasury had been overruled. The result (testifying forcefully to Madison's influence) was a prompt notice to Trist that the President had "thought fit to direct" a revocation of the shipping ban. Baton Rouge and other settlements held by Spain were to be regarded as foreign ports.[15]

As soon as this violation of Spanish sovereignty was rescinded, Madison replied to Yrujo and drew the Mobile Act into the narrow compass approved beforehand. Section 11 was subordinate to Section 4, which applied to places "lying within the United States." Although, by Section 11, the President had power to extend the new customs district to places beyond the *acknowledged* limits of the United States, if within the claimed limits, it could be inferred from the two sections taken together that Congress did not look on Section 11 as necessarily comprehending places

south of the 1795 boundary. The term "Bay of Mobile" applied
to places above as well as below that boundary.[16] He could promise that the only actions which required United States jurisdiction
(establishing posts and a postroad to New Orleans, under another
new law) would not be taken in advance of friendly adjustments
with Spain.

Admitting, Madison continued, that Section 11 embraced places
south of the 1795 boundary, such a construction was warranted
by the treaties ceding Louisiana to France and to the United
States. However, the discretionary terms of Section 11 furnished
satisfactory proof of the respect meant by Congress to whatever
titles Spain might urge. An executive discretion which could
be justly exercised would not be employed unjustly. Necessary
negotiations would be conducted at Madrid but the door was left
open to further communications from Yrujo "on the indispensable condition that the language of decorum . . . be not again
forgotten."[17]

These assurances absolved Jefferson, but Madison's effort to
clear Congress made Yrujo angrier than ever. The insult of the
jurisdiction claimed in the act, he replied, was not altered by the
President's promise not to exercise it. Section 11 was worded as
it logically would be if the United States held quiet possession of
the entire Mobile country. Either it explained the intentions of
the government or it did not explain them. If it did not, the
United States owed it both to itself and Spain to annul the section or alter it to remove the insult. Picking up Madison's remark that West Florida was "understood" to be included in the
cession, he replied that Spain held both of the Floridas in their
whole extent, beyond dispute, and "the United States should
prove its right before passing laws."[18]

These were powerful arguments, yet they actually confirmed
Madison's interpretation of Section 11. Its object (as he saw it)
was to enable the President to extend jurisdiction over any part
of the Floridas that should come into quiet possession of the
United States by agreement with Spain. That being the case, the
President could legitimately confine his discretionary authority
to places within the *acknowledged* rather than the *claimed* limits.

If the hoped-for agreement should take place, the claimed limits would become the acknowledged limits, prior to any act of jurisdiction.

Aside from the basic dispute as to ownership, there were two points at issue between Yrujo and Madison: (1) whether the Mobile Act was subordinate to a policy of force or of peaceful negotiation; (2) the impropriety of legislating on the subject of a territory held and claimed by Spain. In the first Yrujo mistook the implications for actual purposes. In the second he was right. The impropriety lay in the failure to specify in the act that its provisions were subordinate to negotiations with Spain. That could not be written into law without undermining the ultimate policy, which was to march to the Perdido if negotiations failed. Thus, although the law was designed for pacific use, the aura of force hovered over it—to a greater extent, perhaps, than was intended.

The effort to dissipate this aura reached a climax when Jefferson exercised his discretionary powers on May 30, 1804. Acting under Section 11, he erected a Mobile revenue district with Fort Stoddert as the port of entry. In defining its limits, he inserted and italicized the restrictive proviso of Section 4, "lying *within the boundaries of the United States.*"[19]

This proclamation was not, as various historians have charged, an emasculation of the law in response to Yrujo's attacks on it. It carried into effect the cabinet decisions of February 18, made two weeks before the Spanish minister uttered his first protest. The legal basis for both the cabinet decision and the proclamation can be found in Madison's March 19 note to Yrujo. First, that Section 11 was subordinate to Section 4 and therefore was limited by implication to places "lying within the United States."[20] Second, that presidential action could validly be confined to places within the acknowledged limits of the country. Any further step would have to await the outcome of negotiations overseas.

The meaning of the Mobile Act came into question once more in the drafting of Jefferson's message of November 1804. Overanxious, now, to emphasize its moderation, he wrote as if his Fort Stoddert proclamation represented his maximum powers.

Spain had misunderstood the terms and objects of a law which authorized "a district and port of entry on the waters of the Mobile within the limits of the United States." Madison pointed out that the act authorized, provisionally at least, a port *outside* those limits. Gallatin was more emphatic. What would be said by their political friends who had understood the law as Spain did and defended it on that ground? The declaration might be distorted into an avowal of some humiliating concession. Jefferson made a thorough revision, restricting Spain's misunderstanding to the *object* (not the terms) of the law.[21]

Some historians, assuming that Gallatin was criticizing Jefferson's final text, have treated this part of the message as a deliberate distortion, with Gallatin pictured as the overruled advocate of a frank admission of the truth.[22] In reality the paragraph as delivered to Congress was a Madison-Gallatin correction of an innocent error, plus an outline for the future—friendly negotiations, and no hostile act during them. The revision epitomized what Madison had been saying about this law for eight months, and did it so exactly as to make it doubtful whether anybody else could have furnished the wording.

Twice, during the encounter with Yrujo over the Mobile Act, Madison straightened out administration policy. In the first instance, he persuaded Gallatin and Jefferson to rescind Treasury regulations which impinged on Spanish sovereignty. In the second, with Gallatin's co-operation, he kept the President from unintentionally closing the legal avenue to more aggressive action. Whatever the origin of that controversial law, the Secretary of State charted the moderate use of it, yet left the larger powers unimpaired.

CHAPTER XV

Yrujo Takes a Walk

Addressing Livingston on March 31, 1804, Madison made a point-by-point reply to Yrujo on the meaning of the San Ildefonso treaty. To thicken the main bulwark of the American claim to the Perdido boundary—the cession of Louisiana with the same extent *that it had when France possessed it* in 1762—he amplified the arguments of Livingston, Monroe and Jefferson as to the extent and unity of the province in that year. Then he undertook to defend the American claim where it was weakest—in the alternative wording which retroceded the province with the same extent *that it now has* in the hands of Spain. What was that?

"It is not denied that the Perdido was once the eastern limit of Louisiana. It is not denied that the territory now possessed by Spain extends to the river Perdido. The river Perdido we say then is the limit to the eastern extent of Louisiana ceded to the United States."

No other construction, Madison asserted, would give a pertinent meaning to the term "now." Prior to 1783, when Spain received the Floridas from Great Britain, Louisiana in the hands of Spain was limited eastwardly by the Mississippi, the Iberville, etc. The term "now" fixed its extent as enlarged by that treaty.

Though plausible, this did not fit the history of the clause—a history more favorable to the American claim, but then unknown. Taking up the other theory, that "now" excluded the portion of Louisiana whose name was changed to West Florida during British ownership, Madison said that the splitting of Louisiana into twenty jurisdictions would not change its territorial extent. What counted was the extent in which it was known to other nations, and especially to the nation then treating for it, France, who had known and possessed it only as a unit.

His construction, Madison pointed out, harmonized the two clauses defining the extent of territory ceded by Spain to France. The extent Louisiana "now has in the hands of Spain" became identical with the extent "that it had when France possessed it," instead of being smaller. Consequently the cession to the United States, being identical with that of Spain to France, embraced this part of West Florida under either definition.

Madison took note of the term "retrocede" in the treaties of cession. Spain said it meant that she gave back to France what she received from France, but not the portion of Louisiana which passed from France to Great Britain and then to Spain. As applied to France, Madison observed, the word "retrocede" covered all she had alienated in 1762—that is, all of Louisiana as she then possessed it. Moreover, the part ceded to Great Britain on the same day was actually ceded for the benefit of Spain, to induce the British to restore Cuba to her. It was as if France had ceded all of Louisiana to Spain, and Spain had exchanged part of it for Cuba. The term "retrocede," therefore, fittingly described the return of the entire province to France and supported "a conclusion drawn from the clear meaning of every other term and from the whole context."

In addition, Madison offered a shrewd argument based on the personality of Napoleon. Every circumstance of the cession of Louisiana to France denoted the purpose "to give luster to his administration" and to gratify national pride by reannexing ancient possessions which, "being in the hands of Spain, it was in the power of Spain to restore." The cession of Louisiana as far as the Perdido merely reduced Spain to her original possessions.

Madison was uncannily right in his analysis, even though he did not know that the word "retrocede" was used over and over in French references to West Florida. He did not know that Napoleon's demand for the Mobile country caused the two indefinite, interchangeable descriptions of Louisiana to be placed in the treaty instead of the precise and definite one Spain wanted, "as it was delivered at the treaty of 1763." Had these facts been known, Spanish resistance could not have stemmed the American torrent.

Yrujo's outburst ended his personal influence in Washington—a matter of some moment in view of his ability. Chiefly, Madison noted to Livingston, the correspondence revealed the earnestness and the basis of Spain's opposition to the American boundary claim. That was an urgent reason for seeking the support of France, who should desire to remove the cause of an American collision with Spain and to keep Great Britain from extending the war and seizing the Floridas.

New orders were sent to Monroe—to proceed to Madrid as soon as he could get away from the impressment issue. He was given the draft of a treaty confirming the Perdido boundary and ceding the rest of the Floridas to the United States. It was indispensable, Madison said, to have the Perdido country treated as *already ceded*. Should it be ceded anew, there would be no way to get rid of the enormous illicit land grants made by the Spaniards in New Orleans on the supposition that France was to get West Florida. Should Spain refuse overt recognition of the existing American title, the speculators could still be defeated by a blanket cession of all Spanish territory east of the Mississippi, without names or boundaries. That would enable the United States to treat West Florida as a region not belonging to Spain when the land grants were made.

This instruction took no account of the overwhelming power of land speculators in American politics and courts. It could not govern a controversy which would be settled either through French influence or force of arms. Nevertheless Madison's deep concern (reported also by Pichon) was expressed still more positively after Governor Claiborne reported that many Americans in New Orleans were supporting Spain's title to West Florida because they were involved in Morales' land speculations. Should a new cession be necessary, there would be almost no vacant land for the government to acquire unless the king of Spain disavowed these unjust sales.[1]

Following a July cabinet meeting which stiffened the American demands, Madison sent fresh instructions to Monroe and Pinckney. News was expected daily of an overturn of the British cabinet which would extend the war to Spain. That event ought to make Spain more willing to yield to proper terms which "might otherwise be rejected by her pride and misapplied jealousy." The ministers should concede as little as possible in Texas and nothing at all except in return for a cession of all the Floridas. A sum left blank (the cabinet put it at $2,000,000) was to be offered for the Floridas, but none for the portion west of the Perdido lest it confirm the irregular land grants. They were to seek an interim agreement—the Mobile to be kept open and neither country to strengthen its situation in the disputed territory. Rejection of this, Spain was to be told, would tend to drive the United States to counterbalance Spain's military forces in that area, while refusal of a Mobile guarantee would "commit the peace of the two nations to the greatest hazard."

This anxiety reflected the imposition of a prohibitive 12½-percent duty on American commerce traversing Mobile Bay. The region north of the border, a land commissioner reported, was a roadless wilderness whose sole connection with the rest of the world was by water. Cut that, and the resulting isolation would turn honest settlers into banditti.[2]

Unknown to Jefferson and Madison, the danger of a local clash with Spain had just been diminished by the peculiar genius of General Wilkinson. Encountering Governor Folch of West Florida in New Orleans, the commander in chief of the United States Army demanded $20,000 of him. Spain, he said, had agreed fifteen years before to pay him a pension of $2,000 a year, but stopped doing so after five years. If they would pay up these arrears and arrange for the future, he would act as an adviser on defense and would ascertain and report the plans of Jefferson and his cabinet.

To prove his worth, Wilkinson wrote out a set of "Reflections" on Spanish defense. If Monroe succeeded in buying the Floridas, he warned, the Western frontiersmen "like the ancient Goths and Vandals would precipitate themselves upon the weak defenses of Mexico, overturn everything in their path," and propagate the pestilential doctrines that were destroying the foundations of European monarchy. Folch referred Wilkinson to Spanish Commissioner Casa Calvo, who paid him $12,000 on account and submitted his request for $4,000 a year to higher authorities.[3]

Britain's cabinet crisis came late in May. The aggressive Pitt succeeded Addington as prime minister. With Spain thus threatened, American pressure could be increased. French support of the American territorial claim was less essential, yet might perhaps be obtained more easily, either to keep the United States out of the war or the British out of Florida. All this was seen before Pitt actually took office and found expression in Madison's directions to Robert Livingston.

The latter was pleased at even a partial shift of the Florida negotiations to Paris, but had little patience with Madison's methods. His reply, headed "Private and confidential, to be deciphered only by the Secretary of State himself," was sent to Montpelier, accompanied by a cipher key.

There were two practicable ways of obtaining the Floridas, Livingston believed—immediate forcible seizure, or bribery. "My sentiment still is as it always has been," he wrote, "that we should not hesitate to take possession of West Florida." Napoleon would acquiesce in order to prevent a war. If, without taking possession, the United States should rely on a direct application to France, "a great private interest would defeat your object." Livingston recalled his earlier scheme of satisfying Talleyrand and complained once more that the appointment of Monroe upset those arrangements.[4]

"Whether [he added] we should have made a better bargain by pursuing the path I had chalked out I know not but I think we should. As it was, the sale of Louisiana brought no profit to a shop that has not usually seen a customer pass by. I have reason to think it is still open for the sale of Florida but I have always spoken of West Florida as ours, which has never been contradicted, and of East Florida as of too little moment to afford a *bon pot de vin.*"

East Florida by itself might not be worth enough to sustain the bribe needed to secure it, but the Floridas together would merit a good price and "something may be collected from it for the privy purse." This, Livingston hoped his former letters had made plain, was the cheapest and most certain way of negotiating in France, and he believed also in Spain. Reaching a proper understanding between negotiators, however, was a point of some delicacy. Make up your minds, he advised, as to the sum you are willing to pay for the Perdido boundary. "If this is adequate to the expectation of —— a direct application may be made to the emperor claiming it as part of your purchase and stating strongly the reasons upon which you found your claim."

These reasons, he thought, would be "sufficiently cogent if backed by a million livres" for those who were to smooth the channel in Paris and Madrid. In putting over a deal which must not be known to "any other person than that negotiator and the President," he was well aware of "the difficulty that will arise from the nature of our government." How to get over those difficulties was for Madison to judge. "I can only point out to you the mode in which this business can be most effectually done."[5]

This amazing letter, lying deciphered in the Madison manuscripts, has been open to historians for more than a hundred years. Two sentences have been quoted from it again and again—the advice to seize West Florida, and the remark that the sale of Louisiana brought no profit to a shop usually looking for it—a sentence which, taken out of context, is made to look like a boast by Livingston that he bought Louisiana without yielding to Talleyrand's corrupt cupidity. Bribery proposals by an American diplomat hit a blind spot in scholars who easily recognized French iniquity in the XYZ affair.

By the time Madison received Livingston's proposal, a new American minister was on his way to Paris. The Secretary's opinion of the scheme was made plain some months later, when Talleyrand came to Spain's support. If this deviation from sound policy was an effort "to convert the negotiations with Spain into a pecuniary job for France and her agents," Madison commented, it would no doubt be pushed with singular temerity, but might "finally be abandoned under a despair of success" and give way to something better.[6]

To emphasize his break with Madison, the Marquis d'Yrujo closed his house in April 1804 and left for Pennsylvania without calling on the Secretary. "He and the marchioness called together at the houses of my colleagues," Madison reported to Jefferson in

Monticello, but Sally went alone to say good-by to Dolley. The latter sent cordial regards to her in Philadelphia at the first opportunity. Say a great deal to her, she admonished the messenger, for "I feel a tenderness for her and her husband regardless of circumstances." Also, Dolley would like the news of Philadelphia: "what they say or do—Bonapartee and so forth." A fortnight later the marquis wrote to Madison, with strict politeness, that Spain was withdrawing its protest against the cession of Louisiana.[7]

By midsummer, Yrujo had received such positive support from Madrid, in his quarrel with Madison, that he feared it might stimulate a forcible seizure of territory. He was instructed to notify the American government that no consideration whatever would dispose the King of Spain to cede any part of his American dominions. Yrujo told Merry early in August that he did not intend to carry out the instruction until a squadron of frigates which had just sailed for the Mediterranean was too far on its way to be overtaken and called back. He busied himself in the meantime preparing anti-American articles for anonymous publication in the Federalist press.

Madison and his family left Washington for Montpelier on July 25. The foundering of his carriage horses on the way to Dumfries, due to unaccustomed fatigue and the bad management of his driver, forced the party to transfer to the hack that carried their baggage. The good horses were then sent back from Captain Winston's, near Stevensburg, to bring up the carriage. Under this relay system, the homeward journey took five days. They found grain suffering from drouth, but a five-inch, three-day rain saved the upland crops at the cost of a heavy loss of topsoil.[8]

Before leaving the capital, Madison invited the Pichons and the Merrys to visit Montpelier during the recess. "Mrs. Pichon," he wrote to Monroe, "is in need of every consolation for the loss of her only child, about a year old." The blow was the heavier because Pichon had received notice that a French minister was about to sail for America. Had he arrived, the baby would have escaped the deadly Washington summer. Merry, Madison thought, felt embarrassed by his government's failure to respond to his complaint about etiquette, and he wished to draw the British minister into the circle of private hospitality. "He is at bottom a very worthy man and easy to do business with except that he is excessively cautious." The Pichons, who were in Philadelphia, accepted the invitation, but when the time came to start they could not bear to pass so soon through Washington, the scene of their misfortune. Expecting them, Madison postponed a visit which Jefferson wanted him to make, so the President late in August rode to Montpelier instead.[9]

The wish to get rid of French and Spanish influence in lower Louisiana had just been stimulated by a puzzling missive from Monroe. "I know not what to make of the inclosed letter," Madison wrote in sending it to the President. "The purport of it clashes with every calculation founded in probability and yet it is impossible to disregard altogether the reliance which Col. Monroe seems to place on what he writes." The minister had been told by a person of high authority and character that at the outset of war in 1793 the British government had agreed to replace the House of Bourbon on the throne of France, in exchange for which the Bourbons would help Great Britain recover the United States. The scheme was damped by the defeat of the Duke of York in Holland and had been kept out of sight since Napoleon's victory at Marengo in 1800. It was now revived.

Jefferson termed the account "of an awful complexion," and did not wonder that it made an impression on a diplomat familiar with the immense resources and wickedness of Europe. The Bourbons, he was sure, would agree to anything, but France and England had neither the will to combine nor the strength to restore the United States to British dominion. It would be good policy to let each of them see that it could drive the United States into the scale of the other. Also, it would be wise to give the people of Louisiana full American citizenship at the next session of Congress.[10]

To avert a new clash, the President had recently called a halt to Postmaster General Granger's proposal (violating the assurances Madison had given Yrujo) that an American post office be set up in Baton Rouge, on the prospective post road between Natchez and New Orleans. Jefferson now suggested that Madison instruct Governor Claiborne to propose such an office by mutual consent, to serve both countries.

Madison pointed out that Granger was construing the new post-road law to require postal service for the people living in the Spanish-held portion of the route. "If no regard is to be had to the Spanish possession every law in force in Louisiana ought to be extended into that district." The Secretary of State saw no such obligation in the statute. Therefore, considering the "temper and threats" of the Pensacola government, would it not be well to allow Claiborne the alternative of asking for a simple passage of the mails, without an office? That was done.

In their conference at Montpelier, Jefferson and Madison made final decisions as to government personnel in newly created Orleans Territory (below Arkansas and Mississippi). Commissions were signed and sent to Governor Claiborne. To forestall hurt feelings, the President wrote to Gallatin that he had waited for information until the twelfth hour, and, "on consultation with Mr. Madison," had made the fewest possible changes from what had been provisionally approved by department heads.[11]

Hardly had the President left Montpelier when Madison had unpleasant news from Madrid. The diplomatic situation there, bad from the moment Charles Pinckney was given his well-earned political reward, had been deteriorating steadily. Early in the year, Madison found him "teasing the Spanish government" about the Floridas, which he was not to touch without the advice of Monroe. Spurred on from "an intermediate quarter from motives sufficiently obvious" (that is, by Livingston out of jealousy of Monroe), Pinckney was continually offering to *accept* propositions he was prohibited from *making*. Cevallos turned this against him when he heard of the Mobile Act. Terming Section 11 one of the greatest outrages one power could perpetrate upon another, he plainly intimated that it must be revoked before Spain would ratify the 1802 claims convention. In this conduct, Madison remarked to the President, "we see pretty clearly the passions of Yrujo" and the building of issues on which to restrict Louisiana. Jefferson promptly advised the Secretary of War to send more troops to the Southwest.

The Spanish minister had later news than the State department. Pinckney, in an amazing step, had written Cevallos that if the Spanish attitude toward the claims convention was final, his "instructions and duty" forced him to warn all Americans to leave the country within the period allowed in event of war. When he could fix a date for his own departure, he would ask for his passports. Guessing correctly that no such instructions existed, Cevallos said so in a chiding and unyielding reply which left the American minister self-isolated.[12]

Yrujo now had two critical matters to deal with, each requiring personal discussion. Barred by his pride from approaching Madison, he imagined a danger to his country in doing so. His own and Madison's irritable disposition, he told Merry, would be more likely to inflame than reduce the national disagreements. Addressing the President on September 7, Yrujo wrote that "the conduct of Mr. Pinckney at Madrid" (of which the American government knew nothing) created a need for explanations directed toward peace and harmony. Though well aware that the Secretary of State was the proper channel of communication, he thought "a direct and personal interview with you" would be more effectual. Subject to approval, he and Madame Yrujo were setting out for Monticello.

"Nobody more than myself [he continued] renders to Mr. Madison's head and heart the justice [that] is due to him; but he has in my opinion an extreme susceptibility: unluckily for myself nature has given me a pretty good share of it also. This qualification, useful sometimes, I apprehend may not prove advantageous in the present occasion."

On the day Yrujo forwarded this letter, Major William Jackson of Philadelphia (one time secretary of the Constitutional Convention) made out an affidavit and sent a copy to the President. Jackson, lately ousted from federal office and now a bitterly resentful

Federalist editor, took oath that on the previous day he visited
Yrujo at the latter's request. The Spanish minister told him the
United States wanted war. "But *you* have it in your power to do
much good by espousing the part of peace, which is so necessary to
both nations—and if you will consent to take elucidations from me
on the subject, I will furnish them and I will make you any acknowledgment." "With difficulty," wrote Jackson, "I suppressed
the indignation of my feelings and left the house."[13]

Jefferson, after observing to Yrujo that conditions called for
calm discussion between him and Madison, promised to receive
him with pleasure. Madison sent over Pinckney's letters "that they
may be at hand if wanted." Not knowing of Jackson's affidavit,
now published, Yrujo drove triumphantly to Monticello. "He
passed by the house of the Secretary of State without stopping
there," Pichon reported to Talleyrand. Jefferson, about to leave
for Washington, remained two days out of courtesy. He disavowed
Pinckney's passport demand, said nothing of Jackson's letter, and
invited the Yrujos to stay with Martha Randolph as long as they
found it agreeable.

Not until his return in October did the marquis learn of the
Jackson scandal. "Judge of his embarrassment!" exclaimed Pichon.
Yrujo wrote a long explanation for the President, who referred
him to Madison. The Spanish minister readdressed the communication to the Secretary of State, but published it in the newspapers
before delivering it to Madison's office. This, he explained, was
due to a sudden illness—one which must have struck after he
visited the printer.

The proposal to Jackson, Yrujo contended, was in the American tradition of a free press. Newspapers were full of lies about
Spain, and duty required him to spread the truth and convert warlike editors to advocacy of peace. As for bribery, compensation of
an editor who retailed space by the line was no more indelicate
than paying a fee to a physician. Furthermore, although a foreign
minister might possibly bribe a crown officer, he would not waste
money on an editor "whose sheets are scarcely to be seen across
the water of the Schuylkill." Least of all would he do so for the

mere printing of harmless ideas which had since appeared elsewhere over the signature "Graviora Manent."[14]

This belated admission of authorship hardly made these articles
as innocent as he pretended. Following their mid-September appearance in *Relf's Philadelphia Gazette,* a furious counterattack
was launched in the administration press, with charges that Yrujo
wrote them and calls for prosecution of the editor under the Logan
Act. When the third article appeared, Chief Clerk Wagner sent
word to Madison that Yrujo was incontrovertibly the author. It
was in part a translation of his March 7 letter to Madison on the
title to West Florida. The articles came ostensibly from an American denouncing the policies of his own government.[15]

The Jackson affair finished Yrujo as far as Madison and Jefferson were concerned. Capped by publication of the letter to Madison, it produced a decision to ask for his recall. But how should
that be done? The Secretary had planned, in case the doors were
shut against both Yrujo and Pinckney, to write directly to Cevallos. Instead, Monroe being under orders to go to Spain, instructions were sent to that minister.

Yrujo's offensive conduct, Madison said, had been reported to
Spain in the previous spring. Now there was further proof of his
unfitness. His own explanation "convicts him of an attempt to
debauch a citizen of the United States into a direct violation of an
act of Congress," and into a combination with a foreign func-
tionary against the measures of the American government. He
had used expressions grossly disrespectful to the President. Finally,
there was the publication of his letter to the Secretary of State—an
appeal to the people in which his pretensions were matched only
by his sophistry. "It cannot be necessary to develop or enforce such
egregious misconduct." Monroe was to ask the government of
Spain to substitute "a less exceptionable representative," unless that
had already been done.[16]

Monroe at this time had been several days in Paris, after a stormy
four-day passage of the North Sea. Taking leave of a British government unwilling to settle the impressment issue, he was en route
to a Spanish government unwilling to settle boundaries or spolia-

tions. On the way he sought the aid of a French government which wanted no issues settled unless for its benefit, or for the private gain of its ministers. Should such desires be yielded to? "My present impression," Monroe commented, "is to come off without delay if I find the affair dwindle into a speculating or swindling business."[17]

In Washington, formal relations with Yrujo were not cut off. Receiving, from him, a refusal to give assurances that the 1802 convention would be ratified unconditionally, Madison replied that Spain was demanding exclusion of a clause founded on the responsibility, the honor and self-respect of its king—the clause authorizing later settlement of French spoliations in Spanish ports. The President, he said, was unwilling to believe that Spain would avoid questions which affected the harmony of the two nations. "The mission extraordinary to Madrid ... will accordingly not be interrupted."[18]

The tone of Madison's letter, though not belligerent, was hard and uncompromising. It fairly measured the damage Yrujo had done to Spain through his intemperate zeal and his brash belief that a foreign minister could resort to the newspapers like any domestic politician.

CHAPTER XVI

CANDIDATE IN PARIS

LIVINGSTON's inability to return to the United States in the fall of 1803 did not dash his political aspirations. By this time he was in hot conflict with the three commissioners—John Mercer, Isaac Cox Barnet and William Maclure—who had been appointed by him and Monroe to liquidate the claims against France payable out of the Louisiana purchase money. Voluminous details of this contest came to Madison and Jefferson during the ensuing year, but with so little clarity that they were more inclined to cry "a plague on both your houses" than to probe its political and personal complexities.

Under the convention of 1803, claims up to twenty million francs ($3,750,000) were to be paid by the American minister in Paris after they had been certified both by the American board and the French government. These were claims covered by the earlier convention of 1800, growing out of ship captures and detentions, and sales of supplies to France. Americans having European partners could get nothing. Where prizes had been ordered restored, claimants had to prove that the captors were unable to pay the damages. If the French bureaus insisted on paying any claim to which the American claims agent (Consul General Fulwar Skipwith) objected, the American board was to report on it to the American minister. He would then send his own observations to the French government, whose decision would be final. Livingston asserted that this gave him general control over the board, in spite of the convention wording which directed that body *to ascertain* whether claims were eligible or not.[1]

The vital question was: should the board or Livingston decide whether James Swan was in partnership with a foreigner? The first six cases to come before the board named Swan as agent for six American owners. The board (after postponing these cases for six months) found that Swan was the real claimant in five of them. It rejected these because of his partnership in the European commercial houses of Dallarde, Swan & Co. and Swan & Schweitzer, the latter being purchasing agents for the French government.

The board also rejected the claim of Coster, Coster, Laurence & Wanland, New York merchants, for 962,500 livres, on the ground that they had not proved the bankruptcy of the captors of the ship *Nancy*. The real owner was John R. Livingston and the agent for this claim was J. C. Mountflorence, whose intended appointment as private secretary to Minister Livingston was so bitterly protested by Secretary of Legation Sumter.[2]

Publicly, Livingston's dispute with the board related chiefly to the order and slowness of its actions. Under the rules set up, Skipwith was to examine claims in the French bureaus and furnish correct copies. The American board would then certify them to the French bureaus as eligible or ineligible. The French board would accept or reject them without being bound by the prior American action, and fix the amount to be paid. Those approved by both boards were then to be sent to Livingston, with a final certificate from the American board authorizing payment.

Livingston wanted swift action. In July 1803 he printed Treasury bills payable "two months after exchange of ratifications," and wrote to Madison to be prepared to receive them at an early date. His plan, he explained later, was to enable creditors to convert the bills into money "the moment the news arrived of the ratification." The board upset this by voting not to issue any final certificates until it was known that the treaties had been ratified. They did not want early payees to exhaust the fund before it was known whether there would be enough for all.[3]

The 1803 convention referred to a "conjectural note" which was to identify claims covered by the convention. It was not attached, but Livingston certified a copy to the board—122 named claims and 105 for unnamed embargoed ships, totaling 19,889,303 livres. With several years' interest added, this would greatly exceed the twenty million francs[4] available for payment. Many other eligible claims were not on the list at all—none, for instance, based on captures at sea.[5]

On the conjectural note, the named claims were arranged in three classes: (1) "allowed" *(reconnues)* by the old French board, (2) "reported on," (3) "not yet examined." The board voted to give priority to all the claims on the conjectural note, and to follow its numerical order. It speedily approved seven claims, including one of 330,786 livres by John R. Livingston for hides sold to France. Skipwith, searching the French records, then discovered that claims marked "reconnues" had not been allowed and the whole list was in a chronological jumble. The board decided to ignore the categories, dig out the dates of origin and be governed by them. Livingston protested violently, both against the delay and the deviation from the conjectural note. Even the order of listing, he insisted, was made binding by the convention.

A few months later Livingston denounced the board for adhering to the conjectural note. That list of claims, he said, had been rejected as inaccurate when the convention was being drafted, but in the hurry they forgot to place that notation on it. Marbois and Monroe confirmed this. The commissioners hurled a question at Livingston: why did he certify this invalid list to them and tell them that deviation from it would violate the convention?[6]

That question was not answered, but the reason is clear enough. James Swan, John R. Livingston and Peter W. Livingston had total claims, in and out of the conjectural note, amounting to 4,084,188 livres—Swan 2,500,000, the Livingstons 1,500,000. That was one fifth of the twenty millions payable to several hundred American claimants, and more than the combined claims of two hundred of them. The total fund being inadequate, the order of payment might determine whether a claimant got all or nothing.

The conjectural note opened with eighteen claims marked "allowed" by France, totaling 3,459,778 livres. Of these, 2,182,352 livres, or two thirds of the total, were in the claims of Swan and John R. Livingston. The American board allowed the Livingston claim of 330,786 livres, but rejected Swan claims totaling 851,574 livres. Swan then withdrew another claim for "about 1,000,000 livres" due him as a French agent and reoffered it in new claims of 928,512 livres as an American merchant and 163,738 as a French agent.

With John R. Livingston's claim approved and those of Swan rejected or transferred, the Livingstons and Swan no longer had any interest in the conjectural note. Outside of it, however, Swan now claimed 1,284,504 livres, the two Livingstons 1,147,309.[7]

The Swan-Livingston interest in the conjectural note vanished on February 3, 1804. On February 24, dropping his contention that the note was unalterably binding, Livingston asked Talleyrand to confirm his assertion that it had been rejected as erroneous at the signing of the treaties. Support of that true statement was easy to obtain, for it would help France throw Swan's claims as a French purchasing agent onto the United States.[8]

Minister Livingston won quick support from a group of American claimants living in Paris. On November 4, 1803, Swan, Peter Livingston and thirteen other "merchants and captains" addressed a joint letter to him, complaining of the delay in liquidation, and asked him to relieve their "total ignorance" of the causes. This allowed Livingston to remind them of the public meeting at which he had read Talleyrand's promise to pay the claims fully and promptly. Nothing could induce him to withhold his correspondence with the three commissioners "but an apprehension of affording some handle for malevolence to take hold of."

Assured in this fashion that the three Brutuses were all honorable men, the claimants condemned their "refusal" to execute their official duties and eulogized "the great and virtuous actions" of Livingston, who "by his unabated zeal and unceasing solicitude effected the cession of Louisiana to the United States and . . . secured the means of a speedy discharge . . . of American claims." By a strange coincidence, the resolutions resembled the pattern and wording of two denunciatory letters Livingston had just written to the board. It was the more remarkable because the phraseology of Livingston's correspondence had similarly crept into Swan's letter sent to the American press praising that minister and slurring Monroe.[9]

Livingston now had ardent political support in Paris, but, with winter storms at hand and no letter of recall, he could not get home ahead of the congressional caucuses. Also, if he departed, Swan's claims (not yet rejected) would be at the mercy of the board and of Skipwith, the only man whom he could make chargé d'affaires. On November 15 he wrote to Madison withdrawing his request to be recalled. At "the present critical moment" he felt "bound to make some personal sacrifices."

The minister then sent a note to his brother Edward: "To my friends who are upon the spot I wish to leave the direction of my future career in politics." In any case he would like public approbation, particularly from the creditors of France, whose claims he had snatched almost from annihilation.

Hardly had this been dispatched when a stunning blow fell. Opening a letter from Madison shortly before Christmas, Livingston read the glad news of the Louisiana treaty ratification. Then a postscript: difficulties, it was learned, had arisen respecting the true construction of the convention. It seemed doubtful whether the twenty million francs would cover all claims. The minister was ordered to seek *at once* the consent of France to suspend all payments until it was ascertained whether the fund was adequate or not. This would give time also for "mutual explanations and arrangements" concerning which he would receive additional instructions.[10]

The blow was a multiple one. Early claimants, instead of getting principal and interest before the fund was exhausted, were likely to suffer a pro rata reduction. Gone was the chance of political gain from the Livingston signature on Treasury orders. Responsibility for further delay would be shifted from the board to the minister. Most disconcerting of all, Madison and Jefferson were acting on information from others—from the board or Skipwith.

This was too much. Livingston withdrew the withdrawal of his resignation and asked to be replaced by April 15, also that a blank commission for a chargé d'affaires be sent him. This would enable him to appoint somebody from outside the diplomatic service, by-passing Skipwith.

Now he had a new problem—how to avoid carrying out Madison's instructions. Bonaparte, the minister reported on January 1, 1804, was greatly displeased at the delay in receiving the Louisiana stock. (It was due to be delivered *in the United States on January*

21.) This made it dangerous to seek a delay in payments to Americans. "He will certainly view with astonishment the United States . . . checking the progress of the business, and continuing the distress of their citizens." These were almost the words in which Livingston had been denouncing the board.

A fortnight later he explained why he had not obeyed the stop order: "Since the board have stopped their proceedings it will be unnecessary." (In reality, ignorant of the order, the board was speeding up.) Better, Livingston added, let the responsibility rest on them than lay it to the American government. (That is, "Let the claimants blame them, not me.")

On January 30 Livingston told of frightful developments which made it inadvisable to comply with Madison's instructions until he should receive later ones. His dispatch was so fantastic that only a ciphered copy was placed in the State Department files, where it remained undeciphered until 1952.

Marbois, a few days before, told him that Talleyrand "has a message for you from the First Consul about which he wished me to speak to you, but as it was not my business I told him I would not interfere."

What was it? asked Livingston.

"The First Consul has directed him to tell you that if the stock was not delivered by the twenty-first of this month, which completes the three months from the ratification, he would consider the treaty as void."

The story went on endlessly, Livingston arguing with vigor that the payment (already made) need not be made until March 20—three months after possession was taken. "You may judge by this," he concluded to Madison, "how delicate a business it will be to ask any modification of that treaty till they get their money." Talleyrand, a man not given to disobeying orders, said nothing to Livingston. So his "little anecdote," useful if it scared Madison into allowing a speedy payment of favored creditors, had no diplomatic status.[11]

To further the withdrawal of the stop order, Livingston played down the amount of the claims. Principal and interest of those on the conjectural note would not have a liquidated value of ten million livres. If all claims should exceed twenty millions, would it not be better for the United States to pay the excess and ask France for it later? What was he to answer when creditors asked him for their money?

"The convention is now the law. . . . Will it be sufficient for me to plead an instruction for a breach of the law?"

Learning that Skipwith had sent Madison a claims estimate of 31,000,000 francs—fifty per cent more than the available fund— Livingston protested: "The impropriety of his corresponding directly with you on public measures, without submitting his correspondence to my inspection, is so obvious that I trust it will receive your marked disapprobation."[12]

Some time later, finding Skipwith in Marbois' office, Livingston denounced him for sending the list and received the reply that he had done so in response to orders from Washington. The quarrel flared high. Observing a copy of the 1803 convention in Marbois' hand, Livingston expressed his surprise that "an agent who held office at my pleasure," should seek to discuss a treaty with a French minister or that the minister should enter into a discussion with such a person. To Marbois' mild suggestion that the three of them have an informal talk, Livingston replied that he would take no part in a discussion which originated at the request of "an inferior agent." The aftermath was an exchange of letters, totaling about forty pages, which could have been boiled down to the following extracts from them:

Skipwith: "I never shall learn, sir, that a minister of the United States ought to have felt displeasure at finding a consul from his own government, however subordinate his station may be compared to yours, conversing with a minister of France on the subject of a treaty. . . . Your most dignified course I apprehend, sir, would be to degrade me personally by displacing me, and not officially, by insulting the public character I support."

Livingston: "In what, sir, did the insult consist? Are you not an inferior officer?"

Livingston did something more painful than firing Skipwith—
he cut a thousand dollars off his salary and transferred it to his
own staff. "I am at a loss to know," wrote Madison to the President, "by what authority he undertook to give a part of Skipwith's
salary to an additional secretary for a purpose not included in the
business allotted to Skipwith." Probably he consulted "his feelings
rather than his instructions."[13]

A brilliant idea now struck Livingston. Since he would reach
home too late to be nominated for Vice President, why not create
a vacancy in the office of Secretary of State? Marking his letter
private and confidential, to be deciphered only by Madison, he
wrote on February 8:

"If it were possible to spare you from where you are, you can
render your country essential services here. Should I have designed to stay myself, I should have asked the rank of ambassador,
which gives some advantages and is attended with no inconven-
ience. . . . Should you come, I would recommend these objects to
you as of more moment than you appear to think them, and your
rank and political standing would render them proper."

The day before Livingston issued this invitation to bankruptcy,
Madison invited him to come home. The Secretary had not replied to the minister's request to return by September 1803. Recent letters on the subject had not arrived. Madison recalled, however, that Livingston had set the spring of 1804 as the limit of his
service:

"None of the letters received from you for a long time have said
anything with respect to the period of your stay in Europe. Having been in constant expectation of hearing whether you persisted
or not in the intention last expressed of returning home next
spring I have thus far delayed sending you a letter of leave, which
if not to be used I considered as most proper not to forward."

However, the minister had another letter which could be used
for leave-taking, and, "however agreeable it might be that your

public services should be continued at Paris," the President expected him to use that letter should occasion require it.

On receipt of this semirecall, Livingston redoubled his efforts
to create a cabinet vacancy. Marbois, he wrote, was losing in favor
because of his defeat in the Louisiana bargaining. (Napoleon
punished him with a present of 192,000 francs.) Talleyrand was
all-powerful. Nobody less talented than Madison should be sent
to deal with him. Indeed, the minister knew no other who possessed the necessary rank and dignity, diplomatic talents and information. Never was there a court, he went on (the portrait of
Madison vanishing in a self-portrait of Livingston), in which
more self-possession, suppleness and speed of action were needed.
"Everything here passes as rapid as lightning," wrote the man
who had complained for years of French slowness and stalling.

"I again repeat to you as the result of my own experience that
much may be done here by the man who anticipates the wishes
of the court and knows in time to approve of them. . . . Such a
minister, if he understands the interests of his country and is invested with extensive powers and *proper* means may effect important objects."

Livingston's concept of *proper* means ("nor must these means be
small") had just been placed in the State Department files undeciphered. Would it not be good policy, he asked, to disarm
Spain's jealousy "by exchanging a part of our territory on the
southwest of Louisiana against Florida and obtaining at the same
time a sum of money in addition thereto?" Outlining a possible
exchange, to be achieved by French pressure on Spain, he concluded: "Indeed with half a million at my disposition I would
undertake to make a treaty for you upon that ground."

Livingston's previous plans for buying Talleyrand had hinged
on collusive land grants or the secret buying up of depreciated
spoliation claims. This was the first specific proposal of a money
bribe. Reverting to the theme two years later, he lamented that
Madison had not devoted his "rank and standing in society," his

"prudence, abilities and address" to the Paris diplomatic post, and added:

"Had a *pot de vin* been given on the acquisition of Louisiana, the expectation of a second would have smoothed the way to the acquisition of Florida. But these things are difficult if not impossible in our government, and must therefore be counterbalanced by the superior address of a minister."[14]

By early March the American board had certified forty-six claims for liquidation and rejected forty. None of the approved claims had come back from the French bureaus for payment, so the board appealed to Livingston to intervene. Haste, however, was something the minister no longer wanted. As long as the claims remained in the French Treasury, he would not have to obey Madison's instructions, nor confess to creditors that he had no power to pay them. Chiding the board for having sent the forty rejections to the French bureaus instead of to him, he submitted a letter from Marbois expressing the opinion that the American commissioners were wholly subject to the minister's direction. The board sarcastically replied:

"Report tells us that certain individuals whose claims it is our duty to reject . . . hear from you . . . that the appeal being ultimately with you and the French government, all our mischief will be remedied. But we will not do you this injustice."

In effect, Livingston and Marbois were ruling that Livingston could overrule the board's decision that debts due to Swan as a French agent could not be paid out of a fund covering injuries to American commerce. Livingston, a board member wrote, "is completely at the feet of Swan."[15]

Faced with the request for action, Livingston answered that he could do nothing because he did not know the form of the board's certificate (which he himself had approved before it was printed). Also, "personal delicacy" restrained him. The claims liquidated by the French board, but not returned, included one of his brother's and he did not choose to expose himself to censure by giving him a preference. The board responded that it had the same feeling and gave the reason:

"Having been informed that an application had been made with your knowledge by a member of your family to the French Treasury upon the subject of the claims which you speak of, we were desirous of seeing all upon which liquidation had been directed placed upon the same footing."

Infuriated, Livingston replied:

"It is not, gentlemen, by insinuations like this that you can wound the feelings of a man conscious of his integrity, or hurt the character of one who has faithfully served his country in high and trustworthy offices for more than thirty years successively."

The fact was, he went on, that "the certificate of my brother with that of Mr. Sadler were presented by Col. [Edward P.] Livingston," who asked only what other forms were needed to secure the final order. R. L. Livingston, another secretarial son-in-law, was the registered agent for Livingston and Sadler claims totaling 835,685 livres. Maclure put the acid in the board's charge of self-interest. Mercer, a gentler soul, wrote to Monroe:

"In my colleagues and Mr. Skipwith I have met with nothing but integrity, independence and propriety as far as I could judge of it. In the other [Livingston] I have witnessed only imbecility of mind and a childish vanity mixed with a considerable portion of duplicity. He is however the representative of my country, and . . . commands my silence—only to you have I thus freely spoken of him."[16]

April was nearly gone before Madison's supplementary instructions reached Paris. Reiterating that no drafts were to be issued until it was known whether the $3,750,000 was enough for all, the Secretary said that if it fell short, there should at least be an apportionment of it. Preferably the treaty should be construed or revised:

1. To bring in claimants said to be omitted from the 1803 convention but included in that of 1800.

2. To insure the spreading of the money among all classes.

3. To have France make up any deficit in the sum required for full payment of all. But the total liability of the United States must not be increased above $3,750,000, "nor above any lesser sum to which the United States would be liable under the board's construction."

These were State and Treasury matters. Put together, they were unrealistic. France would be willing enough to admit new classes of claims, but not to pay the resulting deficit. With the fund inadequate even before the asked-for broadening, the reference to "any lesser sum" was fanciful. It served, however, to stir Livingston's anger. The effort to save part of the purchase fund, he told Madison, was as futile as it was disreputable. "You are willing that justice should be done if it cost you nothing." All that was needed was to fire the American board and be ready to advance an extra million dollars. He did not add that without such an addition, the proposals might cost the Livingston family many thousands of dollars in proration of awards.

The minister assured Madison that he had begun to comply with his instructions, now four months old. He had notified the American commissioners that they must govern themselves by the Marbois note, which assented to "that liberal construction of the convention that the President's wishes ... require." (Marbois upheld Livingston's power to override the board's rejection of Swan's claims.) Should the commissioners refuse he would probably suspend them.

As to further obedience to orders, caution was necessary. Napoleon was dissatisfied with the slowness of the American board. (It had then certified more than 150 claims, which were being detained in the French Treasury to give French creditors time to put debt liens on them.) The whole business had been taken out of Marbois' hands. (A total falsehood.) If peace should suddenly be patched up in Europe, "the whole treaty would be rendered doubtful for our nonperformance of this essential part of it."

It would be dangerous, Livingston explained, for him to urge

Private.

Monsieur.

Permettez que sur le point de quitter les Etats-Unis, je vous adresse deux mots pour vous remercier des attentions que vous avez bien voulu me témoigner pendant mon séjour à Washington. — Les choses importantes que j'ai eu l'honneur de vous communiquer alors, resteront je ne doute pas, dans le plus profond secret jusques au résultat final de cette délicate affaire. J'ai agi ici dans cette supposition, en me conformant en tout aux intentions du Gouvernement, que j'espere avoir saisi et observé avec exactitude et discrétion.

La lettre cijointe contient un livre que j'ai promis à Monsieur le Président des E. U., et que je vous prie de lui transmettre.

Ayez la bonté de présenter mes complimens respectueux à Mad.

× what passed with the Brit: Gov.t
† not true

Madison — et de me croire avec estime, et une haute considération.

monsieur.

votre tres humble et tres obéis.t serviteur

Iran: de Miranda.

July 22. 1806

New-York ce 22 Janv.r 1806.

The Hon.l James Madison, Esq.r — &c. &c. &c.

LETTER FROM MIRANDA
With two marked notes by Madison. "July
22, 1806," also in his writing, is a later mis-
reading of "22 Janv."

Sir.

Personal Friendship for you and the love of my Country, induce me to give you a warning about Cl. Burr's intrigues. You admit him at your table, and you held a long, and private conference with him a few days ago after dinner at the very moment he is meditating the overthrow of your Administration and what is more conspiring against the State. Yes, Sir, his aberrations through the Western States had no other effect. a foreing Agent now at Washington Knows since Febuary last his plans and has secord'd them beyond what you are aware of.— Mistrust Burr's opinions, and advice: he thoroughly persuaded B, is a new Cataline. Watch his conexions with M'M...y, and you will find him a Bristish Pensioner, and Agent with all the activity of ambition, and the wickedness of discappointment.

altho anonimous

Your Friend.

ANONYMOUS WARNING TO JEFFERSON
Received December 1, 1806

France to deliver the 150 liquidated claims, for that would either force him to pay them, in violation of Madison's orders, "or take upon myself the charge of breaking the convention." To avoid stirring up Napoleon, he intended to go to England for a month. During that time, he hoped, the President would have displaced the commissioners and given him more precise orders. In other words, he would obey his instructions some day, maybe.[17]

Livingston went to England, where his mysterious presence threw press and Parliament into an uproar. Conferring secretly with opposition leaders who had been excluded from the new Pitt ministry because of their pacifism, he created an impression that Napoleon had sent him with peace overtures—a rumor which forced the French government to a public denial.

On his return to Paris, finding that the American board was moving with speed toward the end of its work, the minister obeyed Madison's instructions in one of the briefest notes he ever penned. France was asked to define claims broadly and, should they exceed 20,000,000 francs, to agree to apportion this amount and "such further sum as may be due from the French government." The reply came instantly that the scope of claims could be expanded provided nothing extra was charged to France. As to the supposedly dangerous request that payments to American claimants be postponed, the United States, Talleyrand remarked, no doubt would pay them when it was convenient to do so.[18]

Thus ended a full year of maneuvering by Livingston—maneuvering designed to favor the valid claims of his relatives and the invalid ones of Swan. A delay for which the American board was responsible at first was dragged out for months by his unwillingness to obey instructions.

Livingston's successor already was chosen when word reached Washington of a *faux pas* reminiscent of the attack on England in his Louisiana memoir. He had made an unneutral public reply to a Talleyrand circular accusing a British diplomat of conspiring to overthrow the French government. To forestall the expected protest, Madison sent for Merry and assured him that no instructions sent to Livingston "could have furnished him with grounds for expressing himself in such a manner."

President Jefferson offered the Paris post to Senator John Armstrong of New York. General Armstrong had begun of late to boast, rather than admit, that he was the author of the anonymous "Newburgh Addresses" which stirred the officers of the Continental Army to mutiny in 1783. Merry described him as "an artful man, of tolerably good talents, and perfectly without principle," more dangerous than Livingston because he could disguise his purposes better. When news of Livingston's recall reached Paris, Commissioner John Mercer saw only the political angle:

"The scheme for making him Vice President originated with himself. Under the hope of being the candidate he requested his recall, but finding another fixed upon he was desirous of remaining here. The administration took him at his word. He will retire disgusted with himself."

Pichon saw a residue of political hope for him. "By some rather equivocal indications," he wrote, "it still seems that he will be in the lists for Vice President at the next election." He referred presumably to some forlorn scheme of the Federalists to chicane the election.[19]

By mid-August, Madison and Jefferson were being deluged with the mutual criminations of Livingston and the claims commissioners. Forced to wade "through tedious pages" of the minister's letters, and disgusted with the illegible press copies sent by his "lazy and disrespectful" secretary, Madison exclaimed to the President that the disputes had "reached their *ne plus ultra.*" He liked neither Livingston's conduct nor the board's narrow construction of the treaty, which took no account of its ambiguity or of the interests of the United States.

Jefferson's reaction was more violent. "A more disgusting correspondence between men of sense" he had never read. They all deserved removal for suffering their "old-womanish quarrels" to influence their public duties. The quarrelsome disposition of Livingston was a trait previously unknown to him.

"He has quarreled with every public agent . . . with his colleague Monroe, his secretary of legation, Sumter, our consul at

Paris, Skipwith, with the commissioners, and his letters to the Department of State have been rising in the arrogance of their style, till that of May 3 is such as, had he not been coming away, would have justified our informing him that we should make no further use of his services."

The minister's way of reasoning puzzled Madison, who wrote to the President:

."Mr. L now admits that the debts will exceed 20,000,000 livres. How he calculates two millions of interest as the effect of the delay, which is less in every view than a year, or how he can charge the delay on the United States when he admits that the French government forbear to take the steps depending on them, or how he makes out an obligation on the United States to enlarge the payments from the Treasury in favor of those not embraced by the last convention more than of those abandoned by the preceding one, I am unable to divine."

The Secretary of State remarked that Livingston was "again a volunteer in diplomatic projects." Proposing to the Russian chargé d'affaires that they draft a Russo-American commercial treaty, he drew a refusal to discuss a subject "absolutely foreign to the mission on which I was sent." The answer, Madison commented to the President, "involves an admonition which would be useful to him if he had modesty enough to understand it."[20]

Madison's attitude both as to favoritism and the board's powers was made clear a couple of days later, when he received a protest from Captain Joshua Barney that the board had rejected his claims (for 965,975 livres) on the ground that he was not an American citizen. This seemed erroneous, Madison remarked to the President, unless Barney's citizenship was suspended *"quoad* certain purposes" by his temporary employment in the French navy. But that was "a question more proper for judicial and executive inquiry and therefore falls naturally within that of the board." Furthermore, besides being "an interference with the functions of the board of commissioners," a patronage of one claim by the Executive might be injurious to others because of the limitation of the total sum. The claims convention, Madison observed, had provided for its own exposition and execution. The Executive, therefore, could act on it only diplomatically or by furnishing additional information:

"This course has been taken in the case of both Barney and Swan. Documents . . . were . . . forwarded to Paris with an intimation that it was an act of justice to fair claimants not to let in unfair ones for a share in the twenty millions, which were likely to be insufficient for the former."[21]

Madison thus agreed with the board that it was an independent judicial body. He accepted the premise on which the board had rejected both the Swan and Barney claims—that contractual relations with the French government destroyed claims based on American citizenship. He sent a warning about the injury which allowance of improper claims would work upon just claimants. But in refusing to intervene he left both power and responsibility in the hands of the minister who was misconstruing the convention.

Livingston was not distrusted in financial matters. Gallatin authorized him to word a voucher because, "knowing precisely what constituted an award under the convention, [he] would conform his drafts to the true construction of that instrument."[22] The effect was to give Livingston (or Armstrong) full power, with Marbois, to do what they liked with the Swan and Barney demands, even on the points which Madison regarded as solely in the province of the American board.

The board in July had thrown out the last of Swan's fifteen claims. The French board was determined to pay eight of these, including all in which the French government owed money to Swan as its purchasing agent or as pretended owner of ships chartered by France. Livingston's interest was divided. Swan was his closest ally, but allowance of the Swan claims would cut down the payments to John R. and Peter Livingston. From that dilemma, the logical escape was a new appropriation from the United States Treasury—hence the desperate appeals to Madison.

These failing, Livingston stood with Swan. Before he and Marbois could overrule the American board, Claims Agent Skipwith must notify the board that the French bureaus insisted on payment. Skipwith held off. Livingston postponed his departure for America, telling Madison that "the aversion that the Americans have to Mr. S[kipwith]" made it impossible to appoint him chargé d'affaires. Not until October 12—nine days before the American board was due to go out of existence—did Skipwith report on the Swan and Barney claims. The delay kept Livingston from passing on them, but he had no need to worry. By staying in Paris, he avoided a hiatus between his powers and those of his successor. Robert Livingston was perfectly willing to let his brother-in-law, General Armstrong, make the decisions.[23]

CHAPTER XVII

THE YAZOO COMPROMISE

As THE PRESIDENTAL campaign of 1804 approached, Republicans felt the confidence that grew out of mounting majorities and a sense of achievement. Federalists displayed the fury of despair. In midterm there had been a brief uncertainty about the President's intentions. "Some affect to believe," Thomas Law wrote in 1802, "that Mr. J. is to decline at the next election and Mr. Madison is to be offered as a candidate—is this true?"

Jefferson observed to Governor McKean of Pennsylvania, in January 1804, that the abominable slanders of his enemies forced him to postpone "the repose I sincerely wished to have retired to now." Another motive had already been stated to his son-in-law. On account of old debts and recent land purchases he would be well satisfied "if by the end of my second term of office (which will certainly be my last) I can see all of us out of debt" and the mill and farms in good shape for the future.[1]

On political issues, the Jefferson administration was unbeatable in 1804. It had bought Louisiana, lowered taxes, reduced the public debt, cut down the Army and Navy and punished the Barbary pirates. Congress was Republican two to one. The achievement hated most in New England—the Louisiana Purchase with its westward swing of power—lifted the President's popularity elsewhere to its zenith. Hopeless of a party victory, the Federalists saw only the chance of a punishing personal blow. By throwing their own electoral votes to the Republican nominee for Vice President, they might make him President instead of Jefferson.

This nominee would not be Aaron Burr, whose 1800 intrigue ruined him in his own party. Facing reality, Burr went to the President a month before the 1804 nominating caucus and complained that his enemies were using Jefferson's name to destroy him. It was necessary for him (as Jefferson afterward recorded the talk) to receive "some mark of favor from me, which would declare to the world that he retired with my confidence." The President promised only neutrality. In his *Anas* he added that he had long distrusted Burr and "habitually cautioned Mr. Madison against trusting him too much."

The Federalists were active for Charles Cotesworth Pinckney and Rufus King, but with the reported intention of voting for Governor McKean and electing him over Jefferson, if the Republicans should nominate the Pennsylvanian for Vice President. Hoping to disgust the people with the ruling party, wrote British Chargé Thornton, they were willing to be governed for four years by an incomparably inferior man of headstrong and ungovernable passions, whose conduct would degrade the country and expose it to contempt. Joseph Hopkinson expressed the feelings of that group: "We have no other hope now than that of desperation. . . . The abandoned folly and wickedness of these devils will drive them to such . . . acts of oppression and weakness that they will be no longer endured."[2]

The most devilish act was performed by Congress. In October 1803 it submitted the Twelfth Amendment, which requires presidential electors to vote separately for President and Vice President. "A torrent which sweeps all before it is in its full flow," lamented a Southern Federalist as he watched ratifying legislatures carry away the barriers "against the evils of levelling democracy."

On February 25 the Republicans in Congress held the caucus which served as a national convention. Governor McKean had refused to be a candidate, whereupon (a Federalist reported) the cabinet members with a few others agreed upon Governor Clinton of New York for Vice President. After a "long and acrimonious debate" the caucus gave sixty-seven votes to Clinton, twenty to Breckinridge of Kentucky, and divided another twenty among a trio of New Englanders.

The Virginians, Senator Plumer recorded, were zealous for Clinton, wishing "to elect an old man who is too feeble to aspire to the Presidency." Breckinridge supporters, according to John Randolph, wanted "such a man say they as on Mr. Jefferson's retiring may boldly challenge the chair of government"—a description, he thought, which hardly fitted the Kentuckian. Of the two recognized avenues of approach to the Presidency—the offices of Vice President and Secretary of State—Madison now held one; the other was sealed off by Clinton's age, not by the absence of ambition.[3]

John Randolph was not influenced by friendship for Madison when he cast his vote for Clinton. He was still talking of political unity and assuring the President of his "highest esteem and veneration," but other words betrayed other thoughts. Every Federalist engine, he commented to Monroe, "is at work to infuse jealousy among us. They affect to talk of the prodigious weight of particular individuals merely to excite the personal feelings of individuals whom they believe indisposed to be considered as secondary characters."[4]

To Randolph, men more prominent than himself consisted of those who made him feel secondary and those who did not. Jefferson, Madison, Monroe and Gallatin were the only Republicans of sufficient political weight to stir his envy. Jefferson looked on him as a valuable agent, to be treated with friendship but not flattery. Gallatin maintained personal intimacy and Monroe a cordial correspondence from overseas. Madison, having no public or social motive for frequent contact, sought none. That was enough to make Randolph his enemy, and, Jefferson being impregnable, the resentment felt against their joint primacy was channeled into burning hatred for the Secretary of State. Monroe and Gallatin, giving minor satisfaction to Randolph's ego, were rewarded with a temporary fealty disproportionate to any effort they made to win it.

For all of this there were tragic physiological reasons. "You would think from his voice," Senator Mitchill's wife wrote of Randolph, "that he belonged to the feminine gender." George Ticknor told of the shrill and effeminate sounds "occasionally broken by those tones which you sometimes hear from dwarfs," and gave this account of his strange appearance:

"My eyes rested on his lean and sallow physiognomy. He was sitting and seemed hardly larger or taller than a boy of fifteen. He rose to receive me as I was presented, and towered half a foot

above my own height. This disproportion arises from a singular
deformity of his person. His head is small, and until you approach
him near enough to observe the premature and unhealthy wrin-
kles that have furrowed his face, you would say that it was boyish.
But as your eye turns towards his extremities everything seems to
be unnaturally stretched out and protracted. To his short and
meager body are attached long legs which instead of diminishing
grow larger as they approach the floor until they end in a pair
of feet, broad and large, giving his whole person the appearance
of a sort of pyramid. His arms are the counterparts of his legs; ...
drawn out [from small shoulders] to a disproportionate length
... and at last terminated by a hand heavy enough to have given
the supernatural blow to William of Deloraine, and by fingers
which might have served as models for those of the goblin page."[5]

After Randolph's death, an examination by his physician revealed that his seminal organs were rudimentary. An early biographer hinted at the reason, quoting Randolph as saying: "My
apathy is not natural, but superinduced. There *was* a volcano
under my ice, but it is burnt out." Isaac Coles, Jefferson's private
secretary, told Senator Plumer in 1805 that the beautiful Maria
Ward of Virginia broke her engagement to marry Randolph when
the latter revealed to her "that some years since he was grievously
afflicted with the mumps—that they ... destroyed his manhood."
Randolph's engagement and occasional love talk fit into the pattern of attempted compensation which included his intense devotion to ill and retarded nephews, violent attacks on public men,
flourishing of pistols and notorious obscenity at dinner gather-
ings.[6]

On the very day that Randolph reported the Federalist plot to
make him jealous, Senator Plumer wrote that the Ways and
Means chairman acted as if he no longer possessed the confidence
of the administration. Plumer told of Randolph's insufferable "insolence and abuse" of Congressman Alston in a debate on Georgia
lands. Renewing the attack at a dinner table, Randolph, after the
ladies fled, smashed a glass of wine on Alston's head and threw
the bottle at him, then apologized to everybody except "that
damned puppy." There was much talk of pistols and surgeons,

but a judge conveniently bound both men to keep the peace. Although Randolph had a talent for provoking duels that never reached the field, people did not scoff at his boast that "he would shoot an impertinent fellow down as he would a mad dog."[7]

In the affair with Alston, Randolph was making a vicarious assault on Madison, the prelude to a decade of vituperation. Had it not started over Georgia lands, it would have begun in one of the other fields to which it was transferred later. Peace with a man who outstripped him politically was no more possible to Randolph than marriage.

Soon after Jefferson became President, he named Madison, Gallatin and Attorney General Lincoln as new members of a federal-state commission to arrange a cession of Georgia's western lands. This grew out of the famous Yazoo land sale of 1795. Repeal of Georgia's act of sale in 1796 caused heavy loss to New Englanders and others. This induced Congress, in 1798, to ignore Georgia's somewhat dubious jurisdiction and place much of the disputed country in Mississippi Territory, then being set up. Federal land grants were to await either a boundary agreement with Georgia or a land cession by the state, after which the federal commissioners were to make a report on private claims.[8]

The joint commission reached an agreement in April 1802, Georgia ceding most of the present states of Alabama and Mississippi to the federal government for $1,250,000. The United States agreed to grant statehood, extinguish Indian titles, and confirm land grants to actual settlers. Remaining lands were to be a common fund for the nation except that the United States might appropriate up to 5,000,000 acres, out of the 57,000,000 total, to satisfy other claims.[9]

Madison, Gallatin and Lincoln proceeded to examine private claims. They found only 350,000 acres covered by fully completed grants. First claim on the reserved 5,000,000 acres, they advised, should go to residents holding incomplete grants. Squatters might pre-empt up to 640 acres. Next came the thorny claims of seven Yazoo land companies.

The three oldest, unrecognized by Georgia, were thrown out

completely. The commissioners then told of the sale of about 35,000,000 acres to four companies in 1795 for $500,000, and the repeal of that action next year by a new legislature, on the ground that the old one had been bribed. Between the sale and the repeal, it appeared, most of the land was resold to third parties. In general, the original speculators who bought the land for a cent and a half an acre resold it for an average of twelve cents and took their profits. Some resold to themselves in new companies. Most of the claimants were innocent purchasers; some of the biggest were "innocent."

The commissioners verified the 1795 bribery, presenting proof that all members of the Georgia legislature except one (Robert Watkins) were "interested in and parties to the purchase." They rejected a claimants' offer to settle for twenty-five cents an acre— about $8,500,000. Without affirming that Georgia was competent to repeal the sale, the commissioners expressed their belief that the title of the claimants could not be supported.

"But [they] nevertheless believe that the interests of the United States, the tranquillity of those who may hereafter inhabit that territory, and various equitable considerations which may be urged in favor of most of the present claimants, render it expedient to enter into a compromise on reasonable terms."

Their proposal was that, after actual settlers were satisfied, the remainder of the five million acres be divided among the claimants to the land sold by Georgia in 1795. Or, at their option, these claimants might receive their proportionate share of land certificates totaling $2,500,000 with interest or $5,000,000 without interest, to be paid off after Georgia received its $1,250,000. This, the cabinet members said, would not give a full indemnity to every claimant, but would nearly repay what all of them had paid in the aggregate.[10]

Neither this report nor the preceding act of cession was written in a political vacuum. The Yazoo land companies had the solid backing of New England congressmen. Georgia wanted its lands or its money. "Much longer delay of compromise," wrote Senator Jackson (the Georgian who upset the sale in 1796) would lead his state to repeal the commission's power.

To find a solution was imperative. Failure would leave state and nation to struggle for possession of a region claimed by both, controlled by neither, and filling up with settlers in dangerous proximity to Spanish power. A simple act of cession, in effect barring the Yazoo claims, would have pleased Georgia. It also would have violated the intent of the federal law of 1800 and raised a new ferment in New England and in Congress. The mildest alternative was to cede the land with a reservation to cover unsettled private claims, thus pacifying both sides and insuring acceptance. That is what the six men agreed to. Georgia quickly ratified and Congress reached the same end by defeating a motion to reject.

Both the act of cession and the federal report were so worded as to put no obligation on Congress to satisfy the Yazoo claimants. Madison, Gallatin and Lincoln rejected their legal title and presented the compromise as a voluntary concession based on national interest and the innocence of most claimants. Advising reimbursement of the average amount paid, they held down profits so sharply that on the average there was none at all. Critics of the compromise saw what the "Yazoo men" were gaining. The claimants saw with grief that they were to receive less than one acre for every six they had bought. The proprietors, one of them lamented to his congressman, were not even notified of this "act of real tyranny" so that they could protest against it:

"No; government proceeded with the same disregard to legal or constitutional rights as old Catherine, old Frederick and the emperor of Germany when they declared that the conduct of the poor Polanders was corrupt—and therefore they would divide their country—and each robber took his share of the land accordingly. The two transactions appear to be equally naked despotism."[11]

In Congress, both sides found ammunition in the report. Opponents could quote the commissioners themselves, who denied

the legal title of the claimants and documented the original corruption in Georgia. Supporters could affirm that the claims were
binding, or that sectional tranquillity and the innocence of most
claimants made it good policy to pay them a fraction of what they
were demanding.

Randolph undoubtedly was opposed in principle to any payment. But why, asked the Richmond *Enquirer* after the matter
got into presidential politics, was all the congressional fury directed at Madison, with none for "Mr. Gallatin, who certainly
drew up the report?" Some puzzled observers have pointed to the
fact that Dolley Madison's brother-in-law, Representative Jackson, was a leading supporter of the compromise. So, too, at the
outset, was Gallatin's brother-in-law, Representative Nicholson:
he wrote the bill to carry it into effect.

When Senator Giles belabored the compromise at a French legation dinner, directing his remarks to Madison, the latter "appealed
to the agreement between the United States and Georgia, and the
reservation of lands made for the express purpose of quieting these
claims." This entry in J. Q. Adams' diary has been taken as evidence that Madison stirred Randolph's wrath by actively defending the compromise while Gallatin saved himself by keeping still.
The explanation lies in no such trivialities, but in the realm of
psychiatry.[12]

Nicholson's bill, quickly passed, granted lands to actual settlers
and appropriated the rest of the 5,000,000 acres to satisfy claims
which Congress might approve in the future. Madison, Gallatin
and Lincoln were directed to receive "propositions of compromise
and settlement" from the land companies and report on them at
the next session.[13]

While this measure was before the House, the compromise was
assailed by the largest of the claimants—the New England Mississippi Company, in which former Secretary of the Treasury Samuel
Dexter was the leading figure. Asserting that fraud by the Georgia
legislature could not defeat the rights of innocent purchasers, the
company told Congress that its shareholders ought to receive their
entire 11,000,000 acres. Conceiving, however, that a compromise
was intended, they merely asked that instead of limiting the land

companies to $5,000,000 derived from the sale of five million acres, Congress pay them the total proceeds of such a sale up to $2 per acre. In effect they were saying: Madison, Gallatin and Lincoln offer us our purchase price, $1,100,000. We are entitled to $22,000,-000, but will settle for a possible $2,200,000. The commissioners quickly knocked down this hope. Inviting the company to present its case, they said it seemed desirable that the claimants be "fully reimbursed for the moneys actually paid by them." But—

> "It is not our intention to report in favor of a compromise grounded on a purchase or on a confirmation by the United States of your title to any considerable portion of the lands you claim. . . . We do not intend to recommend anything farther than an indemnity to be paid out of the proceeds of a certain portion of the lands and which shall not bear interest."[14]

Randolph launched his attack on the Yazoo compromise in February 1804. On a committee report by Nicholson, the House voted, 62 to 56, that the commissioners should have power to receive propositions from the land companies "and finally to adjust and settle the same." There was no division along party or administration lines. New England Federalists and Republicans alike were for it. Virginia voted six to twelve in the negative, with both of Jefferson's sons-in-law among the opponents.

When Nicholson incorporated this decision in a bill, Randolph struck at it in eight resolutions. These attacked the 1795 sale as a corrupt violation of Georgia's constitution, affirmed the state's inalienable right to rescind the action and resolved that Congress forbid compensation. The obvious purpose was to bring up the touchy issue of state sovereignty. The resolutions were so shrewdly drawn that the commissioners themselves would have agreed with the first seven of them, and these led with seeming logic to the eighth. That was because they omitted the reasons for the compromise—recompense of innocent victims and the need to soften New England bitterness at a time when the spirit of secession was rampant there.

The attempt to write Randolph's prohibition into the bill was beaten, but Nicholson was having second thoughts about the commissioners' *final* power to settle. He moved that Congress be allowed six months in which to disapprove a settlement. Over-eager New Englanders defeated the motion and turned Nicholson against his own measure. He helped to postpone both the Randolph resolutions and the bill to the next session. Aided by absenteeism, Virginia's 15-to-3 division produced the total majority of ten against the bill—a personal triumph for Randolph.[15]

Renewing the fight in February 1805, the Virginia congressman inched nearer to an open break with the administration. Postmaster General Granger, a claimant himself, had become lawyer-lobbyist for the New England Mississippi Company. This made it easy to level charges against the administration, although Granger acted on his own account and was not a cabinet member. In "the most abusive strain of invective ever witnessed" in a legislative hall except under Robespierre, Randolph and Matthew Lyon called each other jackal and ape, while President and cabinet came within the Virginia orator's less animalian denunciation:

"If Congress shall determine to sanction this fraud upon the public, I trust in God we shall hear no more of the crimes and follies of the former administration. . . . I should disdain to prate about the petty larcenies of our predecessors after having given my sanction to this atrocious public robbery."

Unready to attack Madison by name, unwilling to attack Gallatin at all, Randolph absolved them personally when it was proposed again that any settlement be reviewable by Congress:

"Do we expect to get commissioners more able; men of greater talents; of more sagacity; more tried fidelity, or more impartiality than they were? . . . They have told you that there was fraud in the original contract; that it was void *ab initio;* . . . yet they recommend a settlement. . . . When I first read their report, I was filled with unutterable astonishment—finding men in whom I had, and still have, the highest confidence, recommend a measure, which all the facts and all the reasons which they had collected, opposed and unequivocally condemned."

The House resolved, 63 to 58, that the commissioners proceed to make a final settlement, but a bill writing this into law did not come to a vote in the brief period before adjournment, and allowed Randolph more time to develop his political vendetta. He staved off action until the Supreme Court, in *Fletcher v. Peck,* denied Georgia's power to rescind the 1795 sale. That 1810 decision proved with stunning force the wisdom of the Madison-Gallatin-Lincoln compromise, which Congress then proceeded to enact into law. Without it there would have been no Georgia land cession, and the claimants could have taken possession of an area one fourth larger than the State of Mississippi. Profits of 600 to 800 per cent would have taken the place of bare reimbursement of their capital. The New England Mississippi Company (chief beneficiary of what Randolph called "this atrocious public robbery") fought for half a century against the compromise, meeting final defeat in the Court of Claims in 1864.[16]

Such matters had no place in the thoughts or plans of John Randolph. His ten-year assault on Madison as a "Yazoo man" was a calculated prostitution of the truth to political demagogy and neurotic jealousy.

CHAPTER XVIII

Political Currents and Eddies

Madison and Gallatin did not always stand together. When Dr. Edward Stevens went to Washington in the winter of 1803-04 to settle his accounts as "ambassador" of President Adams to Toussaint Louverture, the Treasury head objected. He had been sent to a revolted colony, not to a sovereign state; so there was no fund from which to pay him. Madison argued that the foreign intercourse fund was applicable. "With this last I concur," Jefferson wrote in his cabinet notes, but instead of saying so he asked them to get together.

Besides defending the oral contract, which Gallatin thought insufficient, Madison contended in his later brief that any expense, fairly within the idea of intercourse with foreign nations, was legally allowable. To limit expenditures to cases designated by law "would narrow the authority of the Executive more than would consist with the public interest, with the probable intention of the legislature, or with the uniform course of practice."

Sending this to Gallatin, Jefferson remarked: "I presume I must decide between the opinions, however reluctantly." Gallatin was still unconvinced but said he would not put the President to the trouble of a formal decision. "If in this business I have been too zealous or obstinate, I feel a confidence that you will ascribe it to the proper motive and not to want of due respect for the opinions of others."[1]

Madison was becoming dominant in the cabinet, but the general unity between him and Gallatin made them joint targets for most party dissidents. Gallatin was under open attack by Editor Duane and Congressman Leib of Pennsylvania, who had no more use for Madison. Moderation in removals from office, and unwillingness to give Duane all the public printing he asked for, were their crimes. The fate of the Union, as well as Madison's political future was involved in Oliver Wolcott's appraisal of conditions below the Potomac:

"There is one consolation ... some of the great fiefs of Virginia will renounce her pupilage. This wicked state has been the principal cause of all our divisions. The dominion of a community composed of beggarly Palatines and insolent slaves is intolerably odious; almost any change must improve our condition."

Wolcott was ripe for secession, as were Griswold, Pickering, Jedidiah Morse, Hillhouse, Plumer and many other New Englanders, but they preferred intrigue to bloodshed. Many wanted to know, Wolcott wrote to Griswold in March 1804, if support of Burr for governor of New York would bring Northern Democrats into a union with the Federalists "to free this part of the country at least from the abhorred domination of the perfidious Virginians." In particular, Wolcott asked Rufus King, would Burr pledge himself to a separation of the states, or would he "gain New York merely to gain the Presidency"? Griswold reported Burr to be talking eagerly of a northward union to resist the Virginia faction, but all he would promise was a New York administration "satisfactory to the Federalists." On that meager pledge, and against the urgent advice of Hamilton, they supported him. Congressman Mitchill (soon to succeed Armstrong as senator) reported the outcome to Madison:

"We have had a most singular exhibition here of Burrites, malcontents and Federalists but we have had a strong expression of the public voice against all their machinations. After a very hot and angry election all is growing cool and calm again."

From Congressman Richard Cutts of Boston, just married to Dolley Madison's sister Anna, came a report of the Federalist reaction to this setback. "The great hue and cry of the Essex Junto is the overbearing disposition of Virginia and the Southern states." They were saying that only a division of the Union would save New England, but the public mind was not prepared for such an event. More likely, Jefferson would carry Massachusetts.[2]

The festivities at Anna Payne's wedding in March 1804 were followed by a sad letter from President Jefferson telling of the death of his daughter, Maria Eppes—"a girl," wrote Dolley, "so young, so lovely—all the efforts of her father, doctors and friends availed nothing."

For some weeks Dolley and Anna had been in the political storm by virtue of a whispering attack, slightly on the comic side, against their chastity. As the story was passed along by Chief Justice Jeremiah Smith of New Hampshire, Postmaster General Granger came loudly to their defense against some derogatory remarks ascribed to New Hampshire's Congressman Samuel Hunt. The latter challenged Granger to a duel. Granger declined, whereupon Madison "waited on Mr. H. with the compliments of the two ladies and an invitation to dine *en famille*."

Senator Plumer, to whom this account was written, replied that he loved libelous anecdote and assured the judge that "Mr. Hunt is a great favorite with Mrs. Madison and sisters, and is well received by the Secretary of State." Men of chivalry and even the ladies in question approved Hunt's conduct, he told another correspondent, "but censure and ridicule the Postmaster General."

Ten years later the slander was still traveling. By that time the New Hampshire congressman had been metamorphosed into "Colonel Hunt . . . a man of note in the Mississippi country," and instead of being the defamer, he was now Granger's agent in notifying Madison of the ladies' misdeeds. "True or lie I know not nor do I care," wrote the spreader of the moth-eaten tale, but he had been told that Jack Randolph knew about it "and Jack says he will make the hairs of Congress stand erect" like the quills on the porcupine.

A unique variant of the same theme was conveyed to Pickering by Federal Judge Richard Peters of Philadelphia, a friend of Madison in the Continental Congress. An extreme Federalist, Peters was also a wit who acknowledged a gift of tobacco from Madison by regretting that he couldn't return a "quo" for the "quid." He probably felt less animus than pride in his cleverness when he wrote to Pickering:

"You should not have forgot to give precedence to the insatiability of democratic women. The leader of the ceremonious flock you mention carries with her if not the thing itself at least the appetites of the second of the four insatiable things mentioned in the thirtieth chapter of Proverbs, verse 16."

The implied reasoning ran thus: Although Dolley Madison had two children by her first husband, she had none by her second, therefore she must have the sexual insatiability resulting from sterility. Apparently it did not occur to Peters that the same reasoning applied to those idols of his party, Martha and George Washington.[3]

Looking beyond the political discord of the moment, Madison saw no reason to worry. "Our affairs continue in a prosperous train," he wrote to Monroe in July. "The tide of opinion is more and more favorable to the administration." New Hampshire had changed its majority, Massachusetts was in balance, the Connecticut masses were unresponsive to Federalist whips. Tennessee was expected at any moment to ratify the Twelfth Amendment, putting it into effect and ruining anti-Jefferson intrigue.

"If we can avoid the snares which our folly or foreign arts may spread for our peace, we can scarcely fail to flourish and to effect by degrees more of concord than has for some years been seen or thought practicable in the great body of the nation."

Madison related a few steps he had taken to reduce their silver-plate account. A shortage of renewal notes signed in blank made it impossible to extend Monroe's $2,250 debt at the Bank of Alexandria. Madison paid $250 on the principal, indorsed the $2,000 note of the original cosigner and paid about $750 of other Monroe debts.[4]

Impersonally, with Jefferson and Gallatin, Madison was engaged in relieving the distress of the Marquis de Lafayette. To the latter, in the spring of 1803, Congress voted the 11,520-acre bounty of a major general in the Revolution. "We are anxious," wrote Madison to Monroe, "that a clause may be inserted authorizing the President to locate the tract wherever he pleases. Should this idea succeed, the grant may become of great value, perhaps beyond the contemplation of the Marquis or his most sanguine friends." More value was added by Jefferson's idea that the location be in Orleans Territory instead of north of the Ohio.

News of this unsolicited gift reached Lafayette during a five-months' siege with a broken hip. Expressing his gratitude for "the bountiful, flattering grant," he wrote to Madison that "the President and you being my intimate friends," he wished the affair to be entirely in their hands. Enclosed was a blank power of attorney, with which "as well as with the whole affair, I request you my dear friend to do as you think fit." Madison's name was put into it in Washington.

Further explaining his situation, Lafayette observed to Madison that while the storms of the French Revolution had washed away his fortune, debts had piled up during his captivity and he returned to La Grange (his country seat) "as destitute as if it were in a foreign land." To relieve his most pressing debts, Daniel Parker and Banker Baring had lent him 150,000 livres at five per cent (half of their usual return) on a mortgage to be placed in Madison's hands covering lands yet unlocated. He needed as much more. Entrusting the selection of lands to a French immigrant, Duplantier, Madison informed Lafayette that, on the President's initiative, an effort was being made to obtain an overlooked public tract on the Carondelet canal at the edge of New Orleans. "The rapid growth of our American cities has made the fortunes of all proprietors of adjacent lands," Madison commented.

Learning from Lafayette, in the summer of 1805, that he would soon need 300,000 livres to clear his debts, Madison thought of American banks as a recourse. They would lend nothing on real estate, Gallatin told him. "Everything depends on some fortunate extraordinary location." Four years later, Madison, Gallatin and Duplantier were still engaged in acquiring Lafayette's lands, while others carried his debts. By teamwork comparable to that which won the American Revolution, the French hero was finally saved. His New Orleans lots were found to have a value of

$200,000, almost the exact sum he had spent in behalf of American independence.[5]

The most sensational event of 1804 produced a brief and noncommittal remark by Madison to Monroe: "The newspapers which you receive will give you the adventure between Burr and Hamilton. You will easily understand the different uses to which the event is turned." It is evident from the word "uses" that Madison had the same thought that Gallatin put into words, a week after the fatal duel on the New Jersey shore:

"Much real sympathy and sincere regret have naturally been excited by that catastrophe. But unquenchable hatred of Burr and federal policy have combined in producing an artificial sensation much beyond what might have been expected; and a majority of both parties seem disposed at this moment to deify Hamilton and to treat Burr as a murderer."[6]

Senator Plumer wrote a few months later: "The Secretary of State, Mr. Madison, formerly the intimate friend of General Hamilton, has taken his murderer into his carriage, . . . accompanied him on a visit to . . . the French minister." Madison was drawn further into the discord by the post-mortem tendency to credit Hamilton with the origin and much of the content of the Constitution. This began indeed before his death, when partisan attacks on Hamilton as an advocate of life tenure for President and senators were met by the untrue countercharge that Madison's plan had been the same or worse.[7] Noah Webster, remembering his own call for a new government, didn't like it when funeral orators ascribed the start of it to Hamilton's work in the Annapolis Convention eighteen months later. He reminded Madison that the latter had read the Webster pamphlet at George Washington's home in the summer of 1785, and added his belief that the Virginian made the first legislative proposal in the following December.

The general proposition, Madison replied, "grew up in many minds, and by natural degrees, during the experienced inefficacy of the old confederation." He testified to Noah Webster's part in it, understated his own, and said that "the discernment of General Hamilton must have rendered him an early patron of the idea." There was fairness, but no residue of the ancient friendship, in this appraisal.[8]

The 1804 campaign was a slander-fest against Jefferson in press and pulpit, met by newspaper diatribes against the Federalists. Jefferson and Clinton won all but fourteen electoral votes. The Federalists carried Connecticut, Delaware and one district in Maryland. Prosperity, democracy and the Louisiana purchase carried everything else. New England's secession talk was smothered in the landslide, but the momentary silence was no proof of unity or serenity. Awful indeed was the crescendo of evils described by Senator Plumer to a Salemite when Congress reconvened in November:

"The high office of the President is filled by an infidel, and that of Vice President by a murderer, and to increase the gloom, the House of Representatives have this moment elected Mr. Bentley of your town their chaplain!"

The Republicans were not entirely happy, even with an overwhelming majority in Congress and a partisan chaplain. In Pennsylvania, their radical wing had defeated a third party composed of moderate Republicans and Federalists, but nobody knew on which side the national administration stood. "Thank heaven our election is over," exclaimed Dallas. "The violence of Duane has produced a fatal division. He seems determined to destroy the republican standing and usefulness of every man who does not bend to his will."

Griswold, an extra tough Federalist, felt that their great objective should be "the disgrace of the Virginia faction." This might come about, he thought, from Southwestern disturbances. Spanish troops had dispersed a party of American insurgents who seized Baton Rouge. Edward Livingston and Creole politicians were denouncing the Louisiana governor and demanding immediate home rule. Should this lead to dismemberment of the American empire, Griswold believed, downfall of the Vir-

ginia dynasty was certain, wherefore he would work with enthusiasm to give Louisiana "the full power of self government without admitting them into the Union."[9]

More acrimony was engendered by a resolution of the Massachusetts legislature calling for abolition of the five-three ratio
by which slaves added to the number of Southern representatives
and presidential electors. The gesture was really a tapering off
of secession talk—an attempted answer to Pickering's rhetorical
question: Otherwise, how get rid of Negro Presidents and Con-
gresses? Jefferson feared a passionate rejoinder by Virginia.
It was agreed that Madison should draft as weak a reply as he
thought the angry legislators could be induced to accept. He did
his worst and Jefferson's new private secretary, W. A. Burwell,
who was also a member of the legislature, placed the result in
the hands of Committee Chairman James Barbour. The latter
posed as the author and put the milk-and-water composition
through the assembly.

"How often [wrote Burwell in retrospect] have I heard gentlemen wish Mr. Madison would have been called on to answer
the Assembly, and lavish the most unreserved abuse on poor
Barbour for a composition which would probably have passed
current with all its defects if the real author had been known.
Such is the propensity of men to pay homage to names. . . . I
certainly concurred in censure of the piece. I thought it remark-
ably feeble and unintelligible."

This effort to mollify Massachusetts was in effect the opening
of Madison's campaign for the Presidency. Hearing that Jefferson intended to retire at the end of his second term, John Taylor
in December 1804 begged him not to: he was the terror of the
monarchists, the reliance of the firm and faithful. The habit of
voting for Jefferson might continue to sustain wisdom instead of
folly, but would jealousy and ambition allow Virginia three out
of four successive Presidents? Might not these feelings inspire
"an alliance against the most resplendent merits" in any other
Virginian?

Jefferson's reply avowed his intention to retire. "The danger," he wrote for private but general circulation, "is that the indulgence and attachments of the people will keep a man in the chair after he becomes a dotard, that reelection through life shall become habitual, and election for life follow that." He would follow Washington's example, hoping that a few more precedents would fix the custom and perhaps lead to a constitutional amendment limiting tenure to eight years. Only one circumstance could alter his decision—"to wit, such a division about a successor as might bring in a monarchist. But this circumstance is impossible."[10]

The visible hazard to Madison, prospective beneficiary of Jefferson's decision, did not come from Federalist troglodytes but from the feeling against a Virginia dynasty and the disruptive influence of Randolph. The power of this erratic Virginian was put to a new test when, at Jefferson's suggestion, he undertook the impeachment of Justice Samuel Chase of the United States Supreme Court. The House produced eight articles of impeachment and made Randolph chairman of the five managers who opened the trial before the Senate on February 4, 1805. Chase was accused of misconduct in the treason trial of John Fries, the Pennsylvania German farmer who was sentenced to death for speaking unkindly of President Adams (who pardoned him); of coercing the trial of James Callender for other seditious remarks about Adams; of delivering "an intemperate and inflammatory political harangue" to a Maryland grand jury with intent to incite the people against their government, and lesser offenses. It was easy to prove that he was unfit to be a judge, but when it came to showing that his misconduct constituted "treason, bribery or other high crimes or misdemeanors"—the constitutional grounds of impeachment—Randolph's glittering oratory was less effective than the cold legalism of Chase's battery of big lawyers.

The Senate's verdicts ranged from unanimous acquittal on one count to 19-to-15 for conviction on the Maryland address. All Federalists were for acquittal and a similar vote by six Republicans (five from the North) prevented the needed two thirds from being reached. Senator Cocke of Tennessee, who voted for conviction, rejoiced at the result as a rebuke to the premature boasting of Randolph, whose "excessive vanity, ambition, insolence and even dishonesty" were hard for senators (who had none of these traits) to stomach. Senator Adams told how Randolph rushed back to the House and offered constitutional amendments for the removal of judges and recall of senators. Wrote Adams:

"I had some conversation on the subject with Mr. Madison, who appeared much diverted at the petulance of the managers on their disappointment."

An agitated Republican asked Madison where the cabinet stood on this matter, and was it true that Jefferson had written that "many of his best friends were third party men"? No, Madison answered, the President had said that certain newspapers were denouncing his best friends in that fashion. He continued:

"As to the heads of departments approving or disapproving the acquittal of Judge Chase, they did not I believe intermeddle during the trial with a subject exclusively belonging to another department, and now that the constitutional decision has taken place, it would be evidently improper for themselves to pronounce for public use their opinion of the issue, however little disposed they may be to reserve, beyond the rules of official decorum."[11]

Madison's private departure from decorum anticipated the decline of John Randolph's star. The Virginia congressman's envy and hatred would henceforth be more virulent but less dangerous. To Jefferson, the Chase acquittal and roar of Federalist rejoicing did not make pleasing music. However, they must have increased the relish with which he delivered his second inaugural address three days later. Lest (he explained in a memorandum)[12] barbarism, bigotry and despotism recover lost ground, he decided to make this theme a major one. But to avoid direct warfare, he made his remarks apply immediately to American Indians, with a wider extension by inference.

This explanation overstates the planning and understates the vigor of his feelings. From various repetitions in the rough notes of his address, it is quite evident that the Indian tour de force occurred to him during the writing. In this draft, also, Jefferson fairly burned up the Federalist press for charging him and his associates "with everything which malice could inspire, fancy invent, falsehood advance and ridicule and insolence dare." Treason itself had been in full activity—trying to bring on wars, disunity and distrust. On the advice of Gallatin and Madison the President toned this down and struck out a statement that his election victory made a third appeal to the people unnecessary.[13]

Minus the satire, Jefferson's commentary on Indians apparently had its origin in a talk between Madison and Thomas Law, the Englishman from India, in the previous July. "In consequence of your observation last night," Law wrote, he had tried to trace the first transition from a pastoral to an agricultural society. Applying to the Indians what Tacitus said about the Germans, "you might easier persuade them to expose themselves to wounds than to cultivate the lands," he continued:

"I have only been prompted by a desire to prevent the extinction of all these noble spirited, well formed handsome Indians, by suggesting a recommendation from the benevolent President to agriculture. His words will make a deep impression on their minds, and as their chiefs have experienced their diminution in numbers by constant warfare, they might listen to persuasion and attempt more agriculture, and thus the obstacles of habit might at length be surmounted."

Not only did Jefferson put agriculture forward as the only alternative to extinction, but the "obstacles of habit" became the foundation of his satiric assault on the Federalists as Indians. The first draft of his address contained a veiled thrust at New England clergymen ("pure and sinless" Indian teachers) which both Madison and Gallatin found objectionable. Gallatin urged the President to omit the entire Indian parable, while Madison offered a substitute wording which helped set the final style of the piece: "who feeling themselves [something] in the present order of things and fearing to become nothing in any other, inculcate a blind attachment to the customs of their fathers in opposition to every light and example which would conduct them into a more improved state of existence."[14]

The President told the people that in dealing with foreign affairs, the effort had been to cultivate friendship. Acting on the conviction that sound national interests were inseparable from moral duties, the American government was fortified by the testimony of history "that a just nation is taken on its word, when recourse is had to armaments and war to bridle others." Spain and the Indians, it may be suspected, had some doubts about this. However, it was a fair statement of administration policy toward France and Great Britain, provided one added the threat of war to the dictates of morality.

Jefferson rode on horseback from his white palace to the Capitol and delivered his address in a voice too low to be heard. He then held a levee. "All who chose attended," wrote Legation Secretary Foster, "and even towards the close blacks and dirty boys, who drank his wine and lolled upon his couches before us all." All men, the President seemed to think, were created equal.[15]

Quite different were the feelings of Aaron Burr. Surrendering the office of Vice President to Governor Clinton, he went almost directly to the British legation and asked for British help in fomenting a Western insurrection against the United States. The inhabitants of Louisiana, he told Minister Merry, were determined to be independent, but were delaying their action till they could obtain foreign assistance and link their revolt with a similar movement in the Western states. He needed a loan of about 100,000 pounds for immediate purposes, with half a dozen warships to prevent an American blockade of the Mississippi. To avoid "any suspicion of His Majesty's government being concerned in the transaction till after their independence should have been declared," he suggested a secret transfer to him of one half of the £200,000 which the United States was to pay in July as an installment on pre-Revolutionary debts.

Merry was not surprised, for Burr, through an agent, had made a similar proposal in August 1804, a month after he killed Hamilton. Burr was ready to help Great Britain "effect a separation of the western part of the United States from that which lies between the Atlantic and the mountains, in its whole extent." Burr's agent, Colonel Charles Williamson of England, was sent to London but Merry didn't become enthusiastic until the retiring Vice President showed up in person. "Notwithstanding the known profligacy of Mr. Burr's character," he wrote, he was encouraged to report the matter because of evidence of disaffection among Louisiana deputies. A month later Burr notified him from the West that all was going well and he would soon send "a confidential person charged with ample communication on the subject." The No. 2 conspirator "proved to be one of the senators of the United States whose time of service expired last year"—*i. e.,* Jonathan Dayton.

Duels, political disgrace and retirement from office opened the high road to treason and complicated the affairs of government and people.[16]

CHAPTER XIX

IMPRESSMENT

A NEW era in Anglo-American relations began in the summer of 1804, when British naval officers apparently decided that American harbors were part of the high seas. On June 23, Madison summoned Minister Merry and told him that officers of the warships *Cambrian* and *Driver* had been guilty of intolerable violations of the country's territory, laws and neutrality. He asked for the restitution of fourteen seamen taken by force from the *Pitt,* a British merchant ship, in New York harbor. He also wanted an apology, and the delivery of a lieutenant who had resisted and insulted revenue and quarantine officers.

That night, news arrived that Mayor DeWitt Clinton, invoking the federal "twenty-four-hour rule," had ordered the British warships to remain until that long after the departure of two French frigates which were to sail on the first fair wind. Merry termed this a breach of neutrality, designed to cover the departure of Jerome Bonaparte and his wife. The mayor, Madison replied, had been too lenient rather than too strict.

"If our harbors are to become the rendezvous of an armed force bidding defiance to our laws, insulting the officers in the duty of executing them, committing violence on persons within their protection ... and by violating the neutral regulations of the United States ... you will see sir that the United States must be driven by the most imperious circumstances into precautions as disagreeable to themselves as they may be inconvenient to those who fail to render such measures unnecessary."

This "high language," Merry informed his government, probably carried a threat of total exclusion of all British ships of war from American ports. Exactly that was in Madison's mind. Pichon, he wrote to the President, had made a well-founded complaint against the action in New York, but went too far in de-

manding effective surveillance of the entire coast. Even the po-
licing of the harbors would require a force beyond American
policy "and render our exclusion of belligerent ships altogether
the more eligible horn of the dilemma."

Madison, it seemed to Merry, showed an ill disposition. He
alone was dissatisfied with an apology which the squadron commander, Captain Bradley of the *Cambrian,* had made to the
New York port authorities—an "apology," Madison noted in
reply, which disputed the sworn testimony of those officials.
Bradley forcibly prevented a United States marshal from arresting one of his officers, then defied the detention order and moved
his ships down to Sandy Hook. There they cruised for weeks,
holding the two French frigates in port and firing right and left
as they impressed seamen and passengers from American ships.
At times they had two dozen vessels held up. Protesting this
blockade, Madison contended that the American flag gave immunity to British seamen voluntarily sailing under it. Merry defended Bradley's tactics (though he begged the captain to cease
them) and expressed the deep concern he felt at seeing Madison
take so much pains "to criminate the King's officers and magnify
their offenses." No attention, he complained, had been paid to
the activities of French press gangs in Baltimore half a year
earlier.[1]

From Monroe, Madison had just heard of irritating unfriendliness in Lord Harrowby, the new foreign minister. Merry's answer, the Secretary remarked in forwarding it to Monticello, "co-
incides with though it cannot be the offspring" of Pitt's administration. He would investigate the Baltimore affair, unheard of
till then, but "this specimen of Merry shows him to be a mere
diplomatic pettifogger."

Jefferson reacted by asking Secretary Smith when the Navy's
new gunboats would be completed. Were they ready, "I should
certainly make a proposition [to the cabinet] to send the whole
to New York to clear out the harbor," and should the armed
ships still be there in the winter "we might consult Congress on
the subject." This represented feeling rather than purpose; but
also revealed two facets of Jefferson's thinking: a belief that the

Executive could use force against foreign warships without waiting for congressional approval, and readiness to submit all such questions to his cabinet.

Quite different was the immediate action. On going to Montpelier, Jefferson approved a reply by Madison expressing surprise that Merry should assert a right to impress British seamen within American sovereignty. More astonishing still, the minister sanctioned Bradley's amazing claim "to a dominion of his ship over a certain space around it" (the length of its anchor chain) in an American port. Further discussions with him being useless, they would be transferred to London, where, Madison hoped, the matter would be seen in a more friendly light.

So it was. On the very day this was written, before any complaint had reached him, Harrowby notified Monroe that Bradley had been removed from his command and ordered home.[2]

In the following winter, Jefferson obtained a law giving him power to forbid and repel the entrance of armed foreign vessels, also to cut off supplies if they refused to depart. Passage of it shocked Merry the more because Madison had shown so little heat in talking about Monroe's ill success on impressment. Asked now for an explanation of the new law, the Secretary of State gave a "vague explanation" of the President's powers, promised that they would be used with friendly propriety and said "it would be time enough to complain" when inconveniences were felt. Could Merry transmit these assurances to his government? Though without specific authority, Madison answered, he could safely say yes.

What, Merry asked, was meant by the exclusion of a warship because of "any trespass . . . or vexation of trading vessels"? That was to forbid the impressment of British subjects on American vessels. Washington and Adams had maintained the same doctrine and "no administration would dare so far surrender the rights of the American flag." The long talk ended with the British minister promising lenity but clinging to the right of impressment and Madison "maintaining to the last" (Merry wrote) that it could not be admitted.[3]

Tension increased when the British sloop of war *Busy* im-

AARON BURR
Drawing by James Sharples

Independence Hall Collection, Philadelphia

GENERAL FRANCISCO MIRANDA

JAMES WILKINSON
By Charles Willson Peale

Montpelier in Early Nineteenth Century

pressed seamen from three American vessels, just outside New York, stripping one of more than half its crew. Considering the number of American citizens known to be taken, Madison wrote to Merry, it was a proof of habitual mildness that the New York authorities were so courteous as to apply to the consul general for their restoration. In return, as Madison described it, the British commander made the astonishing offer "to commute the forcible detention of citizens of the United States in their own country, by a foreign officer," in exchange for a release of his ship from legal penalties for his misconduct.

He denied that American seamen needed to carry evidence of citizenship, or to prove they were not British subjects. That would not only shift the normal burden of proof and authorize the general practice of impressment; it would support the inadmissible claim that while Americans serving voluntarily on British warships could be held to their engagements, British seamen serving voluntarily on American ships could not be held to theirs. He challenged Consul General Barclay's assertion that as many British subjects as Americans held certificates of American citizenship—a claim "so manifestly incredible and disrespectful that it may be safely left for its comment to your own candor."

Madison's flag-protection doctrine would have wiped out the stock defense of impressments on the high seas—that British subjects were enrolled in American crews. The State Department was jubilant when it discovered a 1739 resolution of the British Parliament going much farther in denial of the right to search British ships:

"Resolved that the subjects of Great Britain have an evident right to navigate the American seas . . . and that it is a manifest violation of this right to visit such vessels at open sea, under the pretext that they are freighted with contraband or prohibited merchandises."

It made a lot of difference, however, whose bow was fired across. With comments on "the increasing acrimony" of the Secretary of State, Harrowby already had written: "The pretension advanced by Mr. Madison that the American flag should protect every individual sailing under it on board of a merchant ship is too extravagant to require any serious refutation."

For ages, Merry said in relaying the rejection, British kings had exercised the right of reclaiming their subjects on the high seas. This made it necessary to inquire into the citizenship of American crew members. He admitted that Barclay (a Loyalist embittered by a New York bill of attainder) had exaggerated the fraud in American certificates, but the existence of it was notorious.[4]

In rejecting flag protection, the Foreign Office threatened that if Congress passed offensive bills for the protection of seamen, Great Britain would withdraw an offer to extend the treaty of 1794 and would adopt a policy of retaliation. That was not likely to influence Madison, who had led the fight in Congress against Jay's treaty. Also, Britain was already imposing discriminatory port duties and there were other signs of a major change in trade policy hurtful to the United States.

Not all of the Merry-Madison exchanges were compounded of frowns and menaces. When Madison notified the minister that the British Navy had seized the ship *New Orleans,* containing a consignment of French wines and four jars of preserves for the President, Secretary of State and Senator Butler of South Carolina, there was a commotion in the legation. Merry wrote to the governor of Nova Scotia, who got in touch with the vice admiral, who was joined by the admiralty judge and the captor's captain in a unanimous agreement to exempt this part of the cargo from confiscation. A Halifax merchant offered to break a voyage to Trinidad and land the stuff in New York free of charge—but bring it back, he ordered, if they try to impose port charges on the vessel. "The effects belonging to the President and Mr. Madison have been liberated," wrote Merry to the latter in June 1805. To be sure, one jar of preserves was broken, and the recipients had to pay $45.05 in customs duties (not even the senator escaping), but there was at least a liquid measure of good fellowship between the two governments.[5]

Finding himself in a deadlock on impressment, Monroe in the

fall of 1804 exercised the discretion given him and left London for Madrid to work for a cession of the Floridas. The day before he sailed, ominous dispatches reached him from Livingston. The French were now saying emphatically that West Florida was not included in the Louisiana Purchase. In reply, Livingston told them that the United States would take possession of the disputed territory and might be led into alliances to support the claim. "I find them a little startled at this idea." They need not have been. His precise threat—an Anglo-American alliance to emancipate all Spanish-American colonies—was the same that Madison had made through Pichon, with French colonies included, to encourage the original cession.

Monroe was induced to go ahead by the imminence of a British declaration of war on Spain. (Hostilities began before he arrived.) In Paris, Livingston told him more about his August maneuver. It was a counterstroke against the Spanish ambassador, who had asked for and received Talleyrand's endorsement of Spain's title to West Florida. It now seemed indispensable, wrote Monroe to Madison, to seek to change the French attitude. Monroe therefore drafted a defense of the American claim to the Perdido boundary, coupled with a request for French support of a transfer of all the Floridas to satisfy American spoliation claims.

Livingston, whose own note had been far more aggressive, protested that this would stir French hostility. However, he delivered it to Talleyrand with a good supporting letter after the action had been approved by his newly arrived successor, General Armstrong. Weeks passed without an answer. Under the instructions from Madison, this rebuff should have halted Monroe's journey to Madrid. He had been told that his departure ought to depend on "active co-operation or favorable dispositions from quarters most likely to influence the counsels of Spain" and that it was "of peculiar importance to ascertain the views of the French government." Disregarding that advice, he went forward to certain defeat.

Monroe traveled from Bayonne by relays of mule teams. This cut the time in half and reduced the danger of being stripped by

Spanish bandits who specialized on ambassadors. In Madrid he found Charles Pinckney in a state of levitation. He had asked for and received his passports, then decided to stay but was performing no ministerial duties. Monroe patched up a peace and they undertook their work in harmony.[6]

While waiting for word from Madrid early in 1805, Madison received disquieting reports on French policy. From Livingston he learned that in the previous fall, Marbois suggested an American offer of sixty million francs ($11,250,000) to Spain for the Floridas. Presumably Spain was to use it to pay her delinquent war subsidy of 6,000,000 francs a month to France. Monroe then wrote that during his stay in Paris, Livingston proposed that the United States ask for the disputed province in return for a loan to Spain of seventy million francs, repayable in seven yearly installments. Thus, said Livingston, we would get West Florida and perhaps East Florida as well, "without paying a farthing for it." Monroe replied that this would "terminate in paying twice for the same thing," as the money would never be repaid. To Madison, Monroe wrote that he thought Livingston patriotic and attached to his country, but he believed that if France cherished hopes of getting whatever the United States might pay Spain for Florida, "such expectations have been countenanced if they were not fostered by him." Monroe had at last received a reply from Talleyrand—promising nothing, but better than expected. It did not occur to him that if he expected nothing or less, he should under his instructions have stayed out of Spain.

From Armstrong came a blunt description of French policy on Florida. "This country," the new minister wrote in December, "has determined to convert the negotiation into a job and to draw from it advantages merely pecuniary to herself or in other language, to her agents." This venality, he said, explained Talleyrand's marked discourtesy to Monroe, who had indicated that no money would be paid to Spain.

"Since his departure repeated intimations have been given to me that if certain persons could be gratified the negotiations should be transferred hither and brought to a close with which we should have no reason to find fault. My answers . . . have uniformly been . . . that it was quite impossible that the measures of a nation like this could ever be influenced, much less determined, by considerations that would equally dishonor them to offer and the United States to hear."

Talleyrand's attitude left no doubt that he would sabotage the Madrid negotiations—he could get nothing if they succeeded. However, the new minister's letter formed so welcome a contrast to the bribery schemes of Livingston and Talleyrand that Madison burst into praise to the President: "Armstrong . . . I am pleased to find understands the language in which the honorable and honest policy of this country ought to be expressed." Jefferson agreed but noted that the minister was already forgetting the temper of his country and catching the hue of those around him. There was admonition as well as praise, and a vivid memory of Livingston's lapses, in the way Madison conveyed this indorsement to Armstrong:

"I have the pleasure to observe to you that the President entirely approves the just and dignified answer given to the venal suggestions emanating from the French functionaries. . . . The United States owe it to the world as well as to themselves to let the example of one government at least protest against the corruption which prevails. . . . It is impossible that the destinies of any nation, more than of an individual, can be injured by an adherence to the maxims of virtue. To suppose it, would be to arraign the justice of heaven, and the order of nature."

Proceeding in this plain path, "we shall, in the end, be found wiser than those crooked politicians, who, regarding the scruples of morality as a weakness," make the vices of others the instrument of their own.[7]

Madison did not "entirely despair" when he read (in March) Talleyrand's reply to Monroe's request. By remaining silent as to the western boundary of Louisiana, he had left the way open for a trade of Texas for West Florida. There was a chance, the Secretary wrote to Jefferson at Monticello, that "as soon as France despairs of her pecuniary object" she might transfer her weight to the American scale. If, however, she continued to claim that West Florida was no part of Louisiana, it would place the American claim on grounds which "could not be approved by the world" nor justify the use of force.

"The world would decide that France having sold us the territory of a third party which she had no right to sell, that party having even remonstrated against the whole transaction, the right of the United States was limited to a demand on France to procure and convey the territory or to remit *pro tanto* the price or to dissolve the bargain altogether."

One of those steps, Madison averred to Armstrong, was just what France ought to take—either deliver the territory or remit part of the price. He did not admit that the title was invalid. Since France had sold Louisiana "as described in the conveyance to her from Spain," the American title was good against both countries unless it could be shown that the United States was notified in advance of the omission of part of the lands described. On the contrary, he said, both Talleyrand and Marbois at the outset had impliedly corroborated the American construction. Unluckily, such legalistic logic was of little avail in settling an issue whose outcome depended on Talleyrand's money hunger and Napoleon's ambition.

In May, reading Armstrong's letters to Monroe, Madison concluded that the Madrid negotiations were doomed. It was evident, he instructed Monroe, that France would not permit Spain "to bend to our claims to West Florida and French spoliations." French silence as to the western boundary of Louisiana might indicate support on that issue. However—

"There is so little reliance to be placed on the temper and views of France as lately developed, that a failure of your efforts ought to be anticipated. The alternative presented by this event is that of war, or a state of things guarding against war for the present, and leaving in vigor our claims to be hereafter effectuated."

Against war, he went on, the considerations were obvious and powerful. It was moreover a question which belonged to Congress, not to the Executive.

"That consideration alone forbids any step on the part of the latter, which would commit the nation, and so far take from the legislature the free exercise of its power. And it may be fairly presumed, considering the daily increase of our facilities for a successful assertion of our rights by force, that neither the nation nor its representatives would prefer an instant resort to arms, to a state of things which would avoid it without hazarding our rights or our reputation."

How could a resort to force be postponed without national humiliation? First, both Spain and the United States should forbear to augment their settlements or strengthen their military establishments within the controverted limits. Secondly, Spain must not obstruct free access to the sea through the Mobile and other rivers. With settlements and crops expanding north of the boundary, "every moment of delay threatens collisions which lead to war." Monroe and Pinckney had been instructed on these points before, Madison observed, and their silence left it uncertain whether they had presented them. If not, and in the event of a failure in their general negotiations, they were to "pursue without delay the course herein prescribed."

Privately, to Robert Livingston on his return from Europe, Madison remarked that "when France finds she cannot get her hand in our pocket," she might promote an adjustment with Spain in order to keep the United States out of the British scale. That ought to come about unless a military triumph "should place her above all such considerations." But whether Madrid or Paris was the theater, "the issue, it would seem, depends equally on her influence, or rather authority over the Spanish cabinet."[8]

The instructions of May 23, 1805, produced no effect whatever. Monroe had not received them four months after he left Spain. Yet they form one of the definitive policy statements of the Jefferson administration and throw a brilliant light on Madison's views and talents.

Months ahead of definite word from Madrid, he anticipated the outcome there from the attitude of France and began to salvage the wreckage. He knew that Monroe had disregarded his advice to make sure of French support before going to Spain. He guessed correctly that Monroe and Pinckney had failed to present the *status quo* and Mobile demands which were to cushion the damaging effect of a failure on main points. On this, too late for effect, he sent a peremptory renewal of the President's orders.

In more basic policy, Madison reaffirmed the administration's devotion to peace and laid down a constitutional principle which was to affect his own Presidency and mount in importance (through violation of it) in later generations. The Executive had no right to commit the nation to war, nor take any steps which would deprive Congress of a free choice between war and peace. He laid down, toward Spain, the same policy he had utilized in 1802 to discourage France from holding Louisiana: avoid a choice between immediate war and loss of reputation, and let the ultimate use of force be timed by "the daily increase of our facilities" for exerting it. If results could be speeded up, it must be through a shift in French policy, but here lay the hazard of a military triumph by Napoleon.

Using the same set of facts, Armstrong, Monroe and Pinckney were coming to a widely different conclusion. In this month of May 1805, Armstrong wrote to Monroe that France would squeeze the United States and Spain together like a couple of oranges and do the least injury to the one that yielded the most juice. To cope with this, he advised, seize Texas and use it to shape the bargain with Spain. Monroe and Pinckney expanded this idea when their negotiations collapsed late in May. They privately recommended to Madison that the United States take East and West Florida as well as Texas, then negotiate for the retention of them in payment of spoliation claims. This "would terminate the business without war, without an increase of regular force and without much or even any expense." With some ambivalence (Monroe doing the writing) they linked aggression and morality:

"The destiny of the new world is in our hands. It is so considered by Europe and in marking any limits to our course in such a movement it should appear to proceed in a consciousness of that fact, from a spirit of moderation, of justice, and love of peace, not from the dread of any power and in any view of the consequences."[9]

Madison was not likely to be impressed by advice to seize an empire out of love of peace, nor would he or Jefferson assume that such action would terminate without war with both Spain and France. But those dispatches and the events behind them placed the issue of peace or war squarely before the government.

CHAPTER XX

The Minister from France

THE HARDENING of French policy under the Empire was appropriately matched in its American legation. The new minister, General Louis Marie Turreau, debarked at Annapolis on November 16, 1804, aided by an artillery uproar of two fifteen-gun and two twenty-one-gun salutes. Three days later the people of Washington were gazing at his huge mustachios, fierce red face and fiery eyes. A report by Armstrong on this forty-seven-year-old "butcher of Vendée" was then on its way to Madison:

Habits in private life? Very profligate. Talents and cultivation? Possesses neither. Devoted to emperor? Pretends to be, but probably sent away as a bad risk. Temper in discharge of public duties? Bad. Character of public services? Most atrocious—an ex-Jacobin notorious for cruelty in war. Toward the American government he professed "sentiments the most friendly and respectful." Americans found him handsome, soldierlike, civil and attentive, but, said Senator Plumer, "I have never yet beheld a face so cruel and sanguinary."[1]

Turreau was instructed to work for good relations between Spain and the United States. The first step, he thought, was to re-establish them between Madison and Yrujo. At the latter's request, he made an appointment for all of them to meet at Madison's house. It was not hard to perceive that the two "detest each other cordially, and that in discussion, their passions take the place of reason." Yrujo, Turreau reported to Talleyrand, had injured himself by joining Merry in "the wretched quarrel over etiquette" and then sulking in Philadelphia. However, the failure of reconciliation was due entirely to Madison. "He is abrupt, spiteful, passionate, and his private resentment rather than difference of policy will hold him away from Mr. d'Yrujo for a long time."

Turreau's words were *"sec, haineux, passioné."* Historian Henry Adams translated *"sec"* literally as "dry," thus making Madison a sapless (though passionate!) individual for whom Turreau, with his "keenness of insight," felt "no high respect." Was that the truth? A French-born language consultant of the Library of Congress, when asked to translate *"sec"* in this context, replied: "It means that he spoke abruptly. When he talked it was Yes! No! Like cracking a dry stick with a cane." What Adams furnished was not Turreau's opinion, but his own, drawn from and reinforcing ancient Federalist slanders.[2]

Meanwhile, as the French minister owed Madison a dinner, he brought the two adversaries to his own table and made a second attempt at reconciliation. "Mr. d'Yrujo would have consented but the Secretary of State does not know how to forgive." Yrujo, a tavern dweller, was now dining every day with Turreau, who hoped the Spanish government would reject the demand for his recall. "These people," he remarked, "have been well spoiled. It is time to put them back in their place."

Turreau was a lavish spender. His great dinners were the talk of Congress, his gilded carriage was the talk of the town, chiefly because he rode so often in it to the home of "a woman of easy virtue." For some months, this was forgivingly attributed to the slow journey made by his wife, who sailed from Nantes with the legation staff in September and landed in Charleston, South Carolina, late in March. People were puzzled, though, that all his worry was over his missing shipload of wines. Legation Secretary Petry of Madame's party, writing during a several-weeks layover in the Azores, informed Turreau that the American consul there had written to Madison about an alleged mutiny of passengers who sought to depose Captain Goodfellow of the *Shepherdess.* The story was false, he said, and no less untrue was the accusation that Madame Turreau had tried to "seduce the captain and sailors." This was impossible because "Madame your wife does not speak English, and there was on board only one sailor who understands French."

The consul told Madison that Madame Turreau and other passengers refused to continue their voyage in the *Shepherdess,* alleging without warrant that it was in a sinking condition. The ship sailed without them and never reached port.[3]

Madame Turreau, according to accounts which seemed to stem from the minister, was a Paris jailer's daughter whom he had married because she saved his life (a great mistake on her part), but a French traveler (John Boussuier) asserted that she saved him from poverty, having inherited a fortune made by her first husband through "the horrid practices of the Revolution." She had been two months in America (and was five weeks pregnant) when Dolley Madison wrote to her sister:

"Since I wrote you two days past, I have heard sad things of Turreau—that he whips his wife, and abuses her dreadfully; I pity her sincerely; she is an amiable, sensible woman."

In that same month Minister Merry described the diplomatic impact of the affair and told of efforts by Madison at mediation:

"The proof which this government have now had of the minister's immoral conduct and of the violence and ferocity of his temper and the personal detestation in which he is held by all classes of people can hardly fail to have some degree of influence (happily unfavorable . . .) on his political intercourse and transactions. . . . His treatment of [his wife and children] was carried latterly to so barbarous an excess as to oblige them to fly from his house and only the mediation of, as I believe, the Secretary of State, aided by the necessity of the case, was sufficient to bring them again all together under the same roof."[4]

Some Washington ladies felt that Madame Turreau brought too much kitchen language into the parlor, but sympathetic anger flared high after her husband "beat and bruised her much" because she objected to his bringing prostitutes into the house, half a dozen at a time. On one occasion, when Madame Turreau hit her husband with a flatiron and he clubbed her more violently than usual, a quick-witted secretary who doubled in brass tried to drown her cries by closing the windows and playing loudly on the French horn. Before midsummer the happy couple left for a five-month stay in Baltimore. There, Dolley Madison wrote in July, they were "going on in the same way they did here, fighting and exposing themselves."

Recording these events, William Plumer remarked: "The ladies of the head of department are so much incensed against him, that they scarcely speak to him on any occasion." That feeling did not prevent invited senators from attending a magnificent dinner at the French legation on January 25, 1806. "I never saw so much rich heavy plate on one table," Plumer reported, all gold and silver, and they had calves' heads in turtle fashion, fine jellies and custards, sweet and white wines. Then this remark: "Mrs. Turreau was the preceding day delivered of a son." Many guests as they drove home, must have thought with the senator from New Hampshire:

"What an astonishing contrast between this man and the late chargé des affaires who preceded him! Pichon was a man of talents, of information, of courtly insinuating manners and the most pleasing address. His company was sought for with avidity!"[5]

When Turreau arrived in America, he brought with him an official notice to Pichon that Napoleon had made him a member of the French Legion of Honor. On its heels came an order, secured from the emperor by Admiral Decrès, that he return at once to France for a financial accounting. Pichon realized what had happened. Reverting from chargé to commercial commissar, he fell under control of the Minister of Marine, whom he had accused of incompetence in financing Leclerc's army. The sudden recall, he wrote to Talleyrand, seemed an action "little befitting the zeal I have taken in this difficult mission for the past four years, and a reward I would not have expected for the sacrifice of health, family and happiness that I have made in this place." When Madame Pichon was well enough to travel, the departing diplomat wrote to Madison (in English):

"We shall ever recollect the many marks of affection and regard you and Mrs. Madison were so kind as to bestow on us. ...I shall ever feel proud of having had the honor of your acquaint-

ance, and I trust deserved in my humble station as a politician your
esteem. Some unpleasant discussions which in the latter times
occurred will not, I hope, have impaired it. This I am conscious
of, that I never had any other object but honestly and sincerely
to promote amicable dispositions in the two nations and governments."[6]

Madison and Turreau got along surprisingly well for many
months. The minister had orders to say that Louisiana, as sold,
did not extend east of the Island of New Orleans, but the western
boundary was uncertain and he should promote an agreement
about it. Finding that Madison thought only about the eastward
limit, Turreau confined himself to putting West Florida beyond
it and recorded the ensuing colloquy:

"But General, replied Mr. Madison, we have a map which apparently carries the eastern limits of Louisiana to the Perdido.—
I would like to see it, sir, since I have one which includes Tennessee and Kentucky in Louisiana. You will understand that
maps are not titles."

Actually, this tended to prove the American case, since the
Treaty of San Ildefonso specifically exempted that portion of
Louisiana (Tennessee, Kentucky and the Ohio country) which
had been given up by Spanish treaties between 1763 and 1800,
but did not similarly exempt the portion south of the Spanish-
American boundary. Although the Ildefonso treaty was worded
to enable Napoleon to take West Florida whenever he chose to
do so, he needed now to prove Spanish ownership in order to
dominate the bargaining.[7]

Just before Turreau reached Washington, the President asked
Congress to restrain the activities of armed ships. Being ignorant
of the situation, the minister left that subject alone but expressed
surprise and indignation that a private American flotilla with
eighty cannon and 700 men had been allowed to sail for rebel
ports in St. Domingo. Madison assured him that a law to prevent
this would soon be passed. Although the pending bill seemed
too weak, Turreau said nothing except when legislators broached

the subject. Then he would hint that Congress itself, without being asked to, no doubt would stop such brigandage by prohibiting every kind of trade with the rebels. Senator Logan offered an amendment to that end but the Vice President broke a tie and defeated it.

Turreau believed he could secure this prohibition in the next session but a talk with Madison gave him the idea that it would be more effective to wait for the execution of some severe measures just taken by the captain general in the Antilles. The Secretary, he said, had offered a long and vigorous protest against General Ferrand's repressive orders. Turreau in turn chided the failure to heed Ferrand's complaints but promised to "make some observations" to the general. This he did—forcefully, he told Talleyrand, yet leaving him completely free.

More effective than anything Turreau wrote home was a newspaper clipping sent to Paris by the New York consulate. This told of a splendid dinner given by Samuel G. Ogden on board the 22-gun *Indostan,* with Rufus King as top man among the hundred guests. It celebrated the return from St. Domingo of "a little navy, nearly or quite equal to the whole force sent by the President" to begin the blockade of Tripoli. It was the same quartet of armed vessels whose sailing had been protested by the French minister. The adventurers rejoiced over a voyage "successful beyond their most sanguine hopes," and planned another. Napoleon blew up when he read the ninth toast: "The government of Hayti, founded on the only legitimate basis of all authority—the people's choice."[8]

Unable to cope with private armaments, Captain General Ferrand vented his wrath on innocent ships. A complaint by Madison about a French privateersman brought a conciliatory reply and counterthrust from Turreau: "I agree with you, sir, that his conduct violates the laws of humanity and the laws of nations." He was doing all that he could against it but was this any worse than the scandalous commerce carried on in St. Domingo?

Turreau, roaring like a dove, was really harder to deal with than the fictional character who, according to the Federalists, scared Madison to death just by looking at him. Augustus Foster, who had no wartime contact with Frenchmen, put that canard in his journal but his evidence failed to support it. Once when Madison and Turreau were "in the midst of a warm dispute, the door was quietly opened, a head thrust in, and Dixon, the barber, announced that he was come to shave and dress the Secretary." The two men forgot their anger in peals of laughter.[9]

It was August before Turreau did anything in diplomacy that fitted his reputation as a wife beater. France's war hero, General Moreau, banished as a plotter against Napoleon, was expected daily in America. Obeying instructions, Turreau wrote to Madison that the exiled officer "ought not to be" *(ne doit point être)* the object of honors "and it is fitting that neither his arrival nor his stay in the United States should be marked by any demonstration that goes beyond the bounds of hospitality."

Owing to previous steps taken by the President, Madison suppressed his reaction and asked for instructions. A year earlier, during the Secretary's absence in Virginia, Jefferson had directed the State Department to send Mayor DeWitt Clinton a Livingston letter on the subject. Talleyrand had told him it was the emperor's wish that Moreau be received with friendship but "any particular parade in his reception would not be well taken" in Paris and, Livingston thought, might injure him. Jefferson added his personal advice that Moreau be received cordially, without public display. Turreau's aggressive letter inspired very different thoughts in the President. On receiving them Madison responded:

"The letter from Turreau appeared to me as to you in the light of a reprehensible intrusion in a case where this government ought to be guided by its own sense of propriety alone. Whether it be the effect of an habitual air of superiority in his government or be meant as a particular disrespect to us is questionable. The former cause will explain it and the latter does not seem to be a probable cause. Be it as it may, an answer breathing independence as well as friendship seems to be proper and I enclose one to which that character was meant to be given."

Just as he finished the draft, Madison continued, Senator Smith of Maryland came in. He thought Turreau friendly, but over-

zealous, and Madison's reply struck him as too hard. Such a reaction from Smith was not surprising. Napoleon was then engaged in breaking up Jerome Bonaparte's marriage to Elizabeth
Patterson, and her uncle wanted no addition to the imperial anger. Madison jotted down some alternative softenings and left
the decision to Jefferson. He called attention to his omission of
something the President had suggested—a denial that the federal
government had power to restrain state or local authorities from
rendering whatever honors they pleased to foreigners. There
could be no need to admit such a federal responsibility, Madison
observed, but "I think it would not be expedient and might not
even be correct, to deny it." Foreign governments certainly never
would be satisfied with such an explanation in case of a real insult
"and such an insult seems possible. A state legislature or city
corporation might resolve and publish that Moreau had been
barbarously treated, or that Bonaparte was a usurper and a tyrant,
etc."

This issue came very close to arising as state and city authorities
welcomed Moreau with great dinners and military parades. Jefferson's earlier admonition to Clinton led to a false report that
Madison had yielded to the French minister's demand. Turreau
himself told his government that the enthusiastic reception was
due to British influence and he testified to Moreau's modesty. Of
his exchange with Madison he said not a word.[10]

Napoleon's enraged reaction to the armed shipowners' banquet
became known in October. Tell the American minister, he wrote
to Talleyrand, "that I can no longer look with indifference on
the armaments obviously directed against France, which the
American government allows to be made in its ports." He
would declare all ships in the St. Domingo trade to be good prize.
The foreign minister notified Armstrong that "this system of
impunity and tolerance could not continue longer" and requested
that the United States interdict all trade with the rebel ports.[11]

Turreau carried the same request to Madison, who ignored
his letter for two months, until the general sent him a copy of it.
Madison in turn sent a copy of a letter written to Pichon a year
and a half before, justifying American trade with St. Domingo

by the precedent France set during the American Revolution. A neutral country, France said then, was not bound to prevent its subjects from engaging in contraband trade or to punish them for it. As to that New York dinner, surely a private indiscretion which the home government had no power to examine ought not to attract the attention of a foreign government.

Turreau replied that the letter to Pichon, though full of sound ideas, was irrelevant. There could be no analogy between maritime independence in general and the "incontestable rights of a mother country over its colonies." This was strange reasoning, since the British colonies had also been in revolt against a mother country. The real difference was between the revolts of white men and Negroes. Turreau, however, was thinking only of results. "I persist in my request," he concluded, "or rather I insist more strongly than ever upon this object."[12]

Senator Logan already was trying to suspend this trade and the administration reluctantly yielded. On Logan's motion, the Senate asked for the letters of complaint from Turreau and Talleyrand. Bayard wanted the American replies. His motion was defeated, Plumer said, because of knowledge that Madison's answer vindicated the right to trade with the island. If produced "it would have a powerful tendency to prevent the passing of the bill."

Congress forbade all trade with the rebels under pain of forfeiture of ships and cargoes, but not all the fear was of France. "The idea of blacks being *free* in that island prejudiced some Southern senators," wrote Plumer. Jefferson's son-in-law Eppes told the House that the independence of St. Domingo "would bring immediate and horrible destruction on the fairest portion of America." Congress would have acted earlier, Senator Smith thought, had the Executive let it know that France was dissatisfied.

"The law of nations [he remarked] is with us; the law of power against us. In our infancy we ought not to commit ourselves to improper risks and unequal contests."

Though Madison disliked the concession, he tried at once to turn it to account. The new law, he wrote to Armstrong, went far beyond the obligations of the law of nations but was deemed expedient for the welfare of the United States. It proceeded (and here he gave a personal reaction contrary to that of Congress) not from any rightful demand by France, "and still less from a manner of pressing it, which might have justly had a contrary tendency." However, its passage must be pleasing to France, and therefore gave a good opening to renew old efforts to get a Dominican trade agreement. Armstrong should propose once more that food be shipped to the island in exchange for its products—a trade "obviously favorable to the true interests of France." This proposal to feed the subjects of Emperor Dessalines was virtually an invitation to France to concede independence to the blacks in order to recapture their trade. Madison's aim, no doubt, was to keep Napoleon from regaining a powerful military base, but this furnished one more proof that he was not swayed by fear of slave insurrections.[13]

Turreau, a military man, was well aware of these strategic factors. Half a year after his arrival, he had made an asked-for report on the policies and war potential of the United States. The country, the general stated, could not wage offensive war successfully. The regular army was small, the militia large but ineffective, and the weakness was made permanent by lack of *matériel* and the prodigious expense of transport over great distances. Another motive for peace was the political effect of individual avarice, "the dominant passion of a people yet new." The party that declared war would lose its popularity and its offices. That was why the administration allowed itself to be outraged by the English and would not start a conflict with Spain. This aversion to war did not depend entirely on the personal character of Mr. Jefferson:

"It is an opinion shared by all the party *coryphées,* even by those who have the best-founded claims and hopes of succeeding the present head of government—such as Mr. Madison."

Having thus stimulated Napoleon's salivary glands, the minister quickly warned that the United States was weak only in *aggressive* war. On the defensive, all moral and physical conditions favored the Americans. To attack them at home, in a vast and difficult country suitable to guerrilla warfare—that was something the most formidable military power in the world could not venture upon with hope of success. A continental attack would stir national pride and instantly unite all parties. The threat to prized possessions would convert avarice from a liability to an asset. "The first obstacle to the success of an offensive war would become the most powerful spring of an obstinate defense. . . . I repeat, the success of their defense does not hinge upon the quality of their troops."

The Americans, Turreau went on, would be subject to prodigious maritime losses even in a defensive war. The navy could put out many privateers, but these would lack trained officers. "The Americans are today the most daring and the most ignorant navigators in the universe." These weaknesses being unconcealed, it seemed to him that the federal government would avoid aggressive war.

"But [he asked] does the system of encroachment which prevails here accord with so peaceful a disposition? Not at first sight, certainly, and yet the United States will know how to reconcile them if the state of affairs does not change. To conquer without war—that is the primary political object."

The Americans, Turreau asserted, had the idea of driving the Europeans from the new world, and then seizing the Caribbean archipelago. Their vast plan was perhaps less difficult of execution than was supposed. Continental colonies brought them in contact with only two nations, Spain and England. The latter never would undertake continental war on the United States—commercial ties were too extensive and important. If war proved inescapable, the British would send five or six naval expeditions across the ocean and then make peace through a treaty of commerce, possibly even giving up Canada in order to dictate terms

favorable to her export trade. Some Americans, the minister remarked, seemed to think the strain of Great Britain's Asiatic
expansion would cause her to abandon her North American
colonies anyway.

"So lacking in reason did this seem to me that it caused me to
express my surprise to Mr. Madison that the projects of aggrandizement which the government of the Union seemed to have
were all directed toward the south, whereas there were still important and suitable countries to the north, such as Canada, Nova
Scotia, etc. 'No doubt,' the Secretary of State replied to me, 'but
the time has not yet come; when the pear is ripe, it will fall of
itself.'"

Turreau commented to his government: "The Floridas are
wanted . . . they are wanted especially as a means of attaining the
place held by Mr. Jefferson, whose political succession is already
devolved by certain journalists on some Virginian," in spite of the
earlier taint on men from that state.

In striving for a Rio Grande boundary, he was sure, they were
trying to get in contact with Mexico so as to sustain the "mis-
sionaries" who would push across the river, organize and take
possession as they were doing along the Florida frontier. The
Spaniards, to counteract this, had advanced their outposts, leading
to "lively complaints" by the Americans and a demand for maintenance of the *status quo*.

The French minister had cordially indorsed the *status quo* proposal when Madison put it before him, but his report makes it
plain that he did so only to hold the Americans in check until
stronger restraints could be devised. When he protested to Jefferson that American settlers had advanced beyond their admitted
Florida limits, the President replied; "We cannot stop our men."
However, the minister observed to Talleyrand, "the intervention
of France in the negotiations with Spain has stopped everything."
Political leaders were affected by it, he reported, but didn't let
him see their discontent. "'Very well,' Mr. Jefferson recently said
to me, 'since the Emperor wishes it, the arrangement [with Spain]
will be postponed to a more favorable time.'"

All this, Turreau commented, presented a strange phenomenon
—a state aggrandizing itself to a limitless degree without an army.
Unless retarded or prevented by Western secession or foreign opposition it would be put into effect gradually but without a check.
Spain, weak at home and overgrown colonially, never could stop
it. Let the Floridas and Cuba be ceded to France, the minister
advised, giving her mastery of the Gulf of Mexico. Garrison them
with imposing French forces, of whom Americans never spoke
but with respect and fear. "France alone can halt the enterprises
of the Americans and frustrate their plan."[14]

Thus a ruthless French general laid down the gospel to an unscrupulous emperor who aimed to rule the world. Taking things
as they were, Turreau's appraisal was sound. But in discounting
American aggressive strength he took no account of growing population and wealth. Also, his advice came three years too late.
Napoleon, by selling Louisiana, put an end forever to the chance
of halting American expansion by military means. A cession of
the Floridas and Cuba to France would have led to an Anglo-
American alliance and invasion, unless England were first defeated, and in that case the reckoning with France would merely
have been delayed.

Superficial, also, was the belief that Florida was placed ahead
of Canada in order to make Madison President. Had his motive
been political, anxiety for a quick decision would have shown up
in his policies. Jefferson's private secretary, Burwell, in a memoir
written after Madison was elected President, said that he always
thought Jefferson stirred the Louisiana boundary question too
seriously, instead of waiting for the country to fall to the United
States with growth and the need of land. Knowing that the President was determined not to go to war, Spain used the controversy
to bully the United States and sink its reputation abroad. "The
mistake," Burwell remarked, "has been repaired with great dex-
terity" by negotiation and delay.

The correction was in timing, not in method or objective. Madison wanted no abortive adventures. At the very time Turreau was
preparing this report, the Secretary of State dissuaded Jefferson
from sending a fast, unarmed ship to overtake a Spanish privateer

and demand the release of the naval storeship *Huntress,* seized as it left with supplies for the Mediterranean squadron. Better rely, he advised, on letters already forwarded by Yrujo to Spanish governors. "Captain Tingey concurred with him," wrote Jefferson to the Secretary of the Navy, "so that on the whole we concluded to abandon the measure." Thus the chance of a greater humiliation was avoided and one more Spanish item was chalked up for the future reckoning.[15]

Jefferson too was willing to wait when he saw that conditions called for such a course. They are in error who see weakness in his remark about postponing Spanish talks to suit Napoleon's pleasure. Madison already had linked the policy of delay with that of ultimate force when he told Monroe and Pinckney to let the territorial issue be decided by "the daily increase" of the American war potential. The "Florida pear" was not yet ripe enough to fall.

CHAPTER XXI

Philadelphia Interlude

Instead of going to Montpelier in the summer of 1805, James and Dolley Madison left on July 25 for Philadelphia. There Dr. Philip Physick, newly appointed head of surgery in the University of Pennsylvania, was to treat an ulcerated tumor on Dolley's leg near the knee, and also overcome the weakening effects of confinement and calomel. Since late May she had not been downstairs save to ride or sometimes dine, except when she was taken to the President's house on the Fourth of July and there "sat quite still and amused myself with the mob." Dr. Physick promised to cure her in a month, using caustics instead of surgery which, Madison reported, would have saved much time. Even with the knife avoided she could not cheer up.

"I feel as if my heart was bursting [she wrote to Anna on the morning of her arrival]—no mother, no sister—but fool that I am, here is my beloved husband sitting anxiously by me and who is my unremitting nurse. But you know how delicate he is—I tremble for him. On our way one night he [was] taken very ill with his old bilious complaint. I thought all was over with me. I could not fly to him and aid him as I used to do. But heaven in its mercy restored him next morning and he would not pause until he heard my fate from Dr. P."

For Dolley, the healing process stretched out for three months. It was a gala though room-bound return to girlhood associations. Old Quaker friends came trooping to the Madisons' "excellent lodgings on Sansom street." Among a host who showed affection, she wrote to Anna, "the Pembertons bear off the palm," and chiefly Betsey. But when Nancy Mifflin and Sally Zane chided her for letting half of Philadelphia invade her sickroom, other memories returned. Her comment (heretofore partially expurgated) ruins the conjecture that she never broke in spirit with the Quaker community after she was expelled for marrying Madison:

"This lecture made me recollect the times when our Society used to control me entirely and debar me from so many advantages and pleasures, and although so entirely from their clutches, I really felt my ancient terror of them revive to disagreeable degree."[1]

A day's journey out of Washington, Madison unwittingly passed the courier who was bringing dispatches from Monroe and Pinckney. Thus he lost a week in learning of the breakdown in Madrid. Spain had rejected the American claim to West Florida and Texas, refused to sell the Floridas, denied responsibility for French spoliations in Spanish territory and would not ratify the 1802 convention settling other claims. "Care has been taken not to commit us to war," Chief Clerk Wagner informed Madison, "by Mr. Pinckney's remaining for the arrival of Mr. Bowdoin," his intended successor. Nobody except the President, Madison and Dearborn saw a private letter giving the drastic advice to seize Texas and the Floridas.

Madison had no desire for a gamble like that, but he could not ignore the loss of face. "The business at Madrid has had an awkward termination," he wrote to Jefferson at Monticello. "After the parade of a mission extraordinary, a refusal of all our overtures in a haughty tone," coupled with the withdrawal of a spoliations settlement already agreed to, formed "a strong appeal to the honor and sensibility of this country." He found his suspicions verified that the envoys had not even mentioned the Mobile or *status quo*—subjects they had been ordered to insist on, even with a threat of force, if their main effort failed.

Under the *status quo* pledge, as Madison outlined it in his 1804 and 1805 instructions, neither country was to strengthen its forces or enlarge its settlements in the disputed territories during negotiations. Since Spain alone had troops and settlers there, she alone was to be held down while American strength increased through settlement of admittedly American territory. Maintenance of the *status quo* was a sure road to annexation.

No doubt Spain would have rejected this. But by failing even to present the issue, or the easier one of Mobile navigation, the envoys deprived the United States of the alternatives Madison had planned in the event of their failure: a minor diplomatic success which would make it easy to wait for a distant victory, or a justifiable reason for local military action.

How could these subjects be reinstated? Bowdoin might be instructed to propose (informally he said later) a suspension of major questions in return for a yielding on these lesser ones. Or, if negotiations could be transferred to Washington, it would look like an advance on the part of Spain. This was the utmost, he told Jefferson, that the Executive could do by itself. If it should fail, "the question with the legislature must be whether or not resort is to be had to force, to what extent and in what mode."[2]

From Gallatin, to whom he sent a short, unvarnished account of the American setback, Madison received a sharp criticism of the whole attempt at Madrid coupled with support of his pacific view. Unless the envoys had taken so high a tone as to jeopardize the country's reputation, it might be well "to wait for a better opportunity before we again run the risk of lowering the national importance by pretensions which our strength may not at this moment permit us to support." Perhaps the most dignified way to preserve both reputation and peace would be to provide for building a dozen ships of the line, "but it will be a doubt with some whether the remedy be not worse than the disorder." At all events, it would never do to go to war for Texas or West Florida after failing to specify them in the treaty of purchase.

For Gallatin, with his past emphasis on naval economy, this marked a decided change of views. Madison's response indicated that he too, without being militant, was extending his thoughts beyond Jefferson's gunboat policy:

"I have long been of opinion that it would be a wise and dignified course to take preparatory and provisional measures for a naval force, and the present crisis gives a great urgency to such a policy."

Madison agreed with his associate's critical appraisal of the Spanish situation. "Your view of it appears to be just." But Gallatin himself felt better after reading the actual dispatches from Madrid. The situation, he commented, "is rather on a more decent footing than I had expected."[3]

For the first time since Madison took office, he and the President were located so far apart, during a period of months, that they had to reach independent judgments on critical matters and thresh them out by letter. Madison's face-saving advice crossed two letters from Jefferson making the same suggestions as to Bowdoin, but asking "whether we ought not immediately to propose to England an eventual treaty of alliance, to come into force whenever (within —— years) a war shall take place with Spain or France." Were the question only about territory or spoliations, the President said after hearing from Madison, he would be for delay, but "I do not view peace as within our choice." Napoleon apparently intended to enforce his will by arms, after peace was secured in Europe, and "we should not permit ourselves to be found off our guard and friendless." Working with his usual tactfulness, Madison presented some drawbacks to the President's proposal:

"Great Britain . . . would certainly not stipulate to continue the war for a given period, without a stipulation on our part that within that period we would join in it. I think therefore that no formal proposition ought to be made on the subject."

An eventual alliance with Great Britain, he agreed, "would be for us the best of all possible measures, but I do not see the least chance of laying her under obligations to be called into force at our will without corresponding obligations on our part." Better, he thought, make frank but informal explanations to England of the state of affairs with Spain. That would have a natural influence on British councils, and would "appeal in a new form to the policy of Spain and France, from whom the growing communications with Great Britain would not be concealed." The latest dispatches from Pinckney, he said, made it quite plain that Spain, though emboldened by French support, was relying on the pacific spirit of America and did not herself want war. This was confirmed by the behavior, in Philadelphia, of Yrujo, who had "multiplied his attentions and with an air of cordiality which I should have thought it not easy for him to assume."

Yrujo compelled Madison to attend a dinner by coupling his name with Governor McKean's in the invitation. Later, the Secretary found himself obliged to write a letter "the tone of which he will probably regard as too hard for that of our later intercourse." It did not prevent the marquis from giving Madison two packages (one for Jefferson) of seed wheat from South America and barley from Spain. Forwarding the President's portion, the Orange County farmer discussed at length the question whether the wheat was green or ripe when Argentine weevils laid their eggs in it.[4]

Jefferson clung to the idea of an English treaty. Saying that he thought Madison had misconceived the nature of it, he restated the matter substantially as the Secretary had understood it. He had no idea of committing the country to war. The treaty should be provisional, to come into force *if* the United States became engaged in war with France or Spain during the war in Europe. "In that event we should make common cause, and England should stipulate not to make peace without our obtaining the objects [rightful Louisiana boundaries and spoliation indemnities] for which we go to war." England should receive an overture as early as possible, to prevent her from listening to terms of peace.

This letter crossed a note from Madison agreeing to the value of "some eventual security for the active friendship of Great Britain," but emphasizing the difficulty of obtaining it without a like security to her.

"If she is to be *bound,* we must be *so too,* either to the same thing, that is, to join in the war, or to do what she will accept as equivalent to such an obligation. What can we offer?"

A mutual guaranty would be useless to Great Britain unless it "involved us pretty certainly in her war," while if commercial concessions were offered, they would have to be an advance payment for aids which might never be asked for or received.

At this stage a dispatch arrived from Armstrong advising (with Monroe's concurrence) that the United States leave West Florida alone, seize Texas and threaten Spain with a commercial embargo. This, the minister to France predicted with confidence, would induce Napoleon "to interpose promptly and efficiently ... to prevent the quarrel from going further." Receiving separate copies of this letter, Jefferson and Madison once more exchanged independent views. The latter wrote:

"He seems to have moderated the scope of his former advice as to Spain. In that now given, there is in my judgment, great solidity. If force should be necessary on our part, it can in no way be so justly or usefully employed as in maintaining the *status quo*. The efficacy of an embargo also cannot be doubted."

To talk of upholding the *status quo* by force was anomalous. It could be forcibly upheld only by an invasion which would end it. The real difference between Armstrong's and Madison's positions was that the former said "invade," the latter "invade if necessary." Jefferson went farther in indorsing the minister's plan but still wanted a British anchor against a Napoleonic gale. Congress, he said, should pass acts giving the President discretionary powers of military seizure and embargo, but there ought to be "a previous alliance with England to guard us in the worst event." He hoped Madison would be able to attend a cabinet meeting in October.[5]

Secretary of War Dearborn was with Jefferson at Monticello when he wrote this, and Naval Secretary Smith endorsed the British alliance. Three days later, however, the President received from Gallatin a 5,500-word brief supporting Madison's view of future strategy but critical of the past.

From the historical record and the wording of the Spanish and French treaties of cession, Gallatin thought, the United States had a good claim to West Florida but not to Texas, which never was French territory. However, the "unpardonable oversight or indifference" of Livingston and Monroe, in failing to obtain a guarantee of the Perdido boundary from France in the Louisiana treaty, robbed the United States of any right to demand the country from Spain. Spain's conduct as to spoliations gave a more just cause of war, but the cost of it would be far greater than the gain. And if haughty, obstinate Napoleon should stick by Spain, "then our fate becomes linked to that of England and . . . the general result of the European war. . . . An entangling alliance, undefined debts and taxes . . . must be the natural consequence."

Having put these abhorred labels on Jefferson's plan, Gallatin advised that territorial negotiations be directed toward a sea front from the Perdido to the Sabine, and that they be with France, on whom their success would depend. The ministers could press Spain on other matters, taking care to avoid a rupture until the United States should build a bigger navy.

Unable to return to Washington because of Dolley's slow convalescence and his unwillingness to leave her during a yellow-fever epidemic, Madison took her to the relative safety of Gray's Ferry on the Schuylkill, arriving the day before other refugees filled up the place. From there he sent a written statement to be put before the cabinet, reiterating both his desire for an eventual coalition with Great Britain and his conviction that it was unattainable without a positive commitment to enter the war.

At Paris, Madison continued, "I think Armstrong ought to receive instructions to extinguish in the French government every hope of turning our controversy with Spain into a French job, public or private," and he should "leave them under apprehensions of an eventual connection between the United States and Great Britain." Bowdoin, who had gone to England, ought to keep aloof from Spain until occurrences should invite him there. On points outside the recent negotiations (that is, on Southwestern military posts, Mobile navigation and recent spoliations) "my reflections disapprove of any step whatever" outside of Armstrong's path or the strong course Claiborne should pursue toward Casa Calvo in New Orleans.[6]

Following the October cabinet session, the President wrote to Madison that they all thought the question of the British alliance too difficult and important to be decided without "your aid and council." A few days later word came of Pitt's third continental coalition against Napoleon—England, Austria, Russia and Sweden against France and her satellites. Though an alliance with Great Britain was less risky now, Madison saw less need for it as the chance reopened to acquire the Floridas by negotiation. Considering, he wrote to Jefferson, the likely extension of the war against France, "the influence that may have on her temper towards the United States," the uncertainty of a satisfactory agreement with England and the damage from abortive overtures, "I think it very questionable whether a little delay may not be expedient."

The President dropped his treaty project. If forced into the war, he replied, the United States could pursue it "unembarrassed by any alliance" and be free to make a separate peace for its own objectives. The expanding continental war would give time too for another effort for peaceable settlement. Where should this be made?

"Not at Madrid certainly. At Paris, through Armstrong, or Armstrong and Monroe as negotiators, France as the mediator, the price of the Floridas as the means. We need not care who gets that: and an enlargement of the sum we had thought of may be the bait to France."

To this he added: "I hazard my own ideas merely for your consideration"—not noticing, apparently, the extent to which those ideas came from Madison and Gallatin. The President's "bait to France" remark ran counter to Madison's objection to a "public job" by that country, but that had been toned down by his advice to take advantage of the changing temper of France under the pressures of an expanding war. With Napoleon in desperate need of funds and Spain delinquent in her subsidies, a payment to one country for the other's benefit bore a more legitimate look than when it seemed a device to put part of the money in Talleyrand's pocket.[7]

Encountering Merry in Philadelphia, Madison undertook explanations about Spain which were to implant the thought of an
Anglo-American alliance. He succeeded only in perplexing the
poor man. The Secretary began, Merry wrote, by discussing Britain's interference with the colonial trade in a much more moderate manner than was expected "from his natural irritability and
the sensation which it had produced." After expressing a hope
that Britain would at least liberate the ships seized before the new
system became known, Madison swung into an account of "the
perfidious and insolent proceedings" of Spanish officers who were
kidnaping Americans along the West Florida frontier, and of
the hazard created by threatening movements of Spanish troops.
Later, in Washington, "a person in a confidential situation" told
Merry that Britain's ship seizures had distracted the public and
made it harder to secure congressional action against Spain. Apparently he did not even then recognize the hint that his country
could lead the way toward an American alliance by adjusting its
naval policies.[8]

In late October, Dolley's leg was nearly well but too tender for
travel over rough roads. Frost had ended the yellow-fever danger.
Madison, rarely apart from his wife for even a day, took her into
Philadelphia and returned to Washington alone. Going part way
in his carriage, he sent it back and continued by stage. Their deep
love for each other, eleven years after marriage, was expressed in
letters as fervent as those of an engaged couple.

"A few hours only," wrote Dolley, "have passed since you left
me my beloved and I find that nothing can relieve the oppression
of my mind but speaking to you in this the only way." Next midnight a watchman's storm warning kept her awake with anxiety.
"Detention, cold and accident seem to menace thee." The knee was
mending, she reported a day later. "Adieu, my beloved, our hearts
understand each other." News of Madison's safe arrival brought
the comment: "To find you love me, have my child safe, and
that my mother is well, seems to comprise all my happiness."

The doctor, Dolley said in one letter, "regards you more than
any man he knows." Madison may have felt that way about the

doctor early in November. To have word that his wife was coming home "gives me much happiness," he wrote, "but it cannot be complete till I have you again with me." Hearing that Richard and Anna Cutts had stopped in Philadelphia to return with her, he closed the correspondence on "the last mail, my dearest, that will be likely to find you in Philadelphia and I am not without some hope that this will be too late."

Madison told Dolley of arrangements made with Bishop John Carroll for admission of her son Payne Todd, not quite fourteen, to St. Mary's College in Baltimore. This was a new school for boys directed by Father (later Archbishop) Louis Dubourg, a West Indian Frenchman of the Sulpician order, and contained many non-Catholic students. The religious aspect of the choice, it is to be suspected, was subordinate to the need for strict discipline over a youth who still called his stepfather "papa" but may have begun to manifest the unpleasant traits of his maturity. Also, it would give him a fluency in spoken French which Madison failed to acquire in his intensive reading of that language.[9]

Nearing recovery, Dolley executed Jefferson's request that she buy "a fashionable wig of the color of the hair enclosed" and other articles for Martha Jefferson Randolph. She collected the rent on the old Todd house leased by Colonel Moylan—less than she expected, net—and heeded (let us hope) her husband's admonition to insure it. She completed the purchase of a new team of carriage horses. The former owner, "well pleased with the payment . . . congratulated me on possessing such a handsome pair." At a farewell gathering in her rooms, the Marqués de Casa Yrujo became "terribly angry" when a lady asked him if it was true, as Major Jackson (the editor he tried to bribe) stated in his paper, that Spain had declared war on the United States. Turreau had come to Philadelphia and was making a sad impression. "He is remembered as the cruel commander at La Vendee, and the fighting husband."[10]

The question of war with Spain was on everybody's tongue. To Dolley, who was anxious to hear "what is going forward in the Cabinet," Madison had written that neither Spain nor England would force a war "if they consult their interest." He reiterated constitutional principles which also served as a buffer against popular pressure:

"The power of deciding questions of war and providing measures that will make or meet it is with Congress and that is always our answer to newspapers."

It was not alone the press that was crying out against "insults and injuries" from Europe. Although "educated a Quaker," Dr. William Thornton was ready to seize the Floridas and Cuba and turn armed vessels loose on British commerce. The Executive, he assured Madison, would be supported by all classes of the people in a benevolent extension of American empire and personal freedom to a larger portion of mankind.[11]

Jefferson and Madison were now in full agreement. On November 12, the President called the cabinet and proposed a money offer to Spain for the Floridas and the Rio Grande boundary, with Spain to pay later for spoliations under her own flag. The normal course would have been to deduct these claims from the purchase price, but that would not have left enough to entice France.

Gallatin, according to Jefferson, did not like purchasing Florida when there was so much talk of war, "lest we should be thought in fact to purchase peace," but he yielded to the view that no such chance might come again. The four secretaries voted unanimously to offer $5,000,000, of which, it was estimated, about $4,000,000 would ultimately be repaid by Spain.

Hardly had this step been taken when Madison received a French proposal from Armstrong. An unsigned paper in Talleyrand's handwriting, handed privately to the minister, offered the Floridas to the United States for $10,000,000. The Colorado River in middle Texas was to be the western boundary of Louisiana. Spanish (but not French-Spanish) spoliations were to be paid in bills on Spanish colonies. The emperor, the note stated, could induce Spain to accept.

Armstrong did not name the intermediary, but it was Daniel Parker. This was sure evidence that Talleyrand and Parker hoped

to divide part of the money, but the method of paying for spoliations gave the offer a more impressive stamp. France was to get
American money while the United States collected the Mexican
or Peruvian bullion whose obstruction by the British Navy caused
Spain to default on her subsidy to France. Jefferson recalled the
cabinet, which agreed to the French proposal but kept the price
at $5,000,000.[12]

Meanwhile, what was to be done about Yrujo? An exceedingly harsh demand for his recall had been made by Pinckney
and Monroe. The Spanish government asked that he might depart voluntarily under a leave already granted. To Madison, these
circumstances suggested forbearance. On the other hand, he reported, Yrujo had told the British minister that he intended to
spend the coming winter in Washington, and this indelicacy, as
well as Spain's general conduct, seemed to plead strongly for peremptory measures. The cabinet agreed on November 12 that
Yrujo should be "made to understand" (through Dallas) that he
was unwelcome in Washington and his departure from the country was expected. Morales and Casa Calvo were to be ordered out
of New Orleans.

To George W. Erving, who was going to Madrid as chargé
d'affaires while Bowdoin remained in Paris, the Secretary of State
sent orders that he take no step whatever to revive the negotiations. He might, however, teach Spain a salutary lesson by disclosing the effect of her "proud and perverse" course on American
public opinion. If, said Madison, she had been jogged into these
follies by "the friend at her elbow," a lesson was at hand in the
coalition against France's imperial career. However, he added:

"England seems as ready to play the fool with respect to this
country as her enemies. She is renewing her depredations on our
commerce in the most ruinous shapes, and has kindled a more
general indignation among our merchants than was ever before
expressed."

Petty indeed these European nations looked to him, "alternately
smiling and frowning on the United States, not according to any

fixed sentiments or interests, but according to the winds and clouds of the moment." His own country would "continue to present a contrast of steady and dignified conduct, doing justice under all circumstances to others, and taking no other advantage of events than to seek it for themselves."[13]

Anger and disgust underlay these expressions—anger born of inability to resent the injuries effectually, disgust that the great belligerents paid no heed to America's rising strength. The justice which Madison demanded and offered was tinctured with national self-interest, but he saw clearly what England and France did not—that by aiming at close and permanent ties with the United States, either of them could gain far more than through repressive action which in time would invite retribution.

As to Spain, while public opinion inclined toward the use of force, the Jefferson administration preferred to negotiate with France as Spain's overlord. Here two major uncertainties lay ahead—the influence of Talleyrand's desire for private gain, and the possible effect of Napoleonic victories or defeats on the continent of Europe. Over all hung the cloud of England's naval policies, now turning severely against the United States.

CHAPTER XXII

EXAMINATION OF A DOCTRINE

ANTICIPATING Monroe's return to England in the spring of 1805, Madison adopted a conciliatory tone toward that country. He approved the minister's passive attitude toward Britain's dodging of the 1804 treaty project, since that kept the way open for "a fair and friendly experiment" in the future. He should inform England of the public impatience over impressment and other irregularities at sea—an indication not of hostile sentiments but of the need for serious efforts to preserve harmony.

Madison called attention to a new law regulating the arming of private vessels. This, he said, was enacted in response to the protests of Pichon, Turreau and Merry regarding St. Domingo. Instead of prohibiting such weapons, the new law required bond to be put up against their unlawful use. (This feature, which Turreau thought too weak, was proposed by Madison himself as a substitute for a still weaker one.) Although France took the lead in asking for this law, Madison commented, it would actually benefit England and harm France by cutting off the flow of contraband to French colonial forces.

British governors in the West Indies, he noted, were cutting down American exports to them in order to force a trade with Canada. Besides the injustice of compelling one colony to subsidize another through higher prices, the move seemed to him especially shortsighted at a time when the United States, by cutting off vitally needed supplies, could force Great Britain either to relax her regulations or sacrifice her West Indian islands. More and more, it appears, Madison's thoughts were turning toward an export embargo aimed immediately at the West Indies, but designed to coerce the major European combatants.[1]

April found the issue of colonial trade right on the Secretary's doorstep. The owner of the American brig *Aurora,* he informed Monroe, brought a cargo of Spanish produce from Havana, landed it, paid the duties and after three weeks reshipped it for Barcelona. The vessel was captured by the British, sent to Newfoundland, and condemned on two grounds:

First, that under the British "Rule of 1756," a trade from a colony to its mother country, closed to other countries in time of peace, could not be opened to them in time of war.

Second, that the continuity of the voyage from Havana to Barcelona was not broken by the landing in the United States and paying of duties which were later refunded under the law governing re-exports. This, it was contended, deprived the cargo of the benefit of the order allowing direct trade between an enemy colony and a neutral country.

Taking up the first contention, Madison pointed out that this rule of 1756 was maintained by no country except Great Britain. Through naval supremacy she enforced or modified it to suit her interest. (Adopted in the war of 1756-63, it had been abandoned in 1778-83, reimposed in 1793, modified in 1794, further relaxed in 1798, stiffened by the courts in 1799 and by the crown in 1803.) This principle, he asserted, was contrary both to the general interest and the law of nations. It was the more unreasonable because nobody denied the right of a country to admit neutrals to *direct* channels of trade which had been closed in time of peace. Moreover, the colonial trade was opened at times for reasons unrelated to war. He noted that it was Great Britain's wartime practice to admit neutrals into forbidden channels of her own trade. To avert captures, she opened her colonies both to neutral vessels and supplies. Finally, British vessels were authorized by Parliament to trade directly with the enemy.

"In this manner she assumes to suspend the war itself as to particular objects of trade beneficial to herself whilst she denies the right of the other belligerents to suspend their accustomed commercial restrictions in favor of neutrals."

To climax the injustice and inconsistency, American cargoes condemned in British courts were sent on British account to enemy ports, even "to the very port of the destination interrupted when they were American property." He pointed out that British and American commissioners, settling claims under Jay's treaty, had reversed British condemnations founded on the Rule of 1756.

"As the reversal could be justified by no other authority than the law of nations, by which they were to be guided, the law of nations according to that joint tribunal, condemns the principle here combated."

On the second point in the *Aurora* decision, Madison affirmed that "the continuity of her voyage was clearly and palpably broken, and the trade converted into a new character." The goods being landed and duties paid or secured, they qualified for internal consumption or for export, and the law was the same during peace and war. This, he pointed out, had been recognized by the highest admiralty authority in England when it was argued in the case of the *Polly* (1800) that landing the goods and paying duties did not prove a bona fide importation. "If these criteria are not to be resorted to," said Sir William Scott in refusing condemnation, "I should be at a loss to know what should be the test." Madison quoted Lord Mansfield's ruling that even a transfer of cargo from ship to ship off a neutral port was equivalent to the landing of goods and "in the case of a landing there could be *no color* for seizure."

In spite of these clear precedents, the Secretary expected the verdict against the *Aurora* to be sustained on appeal. Great Britain was not trying to cut off the supplies of enemy countries but to restrain the rising trade of the United States. If this was her motive in spoliating American commerce, she ought not to forget that the United States would use the same standard in "counteracting her unjust and unfriendly policy."

In June Madison shared the "great sensation" (his words to Merry) over the news that Captain Bradley, recalled for defying American port authorities, had been punished by promotion to a ship of the line. This was no approval, Merry assured him, because naval officers preferred to command a fast frigate. The explanation, reported the minister, had no effect on Madison, who said he would send a new protest to London about "what he still called Captain Bradley's promotion."

In that same month word came that American ships laden with innocent colonial cargoes were being seized on the ground that they had carried contraband on the outward voyage.

An 1803 Order in Council, hitherto unknown, was cited to justify condemnation. The British, Madison conjectured, would not call this a trade restriction, but a *relaxation* of the Rule of 1756, which totally prohibited trade with hostile colonies. He therefore based his immediate protest on the great damage from lack of advance notice of "this hard and unjustifiable clause." Merry defended the action and was asked to forward the protest to London.[2]

This assault on direct trade with French colonies—lawful under every concept except the disputed Rule of 1756—confirmed Madison's belief that he must center his attack on that rule. From the Library of Congress he borrowed the works of Grotius, Pufendorf and Sir William Temple, and volumes of the *Annual Register* encompassing forty years (1758-1797) of British politics, war and trade. Taking this and other material with him to Philadelphia, he began the first thorough inquiry ever made into the "predatory" doctrine "that a trade not open in peace is not lawful in war." It was amazing, he commented to Monroe, that neutral authors had scarcely touched the subject. A few weeks' study showed the theme to be so important, new and involved that he had to go through an even wider field. The result, he reported to Jefferson in October, "will I think fully establish the heresy of the British doctrine and present her selfishness and inconsistencies in a light which it would be prudent in her to retreat from."

Reviewing the judgments of Sir William Scott, he found them more vulnerable than expected. "The decisions are often at variance with each other and the arguments sometimes shamefully sophistical, at others grossly absurd." He wished that some talented lawyer "would undertake to overturn this colossal champion of belligerent usurpations" in order to protect the American judiciary from his prestige. Scott's decisions and even his dicta,

he observed, "are in a manner laws already in our courts and
his authority if not checked will be as despotic here as it is in
England."[3]

By this time, Madison had received Scott's decision in the case
of the *Essex,* reversing his own prior ruling that landing of goods
and payment of duties broke the continuity of a voyage. The
decision, Madison remarked, "has spread great alarm among the
merchants, and has had a grievous effect on the rate of insurance.
[It quadrupled.] From the great amount of property afloat subject to this new and shameful depredation, a dreadful scene of
distress may ensue to our commerce."

Much could be said for Scott's decision, if one admitted the
validity of British orders which forbade direct shipment to France
of noncontraband goods bought by Americans in French colonies.
British Orders in Council forbade that, but allowed such goods to
be exported to the United States. There was of course no ban on
the export of American goods to France, in the absence of a blockade. Scott said truthfully that the landing of colonial goods was
designed to escape the prohibition against direct shipment. But
that had been true when he held it legal under the law of nations.

Madison aimed at a total refutation of the Rule of 1756. If he
could establish the right of a belligerent *to alter its commercial
regulations in time of war,* it would make no difference whether
the trade between colony and mother country was direct or
broken. In January 1806 he published a pamphlet (actually a
book of nearly 70,000 words) entitled *Examination of the British
Doctrine, which subjects to capture a Neutral Trade Not Open in
Time of Peace.* It was anonymous, but everybody knew who wrote
it. Nobody else could have examined the subject with such microscopic exactness, penetrating logic and (in spite of clear reasoning
and pungent paragraphs) such massive unreadability.

Just before his own pamphlet came off the press, Madison received one from England on the opposite side. Entitled *War in
Disguise, or, The Frauds of the Neutral Flags,* it was the anonymous product of James Stephen, a Scotch lawyer who had lived
in the West Indies and was known for his enmity to the slave
trade. Once so devoted to American liberty that he thought of

joining the Continental Army, he was now a thoroughgoing British Tory and imperialist.

The dates printed in the two pamphlets, 1805 and 1806, create the impression that Madison was answering Stephen. Actually, it was the other way around. Madison's earlier attack on the Rule of 1756 had been paraphrased by Monroe to Lord Mulgrave and it was plain enough, as Monroe saw, that *War in Disguise* was "written by a person who saw my note."

Madison contended that the Rule of 1756 was both unknown to early writers and contrary to the law of nations as expounded by them. It conflicted with many treaties, some signed by Great Britain, and the actual conduct of Great Britain had run contrary to the rule more often than in accord with it. Analyzing the shifting court opinions, he declared that this innovation was in truth "a mere project for extending the field of maritime capture, and multiplying the sources of commercial aggrandizement; a warfare, in fact, against the commerce of her friends, and a monopolizing grasp at that of her enemies." Two practices to this end were cited and proved by a mountain of evidence:

"1st. Whilst Great Britain denies to her enemies a right to relax their laws in favor of neutral commerce, she relaxes her own."

"2nd. Whilst she denies to neutrals the right to trade with the colonies of her enemies, she trades herself with her enemies, and invites them to trade with her colonies."

By a series of acts in April, June and August 1805, Madison pointed out, the British government authorized British subjects to import enemy colonial goods during the war, and re-export them to enemy countries, while shutting out Americans. In characterizing Great Britain's conduct, he quoted (not verbatim), a passage from Jefferson's message of December 3, 1805, and heightened the effect with a denunciatory setting:

"And thus, in defiance as well of her treason laws and of her trade laws, as of the rights of neutrality under the law of nations, we find her in the just and emphatic language of the President, 'taking to herself, by an inconsistency at which reason revolts, a commerce with her own enemy, which she denies to a neutral, on the ground of its aiding that enemy in the war.' "

Pursuing and dissecting the shifting justifications of the Rule of 1756 in admiralty courts, the Secretary of State defined the final basis of the doctrine:

"Finding no asylum elsewhere, it at length boldly asserts, as its *true foundation a mere superiority of force.*"

The author of *War in Disguise,* instead of denying or ignoring all these inconsistencies, undertook to justify them. The proper use of sea power was to distress an enemy and gain advantages. For that purpose, the nation controlling the sea could establish one rule for neutral trade with its own colonies, an opposite rule for the enemy's. Having power to prohibit enemy trade altogether, it could enforce or relax that prohibition at will. Relaxations were not rights; they were privileges granted by the superior power for its own purposes. New rules for confiscation of neutral ships were mere adjustments to cope with past evasions. Basically, Stephen was holding that Britannia ruled the waves and neutrals had no rights. Madison's legal case was built on a contrary premise whose sound morality had more to support it in 1806 than in the dark ages of the tenth and twentieth centuries:

"The progress of the law of nations, under the influence of science and humanity, is mitigating the evils of war, and diminishing the motives to it, by favoring the rights of those remaining at peace, rather than of those who enter into war. Not only are the laws of war tempered between the parties at war, but much also in relation to those at peace."

Monroe assumed that *War in Disguise* was written under ministerial auspices. It was in part a criticism of the ministry—a call for more drastic enforcement of the Rule of 1756. Stephen condemned past and current relaxations and seemed to be calling on Pitt to catch up with Sir William Scott. His revealed purpose was exactly what Madison charged against the British government—

war on neutral trade in order to cripple it and take over enemy trade.

Impassioned, plain-spoken and literal, the Scotch writer disclosed his objective over and over again. He devoted pages to proving that because of lower insurance rates and British convoy costs, American ships trading with French colonies could undercut their British rivals. Hostile colonies, by this means, were underselling British colonies in British ports and in the continental markets, thus ruining British planters and the colonial market for British manufactures. To cure this, he would cut off neutral trade in sugar, coffee, cotton, indigo and bullion from enemy colonies, giving British planters, merchants and shipowners a monopoly of these major articles. But "as a voluntary sacrifice to amity" he would allow free trade throughout the West Indies in "those inferior articles of colonial produce, rum, taffia and molasses" consumed domestically in the United States. (Americans chortled when they read his assertion that they did not eat sugar.)

Stephen did not believe in the current practice by which licenses to trade with the enemy were as easily obtained as papal dispensations in the days of Luther. "Should, however, the neutral nations be insane enough to go to war with us for the sake of the colonial trade," or should the United States place an embargo on British commerce, the remedy was easy. A well-regulated British trade with enemy countries, combined with the smuggling of British manufactures across the ill-guarded American coast, "would soon show them their folly."

In short, starting with a call for the full Rule of 1756 as a war measure against France, Stephen reached the conclusion that it must be re-imposed sufficiently to shift the carrying trade from the United States to Great Britain, create a price advantage for British colonial goods and build up colonial buying power for British manufactures. The worst that Madison *charged* was here *advocated,* and in a most dangerous form—an appeal to the cupidity of British merchants as a class, and to the men in government most responsive to the mercantile interest.[4]

It was planned at first that Madison's pamphlet should be sent to Congress by the President, making it an official document. In-

stead, Senator Mitchill informed his colleagues on January 14 that
it would be placed informally on their desks. This was done two
days later, and copies were mailed over the country and to Europe.
It was republished in England and Monroe had it circulated in
the ministry and Parliament.

The reception at home was mixed. "My son is now devouring
it," wrote Dr. Benjamin Rush, father of brilliant young Richard.
"It is spoken of in all the circles in our city with the highest praise
and admiration." J. Q. Adams wrote in his diary on January 22:
"Finished Mr. Madison's pamphlet, with which I am, upon the
whole, much pleased." Plumer probably spoke for others when
he noted on the same day, "I never read a book that fatigued me
more," but few senators would have added as he did: "That circumstance may arise from my want of information on the subject." Rufus King voiced the mercantile verdict: It "shows the
unsoundness of the English doctrine."

Senator Uriah Tracy, growing more bitter as he neared death
from tuberculosis, saw only weakness and evasion—one more
proof that the Jefferson administration was "sneaking behind to
avoid all hazard to darling popularity. . . . By the debauching
force of party, by the fatal effects of demoralizing democracy, by
the babyish nonsense of peace, peace, the watchword of democracy . . . our country is unhinged, is let down to such a degree
that no manly exertion can be expected." Had the Jefferson administration blossomed out with a war policy, nobody would have
denounced it more violently than this senatorial decrier of peace,
peace. Some complained that Madison charted no course of remedial action—which was the same as saying that he should have cut
off all alternatives except the one he might have proposed.[5]

Jefferson's annual message of December 3, 1805, was written to
cover the policy of peace with the tone of war, in order to put
pressure on France to settle the Spanish controversy. In the original draft, the trouble with Spain was outlined at length and quite
belligerently. About England it merely stated that "New principles too have been interpolated into the law of nations founded
neither in justice, nor the usage or acknowledgment of nations,
which, if pursued in practice, prostrate the navigation of the neu-

tral, and make him merely subservient to the purposes of the belligerent."

The message was sent to Madison on November 22 for "a severe correction both as to style and matter." Jefferson's papers contain memos from Madison suggesting many other changes, but nothing about this paragraph. That he objected to it is evident from what followed. "How will it do," the President asked him two days later, "to amend the passage respecting England to read as follows?" He then submitted what Madison in his pamphlet referred to as "the just and emphatic language of the President." Returning the revised paragraph, the Secretary suggested a trivial change and added: "This however is merely for consideration. The passage as it stands has a good countenance and is made of good stuff."

Jefferson then did exactly as he had done on a similar occasion in 1801. He sent the unrevised message to Gallatin, asking for a scrupulous and early revisal so that he could "submit it successively to the other gentlemen," and continued:

"On reviewing what has been prepared as to Great Britain and Spain, I found it too soft towards the former compared with the latter, and that so temperate a notice of the greater enormity might lessen the effect which the strong language towards Spain was meant to produce at the Tuilleries. I have, therefore, given more force to the strictures on Britain."[6]

Comparing this with the action in 1801, it is evident that the note to Gallatin was a paraphrase of Madison's criticism. Jefferson was willing to accept advice, but not to let others know that he did so. Madison's chronic failure to claim credit contributed to the result—a long-unchallenged historical verdict that Jefferson ran everything in his administration.

Foreign diplomats knew that this was not true and there were others who doubted it at the time. Among them was Senator John Adair of Kentucky, who entered Congress after Senator Breckinridge was made attorney general late in 1805. In the following April, Senator Plumer asked this antiadministration Republican whether it was true that the President had lost confidence in Breckinridge. The Kentucky senator, as Plumer recorded their talk, denied this.

"But," said Mr. Adair, "the President wants nerve—he has not even confidence in himself. For more than a year he has been in the habit of trusting almost implicitly in Mr. Madison. Madison has acquired a complete ascendancy over him."

Plumer replied that he regarded Madison as an honest man "but that he was too cautious, too fearful and too timid to direct the affairs of this nation." Adair agreed and expressed the hopeful belief that John Randolph with his "great talents" would "crumble down this administration." Taking up the subject with his New Hampshire colleague a few days later, Plumer received a similar Federalist verdict:

"Mr. Gilman told me that he believed the President was an honest man, but he wanted firmness. That Mr. Madison was much more timid, and yet he governed the President . . . [who] consulted the other heads of department but little."[7]

These characterizations of Jefferson and Madison can be discounted heavily. General Adair was a zealot for war with Spain. The Federalist senators were mouthing party platitudes. But when these men talked of Jefferson "trusting almost implicitly" in Madison, of the latter "governing the President," they were asserting a state of facts which their unflattering opinion of Madison would not have led them to imagine or believe. Those facts overthrow their estimates of character. A firm Chief Executive might yield to superior judgment, a rash one to caution, but a timid man would not be governed by a subordinate who was "much more timid" than himself.

It was not indecision, timidity or want of nerve that made Jefferson lean ever more heavily on Madison. He relied on the Secretary's analytical ability, understanding and judgment, applied to purposes on which they agreed completely. Though cautious in forming major policies, Jefferson was given to impulsive day-by-day decisions. Madison studied the alternatives as in a chess game, thinking of the future. Time after time, the President altered a hasty stand after the Secretary of State pointed to flaws in it. Tenacious of principle, Jefferson had no pride of opinion that held him to a course merely because he had proposed it, but personal pride bade him tell posterity that he alone made the decision to veer.

That this relationship could continue eight years without producing a personal rift is almost inconceivable. There were two reasons why none developed. No difference of principle or basic objective ever separated the two men, and Madison gave not the slightest hint that the policies he was carrying out were to a great extent his own. Their unity made them joint targets in the political world. They became the twin foci of a circling storm that roared around them both, with Madison gradually taking the brunt of it because he was moving toward, not out of, the Presidency. It was not the Jefferson administration, but the one he saw rising beyond it, that John Randolph wanted to crumble down, and for that purpose one issue was as good as another.

CHAPTER XXIII

SAVAGES IN AND OUT OF CONGRESS

THE WINTER of 1805-06 was mild and gloomy in Washington. The gloom was due in part to the scarcity of attractive ladies, in part to Britain's naval victory at Trafalgar and Napoleon's startling successes on the continent. The wiping out of French and Spanish sea power was bound to tighten British control of neutral commerce—a prospect slightly tempered by the death of Pitt and entrance of the "Ministry of All the Talents," mostly concentrated in Foreign Secretary Fox. Exaltation of French land power reduced Napoleon's need to settle Spanish-American differences and made it more hazardous for the United States to exert pressure on Spain.

To liven things up, the capital was invaded by American Indians and a Tunisian ambassador. Senator Plumer recorded in November, after calling on the President, that as he entered he met Madison, who "gave me his hand and very politely inquired of my health." Received by Jefferson, the senator made a mental note for his diary (ragged slippers with his toes out—clean linen but hair disheveled) and then heard a cannonade off Alexandria. That, the President told him, marked the arrival of Ambassador Sidi Suliman Mellimelli, whose ship had been fighting headwinds on the Potomac for three weeks. His mission, it was explained, resulted from the President's peremptory refusal of a Tunisian demand for tribute like that paid Algiers. When Captain Rodgers bluntly asked the Bey what he was going to do about it, the latter said he would send an ambassador to Washington at American expense.

Those pirates always sent their diplomats collect, Jefferson explained, so he had rented Stelle's old hotel and made a food contract with the owner. There might, however, be no net cost, since Mellimelli was bringing several stud horses as a gift, including a fine animal which the Dey of Algiers once sent to the Bey of Tripoli. If Congress was willing, they might be sold for enough to pay all the expenses of the Tunisian mission.

Mellimelli landed next day with his party of eleven, including four Turkish attachés (he himself was a Turk), Negro servants and an Italian band. The ambassador called at once on Madison, followed by the carrier of his four-foot pipe. Mellimelli was a man of fifty, with an eight-inch black beard streaked with gray, who usually wore rich scarlet and gold silks topped by a twenty-yard turban of white muslin. The arrangements for him, he reported, were satisfactory, except for one omission. He needed some concubines. Madison supplied the deficiency with "Georgia a Greek," and charged the cost to the State Department. "Appropriations to foreign intercourse," wrote Madison a few months later on another subject, "are terms of great latitude and may be drawn on by very urgent and unforeseen occurrences."

Soon the Tunisian ambassador set off for the President's house, leading four horses. One had died after landing; luckily not the one with the royal pedigree. Being practical farmers, Jefferson and Madison soon saw the possibility of financial recoupment without a sale of this prize beast. Hardly had the stallion been established in the presidential stables when Representative Joseph Bryan of Georgia wrote to the Secretary of State:

"I applied to the President for permission to put a couple of mares to the Barbary horse sent over by the Bey of Tunis. On Saturday he told me I might send the mares whenever I pleased provided I would agree to be answerable to the government for the payment of the price he should cover at the ensuing season. I sent the mares this morning but the groom refused to put the horse to them without an order—that order I presume must come from you."[1]

The Indians began to arrive in November—not the usual run of "give us" or "don't rob us" petitioners who camped along the swamp between Pennsylvania Avenue and the Potomac, but representatives of powerful tribes from the Southwest and beyond the Mississippi. First came a half-dozen Creeks, from Tennessee and Mississippi Territory, led by their beloved protector and civilizer, Colonel Benjamin Hawkins (Madison's close friend in the Continental Congress). They wore blue coats with red collars, pantaloons, moccasins and gold-laced hats. Next came twenty-one Osage, Pawnee, Sac, Sioux, Missouri and Mississippi Indians (the listing is by Foster of the British legation), mostly sent east by Lewis and Clark. Naked to the waist, with painted bodies, shaven heads and feathered topknots, they rode down the avenue "on miserable little horses with saddles and bridles like our own," singing or bawling and shaking gourd rattles. They took a house across the street from the Creeks, but the Sacs ate separately because their tribe was at war with the Osages. (Merry and Turreau obeyed a similar tabu.) In January, Cherokees joined the Creeks. They too were at war with the Osages, but fell into the evil of fraternization and were amazed to discover what good fellows their enemies really were.

Diplomats and congressmen hobnobbed with the Indians in Dolley Madison's drawing room. When Mellimelli met the red men, he asked (through an Italian) whether they believed in Mohammed, Abraham or Jesus Christ. "We worship the Great Spirit without an agent" was their answer. "Vile heretics" was the Tunisian's rejoinder. He asked Jefferson how he could prove that these men were descended from Adam. "The President replied it was difficult." Mellimelli thought better of the Indians after three or four of their orators said, at the funeral of an Osage chief who danced himself to death, "that God was God, it was his work," but he still would not admit that they were the children of Shem, Ham or Japheth. Probably they came from sparsely inhabited Gemen Arabia.

At Jefferson's New Year reception, Mellimelli and the Indians shared the light with four Federalist sachems (Adams, Plumer, Chittenden and Taggart) who disregarded the decision of a party war council to insult the President by staying away. Minister Merry was so affronted by the President's concentration on the Indians that he left in five minutes, dragging Foster with him.

The presence of Plumer and Adams was not wholly a triumph of politeness over politics. The former had written to his son, "I am still a Federalist . . . but." J. Q. Adams had noted in his diary

that "Mr. Madison . . . expressed himself in very favorable terms
of me" to Dr. Rush and spoke of the President's desire to send
him on some foreign mission.[2]

Mellimelli's demand for annual tribute met a categorical refusal.
The United States would not pay him a single cent, wrote Madison, and was not terrified by his threats of war. The ambassador
then begged for some concession that would save his life. His
king was a tyrant. "If he failed (with fingers at his throat) bow-
string."[3]

From that time on, the problem was to get rid of the ambassador. He was sent to Boston loaded with presents, but three of
his staff rebelled (at American expense) and could not be dis-
lodged from New York. "Coercion alone will rid us of the Tunisians in revolt," wrote Madison to Jefferson in July, but was there
not "room for criticizing the legality of it?" Three months later
word came that Mellimelli was on his way to Monticello and
Montpelier. "I have written to Wagner to save us," Madison informed the President, and word soon came that the ambassador
had gone back to Boston and sailed for home.

What should be done about the three rebels, Secretary Mahomet
Choux, Mustapha the cook and Soliman the barber? "Pay their
passage [to Great Britain] and get rid of them," advised Jefferson. Madison did so. The British cabinet, too late, issued orders
in council restricting the admission of aliens. Letters piled up
between Monroe and British secretaries. Board bills piled up at
the home of a kindhearted London Jew who had the misfortune
to speak Turkish. At last Great Britain agreed to ship the men to
Turkey but asked the United States to pay the six-months' food
bill which had made Mr. Benjamin almost penniless. At that
point the diplomatic record stops, nor is there anything to show
whether the Arabian stud horse covered the cost of the mission.[4]

The United States faced another North African problem in the
person of Hamet Caramalli, ex-bashaw of Tripoli, with whom
Consul William Eaton attempted a 1200-mile march across the
Lybian Desert to knock his usurping brother off the throne and
end the Tripolitan war. Madison looked a bit askance at Captain Eaton (henceforth General) when he came home at the

end of 1803 to recoup his expenditures and obtain additional authority. The Secretary declined to approve Eaton's bribe of $10,000 to the reigning bashaw's secretary, or his payment of $6,921.46 to ransom the appealing granddaughter of a Sicilian count. Eaton financed his preliminary arrangements with Hamet by borrowing $22,000 from the Tunisian finance minister, who was to be repaid on the arrival of an American frigate. When the frigate arrived without the money, the minister collected by holding Captain Morris for $22,000 ransom, which Eaton borrowed from a French commissioner. Madison told him that Congress alone could reimburse him.

The President too showed reserve, but agreed to appoint Eaton naval agent and send him back to undertake the invasion. "Mr. Madison 'leaves everything to the Secretary of the Navy Department,'" Eaton complained. Gathering several hundred Arabs and Greeks in Egypt, he marched five hundred hostile miles to Derne, where American naval guns and marines saved his force from a massacre. The invasion may have helped persuade the Bashaw Yussuf Caramalli to sign a peace treaty which included a payment, to him, of $60,000 ransom for the crew of the shipwrecked frigate *Philadelphia,* which struck a reef off Tripoli.[5]

Eaton received a hero's welcome in November 1805 and denounced Consul General Tobias Lear and the administration for "buying a peace" which he could have imposed by force. Actually, his expedition had failed. Continuance of his venturesome exploit would have cost his life and probably that of the *Philadelphia* crewmen. The Navy now had Hamet Caramalli on its hands. Yussuf held Hamet's wife and children, though pledged to restore them. Hamet had a relief bill in Congress and the Senate had the treaty. The Federalists, for political reasons, supported the first and denounced the second. Aided by a Republican senator, they united these aims in a committee report accusing Lear and Commodore Barron of bad faith toward Caramalli. The Senate was straightened out, and a temporary relief bill passed, after Adams was sent to get a truer story from Madison.

On the morning of April 3, Senator Plumer visited the President, who indorsed the treaty but suggested that ratification be

postponed till the next session, ostensibly to insure the release of
Mrs. Caramalli and her brood, but actually to postpone lapse of
the Mediterranean fund when a Tunisian war threatened. On
that same evening, Madison spent half an hour with Senator
Adams, "pressing the necessity of ratifying the treaty." Plumer
asked Adams how he could reconcile the two conversations. It
couldn't be done, was the reply, "there was no such thing as placing confidence in these men." The treaty was ratified a few days
later.[6]

Mellimelli, Caramalli, General Eaton and the Indians did not
wholly engross public attention in 1806. While Western savages
were behaving like gentlemen, some gentlemen in Congress were
behaving like savages. Having, in his annual message, verged on
a war spirit against Spain in order to alarm France, the President
followed with a confidential message on Spain. He told of the
failure at Madrid, emphasizing Napoleon's part in it, but said that
the current crisis in Europe disposed France to effect a Spanish-
American settlement "on a plan analogous to what our ministers
had proposed." Not a moment should be lost in pressing for it.
Formal war was neither necessary nor probable but "the protection of our citizens, the spirit and honor of our country, require
that force should be interposed to a certain degree." Means would
be needed which Congress alone could furnish or deny. Thus the
emphasis was militant, but the request was for means of negotiating for objects already proposed—purchase of the Floridas and indemnity for spoliations.

The message was referred to a committee headed by John Randolph and including Nicholson and a much-touted new Democrat
from Massachusetts, Barnabas Bidwell. To understand what followed, one must be familiar with several matters involving Randolph. Some weeks before Congress reconvened he informed
Gallatin that he intended to spend several years in Europe and
added:

"On my return a king of the Romans will have been elected and
if he will let us be at peace I for one will promise not to disturb
his repose. I regret exceedingly Mr. Jefferson's resolution to re-

tire. . . . If I were sure that Monroe would succeed him my regret would be very much diminished."

Whether or not Randolph was suggesting that he be put out of Madison's way through a diplomatic appointment, his letter pointed to his availability for the expected vacancy at London. As congressmen gathered, rumors went around that the administration was tired of the eccentric Virginian and intended to make Bidwell its chief agent in the House. The latter, a noted lawyer, could hold his own in a prepared speech, but he was utterly destitute, a friendly critic lamented, "of every quality which fits a man for intrigue" or spirited defense. His ambition and maladroitness were made evident when he attempted to keep a portion of the annual message from being referred to Randolph, and was bowled over by Speaker Macon and Nicholson.

About this time, Nicholson handed President Jefferson a letter received from Major James Bruff. It credited General Wilkinson with saying that the President had written that he would never appoint such violent men as Randolph and Nicholson to office. Bruff's purpose was plain—to hamper the confirmation of Wilkinson as governor of (upper) Louisiana. Jefferson returned the letter without a word. His intention, he said afterward, was to treat "so palpably absurd" a charge with silent contempt, but Randolph and Nicholson construed it as an admission.[7]

Thus, Randolph was fully set to break with the administration and attack Madison for Monroe's benefit. His desire to take the latter's place was increased by his pro-British political slant and an obsessive desire to gild the family lily—to link his descent from Pocahontas with British coats of arms. "He values nobility of birth very highly," wrote Foster, "and is intimately acquainted with all our great families, even to their estates."[8]

Randolph and Bidwell clashed at once in committee. The New Englander proposed a Florida appropriation, which all knew that the cabinet had approved. Randolph protested that the message contained not a syllable on that subject. Obtaining an interview with Jefferson, he was asked to recommend a $2,000,000 initial appropriation. Madison supported the President's request and

Gallatin gave Randolph a detailed financial plan. Rejecting this as a delivery of the public purse to the first cutthroat that came along, the chairman persuaded the committee to propose instead that enough troops be raised to protect the southern frontiers and chastise Spanish intruders. Congress, more responsive to presidential wishes, appropriated $2,000,000 and used the exact language employed by Randolph in 1803 to finance the Louisiana purchase.[9]

On the day this bill passed the House, Madison's pamphlet on neutral trade was distributed in Congress. The President followed with a special message on that subject and impressment. At the Senate's request, Madison furnished a short, clear statement of the adverse changes in British policy. The consequence was a resolution by Gregg of Pennsylvania to prohibit the importation of British goods till these evils were corrected. Senator Smith sent Madison a bill less destructive of import duties. Similar in principle to Madison's 1794 retaliatory system, it proposed to bar a specific list of British goods. With some revision, this formed the basis of a substitute for Gregg's resolution, offered by Nicholson. A few nights later Senator Adams went to a party at Madison's house ("about seventy persons of both sexes") and talked at length with the Secretary.

"His system of proceeding towards Great Britain [reads the Adams diary] is, to establish permanent commercial distinctions between her and other nations—a retaliating navigation act; and aggravated duties on articles imported from her. This is doubtless the President's favorite policy."

Adams found this belief verified when he dined with Jefferson: "His own preference is manifestly for Nicholson's resolution, which is indeed a renewal of his own project in 1794, then produced in Congress by Mr. Madison." This was a typical bestowal of credit. Jefferson had been five years in France when Madison first proposed this system in 1789 and was a private citizen when Madison reoffered it in 1794. It became "his own project" because he indorsed it in a report to Congress between those dates.[10]

Randolph lay low until the debate on Gregg's resolution opened in March. In the meantime his devoted follower, Clark of Virginia, failed in an effort to have him appointed minister to Great Britain. Reports swept the capital that Randolph had applied for the place and been turned down. Both Jefferson and Madison privately denied that he had sought the appointment either directly or indirectly. Clark told the President's secretary, later, that he "discovered Mr. Randolph was on the eve of a rupture with the administration and wished him out of the way, fearful of the consequences." But the historian George Tucker, who knew Madison intimately, had this to say: "Mr. Madison had expressed to one of Mr. Randolph's friends and admirers his opinion of Mr. Randolph's unfitness for the office of minister to Great Britain."

It mattered little whether he actually said this. Failure to act on Clark's suggestion, after Randolph himself had given notice of his desire to spend an indefinite period in Europe, carried the clear implication of unfitness. An epoch which began in envious hatred could only progress to fury.[11]

Toward the end of February, Randolph had his last amicable talk with the President. The time fits a story which Monroe received from George Erving in cipher and placed in his papers without an interlining. Deciphered a century and a half later, it reads:

"It is said that Randolph asked when Mr. Monroe would return home. The President answered, not until his successor arrives. The other bluntly observed that he, Mr. Monroe, would be the next President."[12]

As far as it goes, that may well be correct, but it omits the salient fact that a special envoy was soon to sail with authority to take Monroe's place. Randolph, in his next letter to the minister, rejoiced that he was "about to return." With that in prospect, it was time to attack Madison.

Opposing the Gregg resolution on March 5, Randolph broke completely with the administration and made the Secretary of State his target. Congress was being asked to protect an avaricious neutral trade that would vanish in peace like a growth of fungus. It would be time enough to uphold the American flag against Britain after they were told what was to be done about Spanish invasions and piracies. Whence came this incipient war measure, based on the infatuated belief that the United States could overmatch England on the ocean? "After shrinking from the Spanish jackal, do you presume to bully the British lion?" Gregg, he noted, had said he was uninfluenced by any minister, and Randolph was willing to concede that the resolution was not the product of the cabinet.

"Not of an open declared Cabinet; but of an invisible, inscrutable, unconstitutional Cabinet, without responsibility. . . . I speak of back-stairs influence—of men who bring messages to this House, which . . . govern its decisions. . . . I shrink intuitively from this left-handed, invisible, irresponsible influence, which defies the touch, but pervades and decides everything. . . . I assert that there is no Cabinet."

What proved there was none? Why, Gallatin had told him he was not familiar with the contents of a dispatch from Monroe which the President and Madison, with devilish cunning, withheld from the House until after the Florida appropriation was voted on. Randolph did not explain why it was sent *before the Senate acted* on the $2,000,000, nor why it should have been sent in the briefing on Spanish affairs. Nine tenths of it related to Great Britain and the remainder attracted not a ripple of interest in the Senate.[13]

To identify Madison as the invisible source of backstairs influence, Randolph turned his remarks directly upon the Secretary:

"Some time ago, a book was laid on our tables, which, like some other bantlings, did not bear the name of its father. Here I was taught to expect a solution of all doubts, an end to all our difficulties. If, sir, I were the foe—as I trust I am the friend of this nation—I would exclaim, 'Oh, that mine enemy would write a book.' . . . Has any gentleman got the work?"

Somebody handed him a copy, whereupon, as Senator Smith of Maryland described the scene, "he animadverted severely" on the book, read from it, "then cast it indignantly on the floor." Extolling *War in Disguise,* he justified British conduct and censured the cupidity of American merchants. The performance lasted two and one-half hours, "replete with invective (the most severe that the English language can furnish)" against the President and Madison.

"In truth [said Smith] he astonished all his hearers by the boldness of his animadversions on executive conduct, the elegance of his language and the pointed and fine strokes of oratory. But he has left stings in the breasts of many, that never can be extracted."

The next day, mild-mannered Smilie of Pennsylvania, sixty-four-year-old dean of the House, made the response which Randolph would least like to hear:

"Notwithstanding the contempt with which a certain book was yesterday treated by the gentleman from Virginia, I will venture to predict that, when the mortal part of that gentleman and myself shall be in ashes, the author of that work will be considered a great man."

The distorting rejoinder showed how deeply this shaft cut. Smilie, said Randolph, had pronounced that "a certain book, which seems to be his political Bible . . . will live when he, and I too, sir, are laid in our graves. But, when he considers his own age, and the frailty of my constitution, he will confess that he has allowed but a short span for the existence of his favorite work." Picking up Madison's *Examination* once more, he asked defensively:

"Am I the apologist of Britain because your cause has been weakly defended, or treacherously betrayed? No, sir, this 'Examiner' is her apologist! I have not minutely dissected the work. There was no occasion for it . . . a miserable card-house of an argument which the first puff of wind must demolish."[14]

What Randolph demolished was his own leadership in Congress. Nobody could compete with him in invective, but the foreknowledge of defeat was in his outcry that leadership belonged either to him or "to Tom, Dick and Harry, to the refuse of the retail trade of politics." Arrogance bade him scream to General Thomas, "Sit down, sir, pray sit down, sir, learn to keep your proper level." But the level that changed was his own.

Nicholson's nonimportation resolution was adopted, eighty-seven to thirty-five, only nine Republicans voting no. A bare half dozen followed Randolph into chronic opposition. Jefferson wrote that he had never seen a House more solidly united for the public weal, of which there could be "no better proof than the fact that so eminent a leader should at once and almost unanimously be abandoned."

Randolph's purpose was obvious. Adams recorded it the day after the attack began, "to prevent Mr. Jefferson from consenting to serve again, and Mr. Madison from being his successor." Pickering saw an attempt to decide whether "the feeble timid Madison or the dull Monroe" should extend the system under which "fools and knaves will continue to be the general favorites of the people until the government is subverted." Bidwell, Varnum and most other Republicans from Massachusetts, New York and Pennsylvania, were the friends of Madison, he reported, while Randolph and his special adherents supported Monroe. Merry, little as he liked Madison, saw it the same way. Randolph's assault was an effort "to lower his political character and estimation in order that Mr. Monroe . . . might be the only person looked up to as proper to succeed to the Presidency."[15]

Jefferson quickly warned Monroe to be on his guard against new friends who were "attacking your old ones out of friendship to you, but in a way to render you great injury." Saying that both his station and his friendships prescribed "a sacred neutrality" in coming political events, he advised Monroe to come home before Congress met again. This letter lay for months in Norfolk and was returned. However, the special envoy carried formal papers from Madison authorizing Monroe to come home, and another letter from the President suggesting that he do so in the fall. Very different was the message Randolph sent his candidate:

"Everything is made a business of bargain and traffic, the ultimate object of which is to raise Mr. Madison to the presidency. To this the old Republican party will never consent, nor can New York be brought into the measure. . . . Need I tell you that they (the old Republicans) are united in your support? That they look to you sir for the example which this nation has yet to receive—to demonstrate that the government can be conducted on open, upright principles, without intrigue or any species of disingenuous artifice."[16]

To further these open, upright principles, the "descendant of Powhatan" (as Dolley Madison's congressional brother-in-law called him) raised his tomahawk once more on April 5. To reopen the subject of Florida, he declaimed against the omission of the President's confidential message from the Secret Journal of December 6. Recounting committee proceedings, he told of his endeavors to "protect the Southern frontier from Spanish inroad and insult," but said he found the executive department strangely unwilling to take a decided stand. With this prelude, Randolph delivered the attack on Madison for which his whole maneuver was planned:

"I found what was worse—before I left town to go to Baltimore—from a conversation with what has been considered the head of the first Executive department under the Government, that France was the great obstacle to the compromise of Spanish differences; that France would not permit Spain to come to any accommodation with us, . . . and that we must give her money. From the moment I heard that declaration, all the objections I originally had to the procedure were aggravated to the highest possible degree. I considered it a base prostration of the national character, to excite one nation by money to bully another nation out of its property, and from that moment, and to the last moment of my life, my confidence in the principles of the man entertaining these sentiments, died, never to live again."

At this moment, "with an indignant gesture," Randolph threw his hat across the room. From his remarks, he said, the public would see what members of Congress were disposed to act on "the most authentic information from Europe" (that is, follow Monroe's advice to take the Floridas by force) rather than work through a foreign power, "especially in the shape of a bribe."

Coming to Madison's defense, Jackson presented a denial by Gallatin that Madison had ever attempted to send the $2,000,000 to France before it was appropriated. Findley said Randolph had introduced a system of slander previously unheard-of in Congress.

"It is contrary to good order, it is an outrage on decency, to defame the character, or impeach the conduct, in this way, of public officers or citizens, on this floor. . . . If Mr. Randolph had a charge against him [Madison] he ought to have moved for an inquiry . . . but this would not have answered the gentleman's purposes of slander. The Secretary of State would have had the opportunity of defending his own character."[17]

The repetitious hat-throwing stunt merely called attention to the dishonesty of the whole performance. Three years earlier Randolph had been the legislative leader in furnishing the money with which the United States bought, from France, an empire which France was then bullying out of Spain. In 1804 he introduced the Mobile bill, and criticized the administration for not interpreting it as a directive to take West Florida by force. In December 1805, having decided to break with the administration, his first thought was to attack the President's message from the opposite angle. Near the end of the year Jefferson's private secretary dined with others at the home of George Hay in Richmond.

"Previous to dinner [Burwell recorded] Mr. Hay read to us a letter from Mr. R[andolph] who had just returned from Baltimore to Washington and previous to the report he made as chair-

man of the select committee. In that letter he said the language
of the P[resident]'s message had been loudly applauded by the
F[ederalist]s and they were consistent, that [it] breathed war,
and very eloquently contended against a course which would involve the country in war."

Why did Randolph say nothing to the committee about his
talk with Madison which even Nicholson first heard of in the
April 5 speech? Because if truly reported, it would have aided
the appropriation, and a distortion then would have been detected.
Randolph's original objective was not to defeat the appropriation,
but to force the President to ask for it directly, instead (as he
complained) of throwing the onus on Congress of converting
warlike words into a pacific policy. So little was he concerned
over the money issue that when an intestinal upset kept him from
a committee meeting, he wrote to Nicholson: "If *you* persist in
voting the money, the committee will alter its report."[18]

Then came Madison's rejection of the request that Randolph
be made minister to England—a fearful blow to his pride—and
the discovery, from Monroe's letter sent to Congress on January
17, that his presidential favorite preferred force as a means of
obtaining the Floridas. The congressman who, less than a month
before, had "eloquently contended" against the President's message because it "breathed war" now swung passionately to the
other side, crying out against the prostration of national honor,
denouncing the "poltroons" of the executive department for their
"cowardly behavior." To the same end—to push Madison down
while pulling Monroe up—but with personal rancor as a stronger
driving force, he finally assailed Madison with a distorted version
of something said four months before.

Madison, who usually ignored personal slanders, prepared a
statement "for the public if found expedient," but merely left it
among his papers. "On no occasion, nor with any person whatever," had he ever suggested the use of money without congressional authorization, nor otherwise than "in a bona fide purchase
for a valuable consideration in territory," with payment to the nation owning and conveying it.

Except among Randolph devotees, this story was generally regarded as a canard. Findley told the Virginian that when his habits were considered, the House would feel justified in receiving his assertions as "the dreaming effusions of a vivid imagination, highly disordered." Jackson, because of personal ties, felt debarred from vindicating Madison's character but observed that there was no need to do so. His well-spent life was "a complete answer and refutation of the malignant calumnies which disappointed ambition and prejudice have given rise to," and his conduct and character had "made an impression on the American people, not to be erased by declamation unsupported by fact."

Randolph himself, besides distorting Madison's remarks, revealed his own readiness to go full tilt in any direction. To sustain his objection to buying Florida through France, he demanded that the United States deal with Spain alone. But to prove the greater iniquity of France he cried out:

"Why do I talk of Spain? . . . There exists no such nation, no such being as a Spanish king, or minister. . . . Take [Yrujo's] instructions from his pocket tomorrow, they are signed 'Charles Maurice Talleyrand.' "[19]

If that was the situation, Spain could not sell, and a resort to force against her would mean war with France. The alternatives were to buy through France or invite war with both countries. *That was just what Madison told Randolph.* One could deduce this from the Madison-Jefferson correspondence, but proof of it is in Randolph's second version of their talk. Writing under the name of "Decius" in August 1806, he quoted Madison as saying "that France wanted money, and that we must give it to her or have a Spanish and French war." Here was a twisted version of the alternatives actually faced by the United States. By omitting "if the United States is to obtain Florida," and saying nothing of a purchase, Randolph created the appearance of an American surrender to French demands for war funds. At the same time, by inserting the Franco-Spanish threat of war, he destroyed his original charge that the administration wanted to bribe France into bullying Spain.

GEORGE CLINTON
By Ezra Ames

CHARLES COTESWORTH PINCKNEY
Miniature by Malbone

TIMOTHY PICKERING
By Gilbert Stuart

DR. WILLIAM THORNTON
By Gilbert Stuart

CHARLES PINCKNEY
Attributed to Gilbert Stuart

Why did he change the accusation? Because Napoleon, after smashing the Third Coalition at the Battle of Austerlitz, was reducing Europe to vassalage. Randolph's charge of corruption had fallen flat, repelled by Madison's lifelong reputation for integrity. But with hysteric fear of imperial France beginning to grip those who had once shivered at the French Revolution, a public man might be destroyed by implanting the suspicion that he was subservient to the conqueror of Europe.

Randolph's allies in Virginia took up the attack, but, wrote W. C. Nicholas to Madison, "your life has been so pure that no man who values his own character will venture to make any charge against you that is susceptible of proof." None had made the least impression, he went on, except an intimation that Madison had been trying to unite Republicans and Federalists along lines favorable to the latter. The cited evidence was that he had retained Wagner and Brent, protégés of Pickering and Hamilton, in the State Department, and "it is roundly asserted that much of the scurrility that appears in the Washington *Federalist* is written by W[agne]r." Judging the chief clerk by his later conduct, this charge may have been true, but Madison trusted him. A few weeks earlier, having Senators Pickering and Hillhouse as dinner guests, he brought in Wagner's name, eulogized his work and character, and concluded with the words: "In short, he is fit for Secretary of State." Late in the year, Wagner asked Madison to help him get a collectorship—a political sinecure— saying that "whatever your opinion may be, it will be prized as an evidence of that goodness which I have always experienced from you." He did not get it, and resigned to become one of the most scurrilous Federalist editors in the country, attacking his former chief with a malignancy worthy of Pickering himself.[20]

Eliza Trist had remarked twenty years before that Madison was "too amiable in his disposition to bear up against a torrent of abuse." There was no sign of that during the Randolph attacks, although he was not in good shape physically. Late in January a fall down his front steps dislocated his ankle. Healing took months. In March he wrote to Monroe that "for the last year, especially for five or six months past the weight of business has almost broken me down and robbed me of any leisure for writing to my friends." The purpose of this letter was to tell Monroe that, although high value was placed on his services in the coming joint mission, the President was too much impressed with the reasons given for his return, "already so long suspended, to require a further sacrifice of what you owe to yourself and your family." In other words, Monroe was free to come home and run for President.

If there was any load on Madison's spirit it was not evident when he and Dolley visited the farm home of Publisher Samuel Harrison Smith after the hardest of Randolph's attacks. "Mrs. M[adison] was all that was tender, affectionate and attractive as usual," wrote the hostess, and "Mr. M[adison] was in one of his most sportive moods."[21]

The overthrown leader of Congress did not confine his slanders to Madison. Governed by those open, upright principles which he had extolled to Monroe, Randolph picked up the Federalist whispers against the morals of Dolley Madison and Anna Cutts. Suggesting the calumnies instead of specifying them, he wrote to the London minister:

"There is another consideration which I know not how to touch. You, my dear sir, cannot be ignorant, although of all mankind you, perhaps, have the least cause to know it, how deeply the respectability of any character may be impaired by an unfortunate matrimonial connection. I can pursue this subject no further. It is at once too delicate and too mortifying."[22]

Coming from a man who, after being a house guest at Morrisania, wrote to Gouverneur Morris accusing his wife of incest and murder, this attack showed real restraint.[23] The insinuation against Dolley Madison had too much method in it to be put among the verbal violences which graded into Randolph's later insanity. However, there was something akin to madness in his whole reaction to the thought of Madison becoming President. If he achieved nothing else, he started the campaign of 1808 two years ahead of time.

CHAPTER XXIV

Visitor from Venezuela

The Marqués de Casa Yrujo was Spanish to the point of chauvinism. But as the son-in-law of Thomas McKean, governor, judge and political boss, he knew that the most exalted foreigner had rights equal to those of the lowliest American, and these included the right to tell the government to go to hell. The place to tell it was in the newspapers.

After the State Department modified his ouster by agreeing that he might depart voluntarily, the minister made no move to do so. Asperities softened a little in Philadelphia, during Madison's stay there in 1805, but this did not prevent a roundabout hint in November that his return to Washington would be unwelcome. He responded with a long and savage letter to Madison accusing the President of making false statements about Spain in his annual message.

On January 15 the marquis showed up in the capital. He was received by Madison with silent frigidity. That same afternoon, as he was dining with the French minister, Yrujo was handed a letter from the Secretary of State expressing surprise that he should have returned "as if nothing had occurred rendering such a step improper." His remaining in Washington was dissatisfactory to the President and his departure from the country was expected as soon as winter weather was past.

Yrujo asked Turreau to protest this action in the name of the diplomatic corps, but the French minister "saw a bad augury from his conduct" and refused. The Spaniard notified Madison that his arrival was "an innocent and legal act" and he intended to remain as "long as it may suit the interests of the king my master or my own personal convenience." He then, Turreau reported, "maladroitly recalled his [bribery] affair with Major Jackson," and was foolish enough to visit repeatedly with the British minister, with whose country Spain was at war, just as

323

the Executive was trying to shift congressional hostility from Spain to England. "I tried to calm him," wrote Turreau, "but refrained from giving him advice he did not ask for."

To cap the climax, Yrujo sent a protest to all foreign diplomats against the government's action. This circular and his December 6 assault on the President were delivered to a Federalist newspaper in Baltimore, and he "left Washington suddenly [wrote Turreau] just when everything indicated that he should remain there, especially the order enjoining him to leave."[1]

Publication of these letters (followed by the ones defying Madison and Jefferson) made Yrujo the hero of the hour among Federalists. His secretary Fatio orated to a group of senators at Turreau's house:

"Your laws I know. Your Constitution I understand. I have lived here nearly twelve years and I know that your President, with all his power, hath no authority to send any man, not the meanest malefactor, out of this country without his consent. Much less can he remove an accredited minister against his will from residing in any town or city, as long as he pleaseth."

Yrujo had not been *ordered* to leave Washington, but Senator Adams introduced a bill giving the President power to compel offending diplomats to leave the capital or the country. At a Madison reception that evening, the Secretary "expressed his entire approbation" of the *principle* of the bill. In other words, the administration didn't want it. They had no desire to offend other ministers nor to let it appear, by inference, that the President did not already have this power under the law of nations. Again Adams went to Madison's house, this time to dinner "with the Judges Marshall, Washington and Johnson, Mr. Breckinridge, now Attorney-General," and others, plus ladies and cards in the evening. No more was said about his bill, which both parties joined in defeating some days later.[2]

Recording a cabinet decision, in the following summer, against expelling Yrujo by force, Jefferson noted that "Mr. Madison seemed of a different opinion." Aside from pleasing the Federalists, the Spanish minister's conduct merely laid up trouble for his country. He severed diplomatic relations as completely, at one end of the line, as if the two countries were at war. Henceforth he could act only through the French minister.

The necessity to do so was at hand. For more than a dozen years, General Francisco Miranda had been seeking British and American aid for the liberation of his native Venezuela from Spain. In 1798 Alexander Hamilton, thirsting for military glory, wrote to Minister Rufus King that he wished the United States "to furnish the whole land force necessary" to Miranda's project, the command of which "would very naturally fall upon me."

That plan failing, Miranda once more sought British help, but kept in constant touch with King and Treaty Commissioner Gore. On November 9, 1805, he appeared in New York, bearing a letter from Privy Councilor Nicholas Vansittart to King. British plans to aid Miranda, wrote the Secretary for Ireland, had been given up because of the continental crisis. The general was going to see what resources, public or private, America could furnish. "Your influence will be of the utmost importance to him." Vansittart could not speak officially, but believed that once the expedition was under way, Britain's interest in South American trade expansion would force almost any wartime government to support it vigorously.

Miranda at once found a partner: Colonel William Stephens Smith, son-in-law of former President Adams and surveyor of the port of New York, with whom Miranda had once traveled in Prussia. Smith put him in touch with "Commodore" Jacob Lewis, commander of "two or three stout armed ships" (Rufus King's words) owned by Samuel G. Ogden—part of that same flotilla whose return from St. Domingo had been celebrated so joyously by King and Ogden in the previous spring. Miranda had little money. The British government had spent more than $100,000 on him in 1801-02, but his present resources, aside from a £700 British pension, were limited to a London letter of credit for £800 and a promise of twice that for personal expenses. He and Smith soon found, as Rufus King predicted, that they would not get far unless the government was brought in.

On King's advice, Miranda left for the national capital. To pave the way, King sent the Vansittart letter to Madison. In Philadelphia, Miranda's denunciation of the new American plutocracy helped win him a glowing letter of introduction from Dr. Rush. "He knows your character," wrote the physician to Madison, "and longs to do homage to your principles."

In Philadelphia, also, the revolutionist fell in with Aaron Burr, just back from the West. The two competitors for British money talked warily. Burr, a week before, had asked Merry to tell his government that Miranda was "notorious here and elsewhere for his indiscretion and bad faith" and possessed no talents that could render him useful. Miranda was not yet ready to call his rival (as he did later) a detestable and infamous man.[3]

Vansittart's letter made it certain that Madison would receive Miranda, if for no other reason than to probe British intentions. The South American walked into a cabinet meeting, had two conferences with Madison and sat next to the President at dinner. He then returned to New York and gave an account of the government's attitude which both Madison and Jefferson branded as false when they finally heard about it. Miranda reported (King wrote in a memo) that Madison's manner was encouraging at first but more reserved after the matter was laid before the President. The government could give "neither sanction nor succor to the enterprise." When Miranda remarked that this might deter people from aiding him, "the Secretary replied that the United States was a free country, where every one may do what the laws do not forbid." He endorsed the fitness of Smith, Lewis and Ogden for the expedition. The conference ended with advice "that whatever might be done should be discreetly done and with the understanding on the part of Miranda, that although the government would not sanction, it would wink at the expedition."

Madison's own account, sent two months later to Armstrong, stated that Miranda "disclosed in very general terms his purpose of instituting a revolution" and, expecting a Spanish-American rupture, wanted help. He was told that although the government was "free to hear whatever he might choose to impart to it," there would be no deviation from the rules of amity and neutrality. If hostilities toward Spain became necessary, they would not take place in an underhand and illicit way.

"He was reminded that it would be incumbent on the United States to punish any transactions within their jurisdiction which might according to the law of nations involve an hostility against Spain, and that a statute of Congress had made express provision for such a case."

This warning, the Secretary said, resulted from an apprehension that Miranda might attract individuals with military experience. "It was never suspected that the enlistment of a military corps of any size would be thought of." As to the exportation of arms, the government relied on the law forbidding unlawful use of armed vessels and anticipated that the bill prohibiting exportation of arms would become law before Miranda could do anything along that line.

Miranda's story carries internal evidence of falsity. Knowing that a private filibustering expedition was contrary to law, why would Madison remark that any one could do "what the laws do not forbid"? If he said this at all, he was talking about exportation of arms, which did not violate the law. As for endorsing Smith and Ogden, it was two months before Madison learned that "a Mr. Ogden" owned the ships. His ignorance of Smith's part is evident from a sharp letter asking Collector Gelston why his office had neither reported nor obstructed the Miranda expedition. That duty belonged to Smith. It is fantastic, moreover, to suppose that the Secretary of State would urge Miranda to be discreet, and be so indiscreet himself as to tolerate the participation of a federal official in an act of war against Spain.[4]

It is evident that Miranda was received in friendly fashion and was told that the government would not sanction his enterprise. The rest of his story was invention or distortion designed to help him raise money and men, and is demonstrably false in enough details to discredit the remainder. However, in failing to forewarn Gelston's office, Madison and Jefferson were not only negligent but naïve. They trusted to luck that Miranda would stay within the law and grossly underestimated the effect of receiving him at all. Doing so revealed their sympathy with his purposes and gave the color of truth to any false report he might make to his associates, whom he had every motive for deceiving.

Miranda used his story effectively. Ogden's armed ships, the *Indostan* and *Emperor,* already loaded with contraband, sailed on December 23 under Commodore Lewis for Port au Prince, where they hoped to obtain recruits for Miranda among 2,500 mulattoes under General Pétion, who had appealed to Lewis on his last voyage to save them from Emperor Dessalines' black troops. Ogden agreed to advance $20,000 to Miranda, to help outfit the 18-gun *Leander* for a pretended voyage to St. Domingo. From there it would sail to a secret destination, where Miranda would pay 200 per cent of the total value of the ship and its outfit, disbursements and cargo. In case of success he would pay 300 per cent.

To another merchant, the general sold drafts for $10,000 on Vansittart and John Turnbull, whose acceptance of them was encouraged by fresh exaggerations. The administration, Miranda wrote to the British undersecretary, "gave me a perfect, tacit consent, and left to merchants the option of doing the rest. . . . American merchants are furnishing forty-five thousand pounds."[5]

Colonel Smith, meanwhile, gathered ardent young men "of good standing in society, though . . . of crooked fortunes" (a recruit's description which fitted Smith himself) for a vague adventure which the government was said to smile on. As port officer, he cleared the *Leander* for Jacmel on January 23, evading the armed-ships law by listing her as a foreign vessel. Three days later the ship dropped down to Staten Island, where a couple hundred blue-uniformed youths came aboard, including William Steuben Smith, grandson of President Adams, as aide to the general.

On January 25 Miranda showed his associates two letters predated the 22nd. There was a friendly note to the President, casually referring to South American independence, and as artful a missive to Madison as any man ever penned:

"Permit me, on the point of leaving the United States, to address a few words to thank you for the attentions you have so willingly shown me during my stay in Washington. The important matters which I had the honor to communicate to you then will remain, I doubt not, in the most profound secrecy until the final result of this delicate affair. I have acted here on that supposition, conforming in everything to the intentions of the government which I hope I have grasped and observed exactly and with discretion."[6]

Miranda gave copies of these letters to King and delivered the originals to Smith for belated mailing. Ogden was so thrilled that he accepted Miranda's drafts for $25,000 on two merchants in Trinidad, and bought more munitions. His total investment in the *Leander* was now $72,473.80, for which he was to be repaid either $144,927.60 or $217,401.40,[7] depending on the fate of the expedition. Uneasy recruits, hearing of the letters, were less inclined to believe the "whispers through the ship" that they were embarking on a voyage of desperate piracy. But the supreme art lay in the wording. To Madison, who did not yet know what Miranda was doing, the one to him was an assurance that the general was staying within the law. But to those who knew the truth, it was evidence of the government's complicity. The timing was so perfect that it helped Miranda win men and money, yet reached Washington too late for a stop-order to be effective if suspicions were aroused.

At some later time, Madison penned two footnotes on Miranda's manuscript. The "important matters" were identified as "what passed with the British government" (too narrow a description) and he wrote "not true" below the general's assertion that he had "observed exactly" the intentions of the government.[8]

The *Leander* sailed on February 2. The truth came to Madison, like a blow in the face, four days later. From a Philadelphia "gentleman of respectability" he received an account of Miranda's actions, and on that same evening (unknown to him) an express brought Yrujo's dispatches to Turreau. Madison hurried to the President's house. They had to choose between criminal prose-

cution, with the certainty of being pictured as accomplices, and
the national danger that lay in inaction. The decision was immediate. The next day, February 7, Madison wrote to United States
Attorney Sanford in New York:

"By the express direction of the President, I request you to en-
quire diligently into the facts alleged and any others which may
be made known to you relative to the fitting out and sailing of
the *Leander,* and to report to me as soon as possible, whether any
persons now within the jurisdiction of the United States have
thereby rendered themselves liable to a criminal prosecution, with
their names and a statement of the offenses respectively, which
there may be reason to believe may be proved against them."

Turreau came to see Madison the following morning, full of
suspicion that the government was behind Miranda. The interview became a famous one—made so by Henry Adams' appalling
mistranslation of the French minister's account of it to Yrujo.
Here is what appears in the Adams history:

"I was this morning with Madison. I imparted to him my
suspicions and yours. I sought his eyes, and, what is rather rare,
I met them. He was in a state of extraordinary prostration while
I was demanding from him a positive explanation of the proceedings in question."

A devastating picture! Here is the same passage (plus an
omitted clause) translated in 1952 by a language expert of the
French embassy in Washington, who had no knowledge of the
Adams rendering:

"I was with Madison this morning. I let him know my suspicions and yours. I looked into his eyes, and what is rather un-
usual, I caught the meaning in them: I think that I found strong
evidence to support the subject of our fears. He was very dejected

while I was requesting a positive explanation of the proceedings in question."[9]

The rest of the letter follows:

"He found it difficult to break the silence, and finally answered that the President had acted ahead of my representations by ordering measures against the accomplices still on the continent and against the guilty ones who should return here. I allow you to judge whether I was satisfied with this response and I left him rather abruptly in order to write to him. This I am engaged in doing."

The picture of Madison as a half-fainting, shifty-eyed weakling comes entirely from Adams, not from Turreau. There is no reason to suppose that the historian intentionally falsified this document,[10] but that does not alter the effect. The blunders in this translation, made in gloating innocence, and going uncorrected for more than sixty years, have probably done more to blast Madison's posthumous reputation than all the misrepresentations of his Federalist adversaries. More inexcusable, because deliberate, was Adams' failure to mention Madison's earlier letter to District Attorney Sanford. Yet this letter was lying right under Adams' eyes in the French Archives—two copies of it in fact, one in English, one in French, and he actually copied the dispatch to which the French version was annexed.[11] Failure to mention this letter, especially after the character-destroying mistranslation, could lead only to the suspicion that Madison was lying about the steps already taken, and made all subsequent actions look like a fear-engendered consequence of the French minister's protest.

In a succession of written exchanges Turreau bridged the gap between Yrujo and Madison by quoting long passages from the former's protesting letters. But when he undertook to forward a note addressed by the Spanish minister to Madison, it was returned to the French legation unopened. It ought to be presumed, tartly commented the Secretary, that the Spanish government had too much respect both to itself and the United States "to have employed at this day the writer of the letter," especially as other Spanish agents were available.

To Turreau's remark that "disagreeable conjectures" might be drawn from Miranda's sailing just as a British squadron occupied Buenos Aires, Madison replied that the rectitude of the United States was not to be judged by a casual coincidence of dates—whenever foreign hostilities were judged necessary, they would be conducted in a frank and legal manner. A complaint against the failure of the United States to detect the conspiracy was put into reverse. Madison had seen with regret that the affair was so masked that it escaped the eyes, not only of the federal officers, "but of the foreign agents on the spot, whose viligance must have been particularly excited on such an occasion."[12]

This struck deeper than the Secretary realized. Before Miranda left Washington he met Jonathan Dayton (no doubt primed by Burr to draw him out) and related his version of the talks with Madison. Dayton, to ruin the rival enterprise, promptly relayed the story to Yrujo, who reported it to his government on December 31. It appeared, Yrujo wrote, that the Secretary of State was cold and circumspect, but informed Miranda that although the American government could not do what was asked (furnish six frigates and 3,000 marines), "if private persons wished to take part in the enterprise on their own account and risk, and in a manner which would not compromise the administration of this country, it would close its eyes to their conduct." The Spanish minister thereupon directed Thomas Stoughton, Spanish consul in New York, to watch Miranda and report his activities.

That was the end of it, for Yrujo, until February 4, when he sent his excited report to Turreau based on three letters from Stoughton (the earliest dated January 30, though it reads as if there were earlier ones) and a second one from Dayton. Why was there such a failure in Spanish espionage and preventive measures? Yrujo explained the latter point to his government. He had just been informed by Dayton that Miranda, in December, expressed fear of failure should Yrujo learn of the expedition. Madison replied that Yrujo's recall having been asked for (fourteen months before) he would refuse to treat with him, "and that

once the communication was broken, there would remain no way
for me to thwart the departure of the ships."

This was marvelous indeed! Between December 31, the day
on which he notified Madrid of the Miranda-Madison talks, and
January 24, the day of his rupture with Madison, Yrujo called
on Madison once and wrote two letters to him without even
mentioning Miranda. He visited all other cabinet members and
said nothing. Then he brought on the rupture himself by a newspaper assault on Madison and Jefferson which inspired one editor
to exclaim: "In no other country under heaven would the ambassador d'Yrujo be suffered to remain one hour." And this rupture he called a plot by Madison to keep him from thwarting the
departure of Miranda's ship, which cleared customs the day before the rupture occurred.[13]

Yrujo could have blocked the expedition by telling Madison
what he told his own government. Instead, he went to Washington for the sole purpose of insulting the Secretary of State and
the President. Learning, on his return to Philadelphia, the details he could have known earlier, he took frantic and successful
steps to defeat Miranda by warnings to the Spanish colonies, and
covered his own dereliction by disingenuous reports to Madrid.
Wounded vanity and passionate anger governed the Spanish minister's course.[14]

Early in March word came to Washington that Smith and
Ogden had been held for trial. Through "much noise and mis-
representation," Madison reported to Monroe, vigorous attempts
were being made to turn the affair into a battery against the administration. Miranda "had the address" to make Colonel Smith
and others believe that he had "enlisted the Executive into a secret
sanction to his project." They fell into the snare and, when examined, repeated Miranda's representations.

"The truth is that the government proceeded with the most
delicate attention to its duty; on the one hand keeping in view
all its legal obligations to Spain; and on the other not making
itself, by going beyond them, a party against the people of South
America."

Madison and Gallatin wanted Smith removed from office at once, but Jefferson expressed doubt whether that should be done before a conviction. Gallatin then told his chief that retention of an officer who had admitted his guilt would be considered by Spain and France as evidence of governmental connivance; also Smith had falsified his accounts to cheat the government. He was ousted.

Turreau meanwhile was not precisely happy. Though "little satisfied with the vague, meaningless and involved reply, typical of Madison," to his first note on Miranda, he was not going to sacrifice French interests to help a Spanish diplomat whose "immoderate desire to satisfy his personal resentments has nearly destroyed his political measures." So, waiting until the House passed the bill barring trade with St. Domingo, the French minister prodded Madison for the information he had requested a month before.

In return, Madison gently chided Turreau for not restraining himself "at least until the result of the promised measures could be communicated," and happily notified him of the arrests. Telling of Smith's ouster, he said this officer had aggravated his guilt by his false and self-interested claim that Miranda had the secret sanction of the administration. A government, he observed, ought not to be held responsible for circumstances of which it had neither knowledge nor suspicion:

"It is certain that there never was any suspicion of such a hostile expedition in a port of the United States. It was not improbable, after the arrival and movements of Miranda, and judging by the project which had for a long time been attributed to him, that he might attempt to export certain articles contained in the list of contraband of war. But the laws in force were inadequate to thwart such an attempt."[15]

That gets into the real story. To complete it, add the assertion that the United States observed its legal obligations to Spain, but did not take a stand against the people of South America by going beyond them. Combined, these statements make it evident that

Madison and Jefferson neither sanctioned nor winked at an armed expedition. But they expected military supplies to be exported for revolutionary purposes and had neither the desire nor the legal obligation to interfere with that.

The Federalists now had a field day, repeating and amplifying the tale of government complicity. Aaron Burr gave them effective support. His henchman John Swartwout, as United States marshal, had the choosing of federal juries in New York. For the grand jury he called twenty-two Federalists and two others. The trial jury panel included thirty-three Federalists, three Burrites and six Republicans, the majority being, according to the district attorney, "men of the most decided and violent character in politics." Unable to refuse indictments, the grand jury followed them with a report accusing the district judge of bias against the defendants.[16]

Smith and Ogden spread the charge of governmental connivance by memorials to Congress in which Miranda's story of the talks with Madison was garishly set forth. Presented by Federalists in both houses, all reference to the memorials was expunged from the Senate Journals by almost a party vote. In the House, Sponsor Josiah Quincy made the mistake of saying that other members had information supporting the charges. Forced to retract, he said he had no intention of sanctioning the memorials, which then were unanimously condemned as an interference with a cause in court. Only eight Federalists voted against a resolve that they were "unsupported by any evidence which, in the least degree, criminates the Executive government." The House voted 70 to 13 that they were "insidiously calculated to excite unjust suspicions" against the administration. Deep suspicion, however, was felt even by Republicans, so neatly did Miranda do his work.[17]

Mixing politics and defense, the Smith-Ogden battery of Federalist lawyers issued subpoenas for the entire cabinet—Madison, Gallatin, Dearborn and Smith—as witnesses. "It is perhaps not unfortunate," commented Madison to the President, "that so aggregate a blow has been aimed at the administration, as it places in a stronger view the malice of the proceeding and the incon-

venience to the public business which would result from an attendance of all the heads of departments." Still he found an impression that attendance was inevitable.

The defense, District Attorney Sanford wrote, intended either
to force the cabinet to subordinate its dignity and duty, or raise
a clamor against them if they refused. Not being personally
acquainted with Madison, he asked Gallatin to tell him that his
presence was highly desirable.

"The alleged assent to Miranda's preparations is ascribed prin-
cipally to him and it is in his power to put the tale to silence and
refute the calumny. If he should not attend, inferences the most
injurious, however unjust, will be made and they will perhaps
be of a nature well calculated to catch popular prejudice."

The cabinet was aware, Madison wrote some weeks later, that
to ignore the subpoenas might result in an improper acquittal.
That seemed better, in a permanent view, "than to abandon our
public duties and exhibit the heads of departments as the sport
of party management." If they appeared it would not be to give
evidence, which, being irrelevant, "could not be received, but
rather themselves to be examined as so many culprits." He knew,
of course, that if he took the stand, Miranda's shrewd letter to him
would be dragged in through questions, even though the judges
ruled out its admission in evidence, as they would have done.[18]

The outcome was a joint letter from three subpoenaed cabinet
members (the process-server missed Gallatin) informing the
judges, with regret, that the President had signified that it was
impossible to dispense with their official duties at this juncture.
They suggested that a court commission take their testimonies
in Washington. The defense lawyers rejected this proposal,
which did not serve their purpose, and asked for an attachment
against the secretaries, both for contempt of court and to compel
them to testify.

Supreme Court Justice Paterson (a fair-minded Federalist who
sat with the district judge) replied that the court had power to
compel the witnesses to attend, but their distance from the events

complained of created a presumption that their testimony was immaterial: this would have to be overcome by affidavit. Smith thereupon swore to his belief that Jefferson and Madison knew of and approved the expedition. His lawyers argued that evidence of this would absolve him, or should mitigate the punishment. Paterson replied that the President had no power to authorize anybody to violate the law and the jury had nothing to do with fixing the sentence. Cabinet testimony was held to be immaterial.

The jury didn't seem to agree with the judges. Newspapers informed Madison of the acquittal late in July, just as he was preparing to leave for Montpelier. No details being given, he tried to think of possible legal reasons for the verdict but struck nearer the truth in commenting to Jefferson: "Although I have reason to believe that my departure will be the signal for opening the federal batteries against our letter to the court, I shall postpone it for a few days only." He waited long enough to hear the story told by Pierrepont Edwards, special government counsel.

Attendance of the witnesses from Washington, wrote Edwards, was neither desired nor expected by the defense. The whole farce "was intended to create a prejudice against the prosecution, and thereby prepare the minds of the jurors for that disregard of evidence, law and argument" which displayed itself in the acquittal.

"To disgrace the President and you and the present administration was the point aimed at from the start—and it is a source of infinite mortification to the friends of the administration here that conduct, springing from such motives, should be crowned with so much success and have such cause of triumph."

The verdict was not wholly partisan, for even the Republicans on the jury voted for acquittal. Witness after witness testified to the sale of munitions to Ogden or the raising of recruits for Smith, but every one of them had been told that the government was behind Miranda. Reiteration and the absence of disproof overruled all evidence and nullified the court's instructions, while beyond all this virtually nobody regarded it as a crime to aid a revolution against Spain.[19]

Had Madison attended the trial, it would neither have saved him from partisan assault nor produced a conviction in that partisan-filled atmosphere. It was certainly to be wished, he wrote to Edwards, that a fair account of the interview of Miranda with the Executive could be laid before the public. "It would prove, I believe, that the conduct of the latter was precisely such as became the guardian of the laws and as was required by justice and sound policy." But there were insuperable objections to such a disclosure (meaning presumably that it would complicate the Florida negotiations) and it "therefore must be left to time, which alone will do justice to all parties. . . . It is against all experience that evidence, law and argument can long be borne down by such means as have been employed against them."

Jefferson said he was not dissatisfied with the result. He had no wish to see Smith imprisoned: once "a man of honor and integrity, led astray by distress," while Ogden was "too small an insect to excite any feelings." Swartwout, who packed the jury, was ordered dismissed before the acquittals.[20]

Of all the Americans involved in the Miranda affair, the one most at fault escaped most lightly. That was Rufus King. By sending the Vansittart letter to Madison, and then concealing Miranda's violation of the law, he put his country in jeopardy of war with both France and Spain. British partisans, wrote Tench Coxe to Madison before the trials, "have high expectations of this matter embroiling us with France" because of a letter from "one of the English under-secretaries . . . sent on by Mr. King to Washington." King was not fooled by Miranda's report of his talks with Madison, but virtually told him to his face that it was false. Here is the memorandum he wrote on the back of a Miranda letter dated December 30, 1805:

"Respecting succors: answered verbally, that as our government having an opening to do so, had not intimated to any of my friends in confidence even that the supplies might be made in discretion, and privately, there was a difficulty in making the same which would prevent it being done."

Instead of warning his associates against financial loss and possible prosecutions, he kept silent while they lost thousands of dollars. Scores of Americans went into Spanish prisons in a venture started with his moral support and sustained by a story which he had found by indirect inquiries to be untrue. Yet he sent the general's story to Boston as one "which . . . I fully credit," and he supported it by implication in a pretrial statement before Judge Tallmadge.[21]

Madison and Jefferson, by accepting the political punishment of the Smith-Ogden prosecution, averted the international crisis which was threatened both by their prior negligence, and by the machinations of King. Spain was not mollified, but the trials destroyed the impact of her protests to France. Talleyrand notified Madrid that the emperor (the words are paraphrased by Chargé Erving) "certainly thinks that the United States were tardy in taking measures to arrest Miranda's expedition; but that their subsequent proceedings against those who were implicated with Miranda is a perfect disavowal of any connection with that adventure." Better take advantage of that conciliatory disposition, France advised, to settle the disputes over Florida and spoliations, rather than open new grounds of dispute. Not much reliance, perhaps, could be placed on that hint to Spain, but it put an end to the hazard of war.[22]

CHAPTER XXV

TREASON BEYOND THE MOUNTAINS

AARON BURR'S intrigues were swept into the public eye in the summer of 1805 by some questions in a newspaper: "How long will it be before we shall hear of *Col. Burr* being at the head of a *revolution* party on the western waters?" Was it his purpose to form a separate government of Louisiana and the Western states, to seize and divide the public lands, to take Mexico with British aid?

Minister Merry took the story as evidence of Burr's indiscretion, betrayal, or approaching success. Late in November, he and Jonathan Dayton returned from the West, visited Merry and proceeded to Philadelphia. A few days later Jefferson received an anonymous warning about Burr's intrigues:

"You admit him at your table . . . at the very moment he is . . . conspiring against the state. . . . Watch his connections with Mr. M—y and you will find him a British pensioner and agent."

Burr's chief worry, just then, was that he was not a British pensioner. At New Orleans (he assured Merry) he found the inhabitants "firmly resolved upon separating themselves from their union with the United States." The revolt would start in the spring "provided His Majesty's government should consent to lend their assistance." On that point, "Toujours Gai" could offer no cheer. He had heard not a word from London.

Merry received a glowing account from Burr. All through the West, "persons of the greatest property and influence" were supporting his enterprise. By promising independence, he had postponed a revolt of the New Orleans French. Let a fast British warship bring him £110,000 by March or April, let small armed vessels be sent into the Mississippi, and all would be well. But should action be delayed beyond that time, "the opportunity would be lost; and France would . . . regain that country and annex the Floridas to it."

Burr assured the minister that once he had detached Louisiana and the Western states, the North and South would fall apart "and thus the immense power which has risen up" in the Western hemisphere would no longer be formidable. That, Merry observed, "I readily conceive may happen."[1]

In Philadelphia, after running across General Miranda, Burr sent Dayton to see the "exiled" Yrujo. With brazen nerve, Dayton offered to sell, for $30,000 or $40,000, the details of a conspiracy with England, against Spain. He then described Burr's plot so completely that there was no secret to buy. The Pitt cabinet, he finally declared, had appropriated $500,000 for the venture. Yrujo recognized this as a lie, because, he remarked to Cevallos, had the conspirators obtained that money, he would not have been visited by the "faithful thief," relating a secret which he had reason to conceal.

Burr and Dayton were more subtle than Yrujo thought. The latter followed Miranda to Washington, obtained his version of his talks with Madison, then returned to Philadelphia and betrayed the Venezuelan to the Spanish minister. Having thus established himself as a man of good faith, Dayton was believed when he said that British aid had failed and the plan was changed:

They were going to assemble a force of desperate adventurers in Washington, seize the President and everybody eligible to succeed him, loot the banks and rob the arsenal. If they were unable to make peace with the state governments, they would burn all tied-up naval vessels except two or three frigates, sail in them to New Orleans and proclaim the independence of Louisiana and the states bordering on the Mississippi. There would be no attack on Mexico or Florida.

For one who did not know the United States, Yrujo commented, "this plan would appear insane" but in a country full of ambitious adventurers, without property, "I confess . . . it seems easy of execution." The American cabinet members were men of ability and learning, with little understanding of the human heart. "They have not the least idea of the volcano that is forming beneath their feet." Spain might well spend a million dollars helping to dismember "the colossal power which was growing up at the very gates of her most precious and important colonies." Yrujo paid Dayton $1,500 for the information about Miranda and suggested a pension, but his government warned him to leave both men alone.[2]

Burr's scheme of seizing Washington could be dismissed as a maneuver to lull Spanish suspicions except for one fact. He proposed it also to General William Eaton. First came an invitation, which Eaton said he accepted, to operate against Florida and Mexico; then an expansion, which the ex-consul pretended to accept, to detach the Western states; finally a proposal that Eaton, whose Mediterranean adventure gave him close naval contacts, should try to win Marine Corps support for the capture of Washington. Eaton rejected the offer and asked the advice of Congressmen John Cotton Smith and Samuel Dana. They told him the plot was too chimerical to be dangerous and that if he disclosed it, Burr's prestige would ruin him. Some months later, however, he warned the President and followed with a deposition which told of Burr saying to him:

"If he could gain over the marine corps and secure the naval commanders Truxton, Preble, Decatur, and others, he would turn Congress neck and heels out of doors, assassinate the President, seize on the treasury and the navy, and declare himself the protector of an energetic government."[3]

This differs from the Burr-Dayton statement to Yrujo only in the threat to assassinate the President, and that appears to have been metaphorical. "Hang him!"—"throw him into the Potomac!"—"send him to Carter's Mountain!" (where Jefferson escaped Tarleton's Dragoons in 1781) were the words attributed by Eaton to Burr.

Eaton, the "hero of Derne," was a flashy show-off. According to one of Burr's partners, he strutted around wearing a Turkish sash and tippled in public bars. By turning against Burr, he might encourage Congress to pay his $46,000 Tripolitan claim.

(It did allow him $10,000 a few months later.) But all these circumstances do not alter this basic fact:

Eaton could not have invented a story whose exact counterpart, told to Yrujo, was then on its way to the Spanish Foreign Office. There could be only one reason for placing this plot before Eaton—the thought of carrying it into execution.[4]

To understand Burr's plans one more fact is needed. He either had or expected to have the support of General Wilkinson, commander in chief of the United States Army and governor of Upper Louisiana, with whom he was constantly in touch. In Burr's strategy, as varyingly stated to Merry, Yrujo and Eaton, can be seen four alternative plans:

1. With British financial and naval aid: to form an independent empire embracing the Western states, Louisiana, the Floridas and Mexico.

2. With Spanish aid: to detach the Western states and Louisiana.

3. With or without Spanish aid, but with the help of naval officers: to capture the national capital and set up a Cromwellian dictatorship, fleeing by sea to New Orleans and seizing the American Southwest should the main venture fail.

4. Without foreign aid, but with the help of Wilkinson, to go as far with the first plan as the attitude of western Americans would allow.

Thus the plan was adjustable to the loyalty of the West. If that proved too strong, the conspiracy could be cut down in fact to what it was in appearance—a filibustering expedition against the Spanish colonies. If this too collapsed in the making, the expedition could be reduced to the feature that gave it color of legality—a settlement project on the "Bastrop grant" on the Ouachita River in western Arkansas. To this notoriously worthless Spanish grant Burr had acquired an equally worthless title.

All this allowed great flexibility in recruiting. There was no need to talk disunion to the rank and file: a man's loyalty to the Union could be tested by his response to the suggestion that federal lands were overpriced and should be seized. If a recruit was willing to invade Mexico only with government backing, he was allowed to see a forged letter from the Secretary of War. If he would fight only in the event of war with Spain, that was the program. If his sole desire was cheap land, he signed up for the "Washita lands."[5]

The one absolute necessity, for Burr, was faithful support from General Wilkinson. That gentleman's fidelity to the United States could be measured by his past efforts to deliver the West to Spain. His fidelity to Burr could be gauged by his Spanish pension. If Wilkinson did not still feel the weight of the $12,000 in Mexican coin received in 1804, he was held even more firmly to Spain by the hope of getting more.

Burr's activities came to Madison's attention early in February 1806, when the President received a warning letter from Federalist Joseph H. Daveiss, United States district attorney for Kentucky: "We have traitors among us. A separation of the Union in favor of Spain is the object." The letter could be shown to Madison and Gallatin, but, Daveiss begged: "Mention the subject to no man from the western country however high in office he may be: some of them are deeply tainted with this treason."

Daveiss mistook the conspiracy for a resurrection of old Spanish plots and destroyed his credibility by sending a list of suspects which sounded like a Western Democratic roster: Attorney General Breckinridge, Henry Clay, Senator Adair, Senator Smith of Ohio, Governor (later President) William Henry Harrison and several others.

Later he cleared Clay and Breckinridge—actions which pointed to his sincerity—but after failing in premature efforts to have Burr indicted, he burst into public denunciation of the Jefferson administration. Overheard by a rejected rival for the hand of Ann Marshall (sister of the Chief Justice) his remarks were passed along to the President and led to his removal from office.[6]

The summer of 1806 passed. In September, Congressman Nathan Williams of Utica, New York, wrote to Madison that Comfort Tyler, once wealthy, later penniless, had returned from the West "full of cash." Active and daring, he was trying to enlist several hundred young men for a voyage down the Ohio to a destination undisclosed to them. Tyler named Burr, Dayton,

Samuel Swartwout (brother of the marshal) and others as his associates and said there was "nothing on foot inimical to government."

In mid-October, Madison received a joint letter from General Presley Nevill and Judge Sam Roberts of Pittsburgh, detailing a conversation between Burr and the Morgan family of land agents and militia officers. Predicting and advocating separation of the West, Burr had ceased his military overtures when he met with a sharp rebuff, but left "a strong impression" that a plan was arranged for separating the Union.

Hard on this came a letter which had fallen into the hands of General Eaton, telling of Burr's boatbuilding activities. Eaton forwarded it to Madison, and followed with a full account to Jefferson of the talks in which Burr unfolded plans of treason and named Wilkinson as his partner.

The President and cabinet, decidedly unsettled, took precautionary naval and military steps. These were rescinded when the next Western mail failed to produce alarming news. All that survived was a decision that Madison should put John Graham, now secretary of Orleans Territory, on Burr's trail, with authority to have him arrested.[7]

A sensation was produced by articles signed "Querist," in a Marietta paper, advocating Western secession. Madison's Kentucky cousin, Colonel James Taylor, identified the author as Harman Blennerhassett, a United Irish exile, who was said to be building gunboats (actually transports) for Burr on his manorial island in the Ohio River. Burr's conduct in Kentucky convinced Taylor that he was scheming for a division of the Union.

"I assure you, [he added] I am much surprised to find the idea of a separation meet the countenance it does. . . . The idea of seizing on the Congress lands [the public domain] will be very taking with some, and some others who are unable to pay for their lands they have bought may be misled by a mistaken interest."

Then, by special courier, came a startling message from Wilkinson at Natchitoches, near the Texas frontier. He had just discovered that "a numerous and powerful association," extending from New York to the Mississippi, had been formed to carry an expedition against Vera Cruz. Eight or ten thousand armed men were to gather in New Orleans by December. He was totally "uninformed of the prime mover and ultimate objects of this daring enterprise," (in which he was a real or pretended partner). However, believing that the revolt of Orleans Territory was part of the plan, he intended to make the best compromise he could with the Spaniards on the Sabine, "and throw myself with my little band into New Orleans to be ready to defend the capital against usurpation and violence."

In a separate, highly emotional note to the President, Wilkinson said he was going to bring a suit for slander against a publisher who had called him (though Wilkinson did not repeat the horrible words) an "intriguer and a pensioner of Spain, now associated with Aaron Burr"—associated in the plot whose "prime mover," he had just said, was still unknown to him. He closed with this outburst of patriotic devotion: "It is the highest ambition of my soul, on a proper occasion, to spend my last breath in the cause of my country."[8]

Wilkinson's belated warning followed the arrival at his camp, on October 8, of Samuel Swartwout, bearing a letter from Burr dated July 29. After opening with the unciphered sentence, "Your letter, postmarked thirteenth May, is received," it proceeded to tell him in cipher that all was ready. Burr would move rapidly down the Ohio in November with a vanguard of five hundred or a thousand men and meet Wilkinson in Natchez. Wilkinson was to be *second only to Burr*. Then, on to Baton Rouge, New Orleans and glory in a foreign land! There was no hint of a separation of the Union, which flaring Western patriotism had by this time made inconceivable.

In his dealings with Burr, Wilkinson was like a praying mantis devouring a wasp. From all the letters he wrote to Burr in 1805, he could remember, under oath, only one statement: "I fancy Miranda has taken the bread out of your mouth; and I shall be ready for the grand expedition before you are." What was in his letter of May 13, 1806? He had "not the most distant recollection of its contents." His course, however, seems clear enough.[9]

On June 11, Wilkinson received orders to hasten from St. Louis to Natchitoches, place himself at the head of the troops there, and repel any Spanish invasion east of the Sabine River, fifty miles away. That opened two paths to glory, with riches, perhaps, on one of them. He could add Burr's forces to his own and fight the Spaniards if war broke out (a course he suggested to Jefferson), or he could exaggerate the danger of insurrection and become the savior of both countries. He waited until nearly September before starting south, thus postponing the Spanish crisis until Burr was ready to move. Before the cipher letter arrived, the Spaniards chose peace by retreating across the Sabine. Wilkinson waited another two weeks before sending word of Burr's plot, thus reducing the likelihood of his flotilla being stopped.

The Spanish retreat apparently was due to a written threat by Wilkinson. Five weeks passed before he followed leisurely to the river. After this fifty-mile advance, he signed a treaty making the territory *behind him* a neutral ground which he promised to evacuate and neither side was to enter. This done, he falsely reported to Washington that he had agreed to the Sabine as a temporary boundary, and set off with his troops for New Orleans, to defeat Burr or die.[10]

Before leaving Natchitoches, Wilkinson sent his personal aide, Walter Burling, on a secret mission to the viceroy of Mexico. The purpose, he told the Spaniard who issued the passport, was to put Spain on guard against the Burr conspiracy. The purpose, he told the American government when he demanded $1,500 expense money, was to scout an invasion route to the capital of Mexico. The real purpose was stated in a letter to Viceroy José de Yturrigaray—a letter which, after translation, was to "be torn to bits in the presence of the bearer." It was torn up, but the Spanish version survives.

On his own authority *and by his private means,* wrote Wilkinson, he was endeavoring to check a revolutionary tempest which threatened the destruction of the kingdom of Mexico. An infernal combination of Kentucky and Ohio huntsmen, commanded by distinguished leaders of the American Revolution, was assembling on the Ohio. New Orleans was to be the first victim of their rapacity and they would then descend on Vera Cruz and ravage the country.

"To resist these calamities from which the eye and the spirit recoil in horror, I have thrown myself like a Leonidas into the pass, to defend it or perish in the attempt."

Details of the plot could be learned from Burling, who undertook this mission on "the solemn assurance I have given him that Your Excellency would remunerate him with liberality." The commander in chief continued:

"As for myself, I risk my life, my reputation and fortune by the means I have adopted—My life by the change I have made in military dispositions without the knowledge of my government—My reputation by offering this communication to a foreign power without orders—My fortune by exhausting my own resources and those of my friends to elude, frustrate and if possible destroy the essential plans of the revolutionists."

To break up the bandits on the Ohio, Wilkinson falsely asserted, he had "made an allotment . . . of $85,000, and for the executive dispatch of spies and counter revolutionaries, $36,000." These sums, he hoped, would be refunded to Burling, and "in case Providence preserves my life," His Excellency would surely restore whatever other expenditures "I may be obliged to make in sustaining the common cause of good government, order and humanity."

Yturrigaray was most courteous in reply. He thanked Wilkinson for telling him what he had already read in the newspapers, said he could pay nothing without orders from Madrid, and expressed his sincere desire "that the success of your righteous intentions will happily be attained."[11]

The American commander was ready to die for the United

States for nothing, but wanted $121,000 to die for Spain. To cap his patriotism, he spread alarmist stories in New Orleans about Burr's strength and established a military dictatorship, all the time sending a stream of fervent, death-defying letters to Washington.

On the day the general's first excited warning arrived (November 25) the cabinet took action. It approved the issuance of a denunciatory presidential proclamation, ordered the seizure of Burr's boats and directed Wilkinson to block the expedition and arrest its promoters. Navy Secretary Smith, in a panic, asked that the writ of habeas corpus be suspended, and lamented to Jefferson that his opinions "were not at all countenanced by any of the other gentlemen." Madison was puzzled but felt no alarm. There could be no doubt, he wrote to Monroe, that a military enterprise was being undertaken against Spain, but it was hard to see how it could be financed without a foreign connection and equally difficult to point to any that was probable. Another mischief was afoot—severance of the West—and it was not improbable that the two projects emanated from the same source. "There is no ground to suppose, however, that the general sentiment will countenance either."[12]

The President's proclamation had a vigorous, indignant tone. In the West, the people's response to it, combined with state actions secured by Graham, shattered Burr's expedition and sent its leaders fleeing toward the Ouachita as pretended settlers. In the East, Jefferson's words spread alarm. Federalist congressmen denounced the administration for inaction and gloated over Burr's impending triumph. John Randolph aided with an alarmist call for information, whereupon Jefferson cut down the excitement with a factual recital to Congress. Saying there was no doubt of Burr's guilt, he inclosed a decipherment of the conspiratorial letter to Wilkinson, who, the President said, had acted "with the honor of a soldier and fidelity of a good citizen."

Jefferson's doubts about his military commander had been dissipated with the arrival of Isaac Briggs, the Quaker engineer and agricultural leader, who broke in upon the presidential New Year reception with dispatches from New Orleans. "Is Wilkinson sound in this business?" the President asked. "There is not the smallest doubt of it," Briggs replied. Wilkinson's nobly written letter verified the testimonial. Facing "a deep, dark and wicked conspiracy" about to "shake the government to its foundation," he would confront these seven thousand desperadoes (Burr's maximum was sixty persons) with his own tiny force and let "indefatigable industry, incessant vigilance, and hardy courage" take the place of numbers. "I shall glory to give my life to the service of my country." He did not call himself a Leonidas, but did mention Thermopylae.

A decipherment of the Burr letter, sworn to by Wilkinson as "substantially" accurate, was garbled to eliminate every incriminating reference to himself. When he gave the original to a grand jury, it was found that the unciphered sentence (acknowledging Wilkinson's May 13 letter) had been scratched out and restored in Wilkinson's handwriting. The general explained that he thought of showing the letter to the Orleans legislature, but restored the wording when he changed his mind. Grand-jury foreman John Randolph saw another reason—Wilkinson's penknife had cut through the paper and made it impossible to hide the mutilation.[13]

Jefferson informed Congress that he was awaiting Dr. Erich Bollman and Samuel Swartwout, Burr lieutenants shipped by Wilkinson in defiance of the New Orleans judiciary. On that very day (January 22) the two men were brought from Annapolis and locked up in the Marine barracks. Bollman, at his own request, was taken next day to see the President. Madison wrote out a summary of the conversation, from memory, and Bollman did the same, with no conflicts in the memos but with far more "meat" in Madison's.

Burr (Madison recorded) talked only about an invasion of Mexico. He spoke of seizing all the shipping in New Orleans but not of robbing the bank. Bollman's own assignment was to seek government backing for the expedition. He knew of no plans for detaching the West. Burr told him he was deceiving Yrujo on that point: the Spaniard offered him all the money he might need but he would take none from a man of such "dirty character." Had Burr talked with Merry? Freely, and the British minister "entered warmly into his views," but "not with unfriendly views to the United States." It appeared, Madison commented, that Bollman sought the interview to minimize both his own connection with Burr and the latter's criminality.[14]

On the following Monday evening (January 26) Madison received an urgent note from Swartwout's lawyers, one of whom afterward wrote the "Star-Spangled Banner." They wanted him to enforce their client's right to talk with his counsel. The denier of that constitutional right was the commandant of the Marine Corps, recently vice-chairman of a great dinner for Meriwether Lewis at which the Constitution was toasted as "the ark of our safety." The court committed Swartwout and Bollman without bail for trial on a charge of treason, and gave them free access to counsel.[15]

The Senate, by this time, was raging over the disclosure that a New Orleans judge had freed a man against whom no evidence was offered. In a single day, Bayard alone voting No, it passed a bill suspending the right of habeas corpus in treason cases. The House, vehement on the other side, voted to reject the Senate bill on first reading—113 to 19—an extraordinary rebuke to the body that was created to check hasty impulses. John Randolph could not resist the impulse to pin this obnoxious measure on the main object of his hatred. "Certain members of Congress," wrote Burwell, "insinuated Mr. Madison was the promoter of it—for what purpose every person knew." That is, the purpose of the insinuation was to damage Madison's presidential prospects.[16]

Newspapers published Eaton's deposition, Wilkinson's affidavits and letters, Burr's cipher message—all sent by the President to Congress. The fear they might have engendered earlier was offset by news that Burr had sailed from Nashville with only two boats. Kentuckians who had been shouting for him were now calling him a traitor. Eastern cities were flooded with his worthless drafts.

"The enterprise of Burr," wrote Madison, "has probably received its death blow. Every additional development of it increases the wonder at his infatuation." Bollman and Swartwout would remain in prison until transferred to their place of trial. In this prediction he reckoned without the Supreme Court. Affirming (three to two) its right to issue a writ of habeas corpus, it did so and discharged the men. The evidence against them, Chief Justice Marshall said on February 21, went only to indicate treasonable intentions; there was no showing of overt acts.[17]

A month later Dolley Madison wrote to her sister: "I suppose you have heard that Colonel Burr is retaken and on his way to Richmond for trial. This is all I know about him." She had read, in the *Intelligencer* of March 23, a letter from Cowitah in the Creek Nation saying, "Yesterday Colonel Aaron Burr passed here, conducted (as a prisoner of the United States) by a guard of ten men." Times had changed from that day in the spring of 1794 when Senator Burr told Mrs. Dolley Todd that "the great little Madison" had asked to be brought to see her that evening.[18]

On the day Dolley wrote of the arrest, the Richmond *Enquirer* was full of the story of Burr's arrival there. It told how, fleeing toward Mobile Bay, he had arrived at a tavern late at night, inquired the way to the home of a certain major, and aroused suspicion by refusing to wait until morning before crossing a dangerously flooded stream. Soldiers summoned from Fort Stoddert arrested him. Among Madison's papers is a note from John Graham to the Cowitah postmaster saying that he would have arrived the previous night but was informed "that it was extremely difficult and even dangerous to cross the creek (that was so near taking your man to the other world)."[19]

At the first news of Burr's arrest, Attorney General Rodney set out for Richmond, chosen for the place of trial because Blennerhassett's Island, focal point of the plot, was in Virginia. On the way he learned that Burr and his seven guards had turned south from Fredericksburg. Fatigued by rough roads, and knowing that he was in a race against a writ of habeas corpus, Rodney looked around in that town for somebody he could trust with a packet of depositions. Luckily he ran across Colonel Tatham of Bowling Green, "a little flighty but who had a very faithful servant, I knew." So the slave Joseph galloped across the state of Virginia on a mission too important to be entrusted to his master.[20]

"We this day argued the case of Burr before Marshall, CJ,"

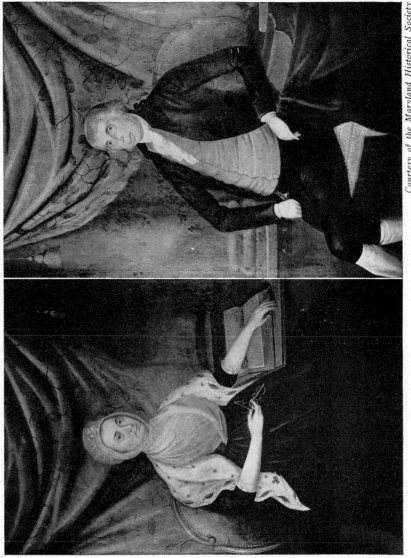

NELLY CONWAY MADISON AND JAMES MADISON SR.
By Charles Peale Polk, 1799

In Senate of the United States.

Be it known, That the Senate and House of Representatives of the United States of America, being convened at the City of Washington, on the second Wednesday in February, in the year of our Lord one thousand eight hundred and nine, the undersigned President of the Senate pro tempore, did, in presence of the said Senate and House of Representatives, open all the certificates and count all the votes of the electors for a President and Vice President of the United States; whereupon it appeared that James Madison of Virginia, had a majority of the votes of the electors as President, and George Clinton of New York, had a majority of the votes of the electors as Vice President. By all which it appears, that James Madison of Virginia, has been duly elected President, and George Clinton of New York, has been duly elected Vice President of the United States, agreeably to the constitution.

In testimony whereof, I have hereunto set my hand, and caused the seal of the Senate to be affixed this eighth day of February, 1809.

President of the Senate,
Pro tempore

Attest,

Saml. Otis _Secretary._

Manuscript in Library of Congress

CERTIFICATE OF MADISON'S ELECTION AS PRESIDENT

wrote Rodney to Madison on March 31. The Attorney General felt sure that the defendant would be held for treason, but sent word next day that the charge was only high misdemeanor—setting on foot an expedition against Mexico. Burr might be indicted for treason later, Marshall said, if evidence of a treasonable assemblage was produced. Rodney did not mention the words, "the hand of malignity," used by Marshall to describe the prosecution—words which the whole audience took as notice that the Chief Justice was renewing his feud with Jefferson. The suspicion of bias was not lessened when Marshall and Burr, a few days later, were both guests at a dinner given by Burr's chief counsel, John Wickham, to celebrate the semiacquittal.[21]

In Rodney's absence, Madison was asked by the President to take all necessary steps to bring witnesses from the West. Those who knew the most, John Graham told Madison, would not tell all they knew. Praised for his work, Graham was appointed chief clerk of the State Department to succeed the resigning Jacob Wagner.

Treason and misdemeanor indictments were secured in June against Burr, Blennerhassett, Dayton, Senator Smith of Ohio and three lesser figures. "But the mammoth of iniquity escaped," lamented Foreman Randolph, after a seven-to-nine failure to indict General Wilkinson.[22]

By this time there were more complaints against Chief Justice Marshall. On Burr's motion, he issued a subpoena ordering Jefferson to appear in court and bring certain of Wilkinson's letters. Both the arguments and Marshall's written opinion on the power to issue the subpoena were plainly designed to insult the President. Jefferson responded by ordering the letters forwarded, while he rejected the subpoena with a discussion of paramount duties that was much more convincing than the belittling remarks of the Chief Justice.[23]

Much of the Ohio Valley evidence was gathered by Dolley Madison's brother-in-law, Congressman Jackson. As soon as Jackson left Richmond, after the grand jury acted, Burr started criminal proceedings against him, charging improper practices in getting affidavits. Returning witnesses told Jackson that Marshall created suspicion against him by saying that the charges should be heard, then had "permitted the author to abandon them without acquitting the accused." Wrote the angry congressman to Madison:

"I have great cause to complain of this outrage: and the more I investigate the conduct and opinions of the judge the more I am convinced that he does feel a dishonest partiality to the accused. ... Why [did he] allege the government wished the conviction of Burr although no evidence of his guilt was exhibited?"[24]

A treason defendant being unbailable, Burr secured an order from Marshall that he be guarded in the house of one of his lawyers. This stirred the hopes of Jonathan Dayton, who through illness, real or feigned, had so far escaped the ignominy and lice of the Richmond jail. If ever once he had made any movement to aid Burr, the No. 2 conspirator assured Madison, "I am willing to be condemned without relief or mercy." Jefferson and Madison exchanged drafts of the replies in which they informed Dayton that only the courts could do what he wanted. On his own draft the President jotted some inquiries:

"Shall I send Dayton an answer as above? Shall I leave out the last sentence but one? Or shall I send him no answer?"

Leave out the sentence, the Secretary advised. It might be regarded as a "covered animadversion" on Marshall for his indulgence toward Burr.[25]

During the to-do over subpoenas, Madison, John Walker, Henry Lee and others were summoned to testify before the federal court in Connecticut, in a prosecution for criminal libel growing out of an ancient affair between Jefferson and Mrs. Walker. This happening of 1768, exhumed by Callender in 1802, had been enlarged into a major political theme by the New England clergy. In 1806, with the aid of Henry Lee, Madison brought Jefferson and Walker together at his house, and they agreed that the matter should be consigned to oblivion. Jefferson gave Walker a statement, attested by Madison and Lee, exonerating Mrs. Walker. Now, in August

1807, came the threatened dragging of it into court. John Nicholas, also subpoenaed, appealed to Madison:

"Our friend Colonel Walker who has just been with me on the subject is extremely perplexed and puzzled to know how to act, between his duty in obedience to the summons and his delicate standing in some of those transactions to which you are no stranger. He therefore joins me most cordially in requesting your prudent aid and suggestions in devising some mode for superseding the necessity of fulfilling this very disagreeable and inconvenient office."

Madison's two letters to Jefferson (received August 24 and 26, 1807) have disappeared, and so have the letters which Jefferson wrote to Gideon Granger of Connecticut on those two days. Enough correspondence survives to show why Nicholas thanked Madison for releasing him "from a disagreeable dilemma." A year earlier, Granger had protested to Jefferson that two Connecticut preachers, two printers and a lawyer-writer were being martyrized by federal indictments for sedition at common law. Recalling that Madison (in 1799) had called such proceedings unconstitutional, he urged that the cases be dropped, but received no reply. Now, informed of the subpoenas, Jefferson told Madison that he had asked Granger to have the prosecution of the "scoundrel parson" dropped, or at least to eliminate the Walker count. As for the subpoenas, the Attorney General had ruled in the Burr case that they were unenforceable outside the district in which they were issued.

Granger's account reveals that on receipt of Jefferson's letter of August 24, he asked the district attorney to drop all of the cases, on the ground that they were unwarranted in law, but found him unwilling to do so until the bearing on the Walker affair was explained. On receiving the letter of August 26, Granger gave the district attorney an additional reason for dismissal—it would be more embarrassing to drop them after introduction of a bill in Congress to broaden the effectiveness of subpoenas. Both of these arguments, it is evident, came from Madison.[26]

Burr's treason trial was a battle of forensic giants competing for public favor and the aid of the Chief Justice. The jury was almost forgotten. Burr himself, Wickham, Edmund Randolph, Luther Martin and lesser lights were arrayed against Caesar Rodney and William Wirt (present and future attorneys general), also District Attorney Hay and a sharp-tongued Scotchman, Alexander McRae. They strove mightily—the defense to break down the popular belief that Burr was guilty, the prosecution to keep that opinion unimpaired. But the Chief Justice disposed of the case.

The government, Marshall ruled, must either prove Burr's physical presence on Blennerhassett's Island during the actual formation of an assemblage in force for the purpose of war, or prove by the direct and positive testimony of two witnesses—not by presumptive evidence from his actions in general—that he *procured* such an assemblage. Only the ringleaders of the plot could furnish that proof. Marshall's ruling stopped the taking of testimony before one tenth of the 140 witnesses had been examined. An angry jury brought in a verdict that Aaron Burr was not proved guilty "by any evidence submitted to us. We therefore find him not guilty." Burr and his lawyers jumped to their feet to demand a correction. Did the jury mean to censure the court "for suppressing irrelevant testimony?" cried burly, red-faced Luther Martin. They did, of course, but Marshall calmly ordered that the verdict be filed and "Not Guilty" be entered on the record.[27]

"Chief Justice Marshall has it seems acquitted Burr," wrote the Attorney General to Madison. "Every lawyer with whom I have conversed is of a different opinion from him." With a misdemeanor indictment still pending, Burr sent a new subpoena to the President, now at Monticello. "Unwilling, by any notice of the subpoena, to set a precedent which might sanction a proceeding so preposterous," Jefferson forwarded the paper to the district attorney and commented:

"I am happy in having the benefit of Mr. Madison's counsel on this occasion, he happening to be now with me. We are both strongly of opinion that the prosecution against Burr for misdemeanor should proceed at Richmond. If defeated, it will heap coals of fire on the head of the Judge; if convicted, it will give time to see whether a prosecution for treason against him can be instituted in any, and what other court."[28]

Jefferson and Madison were hoping to justify the administration by bringing out the testimony excluded from the treason trial. Marshall co-operated by throwing the gates so wide that the new trial became in effect a prosecution of General Wilkinson, making Jefferson surer than ever that the general was an injured innocent. The scenes at Richmond, he wrote to Wilkinson, were "equivalent to a proclamation of impunity to every traitorous combination which may be formed to destroy the Union."

Following Burr's second acquittal, Marshall committed him and Blennerhassett for trial in Ohio, where acts against Spain had been more overt. Jefferson was inclined to push the case, and prosecute Luther Martin for good measure. Cabinet discussions led to a decision to drop all charges and send the proceedings and evidence in the trials to Congress for publication.[29]

Although Marshall's political animus was evident, his fundamental rulings were sound. As treason is defined in the Constitution, a man may commit it by adhering to the country's wartime enemies, or, during war or peace, by "levying war" against the United States. Marshall held rigidly to this definition, and also to the requirement that the crime be proved either by confession in open court or by "the testimony of two witnesses to the same overt act."

Combining the testimony in court with the contents of the British and Spanish archives, it is clear enough that Burr's purposes were treasonable. But his actions were not. Lack of support for the traitorous features of his conspiracy caused him to omit them before any overt act of treason was committed, and warranted the verdict of acquittal. In the long run, Marshall's rejection of "constructive treason" far outweighed the evil of letting a villain escape punishment.

In Congress, Randolph and Daniel Clark of Orleans pointed so convincingly toward Wilkinson's Spanish pension that the general obtained a court-martial to refute the "foul slander." A testimonial from Governor Folch of West Florida acquitted him. The Spaniard had found Wilkinson utterly devoted to the United States and there was *no document whatever in his archives* to show that he ever received a pension from Spain. Privately, Folch wrote to Wilkinson:

"I have sent to the archives of Havana all that pertains to the ancient history, persuaded that before the United States are in a situation to conquer that capital, you and I, Jefferson, Madison . . . and even the prophet Daniel himself will have made many days' journey into the other world."[30]

Proof of Wilkinson's villainy, when these archives were opened, had much the same effect on historians that the suspicion of it had on jurors. It cast doubt on Burr's criminal intent and helped build him (for some writers) into a picaresque hero who tried to swindle foreign governments into financing a project of American territorial expansion.

Madison apparently never doubted that Burr's purposes were treasonable. So he could not have been greatly surprised when, early in his Presidency, he received an anonymous account of Burr's later activities in Paris. Quoting an unnamed high official, "A Citizen of the United States" told how Burr gave Police Chief Fouché a 63-page memorial proposing that France offer England an army of 100,000 men, to be transported in British ships for "the conquest of the northern parts of the United States." Burr wanted to be financed by France in fomenting a division of the West from the East during the 1812 presidential campaign, and in raising an insurrection in Texas and Florida.

This was no idle rumor. The unnamed official was Deputy Foreign Minister Ernest Roux, to whom, at the same time as the talks with Fouché, Burr had outlined a scheme for the retaking of Louisiana and the conquest of Florida and Mexico by France. Fouché, without Napoleon's knowledge, sent his agents Ouvrard and Labouchère to place Burr's scheme before the British cabinet as part of a secret peace negotiation. Napoleon learned of this from Ouvrard and discharged Fouché. Burr, alarmed, went back to Roux and restated his proposals. By omitting the conquest of Louisiana, he eliminated treason from the plan, as yet unanswered, which he had submitted to the Foreign Office.[31]

Here was an amazing repetition of the earlier plot. The proposal to Fouché, to divide the United States between England and France, corresponded to the extravagant scheme he placed before Yrujo and Eaton. His milder, yet still treasonable, offer to the Foreign Office duplicated his overtures to Minister Merry. And when exposure threatened, he cut the scheme down to an invasion of Spanish territory, exactly as he had done in his previous operations. Burr did his work so well in Paris that his second treason plot convicts him of the first.

CHAPTER XXVI

Special Missions in Europe

EARLY in 1806 special diplomatic missions acquired a sudden popularity. Jefferson was eager for one to secure Florida, and the Battle of Trafalgar scared congressmen into asking for another. As a result, ministers Armstrong and Bowdoin (the latter assigned to Madrid but waiting in Paris) were joined in a special mission on the former subject. William Pinkney of Baltimore was named to act with Monroe in negotiating a treaty with England.

Minister Merry reported that the President wanted Monroe to act alone but was pushed by a Senate committee into naming a coadjutor. Monroe was too anti-British to suit Senator Logan, the Pennsylvania pacifist, who had heard Merry tell Madison "that, before we went to war, we ought to be very sure that no other measure of a conciliatory nature remained." Senator Smith of Maryland expected to be the special envoy and hoped after that to succeed either Monroe or Armstrong. Then, suddenly, Jefferson nominated Pinkney, who had just sent Congress a powerful memorial in behalf of Baltimore shipowners. But he was a borderline Republican and the wrath of the house of Smith descended on Jefferson. Ascertaining that his brother, the Secretary of the Navy, knew nothing of this in advance, the senator asserted that Jefferson offered the place to Pinkney privately, "without the knowledge of any of his cabinet; they appeared astonished."[1]

Turreau, reporting to Paris, said he did not believe this at all. "On the contrary, I am persuaded that this strange promotion is the work of Mr. Madison, the habitual wire-puller [*le faiseur ordinaire*]. It is beyond doubt that the Secretary of State entirely directs the cabinet at Washington, and that he seizes all occasions to please the Federalists individually. His influence on the head of government is all the more powerful because the latter courts it."

The minister recalled a remark made by Jefferson when he entered the Presidency: "He never would have accepted such a place, if he had not found in the best of his friends [Madison] all the talents necessary to help him fill it." This infatuation for *un homme médiocre,* Turreau commented, was no surprise to those who knew Jefferson—a man of winning personal qualities who understood his country's interest but lacked energy and audacity and was thrown off balance by the slightest event.

Belief that Madison engineered the appointment was strengthened by a report that Dolley "spoke very slightingly" of Monroe in connection with presidential electioneering. Congressman Nicholson told the London minister that "it was intended to take from you the credit of settling our differences with England." The choice of Pinkney was "a bait to the Federalists," and if that didn't bring them to Madison's support for President they would be allowed to bite at something of higher flavor. (Nicholson himself, a few days later, bit at a federal judgeship.) It didn't occur to anybody that, after Monroe's two recent nonsuccesses, Madison might have thought the minister needed help.[2]

Armstrong's nomination to the Spanish mission was bitterly fought by Senator Smith, who attacked his record in liquidating American war claims. There was fuel for opposition in Armstrong's reported effort to knock out one of the biggest claims—that of the ship *New Jersey*—on the unprecedented ground that the real beneficiary was an insurance company. "It is surmised," wrote Madison to Jefferson, "that Swan in connection with a corrupt member of the council of liquidation has created the difficulty in order to secure his own claims out of a fund that might not be equal to the aggregate of claims." Senator Smith saw a more direct interest. Armstrong's brothers-in-law, the Livingstons, he told Plumer, had bought up the rejected claims of Swan and Joshua Barney. "Douceurs rendered them valid" and Armstrong was building up the value of these and other Livingston claims by excluding the huge *New Jersey* account.

If the Livingstons did make these purchases, there was nothing to indicate it in the official records. However, Armstrong connived with the French minister of finance to make the United States pay debts which France owed to Swan as a French pur-

chasing agent, and opened a terrific campaign against Consul
Skipwith, whose persistent opposition to the Swan claims led to
his expulsion from the country.[3]

Madison sent a letter of disapproval to Armstrong before he
learned that the President preferred to ignore the *New Jersey*
affair. This enabled Jefferson to cite the rebuke as administration
policy when the storm broke in Congress. Although Armstrong
prevaricated in denying to Madison that he had ever objected to
the *New Jersey* award because of the insurance feature, the record
proved that he had withdrawn this objection and justified the
assurance Jefferson gave that it was a momentary error and not
the cause of the adverse action. The Senate divided evenly on
the Armstrong nomination, and the Vice President cast the confirming vote.[4]

The credentials of Armstrong and Bowdoin, addressed "to all
and singular" (*i.e.,* to Spanish agents) gave Bowdoin no official
standing in the French court. Forwarding the draft of a Spanish-
American convention, Madison directed the envoys to show this
to the French government and ask it to induce Spain to send a
mission to Paris. Thus they would work "under the auspices of
a common friend" who controlled the court of Spain and wanted
Spanish-American peace. The convention harmonized with the
unsigned proposals which Talleyrand had sent to Armstrong in
the previous September, but limited the advance payment for the
Floridas to $2,000,000 and the total to $5,000,000. Gallatin excluded graft or private profit by requiring a lump-sum payment
of the $2,000,000 and forbidding the sale of securities below par.

To Armstrong separately, Madison sent instructions based on a
belief that Napoleon would try to cap his victories with a general
peace conference in which Russia might be pulled out of the British orbit. He directed the minister to work for a joint effort by
the French and Russian emperors to put neutral maritime rights
on a sound basis in the peace treaty. But should those gentlemen lay any snares "for entangling us in the politics of Europe"
through an armed guaranty, he must politely repress the effort.
He could say, at most, that "a violation of a system of rights so
precious" to the United States would not improbably cause them

to "avail themselves of the means which they possess in a peculiar degree of making it the interest of commercial and manufacturing nations to respect such a system." In fewer and plainer words, he could predict the use of a nonintercourse law against violators of neutral rights. Jefferson followed with a personal letter to Emperor Alexander (shown to other cabinet members after Madison was asked "to correct it severely") invoking his aid to the same end.

A few weeks passed and Jefferson and Madison were jolted by private advices from Armstrong. When Bowdoin arrived in France, full of honest indignation against "British piracy," he proposed that Armstrong inform France that its help in settling the Spanish troubles might inspire the United States to enter the war. After the minister replied that this was far beyond his powers, only the warnings of a private American prevented Bowdoin from going to Germany in an effort to put the matter before Napoleon. This account, the President observed to Madison, "changes considerably the idea we had formed of Bowdoin's caution and prudence."[5]

Reading Armstrong's report that Napoleon wanted an actual power of decision over Florida, Madison saw little prospect of success. The plan would have been in the nick of time, he wrote to Jefferson in Monticello, had it not been for Randolph's "attempts to assassinate it." On the same day, the Secretary instructed the envoys that, in case of a final and unfavorable turn, "it is thought proper by the President" (whom he had not consulted) that they should work for the military *status quo* and free use of the Mobile. The nation could then wait in peace "for that increase of the power of the United States for which time is wanted."[6]

As summer came on, Madison heard good news and bad from Armstrong. Talleyrand had told of the intention (not fulfilled) to replace General Turreau with General Vial, ambassador to Switzerland, on account of the former's scandalous conduct. Only a desire for harmony could lie behind such belated scruples. Then came another report about Bowdoin. When Armstrong asked for French support of the Florida purchase, Talleyrand showed him a mass of papers sent by Charles IV, exalting the colony as indispensable to Spain. Knowing that its future had been put in Napoleon's hands a few weeks before, Armstrong asked the meaning of this sudden change.

"France [Talleyrand replied] has been represented as usurping over her an entire sovereignty and even as putting her provinces to sale without her knowledge or consent. Do you know that even your own agents have not merely insinuated but asserted this?"

He then disclosed that Chargé Erving, at the request of Bowdoin, had informed the Prince of Peace of the confidential propositions made by Talleyrand in 1805. "You may readily imagine my confusion and astonishment at this discovery," wrote Armstrong to Madison. Some hope remained, since Napoleon and his minister now seemed friendly. But how should he behave to a man who had thus violated the strictest pledge of secrecy? He decided to be cold and silent.[7]

Honesty inspired Bowdoin's bungling. He knew that the Boston speculator, Daniel Parker, had been Talleyrand's emissary in offering the Floridas for $10,000,000, but did not know that Jefferson's cabinet had cut this in two. In January 1806, when Bowdoin as minister to Spain had sole authority to negotiate a purchase, he was visited by Labouchère and Parker, agents of Hope and Company, the Amsterdam bankers who had joined Sir Francis Baring (Labouchère's father-in-law) in financing the Louisiana Purchase. They told him that Spain had hypothecated the Floridas for $4,000,000, to cover a debt guaranteed by France. Napoleon was likely to settle the obligation by taking both East and West Florida. Labouchère, claiming to be Spain's agent, wanted Bowdoin and Parker to work out a purchase of the provinces. The minister offered too little and the talks broke down.

Bowdoin was aware that Hope and Baring had made $1,700,000 by buying the Louisiana stock from France at a 15-per-cent discount and reselling it at par. Parker admitted that the bankers and their agents were out for a new profit. Bowdoin suspected that they came from Talleyrand instead of Prince Godoy. Why, he asked Erving, should the United States pay France $6,000,000 above her mortgage? By confidentially informing the Prince of Peace of Talleyrand's earlier proposition, he could transfer the negotiations to Madrid and get the Floridas for $4,000,000 or less, none of which would go to France.[8]

Any legation clerk could have told Bowdoin that Spain had no power to keep either Florida or the $4,000,000. This being true, the diplomat's foolish move could have no fatal effect unless by angering Napoleon. He found himself isolated. Armstrong cut off personal contact and progressed to sarcastic, sneering letters. Talleyrand, while soothing the emperor, ignored Bowdoin's existence on the front stairs, but not via the back.

On May 6, Talleyrand advised Napoleon that Turreau's reports indicated the readiness of the United States to attack Spain. West Florida would sooner or later be taken by force, the foreign minister believed, unless ceded now. He put in a hint that Napoleon's 1803 idea of maintaining "a germ of division" between the United States and Spain might be more hazardous to the Spanish colonies than to the Americans. He resurrected the emperor's argument for selling Louisiana, that overexpansion would split the United States in two—a theme supported by Turreau's report of a secession conspiracy by Burr and Merry. If, Talleyrand suggested, *Sa Majesté* wished Florida to be ceded, the price should be high, enabling France to escape new taxes. A month later Armstrong was notified that the emperor would aid the negotiations.[9]

A week passed, and Consul Skipwith told Bowdoin that Talleyrand's former private secretary, Dautremont, a native of America, had invited him to his house to dine with his father-in-law, Doyen. Another guest was to be "Mr. Escardo," a confidential agent of the Spanish cabinet. Doyen was called the banker of both Talleyrand and the Spaniard.

Bowdoin advised Skipwith to decline but listen. At their next meeting, Dautremont told the consul that either "Escardo" or Doyen would receive propositions from Bowdoin, "to which prompt and decided answers would be obtained from the *chif source"*—Talleyrand. Bowdoin refused to talk to anybody who lacked credentials, after which "Escardo" blossomed out as Don Eugene Yzquierdo, sent by Spain with special powers.[10]

Talleyrand had forced the Prince of Peace to agree to this, but there was mysterious delay in presentation of the envoy's credentials. Paris was in a ferment. Napoleon made Talleyrand Prince of Benevento—the prelude, rumor said, to his replacement by Champagny. The emperor made peace overtures. When Grenville evaded the trap, Napoleon turned violently on Talleyrand. How had he dared intervene in Madrid? He should never speak of the sale of Florida again. This was the sad word Armstrong sent to Madison on October 10.

Not knowing of this rebuke, the vultures around Talleyrand's table still had hopes. Dautremont told Skipwith that in spite of all denials Yzquierdo really did have power to treat under French directions. But in view of the XYZ scandals, a big land grant to Talleyrand's brother would be more convenient than money in reconciling public measures to private interest, and Skipwith could share in the booty. He refused and Bowdoin repelled the main offer.

The special envoy suspected Armstrong. Madison's March instructions had become known to Parker (consequently to Talleyrand) five days after they reached Paris. This speculator, Bowdoin wrote to Erving, was daily closeted with Armstrong and had "converted himself into a kind of minister of the United States." Much the same had been said of Parker and Livingston in 1802, but Armstrong furnished no tangible evidence, as Livingston did, that he fell in with the schemes of corruption. There was no room for it in his proposal to take Spanish territory by force, and Bowdoin referred to him as opposed to Talleyrand's plan of purchase when he sent it to Washington. However, Armstrong's failure to tell his government about the schemes of Parker, which Bowdoin freely reported, hardly suggests a righteous revulsion against them.[11]

Failure of the Armstrong-Bowdoin mission shifted the focus of American diplomacy to London just as the breakdown of peace negotiations intensified the war. That did not ease the effort of Monroe and Pinkney to soften naval and trade policies. Their instructions, approved by the cabinet in April 1806, were based on those to Monroe in January 1804, but with revocation of the nonimportation act as trading material. To permit this use of it, the act was not to go into effect until November 15. The ministers were to inform the British government that this law excluding certain British goods was decided on before Pitt's death became known. Passage of it, later, did not imply distrust of the Ministry of All the Talents. The law, Madison pointed out, was in form a mere act to aid American manufactures, while its discriminatory features had examples in British practice.

Two orders were imperative. The ministers were forbidden to promise a revocation of the nonimportation act unless the treaty (1) forbade impressment on the high seas, and (2) protected American trade between an enemy colony and the parent country when the goods were transshipped from the United States. Other objectives were to restrict or abolish contraband lists, put an end to "paper blockades," restrain the insults and injuries committed by British warships in American waters, and secure mutual guarantees against commercial and tax discriminations.[12]

Encouraging reports were coming from Monroe and they were needed. The British Navy, apparently, had never heard of Fox's friendly policies. In April 1806, the three warships which had defied New York officials a year before met by chance off Sandy Hook and, said Madison, "renewed their violent and lawless proceedings." Halting American commerce within territorial waters, they killed one seaman by a cannon shot and roused public passions to fury. You will present this to the British government, the Secretary wrote to Monroe, "in terms which equally express the enormity of the offense and the necessity of an exemplary punishment of the offender." Madison summoned Merry and informed him that the President was issuing a proclamation, under a year-old law, ordering the *Cambrian,* the *Driver* and the *Leander* to leave and stay out of American ports. Although Madison "observed much temper both in his manner and language," Merry expected new demands, and they came: Captain Whitby should either be delivered to the United States or be punished by his own government.

To ease the tension, Merry allowed Madison to read a letter from Fox, written after the Gregg resolution was published in England. He would seek at once, by treaty, to remove all causes of dispute. "From the moment and manner of this step," Madison commented to the President, it plainly resulted from the loss of the German market (due to Napoleon's victories), and to fear that the United States might shut the trade door if not soothed by friendly assurances.

The soothing syrup, it quickly appeared, was to cut the pain of a notice, which Merry gave, of a "paper blockade" of German rivers. Madison retorted that he considered every American ship at liberty to enter and depart unless a blockading force was present to invest the port. Britain herself had confessed this by canceling the pretended blockade of Martinique.[13]

London's climate changed with the reprinting there of John Randolph's attack on Madison's pamphlet and the American colonial trade. James Stephen, author of *War in Disguise,* replied to Madison under the title, *Observations on the Speech of the Honorable John Randolph,* etc., proving his own arguments by showing that they were admitted by the leading figure in Congress. With the British cabinet badly divided, wrote Jefferson, "this publication appears and it is feared may fatally arm Mr. Fox's opponents." London newspapers also published, with bitter comments, Randolph's charge that the United States was sending $2,000,000 as a bribe to Bonaparte—an accusation which did serious harm in France too. Our affairs in London, the President commented, "are in danger of being all in the wind."

To make things worse, Merry reported that the nonimportation act was passed in expectation that the clamor of British merchants would induce Great Britain to accede to American pretensions, thus restoring Jefferson's popularity. From "remarks dropped by cabinet members"—that usually meant Robert Smith—the minister found that American policy was grounded in a belief that Great Britain, overwhelmed by debt and military misfortunes, could no longer resist the demands of other powers. Merry, on the contrary, was convinced that the real weakness was in America, so great was the division of parties, debility of government, avarice of the people and dislike of taxes. Reinforce the British squadrons on the American station and all hostile proceedings would evaporate.[14]

Senator Mitchill at this time was begging Madison to entreat the President to station some frigates and gunboats at New York. The Republicans there had just carried the election against the "virulent machinations" of the Federalists, but were tired of telling people that warships were most useful in the Anacostia River. Madison had already sent a refusal, informing DeWitt Clinton that the Mediterranean operations made it impossible to overmatch the British vessels at New York. Such campaign alarms easily misled the British minister. He saw the country through the eyes of the party out of power—a place (said Rufus King) where "every man you meet seems ashamed of the feeble, hypocritical and mean proudness of the Executive"; a place (said future Governor Sullivan of Massachusetts) where Federalists were threatening "that a monarchy must be established even if they wade through blood to do it."[15]

Pinkney landed at Liverpool on June 19, but negotiations were delayed many weeks while Fox struggled against the fatal progress of dropsy. Hearing a favorable report on his health, Madison's confidential friend George Joy undertook on July 4 to ease the task of the envoys. He sent Fox part of a private letter in which Madison expressed his belief that "the mutual interests which ought to bind the two nations together in harmony and sincere friendship" would be promoted by the liberal outlook of the new British administration. When Fox turned the negotiations over to Lords Holland and Auckland, Joy sent Holland both his own letter to Fox and the extract from Madison's, remarking that the whole tenor of Fox's life was a guarantee that he would not take advantage of Madison's pacific desires to raise his own terms.

The pacific assurances became possibly damaging when Fox died in September. Acutely aware of this, Madison mildly rebuked Joy for having disclosed a letter not intended to go "beyond your own perusal," and warned that "the very consideration which promised advantage from the communication would not permit a repetition." He might have felt no better had he read Auckland's note inviting Monroe and Pinkney to his country home, where, "we shall be able to do some good to mankind, if your powers are sufficiently extensive."

Prior to Fox's death the reports sent to Madison were encouraging. Captain Whitby, whose cannon shot had killed an American seaman, was to be court-martialed. Minister Merry was recalled and thirty-year-old David Erskine was to succeed him. The latter had an American wife (née Cadwallader) and was the son of "the celebrated Erskine," defender of free speech, famous wit, and now lord chancellor, whose expectation of revolution in England caused him to invest (and later lose) a great part of his fortune in American property. The chancellor furnished Madison with one of his favorite dinner table stories. Loving Cape wine, and witnessing the exhaustion of a bottle furnished by a stingy host, Erskine remarked: "If we cannot double the Cape, I suppose we must return to port."[16]

In Washington, Merry was complaining about the issuance of American protections to British seamen. Madison saw no reason to shift the subject from London, but thought it might be well to make an inquiry to vindicate the collectors "against testimony which convicts the witnesses of the most hardened disregard of truth." Jefferson was not so sure. Better admonish the port officials to be scrupulously exact in issuing certificates, he advised, "as the contrary conduct disgraces us." Merry notified his government of an alleged admission by American naval officers that nearly two thirds of the seamen in the United States Mediterranean squadron were English. (He did not propose swapping them for the impressed Americans who, an American consul seemed to think, won the Battle of Trafalgar.) The adverse effect was heightened by Merry's account of the nationwide sensation produced by Randolph's newspaper attack on Madison and Jefferson under the name of "Decius." This experiment in the "big lie" was said to be opening the eyes of the people to the underhand proceedings of their government.[17]

When Merry left for England in November, he carried a private letter from Madison to Monroe saying that the circumstances of his return were "not a little mortifying to him." It was hoped that Merry's unfriendly feelings would not "check a spirit of conciliation and liberality in his government." Madison should have read Augustus Foster's remark to Lady Elizabeth, likewise carried by Merry and sure to be circulated by the Duke of Devonshire: "We are feared and respected more than the rabble Republicans choose to believe . . . a mere face of anger is all we need show to these Democrats."

Merry had mentioned the interception of some dispatches from Yrujo, and Madison hoped that it might be possible to find out their contents or even procure a copy. This was just after Turreau informed Madison that the Spanish government wished Yrujo to remain as minister. The rejection was so positive that the general would not even present Yrujo's later request that the United States accept a chargé d'affaires. After Madison's repeated refusals, Turreau wrote to the marquis, "I formally declared to him that I would mix no more in your differences with him." If Spanish and American interests were jeopardized by the diplomatic breach, "the responsibility would fall on those who wanted to shoulder it."

Madison sent a full statement of the Yrujo case to Chargé Erving in Madrid, warning him, however, that, while this would prepare Spain for rigorous steps toward the marquis, it "leaves this government uncommitted as to the time and degree of such a resort. Be careful not to depart from this ground." In other words, the handling of Yrujo was subordinate to the Florida policy.[18]

Reports from the American envoys, arriving in November, indicated a stiffening British stand on impressments. To forbid them, Auckland and Holland asserted, would make the American merchant marine a floating asylum for British deserters. They proposed that American seamen be required by law to carry "authentic documents of citizenship" as a protection against boarding parties. The proposal was rejected as a derogation of national sovereignty.

Madison's reply cherished hope for a favorable result, especially as Great Britain had asked for a postponement (quickly granted by Congress) of the nonimportation law. But to Minister Erskine his manner "indicated disappointment and vexation." He expressed himself in very strong terms upon impressment, "intimating that he did not believe that justice was intended to be done to the United States."[19]

The Secretary had no warning of the shock that came on February 1, 1807, when dispatches revealed that the American ministers, violating their instructions, had agreed to leave impressment out of the treaty. At one time the British commissioners yielded, but the cabinet overruled them and allowed only an informal written pledge that naval officers would observe "the greatest caution" in impressing British seamen.

To Erskine, who hurried over, Madison declared that America never would abandon its opposition to impressment. The injury which resulted from stripping American ships of their crews "infinitely outweighed the inconveniences that might be incurred" by the brief withdrawal of a few British sailors from His Majesty's service. It would be easy to recover the latter when American ships visited British ports. Furthermore, abolition of impressment "had been taken up as a point of honor by the United States." On that point they would never yield, but, once it was conceded, they would give every facility for restoring British deserters.

During that day Madison received a note from the President saying he believed the nation would rather go on without a treaty than take one which omitted this article. He was calling the cabinet to ask whether, under this dilemma, we had "not better take the advice of the Senate." The cabinet's vote was "unanimously not," both on consulting the Senate and accepting such a treaty. To give up the nonimportation act without obtaining security against impressments "would be yielding the only peaceable instrument for coercing all our rights." Pending a study of its effect, no action was taken on Madison's tentative suggestion that the United States bar British seamen from American vessels in exchange for abolition of impressment.[20]

Putting some of his disgust into new instructions, Madison wrote that the British government was "under an egregious mistake" in supposing there were no recent causes of complaint. As to the remedy they offered, what good would it do to *repeat* ineffective words? "The habits generated by naval command," plus naval self-interest, made every provision inadequate which did not take away the discretion of the commanders. If no formal stipulation against impressment could be obtained, no treaty should be signed, but the President would agree to an informal mutual understanding if one could be reached. To support it, he would exercise his power to suspend the nonimportation act from July to December 1807, and (barring unfavorable news) would ask Congress for a further extension. The Secretary rejected a British proposal that the produce of enemy colonies be held one month in the United States before reshipment—a mere device, he said, to favor British colonial produce and promote commercial monopoly.[21]

With European mail requiring about five months for a round trip, it was not surprising that when Madison wrote these instructions, a signed treaty violating them had been four weeks on its westward way.

CHAPTER XXVII

TROUBLE WITH ALBION

ON FEBRUARY 6, 1807, an icy wind of hurricane force blew the windows out of the House and Senate chambers, unroofed brick houses and overturned carriages in the streets. Hardly milder was the impact of a wind from France, bearing Napoleon's decree of total blockade against the British Isles. This decree of November 21, 1806, issued at his Berlin camp, converted all British merchandise into lawful prize. No vessel coming from England or her colonies could be received in any port. Ships that evaded this order would be confiscated. The decree was to be fundamental law until Great Britain stopped seizing private property and restrained the right of blockade to seaports actually invested.

Along with the Berlin Decree, Madison received the none-too-firm assurance of the Minister of Marine to Armstrong that these prohibitions would have no effect on neutral ships except when they entered French ports. Decrès refrained from interpreting the blockade itself.[1]

With these papers, Jefferson sent Congress a newly arrived note which vastly cheered him and Madison. It was from Monroe and Pinkney, hastily written to say that they had just concluded a satisfactory treaty on all points. The inference was that Great Britain, by yielding on impressment, had made a powerful bid for American support against the Napoleonic decree, and Madison was not slow in revealing his satisfaction to the friendly new British minister.

Congress was within a few hours of adjourning sine die, on March 3, when Erskine received a copy of the treaty. He "hurried with it immediately . . . to Mr. Madison" to urge him to induce the President to detain the Senate for ratification. Alas! "I am sorry to inform Your Lordship," wrote the minister to Foreign Secretary Howick, "that . . . the treaty was not as satisfactory to

374

him as he has expressed his expectation that it would prove to be."
Madison's first question was: What did it say about impressment?
At the reply that it contained nothing "he expressed the greatest
astonishment and disappointment . . . he did not think it would
be possible to ratify the treaty."

Erskine handed Madison a supplementary note signed by Holland and Auckland. This alone, the Secretary told him, would
prevent ratification even if the treaty were satisfactory. The note
reserved a British right to adopt the same measures against neutral
commerce that Napoleon did. Furthermore, Great Britain would
not be bound to the treaty unless, prior to receipt of the American
ratification, either France abandoned her violations of maritime
law or the United States gave security that it would not submit
to them.

Madison asked Erskine to leave the treaty with him to lay before the President, "who was at that moment very unwell." Jefferson recovered enough from his migraine headache to tell a
senatorial delegation, that evening, that the treaty would not be
submitted to the Senate at all. To Erskine, next day, he said that
"the influence of Washington himself" would have been incapable
of restraining the people's indignation at being called on by one
country for assurances of what they would do in the event of
gross insult and injury by another.[2]

On receipt of the official text of the treaty, in mid-March, Madison wrote briefly to the envoys. They were to be guided until
further notice by his February instruction to seek only an informal
agreement. In the meantime the President, to show his conciliatory spirit, would further suspend the nonimportation act. By this
time Erskine had given notice of a British order in council retaliating against the Berlin Decree. All trade from port to port
of enemy countries was forbidden—a restriction affecting nearly
the whole coast from Trieste to St. Petersburg. By means of a
"paper blockade," it completely banned a trade in which, as other
neutrals vanished, American vessels had almost a monopoly.

Madison protested against taking so injurious an action before
it was known whether the French decree applied to American
vessels at all. A week later he presented one of those analytical

arguments that were so vexatious to foreign diplomats who could not answer them.

In the absence of a blockade, this coastwise trade was lawful both in peace and war. A real blockade being impossible, the order could be looked on only as retaliating on that of France. Retaliation through a neutral ought not to exceed the injury nor precede an unreasonable failure of the neutral to put an end to the wrongful inequality. So, the British order being peremptory and immediate, its execution might be considered premature and unfriendly even if it were certain that France intended to violate her treaties with the United States by restraints on American commerce. Should that prove not to be the case, the British order would "take the character of an original aggression" and furnish France a like ground for retaliation. It was moreover "a palpable violation of a treaty just signed by the British government," and then expected to be speedily ratified.

Madison said he would not dwell on the fact (but obviously wanted London to do so) that owing to certain British treaties, American immunity to the French decree covered British goods carried under the American flag. Thus, England was cutting off her own avenue to the continent, as well as delivering a destructive blow against American commerce. Cargoes from and to the United States were discharged and gathered from port to port in Europe. To restrain them from this essential right would be ruinous. The President, Madison said, was persuaded that the truth of these observations would be reflected in remedial measures.[3]

To leave the way open for new negotiations, Jefferson reported only the substance of the treaty to friendly senators. Newspapers learned of its main provisions and Federalist editors leaped from one extreme to the other in attacking the administration. The *United States Gazette,* which had predicted that an unknown treaty would be ratified, in deepest secrecy, linked the rejection of it with the twin bogeys of French domination and Madison's political aspirations:

"Whether Mons. Turreau has set his famous whiskers against a treaty with England, or whether Mr. Jefferson fears that the successful negotiation of a treaty would render Mr. Monroe more popular than consists with the views of the executive previous to the next presidential election, we are not informed."

The *Gazette* conceded that French explanations might exempt American commerce from the Berlin Decree and thus end the need for British retaliation. In that case, would it be wise to reject a treaty which was said to protect the colonial and East India trade, merely because it failed to forbid the impressment of *British* seamen from American ships? Republican Senator Smith of Maryland wrote to Madison along the same line. Would there not be loud complaints if the people should like the treaty and ship captures should continue after its rejection? Public opinion, he noted, was decidedly opposed to the rejection.[4]

Smith's conjectural summary of the treaty made it better than it was, and Madison wanted advice on some clauses. The United States was to give up the weapon of discriminatory nonimportation. What did it gain in return, outside of trade with the colonies of Britain's enemies? He sent the other commercial articles to such foreign-trade experts as Senator Smith, Tench Coxe and William Jones (later a Madison cabinet member).

The response was wholesale condemnation. The treaty would destroy the East India trade, since it forbade the indirect voyages needed to gather silver bullion for Oriental purchases. American markets were open to all British goods, but many American goods would be excluded from British markets and could be shut out of others by "paper blockades." The United States totally gave up the right to discriminate, but the wording allowed Great Britain to continue her discriminatory duties on her exports. The Senate, Smith declared, would reject the treaty.[5]

On April 3, just before Jefferson left for Monticello, the cabinet approved a new ultimatum to be translated into instructions. Further consideration was given to Madison's proposal that British seamen be excluded from American ships in exchange for abolition of impressment, but no decision was made, pending a report by Gallatin on their numbers. To promote the idea in London, the Secretary of State swept aside Erskine's complaints by saying that the United States could do nothing about deserters in the absence of a treaty provision.

Madison saw a sharp difference in principle between impressing seamen and reclaiming deserters. In the former case, he observed to George Joy, a foreign officer claimed the right to go on board an American ship and pronounce any person he pleased to be a British subject, "and carry his interested decision on the most important of all questions to a freeman, into execution on the spot." To allow this "is so anomalous in principle, so grievous in practice, and so abominable in abuse, that the pretension must finally yield to sober discussion and friendly expostulation."

His views on desertion were outlined to Judge Peters, an admiralty expert. Desertions from merchantmen, Madison wrote, were merely breaches of private contract, to be enforced or not as the policy of the country might dictate. Deserters from foreign ships of war were "on the common footing of exiles liable to punishment, even to capital punishment, for violating the law," but unlike other fugitives, their only offense was flight. "It is well understood that no nation is bound to surrender them to the angry sovereign, unless by some positive stipulation." Great Britain never did so. With the United States there was no obligation to return deserters, and no reason to enter into a reciprocal agreement, "our navy being so small and so little resorting to foreign parts." As for foreign warships in American ports, if fear of desertions kept them away, so much the better. Finally, "as far as humanity can be justly consulted, it does not plead for the surrender of men to vengeance for leaving a situation such as that of a British ship of war into which they have been engaged by a mode such as that of impressment." The only reason for agreeing to surrender them would be to gain more desirable objects.[6]

With his suspicions thoroughly aroused by the treaty pitfalls already uncovered, Madison began "looking critically into the colonial article" and found it more damaging than he had supposed. American merchants could transship enemy colonial goods "to Europe," and could transship the produce "of Europe" to enemy colonies. No distinction was made between colonies beyond the Cape of Good Hope and those in America. Consequently, he told the President, "nothing from India, China or the French,

Dutch or Spanish eastern colonies can be sent to Spanish America, or the enemy islands in the West Indies: nor can the productions of the latter be sent to Smyrna, etc., or the coast of Barbary, etc., or elsewhere than to Europe." Also, American trade between the Asiatic colonies and China would be abolished.

Pointing out these restrictions to Senator Smith, Madison received the reply that this would complete the ruin of the East India and China trade and strike down that with Turkey and South America. The wording as a whole put American commerce at the mercy of British admiralty judges. Better go to war, said Smith, than submit to such a treaty.[7]

Monroe told the public a year later, in bitter self-defense, that the restrictions did not apply to East Indian colonies because they had not been included in the restrictive practices. If that was true, why did he write in the letter accompanying the treaty: "We endeavored to exempt this branch of the trade with enemies' colonies from the operation of the British principle, but that was found to be impracticable"? It was impracticable because, as Lord Auckland told Monroe, the treaty had to meet the approval of the English East India Company, and "this monopoly, as a losing concern, seemed at present to require peculiar protection." Madison, studying effects, uncovered a purpose which Monroe failed to fathom even when it was spelled out to him. It was not by accident that one of Britain's negotiators was President of the Board of Trade.[8]

With these facts before him, the Secretary concluded that the colonial trade would be better off without treaty regulation. This, he wrote to the President, made him perplexed as to the new instructions. He was beginning to suspect that the treaty should be limited to impressments, but on that subject they would need to offer new material. This was at hand, but not as hoped for, in Gallatin's report on British seamen in the American marine. Basing his estimate chiefly on the federal hospital tax deducted from seamen's wages, Gallatin found a total of 67,000 seafarers. Of these, it appeared, about 9,000 were British, but they constituted nearly one half of the able seamen in the foreign trade—enough to make their withdrawal a serious injury.

Mulling this over, Madison thought of a way out. Under British law, alien seamen who served two years in British vessels were claimed as British seamen. Why not ask Great Britain to apply that both ways? British seamen who had been exclusively in American ships for more than two years would stay there. Before this proposal, informally endorsed by the cabinet, reached Jefferson, Gallatin's estimate caused him to reject the original one. Better let the negotiation take a friendly nap, he advised. The cabinet postponed action until his return, when he readily agreed to offer Madison's "two-year rule" as an inducement to end impressment. The new ultimatum also required a guarantee of American trade rights in the Orient and rejected the claim of England to hinge the treaty on assurances of American resistance to French decrees. Two dozen other changes were asked for.

Madison sent these instructions with no anticipation that they would prevail over "the most unfriendly course" expected from the new British cabinet. There was little to hope for, he observed to the President, unless in "their feeble and tottering situation . . . the intruders should be driven out," or—this to Robert Livingston—unless their instability should make them shrink from the political effect of a rupture with the United States. Overhanging all diplomatic efforts he saw a greater menace:

"But whatever amicable arrangements may be put on paper, harmony and good will between the parties cannot be lasting, if the most efficacious remedy be not applied to the atrocious behavior of the British ships of war on our coasts, and even in our harbors."[9]

Those were prophetic words. Three weeks after Madison wrote them, the 36-gun frigate *Chesapeake,* sailing for the Mediterranean, was followed out of Hampton Roads by the 50-gun British *Leopard,* whose captain signaled that he wished to send a letter on board. It proved to be an order from Admiral Berkeley at Halifax that the *Chesapeake,* if met with at sea, be searched for deserters from British ships. Accompanying it was a demand for three seamen named as deserters from the *Melampus.* This being refused, the *Leopard* poured broadside after broadside into the helpless frigate (whose decks had not been cleared for action) until with masts falling and twenty-two holes in the hull, Captain Barron struck his colors. Writing to Madison an hour after the victims were brought ashore, Brigadier General Thomas Mathews of the Virginia militia reported three dead and nineteen (actually eighteen) injured, and continued:

"The British after the American colors were struck boarded the *Chesapeake* and took four men from her. They refused to have anything to do with the ship [*i.e.,* refused to treat her as a prize] and the officers were compelled for the sake of humanity and their own preservation to bring the ship into Hampton Roads."

With Dearborn and Gallatin out of town, a week was required to assemble the cabinet. In that interval Jefferson drafted a proclamation excluding all British warships from American waters, unless in distress or on diplomatic business. Madison revealed his feelings in the changes he suggested for this deliberately mild document. British warships "on this station" became warships "hovering on our coasts and frequenting our harbors." Jefferson's factual narrative beginning "and recently a frigate" was changed to: "and omitting insults as gross as language could offer, the public sensibility has at length been brought to a serious crisis by an act transcending all former outrages. A frigate," etc. Madison inserted such phrases as "this enormity," "the avowed and insulting purpose of violating a ship of war under the American flag," "a pretext the more flagrant," "her lawless and bloody purpose." Where Jefferson justified the ban as resulting from "a well-grounded despair of any other practicable remedy," Madison linked conciliation with indemnities. Mutual desire to avoid a rupture should "strengthen the motives to an honorable reparation for the wrong" and lead to that effectual control of British naval commanders which alone could justify future hospitality and maintain the existing relations of the two nations.[10]

Jefferson accepted all but the most violent of Madison's revisions, but gave them a further toning down in the final draft, made public while war fever was sweeping the country. To Erskine, the words "honorable reparation" left no doubt of the American government's desire to avoid war. Calling this phrase to the attention of Captain Douglas, he urged the senior squadron commander to refrain from violence and, in particular, to drop his menaces against Norfolk. There, after an enraged populace destroyed water casks sent ashore for filling, Douglas had uttered threats of war and established a virtual blockade with his four big warships.

The city was ruled by a Committee of Correspondence under General Mathews—very useful, Littleton Tazewell wrote to Jefferson, "to fan the holy flame which is kindling in the bosom of every American," but somewhat dangerous when it usurped the government and forbade the British consul to communicate with the squadron. Tazewell, emissary of the Norfolk mayor to Douglas, heard from levelheaded British officers just what Erskine assured Madison: it was extremely improbable that Berkeley's orders were sanctioned by his government. Later, Tazewell headed a naval court of inquiry which found Captain Barron guilty of indecision and negligence.[11]

The cabinet, meeting almost daily, voted to bring all warships home from the Mediterranean and to call on state governors to place 100,000 militia in readiness for federal service. War plans were outlined, ranging from harbor defense to an attack on Montreal. (Robert Fulton, Madison was told, wanted to blow up British warships at once with a newly invented torpedo.) Diplomatic demands on England were approved and the armed schooner *Revenge* ordered to carry them. A special session of Congress was called for October, by which time an answer could be expected.

Drafting instructions to Monroe, Madison laid down a premise: "This enormity is not a subject for discussion." The immunity of a national ship of war from search on the high seas, he said, had never been contested by any nation, and Great Britain would be second to none in resenting such an insult. The spirit pervading the United States was abolishing the distinctions of party (a fact reported also by Erskine) and was demanding in the loudest tone an "honorable reparation" for "the indignity offered to the sovereignty and flag of the nation, and the blood of citizens so wantonly and wickedly shed."

Two things, Madison said, were indispensable: formal disavowal of the deed and restoration of the four impressed seamen. Beyond this, the United States had a right to expect "every solemnity of form and every other ingredient of retribution and respect, which according to usage and the sentiments of mankind, are proper in the strongest cases of insult to the rights and sovereignty of a nation." The multiplied infractions of American rights by British naval commanders, and the failure of past appeals, left no alternative but voluntary satisfaction by Great Britain "or a resort to means depending on the United States alone."

Should reparations be refused, the minister was told, all American vessels in British ports must be hurried home and the Russian ambassador should be notified of the probable resort "to measures constituting or leading to war." This was Madison's second 1807 attempt to revive Russian opposition to British navalism.[12]

Not mentioned in the original draft, but conspicuous in the final July 6 letter, was this imperative requirement: "An entire abolition of impressments from vessels under the flag of the United States, if not already arranged, is also to make an indispensable part of the satisfaction." Inclusion of impressment converted the negotiation from simple reparation for a naval outrage into pressure for a fundamental change of British policy. How could this be hopefully sought from a London cabinet known to be dominated, as Monroe was about to phrase it, by "the ship owners, the navy, the East and West India merchants, and certain political characters," all of whom wanted to extend the ravages of war to the United States? The answer may lie in Madison's belief that the political "instability and imbecility" of that cabinet would make it shrink from a rupture. The purpose is evident in his comment to Bowdoin: "In the present posture of our relations to Great Britain it is prudent to turn them, as much as can be honorably done, to account in our other foreign relations."

In the course of three weeks, Secretary Foster of the British legation reported, a majority of the American people had so swung around that instead of wishing "to see Bonaparte destroyed as the

best pledge of safety to themselves, they now desire the contrary."
Thus popular fear of France ceased to be a deterrent to pressure on
England for a broader settlement.

Writing to Armstrong and Bowdoin, Madison withdrew the
offer to buy the Floridas. Need of money in case of war with
England was the reason overtly given, but others were visible. In
May, the Secretary had written that the Spanish crisis could not
be dragged out much longer. An armed conflict on the Sabine
had been avoided by American moderation but the obstruction of
the Mobile was kindling a flame which soon would be irresistible.
The threatened break with England now suggested two thoughts:

1. Entry of the United States into the war, or even a cessation
of commerce with England, would be such an aid to France and
Spain that the price asked for the Floridas should "be at least
greatly reduced."

2. Hostile relations between the United States and Great Britain
might lead to British occupation of the Floridas "with views very
adverse to the policy of Spain." In a note to be paraphrased for
French and Spanish ears Madison did not add the corollary, stated
a month later by Jefferson, that in the event of war with England,
the United States would occupy Florida ahead of the British.[13]

Thus, though a *disavowal* of the attack on the frigate was essential to maintenance of peace, direct *reparation* for it was subordinated to other ends. Jefferson and Madison were willing to
prolong the crisis, and possibly add to the risk of war, in an effort
to end impressment and gain the Floridas. Danger of hostilities
was not diminished by the "continued spirit of insolence and
hostility" in the British squadron. As Madison described it to
Monroe: "Merchant vessels arriving and departing have been
challenged, fired at, examined and detained within our jurisdiction, with as little scruple as if they were at open sea." Even a
revenue cutter bearing the Vice President met with insult. The
blockade of Norfolk has "amounted as much to an invasion and
a siege as if an army had debarked and invested it on the land
side." Following the President's proclamation, some of the vessels
moved outside the capes or left entirely; others defiantly remained. Citing half a dozen earlier outrages, the Secretary said

they "form a mass of injuries and provocations which have justly excited the indignant feelings of the nation and severely tried the patience of the government." All should be brought into view to augment the retribution for the past and produce securities for the future.[14]

Minister Erskine, during these explosive weeks, protested the President's proclamation, objected to the flag of truce required of British warships seeking communication or supplies, and (at Berkeley's request) asked reparations for the navy's smashed water casks. At the same time he chided the admiral and warned his government that the United States "will engage in war rather then submit to their national armed ships being forcibly searched on the high seas." An apology for the attack by the *Leopard,* he wrote, "would have the most powerful effect not only on the minds of the people of this country, but would render it impossible for the Congress to bring on a war upon the other points of difference."

Madison, Erskine continued, had repeatedly spoken of his government's dissatisfaction over the acquittal of Captain Whitby, whose cannon shot killed a seaman in New York harbor, and of the insulting conduct of Captain Love of the *Driver.* The Secretary foresaw either war or an alternative short of it:

"He remarked to me [wrote Erskine] that all the subjects of complaint would be taken up by Congress on their meeting and that he was confident that unless a satisfactory redress of injuries was afforded that very strong measures of restraint upon the intercourse between Great Britain and the United States would be adopted by the legislature, and that with regard to (what he called) the late insult to the flag of the United States that unless reparation was granted, war must be the consequence, and that preparations for it of the most extensive kind would be entered upon by the Congress."[15]

Jefferson and Madison overruled the executive council of Virginia, which wanted to hold a captured British landing party as prisoners of war. By avoiding a decision that a *de facto* war existed, the Secretary told Monroe, the government left itself free to act according to expediency. The public, rallying to the proclamation, was ready for a determined stand:

"Reparation or war is proclaimed at every meeting . . . and the reparation must . . . satisfy the just feelings of a nation which values its honor, and knows its importance."

The British government, Madison hoped, would not be misled into thinking it could abridge the reparation by the mode of rendering it. "If for example a minister specially sent to disavow and repair the insult, should supersede the ordinary minister and remain here, it would be regarded as a species of subterfuge. His immediate return will be necessary to show to the world that his mission was for the purpose avowed."

Madison disapproved the smashing of the water casks and other excesses, and then found on his desk an unopened dispatch from Berkeley to Erskine. Intercepted by a zealous citizen, it had been turned over to Editor Duane of Philadelphia and forwarded to Washington. Madison sent it to the minister at Philadelphia still unopened, but soon found that its detention by the editor was regarded as a national insult almost comparable to the attack on the *Chesapeake*. The Secretary replied that Duane showed vigilant attention to regulations regarding the British fleet, but that, regardless of this, punishment could not be demanded by a foreign government whose naval commanders had been unpunished for violation of American public dispatches, including the breaking of seals and publication of the contents.[16]

Although Madison denied that the nationality of the four men taken from the *Chesapeake* affected Britain's liability, he furnished numerous affidavits showing that two were natives of Maryland (one an ex-slave who took the name of his white father), while a third, also a Negro, had been brought from South America by a sea captain at the age of six. From Berkeley, through Erskine, came the reply that all three Americans enlisted voluntarily, from American ships, after two of them (the Negroes) had been impressed at sea and restored to their vessel in a British port. Madison made short work of this. Irrelevant to begin with, it confessed to the knowing enlistment of American deserters, without consulting American law. When these men fled from the *Melampus* in Norfolk they were "replaced by their own act within the complete possession of the country to which they owed allegiance" and which "had the same right to their services as to those of its other citizens." The Secretary called the fourth man an American, but the British officers were so sure he was their countryman that they hanged him.[17]

Madison reached Montpelier ahead of a twelve-inch rain which carried away his milldam on Blue Run, along with nearly all others in that part of Virginia. Augustus Foster spent some time with him, borrowed $70 because the floods cut off an expected letter, and wrote back that every spoke in his gig flew out as he jolted through the ruts toward Fauquier Courthouse. Such a road would even "try Mrs. Madison's utmost patience. Indeed, I believe she would be inclined to walk the whole of it."

Foster offered congratulations on the probability, becoming stronger every day, that Anglo-American differences would be settled without a quarrel. Other reports gave Madison a feeling, early in September, that affairs had taken a good turn in London. Replying to an opposition query, Naval Treasurer "Old George" Rose had said in July "that the adjustment taking place with the United States would put an end to the non-importation act." This, Madison commented to the President, implied an end to impressment and security for the colonial trade, since the American instructions linked all these subjects. Rose was badly informed. The treaty revision, never going well, came to a halt the instant the attack on the *Chesapeake* became known. With it perished a boundary settlement in which Madison tried to have Grand Manan Island (New Brunswick) recognized as American territory.[18]

First word of that attack reached Monroe from Foreign Minister Canning, who quickly cut down the acute war hazard. "You will find," wrote Madison, sending the London letters to the President, "that the British government renounces the pretension to search ships of war for deserters, but employs words which may possibly be meant to qualify the renunciation or at least to quibble away the proposed atonement." He suspected this from Canning's irritable tone and the basing of his note on newspaper accounts even though he had received Berkeley's dispatches. "The execution of the fourth seaman and the insulting trial at Halifax," Madison observed, "show that Berkeley is in little dread of resentment in his superiors." He believed that the man was hanged not only to avoid the humiliation of restoring a British seaman but to reverse the dreaded impulse to desertion which that action would produce. The hanging furnished added proof "of the absolute necessity of a radical cure for the evils inflicted by British ships of war frequenting our waters."

To Erskine, who gave notice of the execution, Madison expressed his extreme pain and surprise. Reparation for the attack on the *Chesapeake,* he asserted, required restoration of all the seamen before any question could be admitted as to their allegiance. The execution had rendered satisfaction impossible. The offending officer, Berkeley, had "aggravated in the worst form, the enormity first committed by him." If, in doing this, he carried out the purposes of his government, no atonement could be expected. If he contradicted its purposes, his presumption called for "a still more exemplary punishment than has been provoked by his original guilt." Combined with the continuing defiance of public authority by warships forbidden the use of United States waters, this conduct furnished new topics for redress, distinct from all that had gone before.

Erskine saw plainly that the Navy was ruining all chance of peace with friendship. "I am persuaded," he wrote to Canning in October, "that more ill will has been excited . . . by a few trifling illegal captures immediately off this coast, and some instances of insulting behavior . . . in the very harbors and waters of the United States, than by the most rigid enforcement of the maritime rights of Great Britain against the trade of the United States in other parts of the world." Perhaps it was necessary to watch the whole coast of an independent nation as closely as if it were blockaded, "but it has certainly excited and must continue that animosity towards Great Britain which this government has so often manifested."[19]

As the time drew near for his return to Washington in the fall of 1807, Madison's thoughts went ahead to the special session of Congress. Would it not be proper, he asked the President, to let the *National Intelligencer* publish Canning's disavowal of the right to search ships of war, using his exact words but not quoting them? "This will enable the public to appreciate the chances of peace." Whether the British decree against port-to-port trade in Europe was to be placed before Congress must depend on later accounts from London. And "if nothing changes the posture of things with Spain, very serious questions must arise with respect to that silly and arrogant power."

A week later, the *Intelligencer* told its readers that "the British government has, it appears, signified to Mr. Monroe that"—and the unquoted disavowal followed in Canning's words. In the same issue was a two-column reprint from the pro-American London *Chronicle* telling how the 44-gun American *Constellation* (a ship of 36 guns and out of commission) had answered a warning shot by firing a broadside at the 50-gun *Leopard* which then gave the powerful American vessel a thorough licking. Having thus chanted "Rule Britannia," the *Chronicle* contradicted the Tory press by saying that the British commander was to blame.[20]

Sinister news was in the *Intelligencer* on the day Madison reached Washington, October 5. Great Britain's special ambassador to Denmark, known ever after as "Copenhagen Jackson," had served notice that the British fleet drawn up behind him would bombard the capital unless the country joined England in the war. More than the Danes were menaced by his preliminary declaration: "That in the present disturbed state of the continent it was impossible to distinguish any longer between a neutral and an enemy, but by her becoming an ally or an open foe." Later papers told of the bombardment, which killed hundreds of women and children, and of Denmark's surrender of her fleet, but not of the remark made by King George of England when Jackson described his mission: that it was well the Prince Regent of Denmark received him on the ground floor, "for if he had half the spirit of his uncle George III, he would infallibly have kicked you down stairs."

There was grim fitness in the publication, beneath the announcement of Madison's return, of the report of a House of Commons committee on the distress of planters in the British West Indies. It was due to the low state of the foreign sugar market, "in which formerly the British merchant enjoyed nearly a monopoly, but where he cannot at present enter . . . [owing to] the facility of intercourse between the hostile [French] colonies and Europe, under the American neutral flag."[21]

These were dark portents. England was greeting the defeat of Prussia and desertion of Russia, not by bidding for the friendship of neutrals, but by brutal use of naval power against one of them. Concessions in colonial trade, already offered the United States by the former ministry, seemed about to vanish under the spreading influence of *War in Disguise* and its preachment of commercial monopoly. Since no agreement could be hoped for under these conditions, Jefferson's cabinet voted unanimously on October 10 that the rejected treaty should not be laid before Congress with the President's message.

In writing that message, Jefferson heeded Madison's advice to say nothing about France if the late news from England proved bad. Jefferson's papers contain voluminous suggestions for changes, from Gallatin and Rodney, but none from Madison. Since the message dealt mainly with foreign affairs, this probably reflected their close collaboration beforehand. The first draft impressed Gallatin as "a manifesto issued against Great Britain on the eve of a war," rather than a reflection of the existing uncertainty. It was toned down a little, but when the British minister read the softened document, he found it "most unfriendly."

Erskine asked Madison why the President made no reference to Canning's conciliatory language to Monroe. The reason, replied the Secretary, could be found in that language itself, which left it doubtful whether the injury complained of would be redressed. Madison's unwillingness to grasp an olive branch because of its lack of leaves confirmed a suspicion the minister had been forming. Visiting the President, he sought the reason for demanding a nonimpressment clause in the *Chesapeake* settlement.

It appeared, Jefferson answered, that if security were given against all impressments, it would avoid the separate points of honor and make it easier to give satisfaction for the attack on the national ship. That was true, but it was like saying: "If we first move the mountain, it will be easier to get rid of the boulder." The answer confirmed, for Erskine, what he reported to Canning after his prior talk with Madison:

"It is most certainly the aim of this government, by blending the various grounds of complaint against Great Britain with that of the attack upon their frigate (Chesapeake) to prevent the effect of any apology or redress . . . from allaying the indignation of the people."

The administration wished this kept up, he went on, in order to induce the people to support their government's position in other points of conflict. The accuracy of Erskine's analysis could hardly be challenged, since Madison had outlined that exact line of action to Monroe and Bowdoin months before.[22]

CHAPTER XXVIII

EMBARGO

OCTOBER 5, 1807, was a day for coincidences. While Madison, arriving in Washington, was reading about the British attack on Denmark, Erskine in Philadelphia gave his government a warning. From Madison's letters they would see that great offense had been given by the parliamentary report attacking American trade with French colonies, and by the orders in council prohibiting port-to-port trade in Europe. Impressment and the attack on the *Chesapeake* presented still more critical issues. Erskine was "fully convinced" that unless these disputes were on their way to friendly adjustment by the time Congress assembled late in the month, "a system of commercial restrictions on the trade of Great Britain with this country will be immediately formed and every step short of actual war taken to show their dissatisfaction."

On that same day, the fast ship *Sansom* sailed from Plymouth with the latest London news. Newspapers to that date were carried from Bordeaux by the *Sally-Barker-Windsor*. And on that day, George Joy, Madison's confidential informant in the British capital, re-emphasized his August warning of "a terrible hue and cry from the West India interest" on the subject of American ships in the colonial trade.[1]

The United States had to make a decision, since the twice-postponed act excluding certain British goods was to take effect in December. "If we resort to non-importation," observed Jefferson, "it will end in war and give her [Great Britain] the choice of the moment of declaring it." The President's aversion to war was matched by the country's unreadiness for it. The frigate *Constitution,* arriving at Boston from the Mediterranean, was to have her crew discharged to save expenses. But the men could not be paid off until a new appropriation was made, so the ship was ordered to New York to give Congress time to act. The condition of the militia, as the Secretary of War viewed it, was "really deplorable throughout the Union"—seven cannon in all of Pennsylvania and one musket for each five men.

This did not prevent Madison from adopting a somewhat truculent tone regarding Florida. Talleyrand, he observed to Armstrong, construed a request for France's opinion as to Louisiana boundaries "into an entire submission of them to the decision of the emperor." No such idea should be allowed to take root. The United States was to be kept free "to assert their rights against all parties under the convention of purchase," and "if Spain really wishes to live in peace with us she must be infatuated not to hasten a removal of the obstacles to its continuance."[2]

The *Sansom* whisked across the Atlantic in thirty-six days. Monroe, its captain said, was about to sail for home in an air of gloom. A London merchant wrote that an order intensifying impressment was to be issued at once. The London *Star* was reliably informed "that our government has resolved to retaliate on France by a proclamation, exactly on the model of the French decree of blockade." Seizure of vessels would "settle at once the clamors of the Americans respecting their right to trade with the French colonies."

A few days after this appeared, the *National Intelligencer* published the grist from the *Sally-Barker-Windsor*. The emperor had ordered the capture of every vessel bound to or from England. "This is a mortal blow to the American commerce," wrote a merchant, "and we fear will lead to a rupture between America and France." The same bad news had just reached Madison, and he gave Editor Smith the text of Napoleon's ruling. There were to be no exceptions from the Berlin decree.[3]

With Great Britain and France competing in ruthlessness, Jefferson and his cabinet swung toward the idea of a general embargo on American shipping. That would put both belligerents on the same legal footing, with the heaviest pressure on England, the chief offender. Gallatin, probably thinking of the loss of revenue, suggested instead a general nonimportation act directed against Great Britain, to take effect in two months. That has some "good phases," Jefferson replied next day. "I have only seen Mr. Madison as yet, who objects to it." This marked a change in Madison's position since early 1806, when, replying to Elbridge Gerry's suggestion of a general embargo, he said he preferred selective nonimportation. Such a law, hitting British exporters, was now on the books. Madison wanted to make the pressure on England cumulative, and extend it to France, by retaining the existing law and adding a general embargo, which if effectively enforced would starve the West Indian colonies of both of these marauding powers.

Word came from Monroe ahead of his return (he reached Washington December 22), shifting the locus of negotiation. Great Britain, refusing to link the impressment issue with *Chesapeake* reparations, was sending "Young George" Rose as special envoy to settle the latter dispute. George Joy, posting Madison on Britain's reported decision to declare the French world besieged, reported that two more official *Gazettes* had come out without an order for it.

Madison received the *Gazette* of October 17, proclaiming rigorous impressments from merchant vessels. To Americans, this looked like the prelude to greater outrages. English newspapers called it a craven surrender of the historic right to search American warships. On December 12 the *Brutus* reached New York from Liverpool, bringing word that every English newspaper of November 12 treated the signing of drastic anti-French orders as a verity. They were in fact signed the day before—the historic Orders in Council of November 11, 1807, which led to the War of 1812.[4]

On the day this grim news was published in Washington, the President sent Napoleon's seizure order and King George's impressment proclamation to Congress. To accompany the papers, he drafted a message telling of France's unexpected extension of the Berlin Decree and forecasting the new British orders. It concluded with a question:

"If therefore on leaving our harbors we are certain to lose them, is it not better as to vessels, cargoes and seamen to keep them at home? This is submitted to the wisdom of Congress who alone are competent to provide a remedy."

Barely asking for legislation, and relying partially on things yet to happen, this might have jeopardized congressional action. In place of it Madison wrote a two-sentence message (hastily, for the draft is a penciled scrawl) which Jefferson used after striking out the word "immediate" (offensive to congressional pride) and changing one or two other words:

"The communications now made showing the great and increasing danger with which our merchandise, our vessels and our seamen are threatened on the high seas and elsewhere from the belligerent powers of Europe, and it being of the greatest importance to keep in safety these essential resources, I deem it my duty to recommend the subject to the consideration of Congress, who will doubtless perceive all the advantage which may be expected from an immediate inhibition of the departure of our vessels from the ports of the United States.

"Their wisdom will also see the necessity of making every preparation for whatever events may grow out of the present crisis."[5]

The embargo bill went through the Senate, 22 to 7, on the day the message was read, and the House passed it three days later. Senator Adams remarked in committee that the papers sent by the President were inadequate to warrant so drastic a measure. The law was wanted, replied Smith of Maryland, to aid in the coming negotiations with Rose, and "it might enable us to get rid of the Non-Importation Act." Adams wrote in his diary: "I believe there are yet other reasons." Obviously there were. It was adopted, Madison told Erskine, to forestall the capture of American ships by France "and also from an apprehension of a retaliating order by Great Britain."[6]

Federalists and Quids (dissident Republicans) hailed the Embargo Act with commercial dismay and political delight. "Mr. Jefferson has imposed an embargo to please France, and to beggar us!" exclaimed a Bostonian to Senator Pickering. Let it remain three or four months and it would bring down "curses loud and deep." From Randolph came outcries loud and shrill. America was being dragooned into a French alliance, crouching "to the insolent mandate of Bonaparte 'that there should be no neutrals.' "

Turreau, however, lamented to Champagny that his high hopes of a British-American war had evaporated. Madison told him that France's aggressions put that country on a par with England, and the United States "would provide for its proper security."

When the text of the British orders arrived in January, Madison expected an immediate improvement in sentiment. Observing to Robert Livingston that the embargo had excited no more complaint than was to be apprehended, he added:

"The late decrees of Great Britain, which it anticipated, will probably impose silence in quarters where the measure may still not give satisfaction."

On the contrary, although Republicans rallied to support the embargo, Federalist charges of capitulation to France grew louder. Assertions that the government had heard of the British decrees in advance were treated as evasive afterthoughts. Madison, however, repeatedly assured Professor Tucker "that they knew of these orders by a friendly correspondent in England," and he wrote to Henry Wheaton that a copy of the unsigned orders was lying on the President's desk when he prepared his message. All doubt would have vanished had Jefferson used this draft, with its dramatic assertion that "the whole world is thus laid under interdict by these two nations."[7]

The wording of the British orders confirmed the worst forecasts. With revealing exceptions, all seaports controlled by France were to be subject to the same restrictions as if they were blockaded, and all vessels trading to such ports were to be seized and condemned. Drastically applied, that would have been a retaliatory war measure. Exempted, however, were neutral vessels trading *directly* between their home ports and French colonies; also vessels *which had last cleared from British ports* after paying special taxes and receiving licenses. This was not mere retaliation against the Berlin Decree. It was commercial warfare upon neutrals, with a two-fold design: (1) to destroy the broken-voyage American trade between French colonies and Europe; (2) to supply Napoleon's empire with British colonial goods and home manufactures carried by American ships operating under British license. This completely confirmed Joy's prediction to Madison that if the British cabinet failed to make an amicable adjustment with the United States, "the West India interest would be the real, whatever might be the ostensible obstacle."[8]

Generations later, this was fully proved by the papers of British cabinet members—Castlereagh, Perceval, Hawkesbury and others. Canning could not even persuade his colleagues to "keep out of sight" the provisions which gave the measure "the air of a commercial rather than a political transaction." Perceval, Chancellor of the Exchequer, summed up the purpose after the orders were signed:

"The short principle is that trade in British produce and manufactures, and trade either from a British port or with a British destination, is to be protected as much as possible. . . . Our orders . . . say to the enemy, 'If you will not have *our* trade, as far as we can help it you shall have *none*.' "

Most remarkable of all, this cabinet discussion *began* three days after the London *Star* confidently predicted the *outcome* of it. Castlereagh, who proposed the order, could have furnished that inspired item from the inner circle, but the tone was that of James Stephen, the author of *War in Disguise,* whose system of commercial monopoly was being adopted under the disguise of military retaliation.[9]

Madison's relation to the embargo can best be judged by his previous record. In 1789 and 1791, he broached the plan of retaliatory duties to force England to revise her discriminatory navigation laws. In 1794 he proposed the same method of fighting her wartime depredations on American commerce. The Federalists opposed the move, then were swept by New England's clamor over ship seizures into imposing a thirty-day embargo. Madison's comments both on the provocation and the action could have been repeated in 1807.

"You will find in the newspapers," he wrote to General Gates in 1794, "the havoc made on our trade in the West Indies." But if Great Britain declared war, she would break up the portion of American trade that was useful to her.

"I conclude therefore that she will push her aggressions just so far and no farther than she imagines we will tolerate. I conclude also that the readiest expedient for stopping her career of depredation on those parts of our trade which thwart her plans, will be to make her feel for those which she cannot do without."

That could have been a reply to Perceval thirteen years later. When British and French partisans in Congress united to prevent a renewal of the 1794 embargo, Madison lamented that "its expiration will save the West Indies from famine," ending the pressure on England.

"Measures of this sort [he wrote to Jefferson] are not the fashion. To supplicate for peace, and by the uncertainty of success, to prepare for war by taxes and troops is the policy which now triumphs under the patronage of the Executive. Every attack on Great Britain through her commerce is at once discomfited."[10]

Thus the aggressive argument for the 1807 embargo was stated years before by Madison. Jefferson's view was defensive. "If we had suffered our vessels, cargoes and seamen to have gone out, all would have been taken" and war would have ensued. Better "discontinue all intercourse with those nations till they shall return again to some sense of moral right." Nevertheless, he had long been inclined to commercial pressure. His 1793 report as Secretary of State on foreign-trade restrictions, called for by Congress as a device to avoid action on Madison's 1791 proposals, formed the prelude to the latter's more famous resolves of '94. Commercial retaliation, as a substitute for war, was fresh in Jefferson's mind when he entered the Presidency. He had been in office but four months when he said to Pichon:

"At the first denial of justice, we will close all our ports to the English. We can see the effect this step would produce in the illuminations that took place in London when it was learned that the resolution proposed by Mr. Madison to restrain British commerce alone, had been rejected."

Madison put the subject unofficially before the country in 1805.
Receiving Armstrong's suggestion of a commercial embargo
against Spain, he enlarged upon the efficacy of the system to the
President:

"Indeed, if a commercial weapon can be properly shaped for
the Executive hand, it is more and more apparent to me that it
can force all the nations having colonies in this quarter of the
globe to respect our rights."[11]

A few weeks later, the *National Intelligencer* published a two-
part series of "Remarks on Repelling Aggressions on Neutral
Rights," signed "Washington." The source was unmistakable.
Federalist Editor William Jackson wrote in his Philadelphia *Political Register:* "We hazard the opinion, that this exclusive Manifesto is the production of Mr. Madison." The New York *Evening
Post* wanted to know why the administration smothered the ill
deeds of France and Spain in resentment against England, and
still did nothing:

"If Mr. Madison's celebrated resolutions, of which the party
have vaunted so much in the days of their minority, are calculated
to bring England to terms, they can have no excuse now that they
are the majority, for not adopting them in their utmost latitude.
And let them remember that if they fail to coerce England into
what is right and just, they can no longer lay the blame on the
shoulders of the Federalists."

These comments created a diplomatic situation which could not
be ignored. Editor Smith of the *Intelligencer* told his readers that
he ordinarily took no account of statements that his paper was the
American equivalent of Napoleon's *Moniteur.* But to prevent misconception in Europe he felt it necessary to say that "of these
offensive paragraphs every member of the administration is as
guiltless as the unborn infant. They are from the pen of the editor, and dictated exclusively by his own ideas." Then, in what
Josiah Quincy called "a maneuver very remarkable," Smith added
that "whatever satisfaction he feels in holding the same opinions

with those who are at the head of public affairs, he would not, for any consideration, sacrifice the independent feelings of an American citizen." After taking Madison off the diplomatic hook, the explanation restored the full force of the articles as a guide to administration policy and a possible source of pressure on Great Britain.[12]

These 1805 articles were as surely Madison's as if he had signed them. From beginning to end, they paraphrased the speeches he delivered in Congress on January 1 and 14, 1794. Even the number of Englishmen to be thrown out of work by American reprisals was exactly the same—300,000. "Let them be driven to poverty and despair," said he in 1794, and what would be the result? "They would compel their government to change their policy, or inflict upon it a fatal vengeance," came the reply in 1805.

America's superior ability to apply pressure to England lay in the nature of the trade. "We send necessaries to her. She sends superfluities to us," was the way he phrased it in 1794. Eleven years later: "Our products they must have. . . . Theirs, however promotive of our comfort, we can to a considerable degree do without."

In the earlier period Madison used these arguments to sustain a system of retaliatory duties designed to compel just treatment of American commerce. In 1805 he expounded "an intermediate course between submission and war," with four alternative or cumulative methods of applying pressure on an offending nation:

1. Extraordinary duties.
2. Prohibition of exports to their territories.
3. Prohibition to import or consume their commodities.
4. Prohibition of all intercourse whatever.

The first of these measures would deal a heavy blow to British manufactures. The third would have greater effect of this kind and would "be a solemn indication of the vigorous tone of the national sentiment; of the resolution of the American people to sacrifice their luxuries and even many of their comforts to avenging the insults and injuries so wantonly inflicted upon them." The second method would throw British colonies into a state of insurrection or economic paralysis, while the fourth "would be still more fatal" to the colonies. "Would they not unavoidably be converted into the theatres of want, famine, rebellion and conflagration?"

Against the minor privations to Americans, Madison saw positive advantages in a reprisal policy. "Our own manufactures would be efficiently fostered. . . . No event can be more desirable." It would reduce the country's dependence on Britain, whose government believed, "with some truth, that our citizens would rather crouch to a degree of aggression than hazard a rupture." New channels of trade would be opened. To these gains, which he had cited also in 1794, he added a new one—development of the vast resources of Louisiana, among which "the single article of sugar" would indemnify the country for great sacrifices.

"These," Madison asserted, "are the resources that belong to a pacific policy: resources whose application would strike terror into the hearts of those whose aggressions we at present suffer." Should no "honorable arrangements" be made by the Executive to end these evils, "Congress might direct the above measures successively to be pursued by the Executive, at fixed periods, provided the causes of complaint were not removed." This would convince the aggressing nations that no improper concessions would be made. Should these pacific expedients unfortunately terminate in war,

"Our enemies would know that, the measures pursued being those of Congress . . . the undivided resources of the nation would, if necessary, be embarked, aided by the undivided suffrage of the people. The issue of such a contest the American people need not dread."

Here, put before the country in 1805, was the full line of thought that ran through Madison's retaliatory measures of 1789, 1791 and 1794, through the 1806 nonimportation act and the 1807 embargo, to the War of 1812. If that was "Mr. Madison's War," his too were the policies short of war by which the Jefferson administration sought to avoid it, or to postpone it while the country gathered basic strength. And the supposedly accidental by-product of those policies—the great expansion of American manufactures which followed the cutting off of imports—was set forth by him both in 1794 and 1805 as an argument for such a course.

The day after Jefferson signed the Embargo Act, the *National Intelligencer* published the first of three articles explaining and approving it. Sending this to London, Erskine expressed the belief that it was drawn up by some member of the government. The London *Chronicle* gave it a prefatory note saying that its American correspondent named Madison as the author. George Joy sent it to the opposition leader, Lord Holland, with the comment: "I see enough of Mr. Madison's style, manner and sentiments . . . to be satisfied that the Notes . . . are his."[13]

The embargo, this article asserted, was "a strong measure proceeding from the energy of the public councils"—one which could no longer be delayed without sacrificing the vital interests of the nation. British "interpolations into the maritime code" had brought on retaliation by France, and then a chain of reprisals not yet ended, for it was clear that "Great Britain meditates further retaliations, most probably an interdict of all trade by this country" with her enemies.

Reverting, almost verbatim, to the language he had used in 1794, Madison said that the embargo, besides guarding the country's maritime resources, would "have the collateral effect of making it the interest of all nations to change the system which has driven our commerce from the ocean." Great Britain would "feel it in her manufactures, in the loss of naval stores, and above all in the supplies essential to her colonies." France would feel it in the loss of colonial luxuries, Spain in loss of imported food. But, it was asked, might it not bring on war?

"Certainly not, if war be not predetermined on against us. Being a measure of peace and precaution; being universal, and therefore impartial; extending in reality as well as ostensibly to all nations, there is not a shadow of pretext to make it a cause of war."

He analyzed the argument that foreign ships ought to be allowed to carry on the American trade. This would not only give an exclusive advantage to one belligerent, but would drive American seamen, probably forever, into British service. Ships would be sold for half their value; Great Britain would be given the monopoly for which she was striving. The embargo, then, was the best expedient, and it was only necessary for a people confiding in their government "to rally round the measure which that government has adopted for their good."

The second article undertook to minimize the economic damage of the embargo. Farm prices would drop, but farmers had marketed their 1807 crops and bought their winter supplies. Most of the merchants who failed would be those trading fraudulently on capital drawn from unpaid accounts. In any event, the people had shown their spirit, and their support would arm the nation in defense of the country without the evils of war.

Closing the series, Madison repeated the language of 1794 and 1805: "We shall be deprived of market for our superfluities. They will feel the want of necessaries." The embargo would "extend those household manufactures" which the country particularly needed, and open important new lines of industry that would draw skilled workmen from abroad. But the advantage most to be prized was a death-blow to "the insulting opinion in Europe that submission to wrongs of every sort" would be preferred to a suspension of commerce. The opportunity was at hand for putting an end forever to this misconception of our national character.

"Let the example teach the world that our firmness equals our moderation; that having resorted to a measure just in itself, and adequate to its object, we will flinch from no sacrifices which the honor and good of the nation demand from virtuous and faithful citizens."

In this appraisal, Madison overrated the willingness of the people to make sacrifices to support a policy short of war. He underrated the effect of suddenly canceling a foreign trade whose unnatural height linked the country's prosperity to war in Europe. But he made it plain that in his mind the embargo was a positive instrument of national policy, not an act of submission to any power, and he left no doubt of his faith in the masses of his fellow citizens.

CHAPTER XXIX

Emissary from Canning

THE FIRST month of 1808 was a portentous one for James Madison. Jefferson's public refusal of a third term had brought the nomination of a successor to the point of sudden decision. Monroe left for Richmond on January 3, his ears alert to the suggestions of his "stop Madison" supporters. George Rose, Britain's special envoy in the *Chesapeake* affair, spent two weeks picking diplomatic oakum on the anchored frigate *Statira,* and came in from Norfolk on the evening of the thirteenth.

Jefferson's proclamation of July 2, banning British warships from American waters, expressly exempted those on government business. Instructed not to acquiesce *should restrictions be laid* on the *Statira,* Rose refused to leave it until Norfolk officials obtained written guarantees from Madison and Gallatin that none *would be laid.* He felt better when his journey wound up with a flourish in a Navy barge sent to meet his wind-bound packet below Mt. Vernon.[1]

Men of all parties welcomed Rose, whose coming put it beyond question that England wanted peace. Perceval and Canning could not entirely ignore the conditions which caused Augustus Foster to write to his mother, with a side glance toward Ireland: "War with the world, America excepted . . . we might maintain, but I hope we shall not quarrel with our bread and butter particularly as we are not quite sure of keeping easily our potatoes." Young Dr. Rose was snatched into Washington society. Of "good temper, easy of access and great volubility," he appeared "pleased with everybody and everything," Senator Smith of Maryland said.

Introduced to the President on January 16, Rose informed Madison of two points in his voluminous instructions. He could not discuss the general subject of impressment (a limitation agreed to before his arrival), and he was absolutely forbidden to

begin negotiations until after the proclamation of July 2 had been
recalled. His government's disavowal of the right to search national ships, he assured the Secretary, was full and distinct. Wel-
coming this, Madison said he would regret it if the conditions
Rose laid down should block an adjustment.

That evening, Senator Pickering records, Rose dined with him
"at the table of Mr. Peter, whose lovely wife is a granddaughter
of Mrs. Washington." There or elsewhere, Rose received a brief-
ing on American depravity. "Information, riches and talents"
excluded their possessors from Congress, which included a tailor
and a weaver ("both Irishmen"), six or seven tavern keepers, four
notorious swindlers, a butcher, a grazier, a curer of hams and
several schoolteachers and Baptist preachers. It was impossible
to calculate, he commented to Canning, "how shortlived such
a system must be. But the excess of the democratic ferment in
this people is conspicuously evinced by the dregs having got up to
the top." Perhaps this Federalist doctrine came to him via Foster,
who had just remarked that "to judge from their Congress one
should suppose the nation to be the most blackguard society that
ever was brought together."[2]

Madison left day-by-day notes of his talks with Rose. As published in his *Letters* and *Writings* they mean little. Those of
January 18 and 20 are lumped, transposed and dated February
24, and those of January 29 are marked February 1. Among numerous misreadings of the manuscript one seems inspired. The
word "Talk" is all that the editors got out of Madison's "Falk
[land Islands]."[3]

The President, Madison said at his next meeting with Rose,
learned with regret and surprise of the demand for recall of his
proclamation. To help get around that obstacle, he would like to
learn unofficially whatever Rose could tell about the offer of reparation. The proclamation, Madison averred, was not an act of
redress but a precaution to insure internal quiet. Outrages by other
ships would have brought it on, if the *Leopard's* attack had not
done so, and later insults required its continuance. "At any rate,
every nation must be allowed to legislate for itself." Citing the
persistent refusal of British warships to obey the order, Madison

said he would not conceal the fact that, had the United States possessed sufficient force, "it would have been employed in compelling their submission." Reporting this, Rose commented:

"It is but justice due to this minister to observe, that these considerations were urged in a temper and tone calculated to promote a dispassionate discussion."

Insisting that the proclamation was retaliatory, the envoy asserted that the law of nations gave the United States no right to take such action before reparation was refused or unduly delayed. Britain's disavowal of Admiral Berkeley should have produced a recall of the proclamation without a request for it. He showed Madison a paragraph from the Philadelphia *Gazette,* accusing the President of saying that Rose's delay on the *Statira* "coincided exactly with the wishes and interests of this country." The Secretary, who probably heard Jefferson make the comment (a semifacetious one, that time would make the United States stronger), gravely replied that he was entirely ignorant of the injurious paragraph.

Rose denied that Great Britain had reversed the order of procedure in her disputes with Spain over the Falkland Islands and Nootka. Logically, he argued, his government could have demanded prior revocation of the Nonimportation Act, but it was not doing so. That was pleasing, the Secretary replied.

"Mr. Madison [Rose reported] did not evince much paternal solicitude to defend a measure, which, I have since learnt, originates with him. . . . Nor did I find in him, in this first conversation, either that acrimony of temper, or that fluency of expression, which I have invariably understood to be two of his chief characteristics in similar discussions."[4]

Following a cabinet meeting, Rose was told that the United States regarded the disavowal of the *Chesapeake* attack as a necessary consequence of the attack itself. Great Britain merely disavowed the action of an unauthorized officer, yet asked in return for repeal of an act of the government itself. To revoke it ahead of reparation would degrade the United States in the face of the world. "The government could not submit to the indignity of beginning by submission where it had a right to expect concession." Madison reviewed once more the chain of outrages —the destruction of *L'Impétueux* in American waters, the misconduct of Love and Whitby, the hostile behavior of the Norfolk squadron—proving that there was neither insult nor injury in the proclamation, but necessary precaution.

England, Rose replied, was not seeking redress in the recall of the proclamation, but was trying to end an indignity so that it could treat as with a friendly power. Should the reparation he was to offer prove inadmissible, the proclamation could be reissued. Their views, Madison now remarked, differed so widely that they had better be put in writing. Rose agreed.

Reporting to Canning, the envoy said Madison seemed uneasy and, contrary to custom, had notes to refresh his memory. "I infer that he acted under instructions somewhat different from his own wishes." Rose suspected that Madison didn't like the way the embargo was going. Probably, "as it seems certain that he will be elected President," he shrank from a new storm of which he would have to bear the brunt. Jefferson, on the contrary, "having less reason to look to futurity, and dreading . . . the loss of that popularity, which he has pursued at any expense, will not so readily allow his minister, over whom he has a complete dominion, to recede."

That was a lot to infer from uneasiness and note carrying. In truth, Rose wrote this just after Secretary Robert Smith sent word to him that the real difficulty was to find grounds for recalling the proclamation without exposing the President to criticism and loss of "personal weight." It was earnestly wished that Rose should "make, as it were, a bridge over which he [Jefferson] might pass." It would be necessary to know something about the reparation, in order to decide whether recall of the proclamation would be justified.

Trying to find out how far the United States would go, Rose

had a direct talk with Smith, who said (the envoy reported) that "I must be aware how dear to Mr. Jefferson his popularity must be, and most especially so at the close of his political career ... and he pressed me earnestly to take such steps as would conciliate the President's wish to give His Majesty satisfaction on the point in question and yet to maintain the possession of what was pre-eminently valuable to him." Smith added his own anxiety to see the negotiations succeed because the United States had lost all hope of obtaining the Floridas, and this might enable England to get them instead of France. He assured Rose that if peace was maintained with England, the United States would inevitably become involved in war with France. The Navy chief "informed me," Rose reported, "that all his communications with me were with the President's knowledge."[5]

That the President sent him is certain, but Smith would have been bastinadoed had it been known that he talked as he did, either about Jefferson or in his preposterous Florida statement. It is obvious that he was offering his own private deduction as to the reason for his mission, because even had it been correct, the love of prestige that inspired the President's request would have prevented disclosure of the motive for it, especially to such a notorious gossip as Robert Smith. Rose, indeed, chronicled the collapse both of Smith's version of Jefferson's message and his own guess as to Madison's attitude, in a dismayed entry in his dispatches a few days later:

"Notwithstanding the tone of perfect temper with which this conference was carried on, Mr. Madison, that same evening, at an assembly, asseverated with solemn affirmations, that nothing should induce this government to withdraw their own measure, and eat their own words."

National pride, not the need to protect Jefferson's popularity, inspired that remark. Jefferson, however, was responsible for a great and lasting overestimate of the part Smith played in these negotiations. Defending Gallatin, three years later, against charges that he mixed too much in diplomacy, the retired Presi-

dent asked why no similar objection was offered to Smith's dealings with Rose, who, it was perceived, "would open himself more
frankly" to the naval head than to Madison:

"The whole nearly, of that negotiation, as far as it was trans-
acted verbally, was by Mr. Smith. The business was in this way
explained informally, and on understandings thus obtained, Mr.
Madison and I shaped our formal proceedings."

Since the formal proceedings on the American side consisted
of one letter from Madison to Rose, written after the talks ended,
that made Smith virtually the sole negotiator. If Jefferson's account were correct, it would necessarily be reflected in Rose's
day-by-day reports from Washington. In the 199 pages he wrote
to Canning, describing his oral negotiations in detail, Madison's
name appears 102 times, Smith's three times—once in relation
to the mission, twice in telling of farewell social calls. In the entire narrative there is an account of only one diplomatic talk between Rose and Smith, though he sent several indirect messages.
Smith's sole part in the negotiation was to employ his pro-British
leanings and social standing to drive an opening wedge into
Rose's instructions. Probably the overstatement of Smith's role
was not deliberate, but Jefferson possessed a memory in which
past facts were somewhat fluid.[6]

Canning's ironclad orders forbade Rose to do what Smith asked.
However, he promised that in drafting the note Madison had
asked for he would "give every fair facility . . . for the recall
of the proclamation." On January 26 he sent a letter mild enough
in tone, but proclaiming that he could not begin to negotiate until
the United States had revoked an instrument which—whatever
its purpose—had produced unavoidable "effects of retaliation and
self-assumed redress." If that went into the record, the conference
was at an end, so Madison delayed an answer and secured a promise that the letter would be withdrawn if their informal talks
succeeded. The government, he told the British envoy, could not
sacrifice its honor by recalling the proclamation in advance. He
would regret it if failure of the negotiation led the United States

to assume "a serious attitude," and wished that some way of removing the obstacle could be found. Rose agreed and suggested
that he make a friendly return to England with a report of the
difficulty.

Madison (his notes say) reported this to the President, "who,
on consultation on Monday, decides vs. this idea, and prefers
informal disclosure by R. of atonement and repeal of proclamation to be contemporary acts." Jefferson and Madison have been
sharply criticized by historians for this concession, which balanced
a mere *disclosure* against a *repeal*.[7] Actually it never was presented to Rose. On the contrary, the latter's dispatches reveal that
when he himself suggested almost the same thing a few days
later, Madison turned it down.

During that week end startling news had come from Europe.
Russia, joining Napoleon's continental coalition, had declared war
on England. Dreading now lest the United States enter the war,
the envoy began a retreat. He tried to "convey such impressions"
to Madison as might remove any jealousy about ulterior objects
(nothing up his well-stuffed sleeve), then made a minor concession
which implied, Madison thought, a willingness to go farther. The
Secretary thereupon submitted a proposal: *make the whole negotiation the work of one day.* Rose said he had no objection, provided recall of the proclamation came first: given notice of that, he
would proceed at the same hour to deal with reparations. Madison declined this: "The whole should be simultaneous." All
formal papers should be signed on the same day, leaving their
priority "a matter of uncertainty, and which each party might interpret to his own advantage."

That, Rose answered, would violate his instructions. He would
deviate from them, on condition that, "as an expedient to save
him" (those are Madison's words), a signed and sealed recall
proclamation should be *exhibited* to him, but *not published,*
before they took up the subject of reparations. Madison rejected
this, but restated his own proposition the next day (February 5).
If Rose would come to the Secretary's house that evening, bringing with him anyone he chose, Madison would show them the
draft of a recall proclamation and discuss changes in it. With

its wording agreed on, they would proceed to reach an informal agreement on reparations. That done, the formal proclamation would be put into Rose's hands and he would immediately sign the reparation agreement.

Rose wrote a public letter to Canning saying that no decision was reached and a secret one saying that he accepted. He violated his instructions, he stated, because a direct recall of the proclamation was impossible, Russia's entry into the war made it important to avoid a breach with the United States, and above all, because of the universal (Federalist) opinion that unless the government could keep up the indignation against Great Britain, "it must be very shortly involved in war with France."

That evening, struggling against severe illness, Madison showed Rose and Erskine a draft which was accepted after a trivial change in the word order. Rose then offered the same reparations that were outlined by Canning to Monroe—recall of Admiral Berkeley (already ordered), restoration of three seized seamen, indemnity to the families of the men killed and wounded on the *Chesapeake*. Rose rejected Madison's request for more drastic treatment of Berkeley, and they adjourned with every issue apparently settled.[8]

Too ill to go to his office, Madison shifted the next day's meeting to his house. There, instead of committing their agreement to paper, Rose asked for a disavowal of the conduct of American agents in encouraging the desertion of British seamen. That, Madison replied, was going outside the case of the *Chesapeake*. If they did that, there were plenty of things (he listed them) which Great Britain would be asked to disavow. Also, it raised a question as to naturalized citizens, whom the United States would on no account agree to surrender within American jurisdiction. It was unnecessary—orders had already been issued against recruiting deserters. Rose "retired under doubts as to . . . satisfying his instructions."

The British envoy was in a dilemma. He had not yet disclosed that this disavowal, and others of greater severity which he had not even mentioned, were to be "the express and indispensable condition" of the agreement to reparation. Nor could he confess to his own government that he had concealed this part of his instructions while violating another part. Before discussing reparation, he untruthfully chronicled, "I stated what, in return for it, would be required on the part of the United States; on which Mr. Madison at the time made no observation; and very little difficulty could occur" with respect to it. At their next meeting, Rose continued, Madison "objected entirely to the demand of disavowals, such as I am commanded to require." That was true enough, except that it was at this meeting (February 6) that Rose first brought up the subject.

After a Sunday of rest and contemplation, Rose revealed that he was under positive orders to require the disavowal as to deserters. "This," wrote Madison in his notes, "was a new and unlooked-for preliminary ultimatum, though it had been glanced at in a former conversation, when it was supposed to have been answered in a way putting it entirely aside." He asked Rose to put the demand in writing, to be read informally. The envoy came back with the paper next day.

This note, which had to be sent to London, covered all of the disavowals demanded by Canning, but Rose read only one of them to Madison. He called attention to its moderate wording: the United States was to condemn its agents for *not discharging* natural-born British deserters—"a case different from *not surrendering,* which was not claimed." From Madison came the response that no naturalized citizens would be given up, and if there were to be disavowals, the far greater indignities offered by British ships in American harbors must be included. It was "essential to the honor of the United States" that such an action be mutual. Rose said he had already thought of that. He then read a clause near the end of his paper: "a reciprocal right in the demand of deserters on the part of the United States being admitted by His Britannic Majesty." Madison spurned the concession: "There was no reciprocity between an actual disavowal and a right to ask a disavowal." Owing to his illness, the Secretary of State chronicled, "the conversation was soon ended, with an understanding that I would take the orders of the President, and see him as soon as convenient."[9]

Madison spent four days in bed, during which he "obtained the sanction of the President" to his position, then invited the British diplomat to a Sunday visit. The Secretary "repeated the insuperable objections" to Rose's proposal. Reparation for the attack on the *Chesapeake* must be made a separate act. To ease this, it would be followed by publication of an order, which was to be issued anyway, for the discharge of all British seamen from American warships. Apart from that, some mutual and general disavowal might be worked out as to deserters, or a statement of American policy could be made to Erskine. That would suffice if England merely wanted reassurance, but if "an expiatory act on the part of the United States was the object, it was absolutely inadmissible."

Rose, Madison recorded, "dwelt with expressions of great regret on the situation in which he found himself, tied down, as he was, by his instructions." To all of which "it was simply remarked that the attack on the *Chesapeake* was a detached, flagrant insult to the flag and sovereignty of the United States" and the plain course was to repair it. They could then discuss deserters from warships. This brought from Rose the instruction he so hated to reveal:

"He mentioned, with an apology for omitting it before when he intended to do it, that a disavowal of Commodore Barron's denial that he had such men on board as were required made a part of his instructions."

Madison rejected this instantly. Nothing of the sort could be admitted in any circumstances. Barron was responsible to his own government. His denial that he had such men on board "was wholly unbecoming his station" (that is, he should have refused to discuss the matter), but what he said was true, the men taken off not being the ones demanded. Rose admitted this, except as to Ratford, the man whom Admiral Berkeley hanged. Madison cited evidence from the British consul at Norfolk that this man had deserted from a British merchantman, not a warship. The consul called him John Wilson of the *Herald*.

"After this," wrote Rose to Canning, "I was not very sanguine as to carrying conviction to the mind of the Secretary of State." Apparently the lack of conviction extended to himself, for Madison's notes record him as saying "that if the fact was wrong, he could not found a proceeding [against Barron] on it."

Rose retired to "revolve the subject and his instructions," asking Madison to recall him as soon as his health permitted. "I could not dissemble," Rose reported, "that I left him (which I then did) with the most painful impressions." Madison felt puzzled: "His manner and concluding remarks left it uncertain what determination he would bring to the interview."

In truth, Rose was in a more difficult spot than ever before. His demand about Barron was a watered-down version of what Canning ordered him to obtain—disavowal of that officer's conduct in encouraging British-born seamen to desert, harboring them, refusing to surrender them and denying they were on board. Rose already had told Canning that the first three charges could not be pressed against Barron, since his government claimed that all the deserters were Americans. Now the fourth charge was crumbling, but the instruction was mandatory. Furthermore, he had not yet presented, and never did present, the most drastic of Canning's demands—that the United States solemnly disavow "all acts of violence and outrage committed upon the person and property of His Majesty's subjects," detailed in accompanying papers.

On February 16, two days after their Sunday session, Madison invited Rose to the meeting he had asked for. Instead of taking up the Barron matter again, the envoy went back to his original demand for a disavowal of the conduct of American agents in harboring deserters. He was willing to discuss the form of this, but his instructions required specific disavowals.

"This government [Rose cited Madison as replying] is determined to make no disavowal in return for the reparation of the wrongs committed by the attack on the *Chesapeake,* unless reciprocal disavowals in a correspondent instrument are made on the part of His Majesty."

The United States, he added, could not be expected to make "an expiatory sacrifice to obtain redress, or beg for reparation." Once more Madison pressed the point that Rose was departing from the case of the *Chesapeake,* which he had said he was not authorized to depart from. He "seemed sensible" of this, and apparently wished to modify the demand, "but proposed nothing." Rose could not reveal that when the charges against Barron collapsed, he shifted Canning's charges to nonexistent "American agents." That was what disconnected the matter from the *Chesapeake.*

Madison brought the talks to an end by saying that he would write a formal reply to the envoy's unanswered letter of January 26. This he would do as soon as "health, and some urgent business" (delayed letters to Armstrong and Pinkney) permitted. He rejected a suggestion that the negotiations be transferred to England. The place for adjusting the matter was *here,* especially after what had just taken place.

It was March 5 before Madison's reply was completed—nearly five thousand words in which the *Chesapeake* was barely mentioned. The letter was devoted to piling up evidence of other outrages—thus furnishing grounds for continuing the ban on warships and offsetting the demand for disavowals—and to justifying the American position by precedents drawn from British history.

Rose found it "difficult to conceive that the first minister of the United States should have subscribed his name to what is professed to be a delineation of facts, but in which, besides the perversion of the general complexion of the transactions, he has cautiously and most disingenuously suppressed every circumstance which did not suit the view he chose to give of them." The purpose seemed political. Madison as a candidate for President desired "to touch the popular feelings . . . but the grand object has been to give such a complexion of hostility to the whole conduct of Great Britain as shall impress upon the people the necessity of a prolonged acquiescence in the embargo, under which their impatience naturally increases every hour."

Madison kept his promise that, if the informal talks failed, everything occurring after Rose agreed to violate his instructions should be treated as nonexistent. The British envoy was able, therefore, to write a 4,000-word rejoinder which made it appear that he had never deviated one jot from his orders, and he put in all the wickedness of American mobs, the insults and menaces of the United States toward the virtuous British Navy, that Madison had so sinfully omitted. That done, he said farewell to his Federalist friends and sailed for home on the still-unmolested *Statira*.[10]

Thus ended the weirdest mission in Anglo-American annals. Had Rose disclosed his instructions during his first morning in Washington, he could have started home before nightfall. Why did Canning give him such self-defeating orders? Assuming that the foreign secretary knew what he was doing, his purpose might have been to terrify (as Henry Adams surmised), to win by trickery, or merely to prevent a settlement. The one certainty is that he wanted peace. If his purpose was to trick or terrify, why did he forbid the envoy even to mention his terroristic counterclaims until, by deceptively securing a recall of the proclamation, he should have created a situation from which the American government could escape only by war? Also, why send an envoy who lacked both the iron needed for terrorism and the artfulness for trickery? Finally, if the purpose was to prevent a settlement, why send a mission at all? Rose's instructions probably were a by-product of the same Tory arrogance and navalism manifested in the bombardment of Copenhagen, but with no intention in this instance of doing more than exercise a chauvinist vocabulary. Dr. Rose's conduct supports that view, both in his early intransigence, and in the way he tried to break his own fetters after the Russian declaration of war made him realize the folly of his orders.

Some historians, knowing what was in Rose's instructions, have found it easy to condemn Jefferson and Madison for dragging out a negotiation which was rendered hopeless by what they did not know. "Under any other administration," wrote Henry Adams, the negotiation would have ended when Rose revealed that he was bound to ask for prior recall of the *Chesapeake* proclamation. Instead, "Madison yielded to the British demand on condition that the Executive should not be exposed to the appearance of having yielded." Was that true? On the contrary, Rose violated his instructions and told Canning he did so because Madison would not yield. After the conduct of American officers was made an issue, said Adams:

"So cautious was Madison on his side that he offered to make a part of the required disavowals, provided these should be mutual. Rose declined this offer ... and ... ended the conversation of February 14 by addressing to Madison the usual words of rupture: 'I will not dissemble that I leave you with the most painful impressions.' "

In reality, Madison rejected every demand for disavowal in connection with *Chesapeake* reparations, and offered only to discuss mutual, unspecified disavowals at some future time. The words "I will not dissemble," etc., were surmised by Adams, perhaps correctly, from Rose's statement to Canning that he "did not dissemble," but instead of rupturing the negotiation, he asked for another meeting. When it was over he sent a report to London which totally refutes the Adams version both of the negotiations and the way they ended:

"The discussions broke off on the 16th instant on Mr. Madison's positively declining to accede to the proposal that mutual reparations should be made, and on his insisting that the attack on the *Chesapeake* should be redressed first and separately, and that other grievances on both sides should be disavowed and repaired by bilateral instruments."[11]

In dealing with both major obstacles, Madison brought the negotiations to the verge of success. He devised a fair and sensible method by which Rose could, and did, drop his demand for recall of the proclamation before settling the reparation issue. He repelled the demand for compensatory disavowals by first smothering them with counterclaims, then by pushing them off for separate future discussion. The negotiation broke down because the British envoy, after violating his instructions on the preliminary point of form, dared not disregard their substance, which he had so long concealed. Had the slightest latitude been allowed him, the affair of the *Chesapeake* would have been settled on terms honorable to both nations, and thoroughly satisfactory to the United States.

As it was, Madison notified Pinkney that resumption of negotiations rested with Great Britain. They should be resumed in Washington, but the minister in London could accept reparations if freely offered. Meanwhile, Pinkney should place the Orders in Council in such a true light that the British government must revoke them "unless they mean to violate every maxim of justice or are fixed in hostile purposes." It must be understood, however, "that whilst the insult offered in the attack on the American frigate remains unexpiated," recall of the orders would not commit the United States to remove the existing restrictions on commerce with Great Britain.[12]

CHAPTER XXX

Presidential Nominee

Up to 1808, the Republicans had always been solidly united on a candidate for President. The nomination of Thomas Jefferson by congressional caucus, in three successive campaigns, was a mere political gesture. The real function of the caucus was to recommend a running mate. Now, for the first time, there were rival candidates for the highest office. So it was no routine matter when Senator Bradley of Vermont, previous caucus chairman, distributed a printed circular among the Republicans of both houses, informing them that under authority given him four years earlier he was calling a convention for the evening of the twenty-third to recommend candidates for President and Vice President.

For several years the rival candidacies of Madison, Monroe and Vice President Clinton had been taking shape. Jefferson assured Monroe of his neutrality: his preference for Madison needed no words. Randolph's preference for Monroe and his denunciations of Madison saturated the air. Sixty-eight-year-old George Clinton had the backing of his powerful New York machine and the benefit of a widespread feeling that Virginia had furnished enough Presidents. Madison did no wooing of the men who were to choose the nominee.

"The heads of department [wrote Senator Plumer in 1807] visit few members of either house. Mr. Madison for this two or three years past has entirely omitted even the ceremony of leaving cards at their lodgings. He invites very few to dine with him."

Madison suffered less from aloofness than Clinton did from the intimate contacts which caused Plumer to say of him: "He is old, feeble, and altogether uncapable of presiding in the Senate. He has no mind—no intellect—no memory."

In Virginia, reinforcing John Randolph's pathological hatred of Madison, a belief prevailed among some "old Republicans" that the Secretary of State no longer was swayed by his ancient antipathy to national banks, armies and navies. (They were unaware of some of the evidence of it: in paying for the furniture he had bought of Monroe, Madison was straining so hard to clear the latter's bank loans that he had to borrow his own house rent from Navy Captain Tingey.) "The contest," wrote bank enemy Larkin Smith to Monroe in June 1805, "will be between Mr. Madison and yourself; in which case I conceive your presence to be essential. The satellites revolving immediately about the seat of government are in favor of Mr. Madison, but the great body of your countrymen have more confidence in you."

Among the satellites, presumably, was Gallatin, who was the object of virulent attacks by Duane in his *Aurora*. Replying to a note in which Jefferson likened these assaults to the "malignant and long-continued efforts" of Federalist editors "to produce misunderstanding between Mr. Madison and myself," Gallatin said he was but a secondary object. "You are not less aware than myself that the next presidential election lurks at the bottom of these writings and of the congressional dissensions." His meaning was spelled out in an unused draft of this letter:

"To you my wish may be expressed that whenever you shall be permitted to withdraw, the choice may fall on Mr. Madison as the most worthy and the most capable. But I know that on that point, as well as on all others which relate to elections, no executive officer ought to interfere."[1]

Surveying Virginia during the congressional recess of 1806, Randolph reported all Republicans except Giles to be supporting Monroe. They were talking of an indorsement of him by the legislature at its next session. "Depend upon it," he wrote to Nicholson, "a very large majority of us are decidedly opposed to Madison's pretensions and if the other states leave it to Virginia he never will be President."

Monroe was not yet a candidate. George Joy told a Virginian, in London, of the minister's remark to another visitor that he would "sooner be a constable" than oppose Madison. "He said as much to me," the listener remarked. In reply to the appeals of Randolph, however, Monroe was less definite. There were older men, and one in particular, whose pretensions he usually thought of as higher than his own. His candidacy would tear up ancient friendships by the roots, with the likelihood of ruinous results to the Republican cause.

Such reasons, Randolph replied in September 1806, had no validity when the merit of a Monroe was opposed to "the cold and insidious moderation" of a Madison. "To the great and acknowledged influence of this last gentleman we are indebted for that strange amalgamation of men and principles which has distinguished some of the late acts of the administration and proved so injurious to it." His baneful counsels were causing a relapse "into the system of our predecessors" (the usual term for military expenditures). It was because of Madison's influence that the government "stands aloof from its tried friends, whilst it hugs to our bosom men of the most equivocal character" such as Monroe's new associate William Pinkney.

Monroe's reply showed him still resisting, but less strongly. Things had occurred which hurt his feelings and might change his relations with the men in power. Yet even if he "had a view to an object" which his friends were taking an interest in, he should still advise them to view the conduct of the administration with a favorable eye. Its great features were sound. He revealed his chagrin over the appointment of Pinkney but praised his co-operative spirit and expressed satisfaction that he himself had remained in England to complete the treaty.

Monroe did not talk or act like a candidate at the end of 1806. On June 24 he had received from Madison a letter of farewell to the king, to be used "in case you should persist in your intention of returning after the occasion which suspended it [the joint negotiation] shall be over." Monroe replied: "After that very desirable object is accomplished I shall sail as soon as it may be practicable." He had been notified that Pinkney was commissioned to succeed him. The signing of the treaty in December left him free to depart as soon as winter storms were past. He did not go.[2]

Rejection of his treaty, of which he received notice in June 1807, filled Monroe with bitterness and turned every Randolphian insinuation into self-evident fact. Pinkney was sent to deprive him of credit. The treaty was turned down to injure him politically. The request for revision was to hold him in London while Madison won the Presidency. "The friends of Mr. Madison," Randolph hastened to assure him, "have left nothing undone to impair the very high and just confidence of the nation in yourself." Executive influence might carry Virginia for Madison, but New York Republicans were irreconcilably opposed to him. Pennsylvanians (the Duane-Leib group) were leaning toward Clinton because of the administration's alliance with McKean. "Hypocrisy and treachery have reached their acme amongst us." Monroe's supporter Littleton Tazewell, seeing those same qualities in another quarter, warned him neither to decline nor enter the contest till he reached home:

"Among those who are apparently your most zealous advocates there are some made so by disappointment actuated by sinister views ... not because they prefer you but because they hate you less than others."

In Richmond at the end of May, Randolph encountered Duane, "very averse to Madison," and inclined toward Clinton because he thought Monroe's election impracticable. Randolph checked the new Virginia legislature—most changes for the worse (*i. e.*, for Madison), yet he confided to Nicholson, "I believe our friend will outvote the S[ecretary] in that assembly by a great majority. The election however does not depend upon them." Ex-Speaker Macon, supporting nobody, got down to realities as Monroe's ship was approaching Norfolk in December. To win either first or second place, he must have an alliance with Clinton. But would Clinton sacrifice his own ambition to aid someone else? Would Virginia throw away the Presidency, with Madison, to make Monroe Vice President? The returning diplomat, more-over, had but one issue—the unfair rejection of his treaty. "The extract of the treaty which has been published," remarked Macon, "has injured Monroe more than the return of it by the President."[3]

Supporters of aging and infirm George Clinton had one good issue—too much Virginia—and were on a constant quest for others. According to Robert Livingston they hoped for political profit from the *Chesapeake* war scare. "They think," he wrote to Madison in June 1807, "as he has the name of a military man (without ... military talents) that in case of a war he will be pre-ferred." Like the Federalists, therefore, the Clintonians would urge violent measures and throw contempt on everything done by the President "or you, whom the public voice has named as his successor." The task fell on Madison "to save us not only from foreign aggression but from the disgrace of falling into the hands of ignorant dotage at home."

Clinton's newspapers harped on the Madison-Monroe rivalry as evidence that Virginians saw no presidential talent outside their own state. They assailed Madison for lenity toward Fed-eralists in office. "In his own department, and under his imme-diate control, were fostered a most viperous set of aristocrats, monarchists and tories," accused the Baltimore *Evening Post*. Cheetham's New York *American Citizen* conceded that Madi-son was "a correct and able statesman," but, "Woe be to him who, against right and conscience, is not a determined party man." It charged Madison with causing the Vice President to be excluded from cabinet meetings: "The influence of Mr. Madison over the President is known and harmony in the cabinet probably required that his wishes should be complied with."[4]

In Washington, following Monroe's arrival, Randolph stayed away from him for a few days, not wishing to hazard his future by blending "the fate of a proscribed individual with the high destiny which I trust awaits you." They met in secret before Monroe left for Richmond. Congressman Gardenier of New York saw nothing decisive but summed up the prospect from a Federalist angle:

"One thing however appears pretty certain: Clinton cannot compete successfully with Madison. The latter it begins now to be thought will find a much more powerful antagonist in Monroe, who is said to have a majority of the Virginia legislature in his favor. The Federalists here feel a strong partiality for him."

The high priest of federalism, Timothy Pickering, explained that preference. His own party was so impotent that it could only choose the least evil Republican. If George Clinton became President, DeWitt Clinton would "wield the whole machine of the national government" and rule New York as well. Madison was "as visionary in politics as Mr. Jefferson," who "from the top of Monticello . . . would direct all the movements of the little man at the Palace." Monroe was "inferior in learning and discernment to Mr. Madison; but then he is a more practical man and we think more upright than either of the candidates . . . being also thoroughly cured of his French attachment we greatly prefer him."[5]

Stirred by Monroe's presence in Richmond, his friends talked hopefully of an endorsement by the Virginia legislature, which might sway the congressional caucus. Madison's followers were ready for both tests, but his Washington managers, W. C. Nicholas and Giles, urged delay in Richmond. An endorsement there, ahead of the congressional caucus, would subject him to "carping and captious" criticism as a Virginia candidate. Also, a Washington nomination would help in Richmond, and (said Congressman Burwell) many letters were written "assuring the legislature the other Republican states were decidedly in the interest of Madison."

Monroe's Richmond managers heard the same. The Pennsylvania and New Jersey delegations, Congressman Clopton told them, would be nearly solid for Madison. He had fears of New England also, and "if the Yorkers drop Mr. Clinton they may go that way too. I suppose that even in our own state there will be some division."[6]

With impending adjournment forcing early action in Virginia, Nicholas and Giles persuaded Bradley to speed up the congressional caucus (held in February in 1804). As a result, the caucuses in Richmond and Washington, each designed to influence the other, were held so nearly at the same moment that neither influenced either. At one o'clock on Thursday January 21 the Madison forces circulated a ticket calling on "those members of the General Assembly of Virginia who are friendly to the election of James Madison . . . and they only," to meet that evening at the Bell Tavern. The caucus was limited to supporters in order to make sure of a solid ticket of presidential electors. At four o'clock a Monroe spokesman arose in his seat and invited the entire assembly to meet that evening at the Capitol. Two groups met and voted:

At the Capitol: Monroe 57, Madison 10.

At the Bell Tavern: Madison 123, Monroe 0.

Counting three names signed next day, Madison carried the assembly 136 to 57—a stunning upset of Randolphian predictions.[7]

On January 21, after handing copies to Republican members of Congress, Senator Bradley posted his printed call of a convention for the twenty-third. Hardly had this been placed on the House bulletin board before Congressman Masters pinned a paper beneath it—a notice that he was *not* calling a convention, alias caucus, to which attendance was *not* requested. This was more than a gesture of angry defiance. It signified the failure of an attempted intrigue, indiscreetly revealed some months later by George Clinton's son-in-law, "Citizen" Genet. Writing under the name of "A Citizen of New York," Genet said:

"As some Republicans have dreamt that if Governor Clinton declined, Mr. DeWitt Clinton would be made vice president, under Mr. Madison, and that such a disposition would harmonize the party, I state upon the authority of Josiah Masters, Esq., representative in Congress, from New York, that *such an arrangement* was treated with contempt by Mr. Madison's friends, at Washington, last winter."

In other words, Madison was offered clear sailing for the Presidency in 1808, provided his supporters would put DeWitt

Clinton in a strategic position to win the nomination in 1816. The offer was refused. The caucus was held. There were no rival extollings of "the man who." With ninety-four senators and representatives present, they proceeded to vote:

For President—Madison 83, George Clinton 3, Monroe 3, not voting 5.

For Vice President—George Clinton 79, John Langdon 5, Dearborn 3, John Quincy Adams (who attended) 1.

Ten absentees or nonvoters authorized the caucus secretary to list them as supporters of Madison. So too, under cover, were both New York senators, whose "ungrateful" conduct, Masters wrote to Genet, was "very detrimental" to Clinton. Thus Madison had the support of 95 out of 150 eligible Republicans, while of the other 55, less than half took a stand against him at any time.[8]

On motion of Senator Giles, the caucus unanimously resolved "that James Madison of the state of Virginia be recommended to the people of the United States as a proper person to fill the office of President of the United States." Conscious of the novelty of a choice among contestants, the members declared that they acted as individual citizens and had "been induced to adopt this measure from the necessity of the case; from a deep conviction of the importance of union to the Republicans throughout all parts of the United States, in the present crisis of both our external and internal affairs; and as being the most practicable mode of consulting and respecting the interest and wishes of all, upon a subject, so truly interesting to the whole people of the United States."

As a political philosopher, Madison must have been averse to power in a congressional caucus to recommend a candidate for President. It ran counter to the principle he expressed in *The Federalist* No. 51—that the members of each department of government "should have as little agency as possible in the appointment of the members of the others." The caucus, however, came into being to fill a vacuum created by the unforeseen party system, and the alternative (pending the development of the noncongressional national convention) was to throw every presidential election into Congress by a scattering of electoral votes.

Among those absent from the caucus was Dolley Madison's brother-in-law, John G. Jackson, whose home at Clarksburg, (West) Virginia, was the scene of "miseries . . . past endurance." There, in the preceding October, the mother of Dolley Madison and Mary Jackson suffered "a violent stroke of the dead palsy" and died a week later. Mrs. Jackson, a victim of tuberculosis, grew rapidly worse. Jackson bought a light wagon, intending to carry her over the snowy mountains for a last visit with her three sisters. Late in November, leaving the courthouse, he was clubbed almost to death by the associates of criminals whom he was prosecuting. By the time he recovered from a fractured skull, his wife was dying: all their children except the last-born had died before her. Months passed after his wife's death before Jackson could bring himself to write to Madison:

"You knew my Mary well, yes, you gave her to me at the altar, you witnessed our union and our happiness. You saw the little prattlers that she gave me. In the short period of seven fleeting years all these things took place, and all, all but one—and she the dearest of all has been torn from me in the same period."[9]

Except for New York, every state having Republican members was represented in the caucus by a majority of them. Nevertheless, the absence of Randolph's faction and nearly all Clintonians gave notice of trouble ahead. "If there be a division among the Republicans," pleaded the *National Intelligencer,* "let it be candid, honorable, magnanimous. Let no good man's character be traduced to brighten that of another." Editor Smith approved the choice of Madison as the man "best fitted to guide us through the impending storm" without a sacrifice of the principles America was offering to the world:

"Whether we contemplate his irreproachable morals, or solid talents, we are supplied with the strongest reasons for approbation. While in private life he has invariably sustained the unassuming character of modest merit, his discharge of public duty has been no less distinguished by intelligence, fidelity and zeal. And above all, we consider him best fitted for the highest honors in the gift of his country, because amidst the various public scenes in which he has been engaged, he has invariably displayed a dignity and moderation which are at once the best evidence, and the surest preservative of republican principles."

The one-sided Richmond result, according to Burwell, "gave great joy at Washington." Friends of Monroe charged intrigue 'but "it was clearly understood to be the decided sentiment of Virginia." Jefferson told a son-in-law that Madison's election was "considered as out of all question," but Federalists reported the friends of Clinton and Monroe still talking confidently.[10]

From Virginia friends not using him as a tool, unwelcome advice came to Monroe. Congressman Walter Jones held up the severance of "old, sincere and tried friendships," the danger of further party schisms and "the probable ill-success on your part of a premature competition with a person so well fixt in the public opinion as Mr. Madison." Congressman Matthew Clay was more urgent: "For the public good and your future prospects . . . put a stop to the contest." William Wirt explained his refusal to serve on Monroe's campaign committee. "Although personally more attached to you than to Mr. Madison," he preferred Madison for political reasons and believed that Monroe's friends might permanently injure his political standing by running him in defiance of "the sense of the United States." John Taylor of Caroline, a devoted friend and unselfish adviser, warned him that "a personal and lasting enmity from all or most of Mr. Madison's friends and probably from himself is to be one of your calculations." Federalists would support him only to split the party, or because he was regarded as more friendly than Madison to England. Nothing could be worse than a losing alliance with the faction headed by ambitious, untrustworthy DeWitt Clinton.

"In short," Taylor concluded, "an unsuccessful attempt will probably both close upon you forever the avenue to the presidency and utterly demolish your private fortunes." But instead of withdrawing from Monroe's electoral ticket, he would remain and "contentedly immolate my little popularity in the funeral pile which will consume yours."

Others were unwilling to be scorched. "Almost every *Enquirer* from Richmond," Macon wrote on March 1, "contains the name of some person who declined acting as elector or committeeman for Monroe." He expected the latter's friends either to drop him or run him for Vice President on a Clinton ticket. The latter arrangement, Masters told Genet, was "perfectly understood"— but hardly on the basis Minister Erskine reported: that Clinton was "a very old and infirm man" who would be likely to die in office.[11]

Monroe's own thinking is revealed in an article which he drafted but did not publish. "Mr. Monroe," it began, "has taken a house in Richmond and resumed the practice of the law." Solicited by friends who desired that he be nominated as successor to Jefferson, "he is said to have replied that although he is very grateful . . . he was not a candidate." To the inquiry whether he would serve, should his fellow citizens think proper to elect him, "he observed that they must judge . . . by what they know of his past life and conduct."

"It is evidently Mr. Monroe's opinion [continued the anonymous Mr. Monroe] that it would be improper for him to offer himself as a candidate . . . or even to draw . . . the public attention to him. . . . The public suffrage ought to be left free and unbiased. . . . It cannot however be doubted that he will not withhold his services from his country should his fellow citizens be disposed to give him so high a proof of their confidence."

Monroe showed his friends a postcaucus letter from the President and authorized them to say (as one of them reported it back) that they "had undoubted authority for declaring that Mr. Jefferson was not hostile to you." Others might have seen a plea for withdrawal in Jefferson's words:

"I see with infinite grief a contest arising between yourself and another, who have been very dear to each other, and equally so to me. . . . Independently of the dictates of public duty, which prescribe neutrality to me, my sincere friendship for you both will insure its sacred observance. I suffer no one to converse

with me on the subject. . . . The object of the contest is a fair
and honorable one, equally open to you all; and I have no doubt
the personal conduct of all will be so chaste, as to offer no grounds
of dissatisfaction with each other. But your friends will not be
as delicate."

One piquing remark would draw another, Jefferson went on,
until all restraint was thrown off, and it would be difficult for
the principals to avoid participation in the passions aroused by
their friends. "I have ever viewed Mr. Madison and yourself as
two principal pillars of my happiness. Were either to be withdrawn, I should consider it as among the greatest calamities
which could assail my future peace of mind."[12]

Vice President Clinton was properly horrified by the "illtimed
and corruptly managed" caucus. It had "created jealousies and
divisions that never can be healed," perniciously affecting public
deliberations at a moment when the alarming situation of the
country "imperiously called upon us for union." He himself
had no agency in "this offspring of Quiddism," and he was going
to notify the public that his own "spurious nomination" for Vice
President was without his knowledge or approbation. Moreover,
he was assured that a large majority of the people of Virginia
would vote for the Monroe electors. Even at Washington, "this
sink of Quiddism and corruption, the administration candidate
is losing interest daily or I am much mistaken."

Part of the Vice President's statement was true. Southern
Republicans wanted Clinton in second place to insure New York
for Madison, but the New Englanders (Jefferson stated) voted
for him under the "firm belief" that he had said he would not
accept.

When Clinton published his repudiation of the "spurious nomination" it was not a withdrawal at all—Nephew DeWitt had a
better idea. On March 10, the *American Citizen* published a letter
from George Clinton to an unnamed person, dated March 5, replying to one "of the 1st instant." It was actually a letter of February 18 to DeWitt Clinton, replying to his of the thirteenth,
with a substitute final paragraph. George Clinton took note of

the nominations for President and Vice President and corrected the inference of his friends, "a natural one," that his name was mentioned "for the latter [office]" with his knowledge and approbation. He had never heard of the caucus until he accidentally saw Senator Bradley's summons. His actual letter concluded: "The objections which you have stated against this procedure are in my opinion correct and forcible." For publication, DeWitt Clinton changed this to:

"However correct and forcible the objections you have stated against this procedure may be, yet as it is a business in which I had no agency or participation, and over which I can have no control; it might be considered improper in me, situated as I am, to make any comment on it."

Thus George Clinton *remained Madison's vice-presidential running mate while campaigning against him for the Presidency.* On the day this artful maneuver reached the public, the dual candidate expressed his horror at the depravity of his opponents. "Intrigue and management of the basest kind is resorted to [to] secure success to the caucus nomination." A little later he appraised his party and partner-opponent:

"It is in my opinion impossible that the cause of republicanism can exist much longer under the present visionary, feeble and I might add corrupt management of our national affairs. It is calculated to disgust our best friends and is fast doing so. The meditated successor will improve upon the example of his patron to whom he will owe his election and make our situation still worse if possible."[13]

Nobody with political sense believed that Clinton was unconsulted about the caucus, but his disclaimer allowed his editorial partisans to raise the cry of corruption against Madison. He had "surprised" Congress into indorsing him. The Richmond *Enquirer* raspingly replied to one of these editors:

"Cease sir, 'you bite a file.' No man who knows anything of Mr. Madison will believe your insinuations against him. It is a fact which his friends defy you to controvert that no man had ever less recourse to intrigue and corruption of any kind than Mr. Madison; and that no one ever observed a more decorous or profound reserve towards his most confidential friends than this gentleman pursued during the last winter."[14]

That was really the trouble. He had been too reserved toward the ambitions of DeWitt Clinton. To counteract Madisonian depravity, the nonintriguing Clintonians got to work quickly. Congressman Sloan of New Jersey, who lived near Philadelphia, moved to transfer the national capital to that city. Sloan had voted for Madison in the caucus but told John Quincy Adams that he was switching to Clinton and Monroe. "Light-Horse Harry" Lee wrote to Madison that the purpose was "to draw Pennsylvania to the support of Clinton." After losing in a test vote, 61 to 63, the advocates of the measure kept it alive, and presumably prolonged their coalition, by voting not to consider it.

Exulting Federalists now looked to Clinton as the best instrument for defeating Madison. To Judge Peters, who had expressed a preference for Madison based on long friendship, Senator Pickering wrote that the events of the past two days (during which this maneuver reached its denouement) had altered his opinion of the election.

"I have reason to doubt your little *personal* friend's succeeding the present 'Skipper.' Monroe's friends will put their ship in the best train to outsail him. But an old experienced navigator of the Hudson may supersede both. . . . If he does, it will be on a more liberal basis of administering the government [*i. e.,* more satisfactory to Federalists] than has appeared these last seven years."

Flaring up at the disparaging reference to Madison's size, Peters answered:

"You will not let me have a personal esteem for any one with whom I do not agree in politics. One you dislike because he is *little* and another because he is *big*. . . . The greatest men we read [of] or ever knew were often among the *little* race of bipeds so that there is little in all this. The greatest beasts I ever knew were among the largest men."

Peters asserted that he was not a Jeffersonian or a Madisonian, but an American, and as one, it raised his blood to hear people say that it would have been better to remain a colony and "better yet to place ourselves under English government and protection." (Augustus Foster said he heard this from "almost all the sensible Americans . . . not warped by prejudice.") To talk that way, Peters asserted, "puts weapons into the hands of our political antagonists." The Federalists could not regain the ascendancy under their own name, yet they refused to "join the best of their antagonists in getting a change for the better." It is very likely, he concluded, "that Madison will succeed if his friends stick together. Clinton and Monroe will divide his opponents."[15]

John Randolph undertook to unite those opponents. He and sixteen other caucus absentees published an address to the people, denying the power to hold such a meeting and violently assailing the nominee for President. He obtained the signatures of four personal followers (three from Virginia) who were joined by five from the Leib-Maclay faction of Pennsylvania and seven New Yorkers. It was a union of hatchet men, but their numbers foretold failure.

It was true, "The Protesters" admitted, that caucus nominations had been made in the past, but those were palliated, if not justified, by the need to exert the combined efforts of the whole Republican party. Now the Federalists were so few and feeble that there was no reason why the Republicans should unite on any particular person. If the nearness of war called for unanimity, declaimed the leader of the revolt, the nation should unite on a man fitted to lead it with firmness and wisdom, one who had done no shameful bargaining with Yazoo speculators.

"Is James Madison such a man? We ask for energy, and we are told of his moderation. We ask for talents, and the reply is his unassuming merit. We ask what were his services in the cause of public liberty, and we are directed to the pages of the

'Federalist,' written in conjunction with Alexander Hamilton and John Jay, in which the most extravagant of their doctrines are maintained and propagated. We ask for consistency as a republican, standing forth to stem the torrent of oppression which once threatened to overwhelm the liberties of the country. We ask for that high and honorable sense of duty which would at all times turn with loathing and abhorrence from any compromise with fraud and speculation. We ask in vain."

The personal assault on Madison repeated worn-out calumnies. The call for Republican consistency against "the torrent of oppression" was a charge that Madison would subject the South to tyranny by enlarging the Navy. Randolph wrote this after an exchange of letters in which *Monroe* advocated naval and militia expansion and Randolph replied that "a great warlike apparatus" would lead to slavery, "a mournful truth of which it behooves the southern states to profit."

Former Speaker Macon remarked that the protest would do Madison more good than harm. The reminder that he advocated a Yazoo compromise would aid him in New England, and the attack on everybody who attended the caucus would unite that whole group in his support. William Duane, who had been fighting Madison ostensibly on the Yazoo issue—though actually because of too little patronage—agreed. The Randolphian rescript, he wrote to Jefferson, "has fixed men who were wavering and determined many to act in opposition to its dictates."[16]

On the day the protest was published, Pennsylvania Republicans met in a "harmony convention" at Lancaster. The slate of presidential electors, chosen unanimously, contained men of both factions. Nobody was endorsed for President, and the omission was seized on instantly by Madison's rivals. New York newspapers, vainly trying to stir their legislature to endorse Clinton, claimed all of Pennsylvania's twenty votes. In Richmond, Monroe's committee proclaimed that although a majority of Pennsylvania congressmen were for Madison in the caucus, a majority of the electors were against him, and would be for Monroe if Virginia repudiated the caucus nomination.

Retired Admiral Truxton, addressing Captain Tingey but sending his letter open to Madison, briefed the latter on the Lancaster
meeting. Chairman Thomas Leiper (once Jefferson's landlord
and buyer of his and Madison's tobacco) told the admiral that
they were silent on the Presidency because the vote would not
have been unanimous. When Madison's name came up "they
were inundated with objections arising from letters traducing
him." Many were in favor of Clinton, but Leiper (now an elector) "entertains a hope that on the day of election they will be
enabled to bring about a unanimous vote for Mr. Madison."

Following the caucus, wrote Truxton, there was daily and
nightly caucusing in Philadelphia and Lancaster to throw Madison out, and it was the same in New York "where they are in-
triguing among all classes and political parties" in Clinton's behalf. "How stands the Navy there?" he asked Captain Tingey.
One of the Clintonian accusations against Madison was that he
had caused the appointment of a nonpolitical naval (customs)
agent for the port of New York. Admiral Truxton lamented
that the new man (Dr. Bullus) would do Madison no good against
Clinton.

Leiper himself, hearing "that Mr. Madison is all and all in
the appointments," warned him against naming or retaining Federalists. To Jefferson the Pennsylvania chairman remarked:
"You cannot conceive what injury it has done Mr. Madison here,
his keeping Wagner, Brent and Forrest in his office." Many a
time he had heard the cry that Clinton would sweep out all the
old tories of federalism. "Do by them as they would do by you;
turn them out" was Leiper's advice. "If Mr. Madison expects a
single vote from the tories, federalist and quid he will be mistaken."

The need of the moment, as Truxton saw it, was to line up
Duane, but that "must be done through Democrats of the first
water." His famous *Aurora,* "with all its indecency, is worth
for our purposes all others"—a paper which circulated throughout the United States and was read "in every hovel of Pennsylvania." Duane had no wish to back a loser. Having failed to
knock out Madison by the ricochet of verbal bullets aimed at
Gallatin, he wrote to the Richmond *Argus* after the caucus that

he personally preferred George Clinton for President, with Monroe his next choice, but was "willing to abide by the will of the majority." Prior to the Lancaster meeting he reprinted the Petersburg (Virginia) *Republican's* comment upon the "daily resignation" of Monroe committeemen: "The people are with Madison and 'the voice of the people is the voice of God.'"

Duane took a clear stand the day after Truxton wrote about him. From a Washington letter he quoted a forecast of the electoral vote: eleven states, with 107 electors, certain for Madison; uncertain or divided, six states with 67 votes. Noting that both sides were claiming a majority in Pennsylvania, the *Aurora* commented:

"If the observation and information of the editor of this paper are correct, the votes of Pennsylvania will not be divided, they will be decidedly for Mr. Madison."

That, he summarized, gave Madison 127 sure electoral votes, with a possible 47 against him. At no time, wrote the editor a few weeks later, was there a suspicion that more than two Pennsylvania electors favored Clinton, and those would be ruled by the preference of their constituents for Madison.[17]

From James Main, who wanted either to get a consulship or to establish a newspaper in New York City, Madison received an account in March of the tactics of the Clinton machine:

"By intrigue and slander they have completely subjugated this state and DeWitt manages all its affairs in his own way. His hired libellers are again set upon the scent to defame; and you are the victim they wish to sacrifice because you stand in the way of their overweening ambition."

By "hired libellers" he meant chiefly James Cheetham, the once-radical English *émigré*, whose *American Citizen* perished when the Clintons withdrew their patronage after this campaign. In New York City, Main lamented, Madison's friends had "not the privilege of a single press to counteract the virus of this virulent faction." A month later he was able to report that the *Public Advertiser* had "burst its fetters" and resolved "to expose the hollow hypocritical conduct of the Junto who at present govern our state."

Madison already had been told by an anonymous New Yorker (actually Dr. J. H. Douglass) who wrote to him regularly for a year, how the *Public Advertiser's* support of him had been cut off and resumed. The publisher, "a very needy man," canceled a series of pro-Madison articles when the Clintons gave him city and state printing. He swung back after M. L. Davis made a trip to Washington and obtained, from Senator Giles, a promise that the *P. A.* should officially print the acts of Congress. Pro-Clinton articles reappeared after Clintonian politicians called their loans and threatened the editor with debtor's prison. Madisonians assumed his debts and forced the poor fellow to open his columns to a ferocious attack on himself.

Noting that "the character of Mr. Madison has been assailed with a malignity and scurrility not surpassed even in the annals of federal defamation," and that the editor had refused to insert "antidotes to the poisonous effusions of Governor Clinton's friends," the contributor demanded an explicit avowal: "whether you shall continue to publish whatever malice, venality or aspiring profligacy may invent against Mr. Madison; yet refuse to his friends an opportunity of shielding his fair fame, and of hurling disgrace upon his accusers?"

An editor's note replied that the paper was free and its columns open. The *Public Advertiser* resumed publication of a series by Amicus, whom the Clintonians now alleged to be a high Washington official. "I am known neither to Mr. Madison nor to any member of the cabinet," replied that correspondent. Amicus called attention to the contradictions in the Clintonian disparagement of the nominee:

"In this ridiculous attempt, it has been at one time urged that Mr. Madison displayed an *inability* to fulfill the common duties of his office—and at others, that his *subtlety* and *craft* had so far won the easy submission of the President as to dictate the course of that great man's conduct."[18]

The political storm was matched by the elements when Madison, his wife and the latter's cousin Dolley Winston set out for the Virginia Piedmont on Saturday, May 7. No busy corps of journalists was on hand to record the events which made Dolley Madison write eleven days later: "My limbs yet tremble with the terrors and fatigue of our journey." A high wind, which halted the Potomac ferry, forced the presidential nominee's cavalcade (one carriage and a hired baggage hack) to go by way of the new bridge below Little Falls. To avoid the muddy hills of the "courthouses route," they took the level Stevensburg road and found it "very passable even where slightly covered by water." On Sunday night they were stopped by the high waters of the Rappahannock River. This was crossed next morning in a boat, above Norman's Ford, and they went on to Captain Winston's, where Madison wrote three days later: "I continue rain-bound; and how I am to cross the waters before me I know not." Later he told Jefferson how they crossed the flooded Rapidan:

"I got home on Friday night by taking my carriage to pieces and making three trips with it over Porter's mill pond in something like a boat, and swimming my horses."

Within a few days Dolley was stricken with inflammatory rheumatism and lay in bed for three weeks. "Never had I more extreme sickness and pain," she wrote to Anna Cutts, when finally able to move her arm:

"Dr. Willis bled me and gave me medicine—Nelly and Mother Madison nursed and waited on me with great attention and kindness—but Anna—no language can give you an idea of the poignancy of my misery when I recollected the loss of my dearest friends after fainting in the arms of strangers—for at that time Madison had rode out. . . . What in this world can compensate for the sympathy and confidence of a mother and a sister—nothing but the tie that binds us to a good husband. Such are ours and we ought to be satisfied."

Montpelier was overrun with visitors—fifteen or twenty of the family connections at dinner on Dolley's worst day—but she knew nothing about it. There was mild solace to her in receipt of a year-old letter from John Payne, the only one of her brothers who had not died, disappeared or been murdered. He was made secretary, in 1807, to the American consul in Tripoli, which put him at just the right distance from Washington alcohol and bad companions.

The Madisons, as usual, were to leave for Washington a day or two after Jefferson started back. The President and his secretary (Dolley's cousin Isaac Coles) dined with them on June 8, left at four next morning and drove more than forty miles to Fauquier Courthouse. While the Madisons were en route to Washington, their friend John Strode, "a fine farmer and wealthy" (Jefferson's words) with whom they often stopped, was on his way to Richmond. Arriving there, he was amazed to read in the *Virginia Gazette* that an Orange County gentleman who had bought Madison's 1807 wheat crop was lately dunned for the price of it and gravely sent back the reply: "Go back and tell Mr. Madison if he will take off the embargo I'll pay him for his wheat."

Strode strode to the editor's office. As was known throughout Orange County, said his letter in the next issue, he had bought the wheat from all three of Madison's plantations. The rest of the story was "destitute of the least shadow of truth." So far from dunning him, Madison had told him personally, after prices fell, that he should "be among the last who would ask me for payment." Forwarding copies of the accusation and published reply, Strode remarked: "No incident of my life has afforded me half the pain of this malicious fabrication."[19]

To counteract the handicap of Clinton's age and mental debility, his adherents denied the latter and talked about the delicacy of Madison's health. At Troy, New York, the *Farmers' Register* told how Clinton's strong constitution had withstood all physical strains. Age produced no alteration except to furnish that "calmness, composure and moderation" which everybody else found in the opposing candidate. Madison was described in terms which either resurrected his hysteric illness thirty-five years before, or, more likely, exaggerated the dysenteric spasms of summer cholera. The editor drew on medieval anatomy for the dire prognosis:

"Unfortunately for his country, he is sickly, valetudinarian, and subject to spasmodic affections, which operate unfavorably on his nervous fluid, considered by philosophers as one of the most powerful agents of our intellectual faculties."[20]

Personal canards and health whispers were less dangerous than the widespread, discordant charges of subservience to France, war plots against England, artful domination of the government, indecision, timidity and ineptitude in office. Madison was known and trusted for his work in the framing and amendment of the Constitution, for his opposition to Hamilton's fiscal policies and the Jay Treaty, for his fight against the Alien and Sedition Acts. His pamphlet on colonial trade added to his reputation as a closet statesman. But of his day-by-day or year-by-year activities as Secretary of State almost nothing was known.

In the earlier years of Jefferson's administration, everything that happened was credited to or charged against the President. Madison had the benefit of Jefferson's mountainous prestige among the common people, but that was imperiled now by the embargo, and Madison's candidacy made him the beneficiary or victim of popular reaction to current happenings. This laid him open to all the false reports that could be produced by the inventive genius of Federalists, Randolphian Quids and journalistic attachés of the Clinton machine. Against these there was but one effective countermeasure—to break the prevailing rules of secret diplomacy and let the voters know what he had been doing.

CHAPTER XXXI

Running on a Record

Owing to the British Orders in Council, collapse of the *Chesapeake* negotiations might have been expected to renew the Anglo-American war hazard. France prevented that. On February 22, 1808, just as the Madison-Rose talks were breaking down, Napoleon's Milan Decree of December 17 was published in Washington. Every ship of every nation, if searched by an English ship or forced into a British port, or if it paid the taxes imposed by the British licensing system, was declared to be denationalized and subject to confiscation. Likewise, any ship sailing to or from a British-controlled port anywhere in the world was made subject to capture.

Thus both belligerents threw international law to the winds and made war on American commerce. To declare war on both was chimerical. The embargo rose sharply in popularity and Bonaparte became a greater political bugaboo than ever.

These developments were quickly reflected in the presidential campaign. Monroe's adherents pictured him as the man who could end the trouble with England. Federalists and Clintonians intensified the cry of "French influence" already raised against Madison. Cried Congressman Gardenier of New York: "Do not go on forging chains to fasten us to the car of the imperial conqueror." Campbell of Tennessee replied so vigorously to the "infamous, groundless falsehoods" that Gardenier got a flesh wound in the ensuing duel.

Federalist papers published an alleged dialogue in which Madison, to serve Napoleon, told Rose that the United States would not settle the *Chesapeake* affair even if England dropped her demands. The story spread so dangerously that the Secretary of State allowed the *National Intelligencer* to state, "upon respectable authority," that the conversation never took place.

Against Randolph's damaging protest that Madison lacked en-

441

ergy, the Richmond *Enquirer* asked how he had shown the absence of it. Was it in casting aside the feeble threads which connected the states and substituting that energetic bond of union, the federal Constitution? Was it in the courage and firmness with which, on this topic, he met, fought, "and finally vanquished that boasted prodigy of nature, Patrick Henry?" The *Enquirer* granted that if energy consisted in rudeness, bravado and bluster, Madison did indeed lack it:

"But if true energy be evinced, as we think it is, by the calm and dignified, yet steady, zealous and persevering pursuit of an object, his whole conduct during that period is honorably marked with energy. And that energy rested on the most solid and durable basis—conscious rectitude; supported by the most profound and extensive information, by an habitual power of investigation which unraveled with intuitive certainty, the most intricate subjects, and an eloquence, chaste, luminous and cogent."[1]

This glowing appraisal did not unlock the book of Madison's secretaryship, now being misrepresented on every hand. An avenue of correction opened by accident when senators asked for the correspondence on the Monroe-Pinkney treaty (all written by Monroe) before voting on Pinkney's confirmation as minister to England. Madison suggested a quick conveyance of Pinkney's recent protest against the Orders in Council, together with Armstrong's vigorous objections to the stiffened Berlin Decree. The President should avoid the appearance of "an undue anxiety to make certain impressions" (favorable to Pinkney) and offer them to aid the lawmakers "in appreciating our foreign relations and in judging of the influence these ought to have on their measures of precaution." The advice was followed. Pinkney was unanimously confirmed and a stiffening embargo amendment moved to speedy passage in the House.

By unlucky or lucky chance, Vice President Clinton failed to notice the word "confidential" on Jefferson's message. The letters were read before open galleries with a British secretary present.

Madisonian newspapers blamed this on Clinton's "declining years." To disprove this, the Vice President asked Senate Secretary Samuel A. Otis to certify that the message was not marked confidential. When Otis refused to perjure himself, Clinton "spoke to the Senate in anger" about the President's supposed attempt to ensnare him.[2]

Timothy Pickering, ever alert, saw the chance for a major stroke. On March 9, he addressed an open letter to Governor Sullivan of Massachusetts condemning secrecy and assailing the embargo as an instrument of French policy designed "to excite a war pulse." Was it imposed for reasons found in the dispatches from Paris?

"Why, in this dangerous crisis, are Mr. Armstrong's letters to the Secretary of State absolutely withheld. . . . Are they so closely locked up because they will not bear the light? . . . Has the French emperor declared that he will have no neutrals? Has he required that *our ports,* like those of his vassal states in Europe, *be shut against British commerce?* Is the embargo a substitute, a milder form of compliance with that harsh demand, which if exhibited in its naked and insulting aspect, the American spirit might yet resent?"[3]

The Massachusetts senator endorsed British policy and called on the Northern legislatures to take common measures against the embargo. Governor Sullivan assured Madison (and John Quincy Adams shared the belief) that Pickering was trying to revive the secessionist plot of 1804 and "carry the northern states back again to England." However, the emphasis on French influence left no doubt that he was aiming largely at Madison's candidacy. Publication of both French and British correspondence was now imperative, and that involved Monroe's aspirations. Jefferson, presumably, was not departing from his "sacred neutrality" when he sent Congress, on March 22, a file of letters that would have made a "white book" of 100,000 words. Yet a congressman who visited him a few days earlier drew some conclusions not wholly alien to the presidential race:

"By this full and candid disclosure, the best and ablest answers will be given to the devoted advocates of Britain, and the bawlers about French influence in our cabinet."

Hour after hour, for six days, the clerks in both houses read those letters aloud. Vice President Clinton fumed. Why waste time on "papers . . . of no significance"? But in the House of Representatives there was a feeling that the contest for President was being decided. Macon watched the countenances of his fellows:

"The face generally showed whether the person was for Madison or Monroe. The Clintonians evidently seemed to be on the Monroe side."

John Randolph complained that the letters were numbered (presumably by Madison) to put the Secretary's impression of the rejected treaty ahead of the document itself. They came at last to Monroe's long defense of it—not a true diplomatic paper, but a campaign document written only three weeks before it was sent to Congress. Here Randolph took over and read the letter (a Federalist listener remarked) "with singular propriety and force." The Madison-Rose correspondence followed and the French letters concluded the reading. When it ended, the whole House knew that Monroe's candidacy was dead and Clinton's dying.[4]

For two months these letters were published serially in newspapers of all parties, while Federalist and Clintonian editors combed them for evidence that Madison lacked skill and vigor. To supporters of the Jefferson administration it was all very simple. Madison had given strong instructions on impressment, and Monroe had been unable to carry them out. Madison had outlined a good treaty with England; Monroe and Pinkney had made a bad one. Finally, contrary to a thousand propagated rumors, the Secretary of State had conducted the negotiations with Rose in a way that thrilled the hearts of most Americans. In the jubilant words of the Trenton *True American:*

"He has dared to meet the most celebrated politicians of the British school in the diplomatic field, and has completely vanquished, disarmed and disgraced them."

The Richmond *Enquirer* gave its verdict: "A more valuable body of dissertation on the rights of neutrals and the interests of the U. S. was never before condensed in the same space." W. A. Burwell reported Virginian sentiment: "Upon the subject of the next President there is literally no division." Even the *American Citizen* departed from its usual tactics. "Every man of sense and candor will now admit," admitted Cheetham, "that there was no just ground for suspicion" of a cabinet desire to provoke war with England.

Federalist editors conceded nothing. "Never since the birth of Machiavel," cried Coleman's New York *Evening Post,* "has this game of politics been played so dexterously and so knavishly." From the beginning to the end of the *Chesapeake* affair, "the conduct of the American government has been but a series of chicanery." Their whole effort was to defeat an amicable and honorable settlement, and they began the process in advance when "known deserters were enlisted" on American frigates. As for Madison's offer, conflicting with Rose's instructions, to withdraw the proclamation and settle reparations simultaneously:

"If I acquit Mr. Madison of the indecency of meaning to insult the British minister I must leave it to others to give his conduct its proper epithet."[5]

The editor would have been mightily shocked had he known that Rose agreed to Madison's proposal, and that the Secretary protected him by omitting that fact, after the negotiation broke down on other issues.

The letters from France were skimpy, due to Armstrong's habitual laziness, but the nature of American policy was made clear by his strong protest against seizure of the *Horizon*. The savage cynicism with which he charged and proved Napoleon's violation of the 1800 treaty was enough to wipe out Pickering's allegation of concealed subservience. The *National Intelligencer* advised its readers that they would "be *astonished* at the little these papers contain, and at their absolute disproof of the charges of French influence."

Jacob Wagner, the Pickering appointee whom Madison retained for six years as chief clerk, was now using the prestige of his former office to support antiadministration slanders in his Baltimore *North American*. "The public are triumphantly told," he wrote, "that those wretched shreds of dispatches are all that Mr. Armstrong or others have furnished." If that was true, which he doubted, it proved our foreign ministers "incredibly and most criminally deficient in their duty," while the long concealment of them (Wagner knew that they were published with undiplomatic quickness) suggested "partiality to one nation, and hatred to another," if not a personal intrigue.[6]

Hardly had Jefferson sent these papers to Congress when worse French news arrived. Champagny, replying to Armstrong's protest against the Milan Decree, recited England's aggressions *against the United States* and said that "His Majesty has no doubt of a declaration of war against her by the United States." In fact, he stated, "war exists . . . between England and the United States, and His Majesty considers it as declared from the day on which England published her decrees." Being ready to consider the United States as an ally, the Emperor had "not taken any definitive measures" toward American vessels captured by the French: they would remain sequestered until a decision could be based on the future American attitude.

The President sent this arrogant, blackmailing letter to Congress, in confidence, and with it a recent one from Erskine to Madison, formally communicating the new British orders. The proceedings of both nations, he commented, "indicate designs of drawing us, if possible, into the vortex of their contests; but every new information confirms the prudence of guarding against these designs as it does of adhering to the precautionary system hitherto contemplated."[7]

Randolph saw a weapon against Madison and moved to make

Champagny's letter public. The House voted almost two to one against violating the President's confidence. Two more similar motions were voted down next day, but the continuing agitation created a political hazard which Jefferson ended by withdrawing his request for secrecy both as to this letter and Erskine's.

"The TRUTH is out at last," exclaimed Editor Wagner, treating the Champagny letter as if it had long been held back. The only danger to Madison lay in the fact that the letter, made public within a week of its receipt, had not been answered. Even that hazard would have vanished had he subordinated diplomacy to politics by disclosing his February instructions to Armstrong. Declaring that France's new interpretation of the Berlin Decree violated both law and treaty, the Secretary ordered a formal remonstrance calculated either to "obtain a recall of the illegal measure" or leave in full force the right of the United States to claim damages.

France, Madison observed, was trying to enforce local laws at sea. To claim that such a course was lawful would imply "a degradation of every other nation from its common rights and equal rank." France's conduct was the more remarkable, he added, because her naval weakness made it an empty menace, yet furnished England with pretexts for further retaliations which could be enforced. But, apart from all this, "ought the legitimate commerce of neutrals to be thus the victim and the sport of belligerents contesting with each other the priority of their destructive innovations?"

Champagny's declaration of war by proxy stirred a still stronger reaction. That letter, Madison wrote to Armstrong on May 2, produced all the sensations it was calculated to excite in minds alive to the interests and honor of the nation. To offer the alternative of bending to the views of France against her enemy, or incurring confiscation of the property of American citizens, implied that the United States "were susceptible of impressions by which no independent and honorable nation can be guided." Armstrong should "make that government sensible of the offensive tone employed," but leave the way open for friendly explanations if France was disposed to offer them.[8]

These utterances being unknown, they did not prevent Madison's opponents from enlarging the cry of French influence. The issue was made more dangerous by news of Napoleon's invasion of Spain—the prelude to annexation. The Floridas, Mexico and South America faced French imperialism and British naval power, modified by whatever the United States could do about it.

Randolph's henchman, Congressman Gray of Virginia, put out a circular attacking Madison on the Yazoo issue and resurrecting the distorted version of his argument for the $2,000,000 Florida appropriation: "France wants money and we must give it." Clinton's chief organ used the discretion of rhetorical indirectness:

"Who perceive nothing in the insolent note of Champagny but the disinterestedness of a friend and the tenderness of a lover? The friends of Mr. Madison. . . .
"Who wish to ruin commerce by a permanent embargo? . . . The friends of Mr. Madison."

The embargo, unlike the French canard, was a genuine issue, and Jefferson and Madison were thinking of it when the British and French dispatches were sent to Congress. After the reading of them was completed, Senator Anderson of Tennessee offered a resolution authorizing the President to suspend the embargo against any belligerent that mended its ways. This was referred to Anderson, Adams, Giles, Smith of Maryland and Bradley—all friendly to the idea.

Anderson and Giles, with the committee's approval, consulted Madison, to insure concert with the Executive. Giles told Adams that he wanted Madison to write the report, doubting the chairman's ability to handle "a subject of so much delicacy and difficulty." Madison agreed readily enough, but, seeing another place for delicacy, asked that the committee, and John Quincy Adams in particular, make any changes they deemed advisable.

The two senators brought back "a report ready drawn by Mr. Madison." Adams made a couple of changes, and the discretionary power was inserted in a pending bill (which shot through

Congress) strengthening the embargo. Besides arguments to sustain this power, the report contained two important assertions of "committee opinion"—important because they came from the nominee for President.

1. In case the belligerent powers adhered to their destructive proceedings, an entire suspension of foreign commerce might in a reasonable time be substituted for the embargo.

2. The time might come when the evils of war would be less than the evils of further forbearance.

There was nothing fortuitous about this semiforecast of the War of 1812. Writing to Pinkney of the determination "against a dishonorable acquiescence in the despotic edicts enforced on the high seas," the Secretary said:

"I refer you also to the report made to the Senate, by a committee . . . indicating the spirit which may be expected to influence the future policy of the country, if kept under the excitement resulting from the system now pursued against it."

Madison was looking toward a stronger policy, first in the preferred field of commercial restrictions, second in the realm of military force. The latter alternative had been under cabinet discussion. Jefferson wrote to Madison in March:

"I take it to be an universal opinion that war will become preferable to a continuance of the embargo after a certain time. Should we not then avail ourselves of the intervening period to procure a restriction of the obnoxious decrees peaceably, if possible?"[9]

Jefferson's thought was that both belligerents should be asked to exempt the United States from their decrees, letting them perceive that if only one pursued this course the United States would declare war on the other. Madison's report broached this policy to Congress, and the amended law provided what he had talked about in 1805, "a commercial weapon . . . shaped for the Executive hand." To answer this purpose, the embargo must be enforced strictly enough to make it hurt the belligerents, and one or both of the great powers must be convinced that it would remain in effect until results were obtained.

On these points Madison had high hopes. The British decrees, he wrote to Pinkney in February, were "reconciling all descriptions among us to the embargo." In March: "The embargo continues to take deeper root in the public sentiment, and in the measures of Congress." At the end of April: "No pains have been spared to stop every leak by which the effect of the embargo laws might be diminished." Erskine transmitted Madison's assurance that the embargo would be withdrawn as to any power that ceased its aggressions, and reinforced his appraisal of public sentiment: it would "certainly continue to be approved of by a large majority of the people" unless one or both of the belligerents should withdraw their orders.

The makers of American policy—Jefferson, Madison and Gallatin—reckoned without two factors: the domestic effect of strict enforcement, and the overseas impact of Pickering's letter. This senatorial broadside against American policy, with its tone of disunity bordering on rebellion, was carried to London by George Rose. It was reprinted right in the midst of a campaign, led by Lord Erskine and the Barings, for repeal of the Orders in Council. "Your modesty would suffer," Rose wrote to Pickering, "if you were aware of the sensation produced in this country by the publication." The Washington *Monitor* ran through its London mail and reported: " 'General' Pickering is all the rage in the ministerial prints in England." Private letters said an insurrection was expected. Minister Pinkney called for an offset: "Have you prohibited the exportation of all pamphlets which uphold our rights and our honor?" he asked Madison.[10]

While the pressure value of the embargo was disappearing in England, tightened control of the coasting trade cut off smuggling to the West Indies. The embargo now pinched small Republican evaders as well as big Federalists and the effect was evident in the spring elections. If the shift to federalism was no greater elsewhere than in New York and Massachusetts, Gallatin observed to the presidential candidate in May, all would still be well. "But between this and October the pressure of that measure will daily increase." A month later Erskine reversed his prior report:

"The most violent supporter of the embargo never contemplated its being carried to such lengths as it has recently been by the orders of the President. . . . This arbitrary interpretation [of the new law] . . . is extremely unpopular through the country, so much so indeed as to have worked a complete change in the sentiments of a great many people who were in favor of the existing administration."[11]

If this hurt Madison politically, it also aided him. As Federalists began to talk of a ticket of their own, Republicans closed ranks. Support of Monroe, said the *Monitor,* was a farce designed to produce Virginia votes for Clinton, while "the name of Clinton becomes a stalking horse for federalism." A Philadelphia editor, John Binns, shifted to Madison on that issue. Local conventions all over the country endorsed him. Senator Smith, scoffing at Clintonian claims to Maryland, declared that "not a solitary vote will be given to Mr. Clinton south or west of the state of Pennsylvania, nor do I believe he can get a vote either in that state, Jersey or Delaware."

On July 4, a cavalry troop paraded before Madison's house, and Dolley "presented them with an elegant standard, accompanied by a patriotic address." Binns's *Democratic Press* made a nation-wide survey of Fourth of July toasts, and announced that "the spontaneous effusions of the American people" furnished a forecast of Madison's election. The same positive assurance came to General Turreau "from men deeply versed in the intrigues put into play" in presidential politics. He also sensed an accretion of power in the man he had once called mediocre:

"The secret but well assured and very constant influence of Madison develops and becomes more powerful as the time of his election draws near. . . . It seems to me that it is necessary to act from now on as if he were President."[12]

That was exactly what Turreau was doing. Protesting to Madison, in June, that England was "the prior as well as the greater wrong doer," he divorced himself from Napoleon's coercive policy by asking for friendly assurances *unrelated to an alliance.* England, he suggested, would turn to North and South American ventures as her armies were driven from Europe. The United States could "easily give facilities or obstructions to her revolutionary plans."

Madison's reply, like Turreau's overture, reflected latest reports from Spain. There a mob, enraged by the nation's humiliation, had forced King Charles to abdicate, tossed the Prince of Peace into prison, and put the king's moronic son on the throne as Ferdinand VII.

Controlling Spain, Madison responded, France could make her cede the Floridas to the United States, thus cutting off all direct American contact with Spanish territory. But if Great Britain had designs on Spanish colonies, that would make the United States peculiarly important to her. American neutrality would thus become more essential to France and Spain, "the more so, as the disposition of the Spanish provinces to look to the auspices of the United States was so well understood."

Instead of informing his government that his proposition had drawn this hint of an Anglo-American alliance, Turreau dilated to Champagny on his efforts to win the United States to a common cause with France. The Secretary was so embarrassed, he said, that he had to be pressed three times before "he told me it was the intention of the federal government to observe the most exact impartiality between France and England"—the embargo would be raised in favor of the first power that rescinded its orders.

After a three-hour talk which failed to budge the Secretary, Turreau turned to the President, who assured him that American policies did not put England and France on a parity. The embargo was more prejudicial to the former because of her undersupplied colonies. The United States could do much damage to the British in war, and even if revocation of the British orders forced a withdrawal of the embargo in their favor, this would "not close our differences with them, because never—no, never—will there be an arrangement with them if they do not renounce the impressment of our ships."

Greatly cheered by this contradiction of Madison's position, Turreau sought out the Secretary once more and urged that the United States openly adhere to Napoleon's maritime federation of continental Europe. The result:

"Very well, responded the Secretary of State, what will be our guarantee when we shall be engaged in a war with England?

"You could not have a stronger or more certain one, I said, than the co-operation of all the states of Europe.

"But might you not reach an agreement yourselves with England? I have seen in one of your *Moniteurs* that the difficulties during the war relative to maritime rights need not be an obstacle to peace . . . the *Moniteur* is an official paper."

Turreau "answered offhand" that even though the paper was official, its views could not be balanced against "the authentic promise of the sovereigns of Europe not to lay down their arms" until England adhered to those principles. "Mr. Madison . . . did not seem to be convinced." It was after this experience that Turreau wrote that it was necessary to act as if Madison were already President.

The French minister, Madison advised Armstrong, seemed very anxious to change both the language and measures of France toward the United States. So he was, but the Secretary would have been surprised at the way he went about it. Turreau had a feeling (so he told his chief) that Madison's vanity was hurt by the fact that he owed his presidential prospects to the standing of the Jeffersonian party. He would seek to destroy this impression by some brilliant diplomatic stroke which would make the common herd think that he owed his elevation solely to his talents and popularity. "The acquisition of the Floridas is the object of all of Mr. Madison's prayers." A cession of those provinces still seemed dangerous to Turreau, since it would end all chance of recovering Louisiana. However, if motives of interest made it desirable to treat further with the Americans, France should choose a method which would give an opening to the avarice of the people and "also be a means of popularity for the future President." Should this lead to a decision to transfer the Floridas, France might obtain 20,000,000 francs for them and perhaps open the Mississippi to everybody and restore the west bank, below the Ohio, to Spain. However, Spain should first be compelled to make a secret transfer of Cuba to France, to frustrate American control of the Gulf of Mexico.

Turreau did not know that the emperor, adding bribery to blackmail, had offered the Floridas to the United States as an inducement to enter the war, and Madison had sent back a refusal which opened the way to obtain them by future military action. The United States would not depart from "fair and sincere neutrality" to obtain any separate and particular object, however interesting. But they saw with satisfaction that His Imperial Majesty would approve "a precautionary occupation of the Floridas against the hostile designs of Great Britain," should that become necessary. That reply, coupled with the prior withdrawal of an offer to buy the Floridas, cut off any possibility of a "brilliant stroke"—immediate purchase or seizure for election purposes —but laid the groundwork for decisive policies which took shape two years later.[13]

CHAPTER XXXII

Shades of Robespierre

Before leaving for Montpelier late in July 1808, Madison reinforced prior notices that the United States was not going to war with either England or France at the other's behest. No self-respecting nation, he wrote to Pinkney, "will ever purchase redress from one of its aggressors by gratifying his animosity against another aggressor." In a talk with Erskine, the Secretary commented bitterly on a British naval order that American ships, *even without papers,* should be given unmolested passage to the West Indies if they carried provisions. This deviation from wartime practices he regarded as "holding out encouragement to violations of the laws of the United States and therefore as a measure highly unfriendly and offensive." It was the more so because the food-short West Indies were the most vulnerable point of pressure from the embargo.

No claim could be made that France was obstructing that measure. Quite the contrary! Though the text had not arrived, Madison had read a description of Napoleon's latest act of brigandage— the Bayonne Decree, a cynical order by which American ships were to be captured, wherever found, in order to *assist in enforcement of the Embargo Act.* Such a sweeping stroke at American vessels, Madison remarked to Armstrong, would extend the country's demands for reparation, and was rendered more ominous by the timing of it. "If France does not wish to throw the United States into the war against her . . . she ought not to hesitate a moment, in revoking at least so much of her decrees as violate the rights of the sea, and furnish to her adversary the pretext for his retaliating measures."

There was reason to believe, he concluded, that Great Britain was reluctant to withdraw her orders out of fear that France would do likewise and thus end the danger of a Franco-American war. That thought might be employed to encourage a withdrawal by

France, but with care not to promote British policy by stimulating French passions. Looking at the two belligerents, he found them equally ignorant of American character, or rather, he remarked to Robert Livingston, "of human nature, since each in seeking the means of embroiling us with the other, selects those most tending to widen the breach with itself."[1]

For two months, the candidate for President looked after his farms and kept a watchful eye on politics, while campaign passions raged ever higher in the newspapers. Napoleon annexed the Spanish throne by putting his brother Joseph on it. Civil war burst out. If half of the news from Spain be true, Madison commented, "Bonaparte may find the tide at length beginning to turn against him." Should Spanish America become the bone of contention, England and France would have powerful motives for cultivating peace with the United States.

Quite different was the attitude ascribed to Madison by the opposition press. Old and New Spain, including the Floridas, all would be under Napoleon's control, warned Editor Cheetham. "Thus circumstanced, is Mr. Madison fit to be our President?" Saunders Cragg, New York lawyer, gave the dark cloud a Clintonian lining:

"There are men, deadly as the adder . . . who tell us that France is so powerful that . . . to avert her anger we must purchase her favor. And do such beings breathe the pure air of a republic? Yes, hundreds surround us; and in the midst James Madison stands conspicuous! O my countrymen, this is not the man who will face the storm and the tempest. . . . Clinton is the skilful pilot, the brave general, and the energetic statesman. . . . Place Clinton at your head, and you are safe; but should Madison unfortunately rule, war with England will immediately ensue; honor, glory, happiness and virtue will all bow at the foot of the conqueror."

A Bostonian delved into antiquity. Signing himself "Samuel Adams," as if he were that lately deceased statesman, he declared that he served with Madison in the Continental Congress in 1781 (as Adams did). The Virginian was always at heart honest, the pseudo-Adams conceded, but his excessive attachment to France led him into faults "which would have been as fatal to his country, as if they had been the effect of criminal design." The New York *Public Advertiser* asked in reply:

"How comes it that the transactions of thirty years ago are torn from oblivion at this day? Is there such a scarcity of fact, such paucity of motive, such a dearth of incident to set off against British outrages, that it is necessary to travel to the tombs for *French skeletons to excite terror?*"

A contributor to Binns's *Democratic Press* traveled to the tomb of Washington to rebut that "crafty deceiver" who misused the name of Adams. Madison was "admired, esteemed, beloved and approved" by Washington. Would he have bestowed that approval on a betrayer of his country?[2]

The charge of "French influence" was lifted to a new peak by an article in the Albany *Register* alleging that Jefferson and Madison were naturalized as citizens of France by the communistic revolutionary assembly. The New York *Evening Post* identified the author as "Citizen" Genet, and former Governor Morgan Lewis told Madison that he heard DeWitt Clinton say the same in a large company. The author was referring to himself, therefore, when he declared that "the French ambassador" had delivered the certificates of naturalization to these two men in 1793. Genet added:

"The written answer of Mr. Madison, expressive of his gratitude, his admiration, and his devotion, was transmitted to France by the same minister, and the bloody Robespierre, who opened that memorable letter, was very much pleased at his civism. Mr. Jefferson, an older fox, took care himself of his answer."

Federalist and Clintonian editors pounced on the story. Who, better than this reformed ex-Jacobin, could relate the facts and reveal "the horrid pleasure felt by the bosom of Robespierre"? There were some slight inaccuracies in the story. The revolutionary assembly, a year before Robespierre rose to power, conferred citizenship not on Jefferson and Madison, but on Washington,

Hamilton and Madison, and it was to these three that Genet delivered the certificates. That was unknown to Madison's former chief clerk, Jacob Wagner, as he proceeded to bite the hand of the man who had ignored partisan demands for his dismissal and sustained him through illness. Suppose, exclaimed the Baltimore editor—suppose Mr. Adams, Mr. Pickering, Mr. Hamilton, Mr. Ames, "or any other of the virtuous and illustrious federalists" had been naturalized by the British Parliament. "Would they have been hailed as patriots?" How then could America escape betrayal by a man who had received the boon of citizenship "with those unconcealed marks of gratification, which could proceed only from a breast from which had been previously expelled the exclusive sentiments of patriotism"?

Baltimore's Republican newspaper, the *American,* scoffed at the idea that "the unsolicited deed of a French National Convention" was an *act of naturalization.* To make it effective, Jefferson and Madison would have to appear before a French tribunal and swear allegiance. "INSANITY," was the *National Intelligencer's* comment on Wagner's naturalization theory. To which the former chief clerk replied that the mere tender of French citizenship was enough to imply "mutual deference and attachment," and was probably made in such a form as to render a trip across the Atlantic unnecessary.

Aided or pretending to be aided by a published tip from Genet, Wagner located the resolve of the French assembly. Instead of disclosing the embarrassing fact that it embraced Washington, Hamilton, Madison and fifteen Europeans, he assured his readers that "Jefferson and Madison" were decreed to be French citizens "entirely without condition." However (now that the names of Washington and Hamilton clarified his inner vision) he conceded that the decree could not change the national character of the adopted citizens without their consent. Did Jefferson and Madison actually accept? he asked.[3]

Madison and Jefferson pursued their usual course in the face of personal attack. They said nothing. Had Jefferson exposed the falsity of the story, as to himself, he would have magnified it as to Madison. Had the latter explained that citizenship was conferred on Washington and Hamilton as well as himself, it would have emphasized the fact that he alone accepted. That would have brought out the letter of acceptance, addressed not to "the bloody Robespierre," but to Roland, whom Robespierre drove to suicide. However, 1793 was a better year than 1808 in which to testify, as Madison did, to the "sublime truths and precious sentiments recorded in the revolution of France." A lot of international brotherhood had gone over the dam since he identified that revolution with human liberty and renunciation of prejudices based on "the artificial boundaries of nations."[4]

Left to the political judgment of the people, Genet's charges backfired in the same way that the embargo issue did. By giving the Federalists greater encouragement to put a ticket in the field, they weakened Clinton and rallied the Republicans to Madison. Even the Albany *Register,* which first published the story, broke out of its Clintonian thongs long enough to say:

"When Madison is called a Frenchman, an enemy to commerce, and a corrupt adherent of the Yazoo company of fraudulent speculators, they [the Republicans] view these charges as the offspring of prejudice or a distempered zeal! . . . There is nothing now so obnoxious to the feelings of a thorough-going Essex Junto federalist as to hear that the Electoral Colleges, of the republican stamp, will in all probability harmonize in their votes for the Presidency."

In August the Young Republicans of New York City resolved that by the splendor of Madison's talents "envy is subdued and overwhelmed," while "from the view of his blameless life, malice herself shrinks, abashed and in despair." More prosaically, the General Republican Committee of New York City swung from Clinton to Madison (former Governor Lewis told the latter) because of a "prevailing opinion that the embargo was producing a change in the public sentiment which would give a chance for a federal President." In Clinton's state, also, Governor Tompkins' family connections came out for Madison. New England state elections were going Federalist, but the Southern and Middle states looked almost solid for Madison. The embargo, Joel Barlow assured Jefferson, was the only election horse the Tories could ride, and they would wear it down to the bone.[5]

In August Madison learned that Republican Governor Sullivan of Massachusetts, to avoid outbreaks based on "avarice and anglicism," was disregarding the President's order that he stop issuing permits by which flour was imported for domestic use and then smuggled to the West Indies. Such lawless outbreaks, the Secretary commented, would open the eyes of honest citizens to the real source of the evil but would have an effect of the worst kind abroad. Better, if possible, cope with the smuggling by sending gunboats or the entire Navy to the New England coast. He approved Jefferson's draft of a letter advising Sullivan to reduce the permits to domestic necessity, but altered a sentence which had "the appearance of charging the governor with flinching from his duty" in order to preserve the President's popularity.

Passing through Madison's hands, now, were petitions to the President from New England merchants, asking for a special session of Congress to remove the embargo and calling for trade with a revolted portion of Spain. "Such are the malignant maneuvers for vexing the Executive," he commented to Gallatin. No effort of the President could advance the convening date by ten days, while to mix in the Spanish civil war "would be an infatuation which the most stupid or the most wicked only could suggest."

The Secretary sensed a deadly interplay between Boston and London. With France holding to her decrees, he observed to the President, England alone could open the way to an escape from the embargo. Some striking proof of its success was needed to "arrest the successful perversion of it by its enemies, or rather the enemies of their country." Unluckily, the New England petitions were probably producing a great effect in England, circulating there long before Jefferson's firm answers could reach the British public. To make it worse, the hopes inspired by the uprising in Spain would cause the British cabinet "to raise its tone rather than to revise its errors."[6]

Real political danger developed when London papers arrived in August with the text of a June 24 speech by Canning defending his American policies. Using a system of multiple half-truths (or less), he told Parliament that since the return of Mr. Rose, the United States had made no complaint whatever against the Orders in Council. From this he conjectured "that America has entered into negotiations with France, which are expected to lead to some result" that would affect England. The Rose mission failed because the American government, though apparently satisfied with the reparation offered and the manner of offering it, refused to revoke the proclamation excluding British warships from its harbors.

Canning's speech threw an electric shock into the campaign. Everywhere, Federalist editors accepted his version and denounced Madison and Jefferson for sacrificing American interests to aid France. "There is an unseen hand in all this," cried Congressman Gardenier—the hand of Napoleon.

Chief Clerk Graham begged Madison to give the people the facts about foreign policies, "for the most dishonorable and unfair means are used to deceive them." Without waiting for orders, he furnished Editor Smith with a refutation of the charge about the Orders in Council. True, no protest had been *made* since the return of Rose, but, said the *National Intelligencer,* Rose himself carried Madison's protest of February 23, "a full reply or remonstrance which remains unanswered."

After receiving two private letters from Madison, Graham saw Smith again, also Colvin of the *Monitor,* "and put them in possession of your ideas and of the facts you state." These would enable them "to give useful information to the nation," but too late for the Northern elections. Madison unquestionably wrote part and may have written all of the next day's editorial in the *Intelligencer.*

"From the disgraceful animadversions with which the federal prints abound," said Smith's paper, "it would seem that they had entirely forgotten the black outrage" of the attack on the *Chesapeake.* After it occurred, "even the Essex Junto was awed into silence. The voice of treason was still." Then came the negotiations, not as Canning described them, but with a demand by him that the proclamation be revoked before reparations were dis-

cussed, and an offer by the United States to act on both matters
simultaneously. Madison's authorship of what followed is evident
from its resemblance—except in the indignant tone of politics—
to his remarks in the talks with Rose:

"Will any one, then, dare to say, without exposing his understanding to impeachment, that Britain had a right . . . to refuse
making atonement for a *wrong act* committed by her, until we
had rescinded a *rightful* act of ours? Will he dare to say that the
aggressor has a right to demand redress, instead of the aggrieved?
That the insulted and injured party shall be obliged in the first
instance to make concession? That the midnight robber, who
has broken into my house and stolen my goods, has a right to
demand that I shall unbar my doors, which I had purposely secured against further violations, before he shall be obliged to surrender the goods he had stolen?"

As to Canning's claim that the offer of reparation was in itself
a satisfactory reparation, and was so regarded even though not
accepted: "Has the American government ever . . . uttered a word
to justify it?" Would he have us "sink from the manly language
of demand to the mean attitude of supplication?" Not only did
the government feel the strongest indignation over the outcome
of the talks, but so hostile were the people that, but for the equal
injustice of both the great belligerents, "it would inevitably have
issued in war against Great Britain." Did not Canning know, did
not America know, did not the world know, "that we have demanded reparation in the only terms in which an independent
government can demand it . . . and that every remaining duty
rests with the aggressor?"[7]

Two days later Gallatin wrote to Madison from New York:

"You have heard that New England is lost. If there was an
election tomorrow here it would I think be no better. Of New
Jersey I know nothing and therefore fear the event. In Pennsylvania I have great confidence. South of that state you are better informed than I am."

Even if the Federalists failed to regain power, Gallatin doubted that Congress would continue the embargo. "There is not patriotism and union sufficient to bear with patience, where there is no stimulus." The people, he said, had been taught that the embargo was the *cause* of the stagnation of commerce, instead of being a *shield* against foreign aggressions. The measure was certainly the boldest, as to domestic policy, ever attempted in a popular government, "but I had not anticipated the violations bordering on insurrection which have taken place in so many quarters."

Federalists and Clintonians were now accusing Madison of supporting the embargo and nonintercourse in order to destroy commerce and build up American manufactures. "He is a disciple of Confucius, the lawgiver of China," exclaimed an editor, accusing him of hostility to commerce and agriculture, wanting a nation of shepherds, shepherdesses and manufacturers. Madison himself had told Erskine they would temporarily "pursue the system of the Chinese" by shutting up commerce and preparing to defend themselves.

The false accusation that this was to be permanent cut both ways. Manufacturing societies were springing up wherever mercantile capital was idle. When the Republicans swept Philadelphia in October, the *United States Gazette* lamented that the banks, overflowing with money, had financed so much housebuilding that it offset the distresses of the embargo. At the assembling of Congress in November, scores of Republican members wore homespun suits—"wretched stuff," said Minister Erskine. But in Philadelphia glasses were drained to those wearers of domestic wool. Jefferson was toasted as "the manufacturer of the Declaration of Independence," and Madison as "the manufacturer of the federal Constitution."[8]

Some states had chosen electors when Congress convened on November 7. In New York, Madison was told, his "milk and water friends" were guilty of shameful dereliction. Duped by assurances that Clinton no longer aspired to be President, they allowed the legislature to name thirteen Clintonian electors in a total of nineteen. In the South Carolina legislature, Madison was sure of a three-to-one majority. John Randolph tried to stir Monroe's campaign committee from its "spiritless dejection" and lamented that he didn't have health and industry to "hunt the polecat" himself. Monroe put out a pamphlet of private letters to prove Jefferson's neutrality, but only succeeded, Editor Colvin remarked, in disproving the charge that the President named his successor.

Virginia Federalists, however, endorsed Monroe. Forming "a small and oppressed minority," explained Chief Justice Marshall to the deserted Federalist candidate, they had no other way of exerting influence. "The superior talents of Mr. Madison would probably have placed us in his scale," Marshall added, except for recent evidence that he was even more prejudiced in foreign affairs than his Republican competitors. With the Federalists in all other states solidly behind General Charles Cotesworth Pinckney, and with Clinton and Monroe staying in the field, it became crucially important to rebut the latest attacks on Madison's handling of foreign affairs.[9]

Jefferson's message to Congress outlined a program of internal improvements for the distant future, but carried no plans to meet the current crisis. The original draft stated, rather briefly, that all possible efforts had been made to induce one or both of the great belligerents to revoke "their unrighteous edicts" against American commerce. Neither had done so, hence it had not been possible to revoke the embargo as to either of them. The President was persuaded that Congress, in choosing between "painful alternatives," (he meant embargo or war, he told Erskine), would have faithful regard to the interests of the nation.

Madison sweetened this with a reference to "the sentiments of our constituents," stiffened a phrase or two, and congratulated the country on the shift of industry and capital to internal manufactures. "The extent of this conversion," he wrote, "is far beyond expectation." Cheap materials, low living costs, freedom of labor from taxation, and protective tariffs left little doubt that the new establishments would become permanent. A brief trial had proved the advantage of excluding foreign textiles. Thus, future wants from overseas would "be materially diminished and the nation consequently liberated in an equal degree from that species of dependence."

Gallatin was shocked at this suggestion of benefits willingly derived from the annihilation of commerce. Even if the President believed this, the avowal would "produce a pernicious effect and furnish a powerful weapon to the disaffected." Jefferson promised to tone it down and sent the message back to Madison for a further revision made necessary by the arrival that day (Saturday October 29) of European dispatches brought by the *Hope*. When the President asked for the paper Sunday morning he received a note saying that the remodeling had not yet been done. "JM . . . was prevented last night by company and has but just got up for breakfast."

Madison's revision stated bluntly that the "candid and liberal experiment" of the United States had failed. Both belligerents were adhering to their injurious policies, ignoring or rejecting the carefully balanced inducements to a repeal of their decrees. To get rid of what Gallatin called "a tone of complaint and despondency" in the message, he asserted that the course pursued by the United States "will have demonstrated to foreign nations the moderation and fairness which govern their councils, and have confirmed in all their citizens the motives which ought to incite them in support of the laws and the rights of their country." Jefferson's "painful alternatives" were backed by an assurance hardly consonant with the current revolt against the embargo:

"Nor should I do justice to the virtues which on other occasions have marked the character of the American people, if I did not cherish an equal confidence that the alternative chosen, whatever it may be, will be maintained with all the fortitude and patriotism which the crisis ought to inspire."[10]

Jefferson's message was made a vehicle for the transmission of Madison's 1808 diplomatic correspondence. Once more the newspapers were deluged with official letters disproving the charges of subservience to France and weakness or warmongering toward

England. On the contrary, they revealed that Pinkney, pursuant to instructions, had promised a withdrawal of the embargo against Britain as soon as the Orders in Council were revoked and had stated, as an inevitable consequence, that failure of France to revoke her decrees would lead to war. Publishing Madison's "manly and honorable vindication of the national rights and independence" against the Orders in Council, Duane's *Aurora* exclaimed:

"The man who can read this able and spirited paper, without feeling his pride increased and his indignation excited, ought to suspect his head of imbecility, and his heart of insensibility to virtue or patriotism."

The Clintonian *American Citizen,* after assailing Madison for months as a tool of Napoleon, now bestowed the highest praise in its power. In his reply to the impudent Champagny letter, the Secretary of State had expressed "opinions coinciding exactly with those which from day to day were propagated in the *Citizen."*

The *Aurora* summed up the national reaction by asserting that these documents produced a greater effect on the minds of the people "than, perhaps, ever was produced by any similar publication that ever before appeared." Many had been led to believe by artful insinuations that the President, Madison and their ministers "countenanced, winked at, or connived at the decrees of France; and that they were silent on the subject of the aggressions practiced under those decrees. . . . *That* delusion is now passed." At Salem, Massachusetts, center of the antiembargo agitation, a Republican wrote that even on that subject the people were calmer, so great had been the effect of publishing the diplomatic correspondence.[11]

The choosing of electors stretched from November 4 until December 6, only one day before the electoral college was to perform its work. On November 7, arriving Republican congressmen tallied up 106 votes certain for Madison, not including New York's nineteen. Eighty-nine were a majority.

County by county and state by state, the returns came in. By

November 11, Madison had reassuring word from Virginia. Richmond, where the Federalists endorsed the Monroe ticket instead of their own, went for Madison 110 to 70; Henrico County, 238 to 29. When seventy-four counties were heard from, the vote stood Madison 12,451, Monroe 2,770, Pinckney 435.

By November 21 Madison's victory was assured. The Massachusetts legislature, narrowly Federalist, chose Pinckney electors, but New Jersey went for Madison by a vote of the people and nineteen Pennsylvania counties showed a three-to-one Republican majority. The electors had met and voted on December 7 before it was known in Washington that Rhode Island had gone Federalist by 330 votes and New Hampshire by a little over a thousand.

Then more waiting for news, as postmen or horseback couriers came in from North and South and over the Western mountains. In New York, six unyielding Clintonians split the Republican vote, Madison getting thirteen. In Maryland and North Carolina, where electors were chosen by districts, Madison won over Pinckney, nine to two and eleven to three. He made a sweep of Vermont, New Jersey, Pennsylvania, Virginia, South Carolina, Georgia, Kentucky (where one vote was lost through nonattendance), Tennessee and Ohio. Pinckney did the same in New Hampshire, Rhode Island, Massachusetts, Connecticut and Delaware. Congress counted the votes on February 8, 1809: Madison 122; Pinckney 47; Clinton 6.[12]

In general, the close votes were in states carried by the Federalists. Pennsylvania, Virginia, New York and New Jersey stayed strongly Republican. The South and West were solid: Georgia's legislative vote was unanimous. After all the ferment over "French citizenship" and the embargo, the total vote against Madison barely deviated from spring forecasts.

Madison's election was a verdict of approval on his work and Jefferson's in guarding America's welfare and safety in a world convulsed by warring giants. It was a testimonial to the steadfast faith of the people in the principles of the Jeffersonian party. It was an endorsement, not of all that the administration had done, but of its aims and accomplishments in contrast with those of the

Federalists. It was a vote for the integrity of the American nation, a rejection of dinner-table and cloakroom secessionism. It was a proof of the people's ability to penetrate sham, to laugh at reiterated falsehoods, to appraise a man's record and measure him by it. Above all, it was a tribute to Madison's reputation as an honest man who loved his country and could be trusted to defend it. Integrity of character broke the shaft of slander, and an informed electorate carried him to victory against odds which in appearance were insurmountable.

CHAPTER XXXIII

PRESIDENT-ELECT

CONGRESS listened to the President's message on November 8, 1808, and at once began a flight from the embargo. Jefferson told Erskine, the next day, that the country had three choices—war, embargo or submission—and nobody would choose the last. That oversimplified the matter. The Federalists, advocating plain repeal of the embargo, talked of enforcing American rights at sea, but what they were heading toward was submission to British decrees and a trade partnership against the Napoleonic empire. The Republicans were split three ways, with a war party gaining in strength and the advocates of peace divided between those who would strengthen or weaken the system of commercial retaliation.

Madison desired peace, expected war, and wanted to precede if not forestall it with stronger reprisals. He saw both enmity and folly in the conduct of the British cabinet, rejecting a fair offer and "even sneering at the course pursued by the United States." It was too early to speak positively of the congressional reaction, he observed to Pinkney on November 9. "I shall be much disappointed, however, if a spirit of independence and indignation does not strongly reinforce the past measures with others, which will give a severity to the contest of privations at least, for which the British government would seem to be very little prepared in any sense of the word."

Canning's sneers—inspired by Federalist support and the driving of King Joseph Bonaparte out of Spain—took the form of ironic regret that the Orders in Council, after smashing Napoleon's continental system to "harmless and contemptible" fragments, could not be repealed to save the American people from the injuries wrought on them by their own embargo. Madison and Jefferson revealed their thinking in sending Congress a private letter from Pinkney. The "excellent views" therein expressed, Madison told the minister, "coincided . . . so entirely with the

469

sentiments of the Executive, and were so well calculated to en-
lighten the legislative body," that the rule of privacy was laid
aside.

Pinkney warned against the "improvident thirst for gain" that
made people call for trade with Spain and Portugal during the
temporary overthrow of French power there. It would be a cir-
cuitous trade with Great Britain, nullifying the unrepealed embargo against that power. It would bring on war with France
and thus "place us at the mercy of Great Britain" without a settlement of disputes. To withdraw the embargo from Britain
openly, with the British orders unrepealed, would sanction her
injurious and insulting maritime pretensions and throw us "bound
hand and foot, upon the generosity of a government that has
hitherto refused us justice." Total repeal of the embargo, he declared, would give the United States a fatal choice between war
and dishonor unless some other strong expedient took its place.

"On the other hand, if we persevere, we must gain our purpose
at last. . . . The embargo, and the loss of our trade, are deeply felt
here."[1]

With Congress confused, discordant and flooded with antiembargo petitions, Executive leadership was needed. Jefferson had
decided to leave decisions to those who would act on them and
"be myself but a spectator." Two days after he penned those
words, "Mr. Madison, being unwell," asked Gallatin to request
the President to call a cabinet meeting.

"Both Mr. Madison and myself [wrote Gallatin] concur in opinion that considering the temper of the legislature . . . it would be
eligible to point out to them some precise and distinct course. . . .
I feel myself nearly as undetermined between enforcing the embargo or war as I was on our last meetings. But I think that we
must, or rather you must, decide the question absolutely, so that
we may point out a decisive course either way to our friends."

Two more days passed and former Speaker Macon took the
initiative. He moved to exclude the goods and warships of any
belligerent power which had decrees in force violating the lawful

commerce of the United States. Navy Secretary Smith, as soon as he read this, sent a note to Madison suggesting that it be given prefatory clauses—first a declaration that the rights, interests and honor of the United States did not allow their commerce to be subjected to the decrees of any other nation; then a resolve that "all practicable military arrangements ought to be immediately made."[2]

Within a week, the House Committee on Foreign Relations, headed by George W. Campbell, presented a blend of the Macon and Smith resolutions, supported by a report (approved 7 to 2) which contained the views of the incoming administration. The report was prepared by Gallatin, who was then slated to be the next Secretary of State, but the historical survey was so completely based on Madison's writings and oral arguments as to indicate joint authorship. It even drew on his private correspondence.[3] Through defense and assault, the report came to a set of conclusions, which, though written by Gallatin, can be put down as Madison's position as he approached the Presidency:

"There is no other alternative, but war with both nations, or a continuance of the present system. For war with one of the belligerents only, would be submission to the edicts and will of the other; and a repeal in whole or in part of the embargo must necessarily be war or submission.

"A general repeal without arming, would be submission to both nations.

"A general repeal and arming of our merchant vessels, would be war with both, and war of the worst kind; suffering our enemies to plunder us without retaliation upon them.

"A partial repeal must, from the situation of Europe, necessarily be actual submission to one of the aggressors, and war with the other."

The aggressions of England and France, it was asserted, were "to all intents and purposes, a maritime war waged by both nations against the United States." Permanent suspension of commerce would not be resistance. "It cannot be denied that the ultimate and only effectual mode of resisting that warfare, if per-

sisted in, is war." The unsettled state of the world and the necessity, if war was resorted to, of making it against the two most
powerful nations in the world, induced the committee to leave a
decisive opinion on that subject to the House. They confined
themselves, therefore, to an exposition of facts and introductory
resolutions "equally applicable to either alternative," but making
it clear to every foreign nation "that its aggressions never will be
justified or encouraged by any description of American citizens."[4]

Macon, not knowing who was behind the Campbell report on
his resolution, shared a widespread uncertainty. Jefferson, he
heard correctly, would give no opinion as to proper measures.
Madison was said to be for Macon's plan "with the addition of
high protective duties." Gallatin was "most decidedly for war."
That was at variance with the latter's comment to Jefferson, while
the statement about Madison was absurd. Protective duties would
mean nothing in a period of nonimportation. The views of both
men were comprehended in Madison's remark to Erskine that
"the report of the committee seemed distinctly to announce that
the *ultimate* and only effectual mode of resisting the aggressions
of the belligerents would be by a *war.*"

Historian Henry Adams, who never missed a chance to dispar-
age Madison, noted Erskine's embellishment of this statement
with capitals and underlinings, and called it a tactic to excite
alarm—a tactic in which Madison was perhaps a little the accom-
plice, "for at the moment when he threatened war in language
the most menacing, the future President was trembling lest Congress should abjectly submit to British orders." That is like saying: "Smith is a coward. He hit Jones on the nose and then
trembled with fear lest Jones should run away."

Early in December, Erskine reported "important communications" made to him "by Mr. Madison and several of the members
of this government." They and their party "unequivocably express
their resolution not to remove the embargo, except by substituting
war measures against both belligerents, unless either or both
should relax their restrictions upon neutral commerce." Should
either one relax, "the United States would side with that power
against the other which might continue the aggressions."

Madison acknowledged, Erskine said, that the United States was not prepared for war, especially with so strong a power as Britain, and would sacrifice anything for peace except independence and honor. He did not believe, however, that any Americans would be willing to submit to encroachments on the liberty and rights of the United States; "therefore the alternatives were, Embargo or War." The American people, Madison went on, were beginning to think the embargo too passive and would perhaps soon prefer war "as less injurious to the interests and more congenial with the spirit of a free people."

Erskine hastily consulted Secretaries Gallatin and Smith and "collected from them that their sentiments coincide with those of Mr. Madison." He believed that all of these men had an unfeigned desire to adjust the differences with Great Britain so as to extricate the government and the nation "from the present very distressing dilemma in which they are involved." The people at large wanted the embargo removed; indeed, Erskine doubted whether it could be maintained for another six months, but the outcome of the elections made war more probable than outright repeal.[5]

By the end of the year, New England outcries against the embargo were shaking the fortitude of Northern Republicans. Jefferson remained "an unmeddling listener to what others say," but sent a soothing message to Massachusetts Republicans. He did not tell them, as Madison wanted him to do, that "a greater insult could not have been offered to an honorable state" than the unworthy and subversive Federalist proposals of submission. Gallatin, writing to his brother-in-law, described the dangerous state of affairs:

"A great confusion and perplexity reign in Congress. Mr. Madison is, as I always knew him, slow in taking his ground, but firm when the storm arises. What I had foreseen has taken place. A majority will not adhere to the embargo much longer, and if war be not speedily determined on, submission will soon ensue."[6]

This state of mind did not prevent Congress from passing an embargo enforcement measure (outlined by Gallatin) so drastic that it drove New England farther toward forcible resistance if not secession. A proposal to raise 50,000 volunteers brought an inquiry from Erskine as to the purpose of so large a force. The perseverance of the British and French governments in their edicts, replied Madison, "indicated a spirit of hostility against which it would be the most culpable neglect not to provide." He would say frankly that continued adherence to those edicts would "give them the overt character, as they had long had the real effect, of war, and impose on the United States the obligation of vindicating their honor and their rights by other means than had thus far been resorted to."

The British minister (Madison reported to Pinkney) was then assured that the United States would greatly prefer to see a change in the conduct of the belligerent governments, "and particularly of his own, which would lay the foundation of amicable adjustment." This was an implied offer to join in the war against France in exchange for recognition of national rights at sea. It was backed by a feature of the nonimportation bill which in effect repealed the anti-British *Chesapeake* proclamation by extending the warship ban to France. Erskine reported this last fact to Canning, but not the purpose behind it, and emphasized the hostile aspects of Madison's remarks:

"From his manner as well as from his conversation I could perceive that he was greatly incensed and it appeared to me that he wished that Great Britain might take offense at the conduct of the United States and commence hostilities upon them so as to give this government a strong ground of appeal to the people of this country to support them in a war, unless indeed they could be extricated from their difficulties by Great Britain giving way and withdrawing her Orders in Council."

The language of all the members of the ruling party, Erskine continued, "betrays their anger and their disappointment and their desire to inflame the people of this country against Great Britain so as to lead them into the support of a war against her." The South already was almost unanimous for such a war, and

New England was to be stirred up, he believed, by the arming of merchant vessels and consequent sea fights.

Madison went farther than that in a talk next day (January 2, 1809). "He declared," reported Erskine, "that he had no hesitation in assuring me that in the event of the belligerent nations continuing their restrictions upon neutral commerce, it was intended by this government to recommend to Congress to pass a law to allow merchant ships to arm and also to issue letters of marque and reprisal." If this was not done before the end of the present Congress in March, it would be one of the first measures at a special session of the new Congress in May.

Were it not for the chance of belligerent relaxations, Madison observed to Pinkney, letters of marque and reprisal would probably be issued at once. Congress, he believed, would proceed at once to fix a future date for the beginning of hostilities "against the persevering aggressor or aggressors," except that this might cause the belligerents to adhere to their decrees out of national pride. Impatience under the embargo was becoming extremely acute, especially in Massachusetts, and he saw a preference for war gaining ground everywhere.

Test votes in Congress seemed to warrant Madison's confidence. The Senate, in December, defeated embargo repeal 25 to 6. The House produced a four-to-one preliminary majority for the Crawford committee resolves. Yet Republican unity was at the verge of collapse. President Jefferson's abstention from leadership was coupled with at least a partial realization that his authority, amazingly maintained for seven years, had vanished. A. J. Dallas was distraught by the virulence of Pennsylvania politics when he exclaimed to Gallatin in the summer of 1807: "I verily believe one year more of writing, speaking and appointing would render Mr. Jefferson a more odious President, even to the Democrats, than John Adams." Nevertheless, when the President during that summer gave his protégé, William Short, a recess appointment as minister to Russia, he did so to by-pass senatorial opposition. Now, in midwinter, he was still holding back the nomination to prevent a rejection which, as it turned out, was to carry the rebuke of unanimity.[7]

Madison had not yet acquired the influence that would come from presidential authority, nor did he possess the personal qualities that gave Jefferson his original power. Gallatin, in finance, was the bulwark of his party and the country; in statecraft, he was a distrusted foreigner with a French accent. Their combined efforts barely reversed a congressional decision to throw away Navy operational funds by ordering all gunboats and other vessels to be fully manned—in effect a seamen's work-relief appropriation.

New England's revolt against the embargo flared higher in mid-January with the publication, in Boston, of a "covering letter" from Canning to Pinkney which the President had not included in the correspondence accompanying his annual message. Purporting to describe conversations between the two, it pictured the American minister as having said that he was acting only as an individual, without instructions, when he promised that repeal of the orders would be followed by revocation of the embargo against England, and forecast a resulting war with France.

Pinkney had declared his intention of correcting this and other erroneous statements, and his illuminating reply was sent to Congress the instant the Canning publication reached Washington. It was a complete and convincing refutation, courteously written, not even hinting at bad faith, yet giving strong color to Madison's angry comment:

"This foreign appeal through the press, to the people against their own government, has kindled the greatest indignation everywhere; the more so, as the time and place selected leave no doubt that the object was to foster the discontents breaking out in the State of Massachusetts."

Except for the difficulty of getting information from the printer, and unwillingness to multiply topics of irritation, he thought it "not improbable that the insult would have been taken up by Congress," as the British Parliament once took up the case of an Austrian ambassador. Madison was right in thinking that the copy came from Erskine, who denied it in Washington, but admitted it to London. However, the Secretary mistook the circumstances. The British minister, many weeks earlier, showed the letter in confidence to two senators, to disprove Congressman Burwell's assertion that Canning "insultingly rejected" American partnership in the war. When the tumult started he thought it wise not to find out whether one of them secretly copied it. Canning himself probably intended neither insult nor political intrigue: by misunderstanding Pinkney, he rationalized his acceptance of the Perceval-Castlereagh folly of choosing a trade war against the United States rather than its help against France.[8]

Canning's letter reached the press in Boston just at the right moment to aid Senator Pickering's drive for a New England convention to resist the embargo and, perhaps, dissolve the Union. Led by the Essex Junto and stimulated by inflammatory town meetings, the Massachusetts and Connecticut legislatures set the machinery in motion. With conscious irony, their leaders paraphrased Madison's 1798 call to the states to "interpose for arresting the progress" of unconstitutional laws. But they did not limit themselves, as he did in explaining his attack on the Sedition Act, to constitutional methods of interposition.

Republican congressmen reeled before the sound and fury of the Northeastern uprising. Senator Smith of Maryland, measuring the storm, warned Madison that Congress must vote at once to take off the embargo by June or "we shall lose all the spring elections." Repeal it at once, cried Ezekiel Bacon of Massachusetts, who in November had denounced Pickering for talking the same way. Repeal it at once, echoed his new colleague Joseph Story, who had planned a few months earlier to write a pro-embargo pamphlet, and had recently advised Madison to choose between a continuance of it, or June repeal and war. Repeal it, mockingly agreed David Williams of South Carolina, because "I was so much of a fool" as to think there was patriotism enough, pride enough in the country, "to induce its freemen to be willing to abstain from making money, for the good of the nation."

Late in January, W. C. Nicholas moved for embargo repeal and letters of marque at a blank date (June 1 desired) and inserted a policy declaration which is identified as "Mr. Madison's proposed resolution" on Gallatin's copy. The United States should not delay

beyond a blank date "to resume, maintain and defend the navigation of the high seas, against any nation or nations having in force
edicts, orders or decrees violating the lawful commerce and neutral
rights of the United States."

On February 2, driven by dread of war, apprehension of New
England secession and concern over elections, plus the antiadministration bias of John Randolph and the Clintonites, more than
half of the Republicans joined the Federalists in a 73-to-40 defeat
of June 1 repeal. March 4 was inserted next day with 70 affirma-
tive votes (the negatives not recorded), and repeal on that date
was voted 76 to 40. Randolph then moved to strike out letters of
marque and reprisal and authorize more defensive arming of
merchantmen.[9]

On Saturday evening (February 4) Republicans of both houses
caucused together. "We nerveless seceders," wrote Bacon to the
absent Story, "were pressed by all the force and all the weight
of the government machine to meet on the ground of immediate
or contingent war." It required "nerves of brass" to stand up and
bear the pelting of Nicholas, Giles, Sam Smith, Eppes, Jackson
and half a dozen others, but Bacon and "Judge Orchard" (Cook)
managed to hold their silent followers. They were told at last that
if they would postpone embargo repeal from March to June, the
decision about war would be left to the special session of the new
Congress in May. Bacon replied that he had earnestly pressed the
same proposition before they were driven to extremities; now he
refused to disappoint the expectations created in New England by
Friday's vote. "It has been our misfortune," wrote Nicholas to
Madison, "that the various expedients have been offered too late."
At the beginning of the session they could have coupled anything
with repeal of the embargo.

"The only honorable course was from embargo to war. I fear
we cannot now obtain it and I fear we must submit to the plan
least disgraceful in which we can unite the greatest number of
votes."

At a Sunday meeting, Madison suggested that they combine
March 4 repeal with passage of a nonintercourse law directed

against England and France. In other words, continue the embargo as to those countries and add a ban on imports from them. Writing next morning, Nicholas said he believed they might be able to give the President power to issue letters of marque if American vessels were attacked. He asked for instructions regarding the arming of merchant ships, having understood that Madison connected this with the nonintercourse law. High urgency was in his concluding remark: the success of Madison's administration was inseparable from the issue of preserving the Union and both depended "upon the events of this day and night."[10]

Madison's brother-in-law, Congressman Jackson, held the floor all that day, reviewing and defending American foreign policy, and emphasizing the folly of sending armed merchantmen to sea with "the power of making war transferred to them." If private vessels were to be armed, Jackson argued (presumably coinciding with Madison's view), they must either be given the power of making captures, as part of a decision for war, or their activities must be narrowed by a nonintercourse act, keeping them out of belligerent trade channels. Otherwise "on the day they sail the peace of the nation is gone."

The party caucused again that night and a majority agreed to the trade features of the plan Madison outlined to Nicholas. The crucial question of arming for reprisals went over, and they were voted down next day in Committee of the Whole, 57 to 39. That action, in conjunction with the March 4 embargo repeal, converted the Nicholas resolutions into outright submission to England and France. Their sponsor abandoned them and the subject was referred back to the Committee on Foreign Affairs.[11]

The bill which came from this committee two days later was disliked by both sides. Effective March 4, the embargo was to be repealed except as to England and France, and foreign armed ships excluded from American waters. Total nonimportation from those two countries was to begin May 30. Nicholas informed Madison that all of the New Yorkers would vote for the bill if it and all the embargo laws were made to expire completely at the end of the special session. "You seemed to disapprove of it," he commented, "and I have given no encouragement to the idea."

That limitation, however, was contained in a decidedly stronger bill which Senator Giles offered and the Senate passed. In addition to the House provisions, it gave the President power to proclaim a renewal of trade with either country which should cease to violate the neutral commerce of the United States, and to issue letters of marque and reprisal against the nation that continued its unlawful edicts. The House, taking up this bill in place of its own, struck out the reprisal clause, 74 to 33, and beat down repeated efforts by Representative Jackson to have it restored. On February 27 the bill passed, 81 to 40, Federalists and the Randolph faction voting No. "Between ourselves and it must go no further," wrote Bacon to Story, the administration was "completely beaten" in the shaping of the measure. What came out, as Madison's ally Congressman Montgomery saw it, was the best thing obtainable "from the imbecility and timidity" of Republicans like Bacon.[12]

From Madison's point of view, the one good feature of the new law was the power given the President to suspend it in favor of either belligerent. That was weakened by the early date of embargo repeal (finally fixed at March 15 to give Southern ships an equal start), and by the omission of letters of marque. Most damaging of all was the evidence, broadcast to the world, that Congress would not back a policy of force and that the people would not sustain peaceful coercion if it hurt their pocketbooks.

Mass meetings in Essex County, New Jersey, and Muskingum County, Ohio, might assure the incoming President that they would choose without hesitation between "honorable war or tame submission," and support all measures found necessary in repelling aggressions on lawful commerce. Republican leaders, traveling through New England, might send word to him that the rank and file of the people were far calmer than the Josiah Quincys, the Pickerings and the Hillhouses. "The resolves of Massachusetts and Connecticut legislatures and other seditious newspaper publications deceive the government," wrote Hezekiah Huntington two days before the inauguration, "if they are considered as evidence of the real state of public opinion." Nevertheless, legislatures and newspapers spoke for New England, and it was their language that crossed the Atlantic in accents of domestic rebellion, hostility to French decrees and submission to those of England.[13]

The demoralized condition of the Republican party, as Madison prepared for the short journey from the Department of State to the Presidency, gave ample warning that his future difficulties would not be limited to those arising out of the Napoleonic wars. President Jefferson had entered office at the head of an inexperienced party, so completely devoted to him that dissidents were easily sloughed off or reduced to impotence. In eight years the party had become experienced, disunited, factious and rebellious, but the marvel was that the breakdown of administration control did not come several years earlier. To the extent that disunity resulted from trade restrictions, Madison was more responsible than Jefferson, for the policy was peculiarly his own in the field which caused the most controversy—that of attempted coercion of the European belligerents.

. Both men deserve credit for the greater but less visible benefits of the restrictive system. Through it they refused submission to oppressive edicts, yet avoided the losses, hazards, cost and futility of a war which the country was not yet strong enough to engage in. The financial damage associated with their policy was not caused by it, but by the European conflict itself, and the injuries would have been greater had its lawlessness either been submitted to or allowed to drag the country into war. By refusing to surrender in principle what they could not maintain in practice, Jefferson and Madison left the way open to establish those rights in the near or distant future.

Madison's high prestige as Secretary of State, after eight years in that office, contrasted sharply with the unhappy state of his party and the less than radiant prospect of restoring effective leadership. It was only in the final year that his work really became known to the American people. Before that, Republicans and Federalists had seen him as Jefferson's almost anonymous assistant, carrying out the wise or foolish policies of the President. When the need to fight back in a political campaign forced the administration to lay the full record before the voters, a creative personality came to light. Running through Madison's letters to foreign ministers in Washington, through his instructions to American ministers in Europe, was a brilliance of mind, a consistency of thought and spirited devotion to country which could come from nowhere but within himself.

The people did not know how great his influence had been in shaping the basic policies of government, throughout the Jefferson administration. They knew him as an unceasing worker for the acquisition of Florida, but had not the slightest inkling of the foreseeing strategy with which he worked on France to abandon Louisiana. They did not know that foreign diplomats characteristically began by underrating him, owing to his small person and quiet manner, and progressed to the discovery that he was not only outthinking them but was too tough as well as too agile to handle.

Facts such as these lay buried for generations in foreign archives. But the American people perceived, during that amazing process of political education in 1808, that in every recorded diplomatic encounter Madison showed a keenness of mind and mettle, a fidelity to personal and national integrity, a zealous devotion to his country, that made them proud both of him and of the United States of America. That was why, on March 4, 1809, he was to move from the highest appointive office in the land to the highest elective office.

NOTES AND INDEX

NOTES

The principal manuscript sources of this volume are:

From the Library of Congress: The papers of James Madison, Thomas Jefferson, William C. Rives (mostly from the original Madison papers), James Monroe (including diplomatic letterbook), William Plumer (letters, letterbooks, diary, Register, Repository), Joseph H. Nicholson, Samuel Smith (including letterbook), Augustus J. Foster (including Journal), Joseph Story, the Pinckney Family; Letters in Relation to Burr's Conspiracy.

Columbia University: Papers of DeWitt Clinton.

Connecticut Historical Society: Papers of Oliver Wolcott.

Massachusetts Historical Society: Papers of Timothy Pickering and Temple-Bowdoin.

New York Historical Society: Papers of Robert R. Livingston (including letterbooks) and Albert Gallatin.

Yale University: Papers of Roger Griswold, William Griswold Lane, John Cotton Smith, Simeon E. Baldwin, the Morse Family.

Also the extensive manuscript collections of the New York Public Library, the Historical Society of Pennsylvania, University of Virginia, Harvard University, Essex Institute, Maryland Historical Society, Haverford College.

Letters written by Jefferson are cited by date alone, owing to publication of *The Papers of Thomas Jefferson*. Letters by Madison, Monroe, Gallatin and Rufus King, when cited by date alone, are to be found in their collected writings, listed below, or (except Gallatin) in *American State Papers, Foreign Relations*, which also contain similarly cited letters of Robert R. Livingston, Charles Pinckney and William Pinkney.

Letters of Edward Thornton, Anthony Merry and David M. Erskine, cited only by date, are chronologically located in Foreign Office 5 of the British Public Record Office, those of George H. Rose in FO 5, volume 56. Letters of Talleyrand, Champagny, Louis Pichon and General Turreau, similarly cited, are regularly placed in the *Archives des Affaires Étrangères, correspondance politique, États-Unis* (Paris, with photostats in Library of Congress). Letters of Napoleon and General Leclerc, not otherwise located by citation, are in their collected correspondence.

City names have been omitted from the titles of the Washington *National Intelligencer*, the New York *American Citizen*, New York *Public Advertiser*, Philadelphia *Aurora*, Philadelphia *United States Gazette*. *Op. cit.* applies to the chapter in which it is used. References within parentheses apply to only one item. Abbreviations are employed as follows:

Adams: *History of the United States during the Administrations of Jefferson and Madison*, by Henry Adams.

AHA: American Historical Association.

AHR: American Historical Review.

Anas: By Thomas Jefferson, in *Writings* (Ford), I, containing minutes of cabinet meetings.

ASP: American State Papers, Foreign Relations (1832).

ASP PL: American State Papers, Public Lands.

Bruce: *John Randolph of Roanoke,* by William Cabell Bruce.

CtHS: Connecticut Historical Society.

Cutts: *Memoirs and Letters of Dolly Madison,* by Lucia B. Cutts.

EU: *Archives des Affaires Étrangères, correspondence politique, États-Unis.*

FO: Foreign Office 5, Public Record Office, Great Britain.

Foster, "Notes": Augustus J. Foster, "Notes on the United States," *William & Mary Quarterly,* January 1951 and April 1952.

Gallatin: *The Writings of Albert Gallatin,* edited by Henry Adams.

Haswell: *United States: Treaties and Conventions,* edited by John H. Haswell.

Hamilton: *The Works of Alexander Hamilton,* edited by J. C. Hamilton.

JM-LC: Papers of James Madison, Library of Congress.

King: *The Life and Correspondence of Rufus King,* edited by Charles R. King.

LC: Library of Congress.

Maclure: *To the People of the United States,* by William Maclure.

Madison, *Letters:* Letters and Other Writings of James Madison (1865).

Madison, *Writings: Writings of James Madison,* edited by Gaillard Hunt.

Marbois, *Histoire: Histoire de la Louisiane,* by François Barbé-Marbois (Paris, 1829).

McCaleb: *The Aaron Burr Conspiracy,* by Walter F. McCaleb.

MHS: Massachusetts Historical Society.

Miller: *Treaties and Other International Acts of the United States of America,* edited by Hunter Miller.

Monroe, *Writings: The Writings of James Monroe,* edited by S. M. Hamilton.

Moore: *International Adjudications,* edited by J. B. Moore.

NA: National Archives of the United States (State Department).

NYHS:New-York Historical Society.

NYPL: New York Public Library.

PHS: Historical Society of Pennsylvania.

Plumer: *William Plumer's Memoranda of Proceedings in the United States Senate, 1803-1807,* edited by E. S. Brown.

Robertson: *Louisiana under Spain, France and the United States, 1785-1807,* edited by James Alexander Robertson.

Smith, *First Forty Years: The First Forty Years of Washington Society,* edited by Gaillard Hunt from the letters of Margaret B. Smith.

TJ-LC: Papers of Thomas Jefferson, Library of Congress.

VaU: University of Virginia.

CHAPTER I

(Pages 11 to 22)

[1] George Tucker called this a 1799 meeting in Richmond. Actually, his letter of introduction was dated July 11, 1800 (Monroe Papers). Madison visited Monroe at Charlottesville about August 7.

[2] Madison to Jefferson, January 12, 18, March 15, 1800. S. T. Mason to Madison, January 16, 1800, Rives Papers.

[3] Madison to Jefferson, March 15, 1800. *Annals* (Senate) January 23, March 27, 28, May 1, 2, 10, 1800 (pages 694-5-7, 713).

[4] S. T. Mason to Madison, April 23, 1800, Rives Papers. Richard Hildreth, *History of the United States,* V, 366.

[5] *Annals* (Senate) February 26, March 5-27, May 14, 1800.

[6] Madison to Jefferson, April 4, 1800. J. Dickinson to Jefferson, March 18, G. Duvall to Madison, April 28, 1800, JM-LC.

[7] Jefferson to Madison, March 4-8, April 4, Madison to Jefferson, April 4, 20, 27, 1800, JM-LC.

[8] D. Foster to J. Morse, April 20, 1800, Yale.

[9] James Nicholson to Gallatin, May 6, 7, 1800, NYHS. Nicholson to George Clinton, December 26, 1803, *AHR*, VIII, 511. M. L. Davis to Gallatin, May 1, 5, Gallatin to Mrs. Gallatin, May 6, 1800, NYHS. J. Dawson to Monroe, May 4, 1800, NYPL.

[10] S. T. Mason to Monroe, May 15 (Monroe Papers), R. to M. Griswold, April 8, May 13 (Yale), B. Goodhue to Pickering, May 19, June 2 (MHS), 1800.

[11] Harper to Hamilton, June 5, Rutledge to Hamilton, July 17, 1800, Hamilton Papers. Wolcott to McHenry, July 18, 1800, NYPL.

[12] W. C. Nicholas to Madison, May 22, 1800, Rives Papers. G. Duvall to Madison, June 6, 1800, JM-LC.

[13] Thomas Mason to Norborn Nicholas, June 9, 1800, NYPL.

[14] Jefferson to Madison, April 4, June 13, to Monroe, March 26, 1800.

[15] Jefferson to Madison, September 17, 1800. Madison to Jefferson, September (ca 23), October 1, 1800, JM-LC. H. W. DeSaussure to Pickering, August 12, 1800, MHS.

[16] *Ibid.* Hamilton to McHenry, August 27, 1800, NYPL. Richard Hildreth, *History of the United States,* V, 383-386. R. Troup to King, November 9, 1800, *King,* III, 330. McHenry to Hamilton, November 19, 1800, Hamilton Papers, LC.

[17] Madison to Jefferson, October 21, 1800, January 10, 1801. DeSaussure to J. Morse, November 3, 1800, Yale. Dallas to McKean, December 1, 1800, PHS. J. Marshall to C. C. Pinckney, November 20, 1800, Pinckney Papers, LC. R. to M. Griswold, December 10, 1800, Yale (quoting Pinckney to Marshall). *U. S. Gazette,* December 3, 1800. C. Pinckney to Jefferson, October 12, 1800, *AHR*, IV, 114.

CHAPTER II

(Pages 23 to 34)

[1] Burr to R. Livingston, September 24, 1800, NYHS. Madison to Jefferson, October 21, December 20, 1800.

[2] Gelston to Madison, October 8, November 21, 1800, Rives Papers.

[3] Monroe to Madison, November 6, Jefferson to Madison, November 9, 1800, Rives Papers. Madison to Monroe (two letters), November 10, 1800. G. Jackson to Madison, February 5, 1801, JM-LC. J. Nicholas to Madison, November 28, 1800, Rives Papers.

[4] Gelston to Madison, November 21, 1800, Rives Papers.

[5] Madison to Jefferson, January 14, 1824, Rives Papers. J. Cheetham to Jefferson, December 10, 1801, and memo, MHS *Proceedings*, XLI, 46-51. Cheetham said he called on Madison the day before, but he was ill, so Cheetham wrote out what he had to say.

[6] Peter Freneau to Jefferson, December 2, C. Pinckney to Jefferson, November 22, December 2, 6, 1800, TJ-LC.

[7] J. C. Hamilton (*History of the Republic*, VII, 425-430), declared that a letter from Gunn to Hamilton, December 13, 1800, proved that the tie vote was known then in Washington. On the contrary, Gunn referred to "the commencement of Jefferson's administration."

[8] J. B. McMaster, *History of the People of the United States*, II, 511. Jefferson to Madison, December 19, 1800. Jefferson to Livingston, February 24, 1801.

[9] Dawson to Madison, December 17, 18, 1800, JM-LC. Troup to King, February 12 (*King*), Gunn to Hamilton, January 9 (*Hamilton*), 1801.

[10] Jefferson to Madison, December 19, 26, 1800. Madison to Jefferson, January 10, 1801. H. G. Otis to Hamilton, December 17, 1800, Hamilton Papers. Hamilton to Wolcott, December 16, 1800. Hamilton to McHenry, January 4, 1801, and memo on Burr, NYPL. J. Morse to his father, January 1, 1801, Yale.

[11] R. to M. Griswold, December 27, 1800, Yale. Burr to S. Smith, December 16, in Georgetown *Federalist*, December 31, 1800. Burr to J. Taylor, December 18, 1800, MHS (pledging aid to Jefferson's election when Burr thought tie was broken). Jefferson to Martha Randolph, January 4, 1801. C. Rodney to James Nicholson, January 3, 1801, Nicholson Papers.

[12] On December 17, 1800, the N. Y. *Daily Advertiser* named the South Carolina electors, saying the list was from one of the letters, dated December 2, which reached Washington "late Thursday" (December 11). The electors were named in Freneau's December 2 letter.

[13] Burr to S. Smith, December 29, 1800, in "Aaron Burr: Would-Be usurper," John S. Pancake, *William & Mary Quarterly*, April 1951.

[14] Harper to Burr, December 24, 1800, in J. F. McLaughlin, *Matthew Lyon*, 386. Bayard to Hamilton, January 7, Sedgwick to Hamilton, January 10, 1801, *Hamilton*, VI, 506, 513.

[15] G. Christie to S. Smith (three letters), December 19, 1802, Smith to

Burr, January 11, Burr to Smith, January 16, 1801, S. Smith Papers, LC.
B. Hichborn to Jefferson, January 5, 1801. *Anas,* December 23, 25, 1800,
January 2, 1804.

[16] Jefferson to Madison, December 19, 1800. R. to M. Griswold, January
11, 1801, Yale. G. Jackson to Madison, February 5, 1801, JM-LC.
J. Vaughan to Jefferson, January 10, 1801, TJ-LC. J. Beckley to Gallatin,
February 4, 1801, NYHS. Bayard to Hamilton, January 7, 1801, *Hamilton,*
VI, 505.

[17] W. Dana to Wolcott, February 11, 1801, CtHS. Jefferson to Madison,
Dawson to Madison, February 12, 1801, JM-LC.

[18] J. Randolph to Monroe (after ten ballots), February 11, 1801, Monroe
Papers. R. to M. Griswold, February 27, 1801, Yale. A. J. Dallas to Gallatin,
February 15, 1801, NYHS.

[19] Bayard to Hamilton, March 8, 1801, *Hamilton,* VI, 522. AHA *Report,*
1913, II, 128. M. L. Davis, *Memoirs of Aaron Burr,* II, 106-110, 119-137.
Anas, April 15, 1806.

[20] Bayard to R. Bassett, February 17, 1801, AHA *Report,* 1913, II, 127.
R. Griswold to his wife, February 16, 1801, Yale. F. Maury to Madison,
4 o'clock, February 19, 1801, JM-LC.

[21] Bayard to Bassett, to McLane, February 17 (AHA *op. cit.*), Jefferson
to Madison, February 18, 1801.

[22] Bayard to Hamilton, *op. cit.* Linn to S. Smith, January 10, 1803, S.
Smith Papers, LC. *Anas,* December 31, 1803. Madison to Jefferson, February 28, 1801.

CHAPTER III

(Pages 35 to 47)

[1] W. V. Murray to J. Q. Adams, May 2, 1801, AHA *Report,* 1912, 695.
J. Dickinson to Madison, April 7, 1801, JM-LC.

[2] Jefferson to Madison, December 19, 1800, February 18, 1801. J. Dawson to Monroe, February 23, 1801, Monroe Papers.

[3] Madison to Jefferson, January 10, 1801.

[4] Madison to Jefferson, December 20, 1800, JM-LC, January 10, February 28, 1801. J. Madison Sr. to T. Barbour, February 15, 1800, NYPL.

[5] Madison to ——, March 7, 1801, Madison queries and decree in chancery, March 3, E. Randolph to Madison, March 13, 1803, JM-LC.

[6] Orange Co. Records, August 21, September 21, 1803, May 11, 1814,
January 26, 1818. Madison to Monroe, June 1, 1801. T. Macon to Madison,
July 30, 1804, Robert Taylor to Madison, 1801-1804, JM-LC.

[7] D. P. Madison statement, March 21, 1835, Dolley Madison Papers.

[8] Madison to Jefferson, February 28, Jefferson to Madison, March 12, 26,
to Giles, March 23, 1801.

[9] Jefferson to Madison, December 20, 1800, April 30, 1801, to A. Stuart,
April 8, 1801. Madison to Jefferson, April 22, 1801. W. Cranch to ——,
May 15, 1801, Bass Papers, MHS.

[10] R. Griswold to his wife, December 6, 1800, Yale. John Cotton Smith,

"Washington in 1800," Yale. Forty-five Washington residents to Jefferson (in writing of Thomas Law), received March 21, 1801, TJ-LC. Mrs. H. Cushing to Margaret Bowers, January 29, 1801, NYPL.

[11] Jefferson to T. M. Randolph, June 4, 1801.

[12] Wm. Thornton to Madison, March 16, T. Law to Madison, May 12, 1801, JM-LC. T. Law, memo, TJ-LC 19119. A. J. Foster, Journal, LC. Jefferson to Monroe, July 20, 1801. Madison to L. Lincoln, July 25, 1801, MHS. NA, SD, Day Book (on moving offices). That Madison was about to move from the President's house to the Six Buildings seems implied in Law's request that he "make a temporary sacrifice by a residence rather more distant from the offices than the Six Buildings." M. B. Smith wrote that Madison's first residence was "three miles distant" from her own, which was three miles southeast of the Six Buildings. Smith, *First Forty Years,* 2, 27.

[13] Wm. Thornton to Madison, August 15, 1801, JM-LC. Madison to Gallatin, September 1, 1801, NYHS. Because Madison lived next door to Thornton, who once lived in Georgetown, Madison's residence has sometimes been placed there. Thornton moved to Washington in 1797, renting and later buying lot 7, block 253. An indenture given by Voss refers to lot 8, square 253, as "the same house and lot which the said Nicholas Voss hath rented to James Maddison, Esquire." D. C. Land Records, Book 7, 415; Book 11, 358. Madison's house was on the east half of lot 8, at 1333 F St., Thornton's at 1331.

[14] Pichon to Talleyrand, February 15, 1802.

[15] Anna Thornton, Diary, September 5-25, 1802, LC. D. Brent to Madison, September 3, Jefferson to Madison, September 10, 1802, JM-LC.

[16] Madison to Gates, March 10, 1802, NYPL. Sandy Springs Farmers' Society to Madison, May 8, 1802, Briggs to Madison, January 1, March 30, 1803, JM-LC. Madison to Briggs, January 11, 1803, PHS. S. L. Mitchill to Madison, January 10, 1803, Briggs Papers, LC. W. Thornton to Madison, August 17, 1803, JM-LC.

[17] Foster, "Notes." Tucker, Memoir, Rives Papers. J. K. Paulding, Sketch, Rives Papers. Max Farrand in *Pennsylvania Magazine of History and Biography,* April 1938.

CHAPTER IV

(Pages 48 to 58)

[1] Pichon to Talleyrand, March 31, Madison to Monroe, May 6, 1801.

[2] "Citizen W. Duane" MS booklet, NYHS. Wagner to Pickering, May 30, 1801, MHS. M. Van Buren, *Autobiography,* 421. Wagner to Madison, April 30, (VaU), July 22, November 1, Pleasanton, Crawford and Thom to Madison, July 1, JM-LC, 1802.

[3] J. Yard to Madison, October 28, Madison to Monroe, November 7, 1800, W. Lee to Madison, December 25, 1803, January 5, February 12, 1805, T. Newton to Madison, July 30, 1803, F. T. Wichelhausen to Madison, December 7, 1805, JM-LC.

[4] G. Tucker, Memoir, 53, Rives Papers. For job solicitations, see letters in

JM-LC between March 27 and August 2, 1801, in following order: Ellery, Howell, Irwin, Polk, Haswell, Jackson, Maury, Butler, Sharpe, Coxe, Taylor, Butler, Muhlenberg (*re* Irwin), Gaullier.

[5] J. T. Callender to Madison, April 27, May 7, 1801, JM-LC. Monroe to Madison, May 23, 1801, NYPL. Madison to Monroe, May 6, June 1, 1801. Gallatin to ——, August 20, 1802, NYHS.

[6] Madison to Jefferson, July 17, August 26, to A. J. Dallas, July 20, 1801, TJ-LC. Jefferson to Madison, July 19, August 22, 1801.

[7] Jefferson to T. M. Randolph, June 18, 1801. T. Paine to Jefferson, (rec'd) November 4, 1801, January 30, 1806, TJ-LC.

[8] W. C. Nicholas to Madison, May 1, 3, 1801, Rives Papers. Madison to Nicholas, July 10, 1801. Jefferson to Habersham, March 24, 1801.

[9] Jefferson to E. Shipman and others, July 12, 1801. Gallatin to Jefferson, July 25, 1801, September 18, 1804. Jefferson to Gallatin, July 26, 1801, September 8, 1804.

[10] S. Osgood to Madison, April 24, 1801, JM-LC. R. Troup to R. King, May 27, 1801, *King*, III, 460.

[11] Burr to Gallatin, April 21 (NYHS), June 28, September 8, 1801, Adams, *Gallatin*, 283, 284. Jefferson to G. Clinton, May 17, 1801. Jefferson to W. Nicholas, June 11, 1801. Adams, I, 230-236.

[12] Gallatin to Jefferson, September 12, 1801. Madison to Jefferson, September 17, 1801, TJ-LC. Cheetham to Jefferson, December 10, 1801, MHS *Proceedings*, XL, 46-51.

[13] *Ibid*. Gallatin to Jefferson, September 14, 1801. W. Nicholas to DeWitt Clinton, August 13, 1802, Columbia.

[14] Jefferson to Habersham, September 4, 1801. Habersham to Madison, August 31 (JM-LC), to Jefferson, September 14, 21, 1801, TJ-LC. W. J. Northen, *Men of Mark in Georgia*, I, 140, 141.

[15] Thornton to Hawkesbury, June 2, 1801. W. Jones to Madison, September 13, 1801, Rives Papers.

[16] Jefferson, draft for December 8 message, TJ-LC, to Madison, November 12, to Gallatin, November 14, 1801. *Gallatin*, I, 63-74.

CHAPTER V

(Pages 59 to 72)

[1] Pichon to Talleyrand, May 1, 1801. Albert H. Bowman, "The Struggle for Neutrality: Franco-American Relations, 1790-1801," dissertation for Columbia University, 1953.

[2] Pichon to Talleyrand, May 1, 1801. Yrujo to Madison, September 4, 1801, NYPL. Jefferson to J. Yznardi, March 26, 1801.

[3] Madison to W. Eaton, May 20, Invoice, *ca.* July 20, 1801, NA.

[4] Thornton to Hawkesbury, June 2, July 15, 1802, with enclosures.

[5] Thornton to Madison, July 23, August 1, November 11, 1801, April 9, August 27, 1802, NA. Madison to Jefferson, August 12 (rec'd), 18, 1801, TJ-LC. Jefferson to Madison, August 22, 1801, September 6, 1802. Jefferson to R. Smith, August 14, 1801. R. Smith to Gallatin, undated but

after August 29, 1801, NYHS. Thornton to Hawkesbury, November 25, 1801, September 27, 1802, July 29, 1803.

[6] Adams, I, 377*ff.* Naming Toussaint Louverture's domain is hardly easier than reconquering it proved to be. St. Domingo, the Franco-Spanish hybrid universally used by Americans, correctly reflected the union of St. Domingue (Haiti) and Santo Domingo.

[7] Pichon to Talleyrand, March 20, October 9, 1801. J. Marshall to Toussaint Louverture, November 26, 1800, NA, Consuls, I.

[8] Madison to T. Lear, June 1, 1801, NA, Consuls, I.

[9] Napoleon to Toussaint, May 4, 1801. Pichon to Talleyrand, July 22, 1801 (Nos. 15 and 16).

[10] Madison to Monroe, June 1, to W. Nicholas, July 10, 1801. Joseph Allen Smith to Jefferson, March 22, 1801, and memorial, Smith to Joseph Bonaparte, TJ-LC. King to Madison, March 29, 1801.

[11] Pichon to Talleyrand, July 22, 1801. Madison to Monroe, June 1, to W. Nicholas, July 10, to C. Pinckney, June 9, 1801.

[12] Pichon to Talleyrand, August 11, 1801 (Lear address enclosed).

[13] Livingston to Madison, July 1, 1801, JM-LC. Jefferson to Livingston, September 9, 1801. Pichon to Talleyrand, July 22, 1801.

[14] King to Madison, May 30, June 1, Madison to King, July 24, 1801.

[15] J. Dawson to Madison, August 13, 1797, JM-LC. Liston to Prescott, November 28, 1796, Public Record Office, Colonial Office, Q78, 135. Thornton to Hawkesbury, January 26, 1802. Fauchet to Foreign Secretary, February 4, 1795, AHA *Report*, 1903, II, 559. Adams, I, 357.

[16] Brant, Madison, II, 327, 399, 404. Madison to Jefferson, August 20, 1784, March 20, 1785, to C. Pinckney, October 25, 1801.

[17] In *ASP* this appears, incorrectly, "from Spain to France."

[18] Madison to Livingston, September 28, 1801, NA, Consuls, I.

CHAPTER VI

(Pages 73 to 83)

[1] Pichon to Talleyrand, October 25, November 15, 1801.

[2] Pichon to Talleyrand, January 2, February 9, 15, 21, 24, to Madison, February 9, 1802. Madison to Lear, January 8 (NA), to Pichon, February 15, 1802 (French translation in EU 54, 135).

[3] *Intelligencer*, March 5, 8, 10, 1802. Talleyrand to Decrès, December 20, Thornton to FO, March 6, November 30, 1802 (*re* Fulton).

[4] Madison to Lear, February 26, March 25, 1802, NA. Napoleon to Talleyrand, October 30, November 13, 1801. *Lettres du Général Leclerc*, 269, 274. C. L. Lokke, "Jefferson and the Leclerc Expedition," AHR, January 1928.

[5] Pichon to Talleyrand, March 22 and enclosures, 27, July 1, 1802, followed by Pichon-Leclerc letters, EU 54.

[6] Pichon to Talleyrand, March 28, April 14, 24, 1802. Madison to Villaret, March 25, 1802, EU 54, 265.

[7] Livingston to Madison, December 10, 12, 31, 1801. Madison to Livingston, March 16, 1802. King to Madison, January 15, 1802.

[8] King to Madison, November 20, 1801, followed by treaty in *ASP.* Jefferson to Livingston, April 18, 1802. DuPont to Jefferson, April 30 (rec'd May 3), 1802.

[9] Madison to Jefferson, May 7, TJ-LC, to C. Pinckney, May 11, 1802.

[10] Pichon to Talleyrand, March 22, May 7, October 14, 1802. Lear-Leclerc letters, EU 54, 463, 465. Pichon to Leclerc, May 7 (EU 55), Madison to Pichon, May 6 (TJ-LC), to Livingston, May 7, (NA), 1802

[11] Leclerc to Decrès, May 6, to Napoleon, May 7, June 6, 1802 (rec'd June 12 and September 17).

[12] Napoleon to Decrès, June 4, 1802. Appointment of Otto, June 7, 1802, EU 54. King to Madison, November 30, 1801. Madison to Jefferson, September 11, 1802, TJ-LC. Jefferson to Livingston, August 28, 1801, March 16, 1802. Livingston to Madison, December 10, 1801, NA.

[13] Napoleon to Talleyrand, July 4, 1802. Pichon to Talleyrand, October 14, 1802. Jefferson to McKean, June 12, 1802.

[14] Napoleon to Leclerc, July 1, Leclerc to Decrès, May 8, June 6, 24, July 6, 12, August 2, 6, 9, 1802. Adams, I, 395-397.

CHAPTER VII

(Pages 84 to 97)

[1] Jefferson to Barlow, May 3, to C. Rodney, April 24, 1802. R. Griswold to his wife, December 23, 1801, to D. Daggett, January 1, 1802, J. Hillhouse to S. Baldwin, February 11, 1802, Yale.

[2] W. Plumer to Jeremiah Smith, December 9, 1802, Plumer Letters, I, 495, LC. Pichon to Talleyrand, February 24, 1802. Thornton to Hawkesbury, August 4, 1802.

[3] F. Ames to King, October 27, 1801, *King*, IV, 5. U. Tracy to J. Trumbull, December 10, 1801, CtHS.

[4] Randolph to J. H. Nicholson, January 1, 1801, Nicholson Papers. Randolph to Monroe, January 12, 1802, NYPL. Pichon to Talleyrand, February 24, 1802, February 18, 1803.

[5] Denniston and Cheetham to Jefferson, January 30, 1802, TJ-LC. Pichon to Talleyrand, August 2, 1802. E. Benson to Wolcott, August 9, 1802, CtHS. Troup to King, April 9, 1802, *King*, IV, 103. J. Early to Madison, December 7, 1802, JM-LC.

[6] Murray to J. Q. Adams, April 3, 1802, NYPL. Murray to King, April 5, 1802, *King*, IV, 95. Madison to Gerry, December 22, 1801, PHS.

[7] T. Sedgwick to King, December 14, 1801, *King*, IV, 35. Robert Waln to Plumer, January 17, 1803, Plumer Papers.

[8] Madison to King, December 10, 22, 1801. Troup to King, December 5, 1801, *King*, IV, 27.

[9] *Annals*, December 15, 1801. Madison to King, May 1, 1802, NA. King to Madison, February 5, 13, June 20, 1802. Thornton to Hawkesbury, December 18, 1801, January 2, December 31, 1802.

[10] Thornton to Hawkesbury, April 3, June 24, December 31, 1802, April 7, 1803. Madison to King, July 23, 1802, NA.

[11] Thornton to Hawkesbury, June 1, October 25, November 26, Madison to Thornton, November 9 (NA, Domestic 14), 1802. Thornton to Madison, March 17, 1802, JM-LC (about publishing *Phillidore's Games*).

[12] *Gazette de France,* quoted in New York *Spectator,* June 9, 1802.

[13] Pichon to Talleyrand, July 7, 31, 1802.

[14] Leclerc to Napoleon, October 7, 1802: "It is necessary to destroy all Negroes in the mountains, men and women, sparing only children under twelve years, to destroy half of those in the plains and not leave in the colony a single colored man [mulatto] who has worn the epaulette."

[15] Madison to Jefferson, August 29 (rec'd), September 15, 1802, TJ-LC.

[16] Livingston, memoir on sea power, undated, *ASP,* II, 578-581.

[17] Livingston, Louisiana memoir, *ASP,* II, 520-524, unexpurgated in *Intelligencer,* July 11, 1803 (retranslation).

[18] Livingston to Talleyrand, August 19, 1802 (EU 54, 503), to Madison, June 8, July 30, August 10, 19, September 1, 1803. T. Sumter memo, October 1, 1803, Monroe Papers. H. C. Rice, "James Swan: agent of the French Republic, 1794-1796," *New England Quarterly,* X, 485.

[19] Livingston to Madison, July 30, August 10, 1803, *ASP,* II, 519, 520, and Livingston Letterbook A, NYHS.

[20] Livingston to Madison, August 19, September 1, to Jefferson, October 28, 1802.

[21] Adams, I, 365. Livingston to Madison, November 11, 1802, NA (in *ASP* with errors). Napoleon to King of Tuscany, August 29, 1802.

[22] Livingston to Madison, November 11 (second of this date in *ASP*), Madison to Livingston, October 15, 1802.

CHAPTER VIII

(Pages 98 to 110)

[1] Madison to Livingston, October 15, to Pinckney, November 27, 1802.

[2] Madison to Jefferson, August 14, September 9 (rec'd), 1802, TJ-LC. Jefferson to Madison, September 3, 10, 1802.

[3] Thornton to Hawkesbury, November 30, 1802. Madison to Livingston, December 16, 1802, Haverford.

[4] Livingston to Joseph Bonaparte, December 11, 24, 1802 (NA), January 7, 1803, *ASP,* II, 530, 531 (repeated to Talleyrand), 536.

[5] "Tableau General," etc., Haswell, 339-342. Sumter to Livingston, October 24, 1802, NYHS. H. C. Rice, *N. E. Quarterly,* X, 480-481.

[6] Livingston to Madison, August 10, 1802 (NYHS), February 18, 1803.

[7] Livingston to Talleyrand, January 18, 1803, misdated in *ASP,* II, 531, and EU Supp. VII, 310. See *AHR,* LVII, 863n.

[8] Livingston to Madison, December 20-23, 1802. Madison to Jefferson, March 14, 1803, TJ-LC. Jefferson to Madison, March 19, 1803.

[9] Napoleon to Decrès, December 19, 1802. Adams, II, 5-8.

[10] Livingston to J. Bonaparte, January 7, to Madison, January 24, Feb-

ruary 5, 18, 1803. Talleyrand to Livingston, March 10 (*ASP*, II, 546, misdated), to Bernadotte, January 11 (EU Supp. VII), 1803.

[11] Pichon to Talleyrand, October 16, 1802, January 4, 1803.

[12] Madison to Livingston, January 18, 1803.

[13] *Annals*, January 12, 1803. Plumer, 17.

[14] Madison to Jefferson, September 23, 1801, TJ-LC.

[15] Graham to Madison, September 9 (rec'd November 25), 1802, JM-LC. Madison to Monroe, March 2, 1803.

[16] Jefferson to Monroe, January 10, 13, 1803. Jefferson to T. M. Randolph, January 17, 1803.

[17] Madison to Livingston and Monroe, March 2 (originally dated January 31), 1803. Jefferson wrote to Madison on February 22, 1803: "I return you Monroe's instructions which are entirely right."

[18] Livingston and Monroe "full power," January 12, 1803, NA. Plumer, Repository, Anecdotes, January 19, 1803, LC.

[19] The livre and the new franc were each worth about 18.75 cents.

[20] Madison to Monroe, March 1, 2, 1803. Gallatin to Madison, February 7, 1803, extract, Madison, *Writings*, VII, 30n.

[21] Thornton to Hawkesbury, January 31, 1803.

CHAPTER IX

(Pages 111 to 123)

[1] Monroe to S. Coleman, March 2, 1803, NYPL. Madison, to and from Coleman, J. Jones, T. Swann, J. Mason, Suttle, JM-LC, XXV-XXIX, list, XC, 58. Monroe to Skipwith, March 10, September 28, 1801, NYPL.

[2] Livingston to Madison, March 3, 1803, *ASP*, MS in NA.

[3] Livingston to G. Morris, April 18, 1803, NYHS.

[4] Madison to Monroe, May 1, 1803, JM-LC.

[5] Livingston to the First Consul, February 27, to Madison, March 11, to Jefferson, March 12, 1803. Talleyrand to Livingston, March 10, 1803 (misdated February 19 in *ASP*).

[6] Livingston to Madison, March 11, 12 (NA), 1803. Livingston to American creditors, November 5, 1803, NA.

[7] Livingston to Talleyrand, March 16, to Madison, March 24, Talleyrand to Livingston, March 22, 1803, *ASP*, II, 548-550.

[8] C. D. Yonge, *Life . . . of Liverpool*, I, 106-117. C. L. Lokke, "Secret Negotiations to Maintain the Peace of Amiens," *AHR*, XLIX.

[9] *Ibid*. Th. Jung, *Lucien Bonaparte et ses Memoires*, quoted in Adams, II, 35-39. Marbois, *Histoire*, 301.

[10] Pichon to Talleyrand, January 21, 24 (rec'd March 22, 28), 1803.

[11] Jefferson to P. duPont, February 1, Livingston to Jefferson, April 14, TJ-LC, Pichon to Talleyrand, January 28, 1803.

[12] Talleyrand to Pichon, March 23, 1803.

[13] Pichon to Talleyrand, February 13, 18, 1803. Madison to Monroe, March 1, 1803.

[14] Pichon to Talleyrand, February 13, 20, 1803. Madison to Pichon,

February 8, to Yrujo, February 18, March 10, 1803, NA. Soler, Yrujo, Pichon, in *Intelligencer*, March 7, 14, 16, 1803. Thornton to Hawkesbury, May 4, 1803. Edward Channing, *History of the United States*, IV, 312, 326-327.

[15] Pichon to Talleyrand, February 28, 1803 (rec'd April 26).

[16] Livingston to Talleyrand, *Germinal, an.* XI (month beginning March 22, 1803), EU 55, 389. In *ASP*, II, 534-536, wrongly identified.

[17] Livingston to Talleyrand, "Friday noon" (EU 55, 374), fixed as April 8 in Livingston to Madison (April 11, 1803). N. Y. *Chronicle*, February 23, Monroe to Livingston, April 8 (NYHS), 1803.

CHAPTER X

(Pages 124 to 140)

[1] Livingston to Monroe, April 10, 1803, Monroe Papers. Talleyrand to Livingston (not sent), *Germinal, an.* XI, EU 55, 77. Date fixed as April 10, 1803, by reference to Monroe at Le Havre and conflict with Napoleon's instructions at daybreak April 11.

[2] Marbois, *Histoire,* 285-301. Marbois stated that he put in order materials "prepared long ago." Madison had an impression that Marbois gave some of his notes on the subject to Joel Barlow. Madison to Mrs. Bomford, undated, JM-LC, XC, 68.

[3] Livingston to Madison, April 13, 1803.

[4] Livingston to Madison, April 11, 1803.

[5] Livingston to Talleyrand (in French), April 12, 1803, EU Supp. VII, 340.

[6] Madison to Livingston and Monroe, April 18-20, 1803. Madison to Monroe, April 20, 1803. Adams, II, 17-18.

[7] Yrujo to Madison, July 2, Madison to Yrujo, July 8, 1803, Rives Papers (both in cipher). Pichon to Talleyrand, June 3, 1803.

[8] Madison to Livingston and Monroe, May 28, Thornton to Hawkesbury, May 30, 1803.

[9] Madison to Monroe, May 31, June 25, 1803, Monroe Papers.

[10] Livingston to Madison, April 11, 13, 17, to Jefferson, April 14, 1803. Monroe to Madison, April 15, 19, 1803, Letterbook, LC.

[11] Gallatin to Madison, February 28 (NA RG 59), Gallatin to Jefferson, August 18, 1803. Monroe, *Writings*, IV, 14.

[12] King to Madison, July 8 (NA), Livingston to Madison, April 11, Monroe to Madison, May 14 (Rives Papers), 1803. Livingston and Monroe to Marbois, April 22 (NYHS), to Madison, May 13, 1803.

[13] Madison to Monroe, July 30, 1803. Talleyrand to Napoleon, May 6, 1806, EU Supp. VIII, 217. Marbois, *Histoire,* 300, 335.

[14] Monroe to Madison, May 14, August 11, 1803, Rives Papers.

[15] Gallatin to Jefferson, August, Madison to Monroe, July 30, 1803. *Intelligencer,* July 6, 11, 1803.

[16] Madison to Livingston, July 29, 1803, March 31, 1804. Livingston to Madison, November 15, December 11, 1803, May 3, 1804, NA.

[17] Monroe to Madison, August 23, September 17, 1803, Rives Papers, and variant in Monroe Papers, VIII, 1411. The draft Monroe refused to sign is in Livingston Letterbook C, NYHS, May 28, 1803.

[18] Livingston to Madison, May 12, to Mitchill, July 13 (Plumer Repository, III, 342, LC), to H. Gates, June 8 (NYHS), 1803.

[19] Livingston to Madison, April 11, November 15, 1803, NA. Livingston to Talleyrand, April 12, 1803, EU Supp. VII, 340, copy in Livingston Letterbook, NYHS, redated April 10.

[20] Livingston to J. Bonaparte, January 7, to Talleyrand, March 16, to Madison, February 18, March 24, April 13, May 12, 1803, *ASP*, II.

[21] Livingston to Madison, May 12, to E. Livingston (NYHS) May 25, 1803. Talleyrand to Livingston, March 10 (*ASP*, II, 546 misdated), 1803.

[22] Madison to Livingston and Monroe, July 29, 1803.

CHAPTER XI

(Pages 141 to 159)

[1] Jefferson to Gallatin, January 13, to Breckinridge, August 12, 1803. Madison to Monroe, June 25, 1803, Monroe Papers.

[2] Jefferson to W. C. Nicholas, September 7, R. Smith to Jefferson, July 9 (TJ-LC), 1803. Jefferson, drafts of amendment, *Writings*, (Ford) VIII, 241-248. Madison, drafts of amendment, one penciled on Jefferson's No. 1 draft in NYPL, one in JM-LC, XC, 33.

[3] Jefferson to Madison, August 18, Livingston to Jefferson, June 2, Madison to Jefferson, August 20, 1803, TJ-LC.

[4] Livingston and Monroe to Madison, June 7, 1803. Livingston to Madison, June 25, July 30 (NA), 1803. Napoleon to Charles IV, September 18, 1803. Spain retained French ships because of Spain's dissatisfaction over Louisiana.

[5] Jefferson to Levi Lincoln, August 30, 1803.

[6] J. C. Hamilton spread a story (coming from L. Tazewell) that a letter from his father to Madison converted Jefferson from his belief that the purchase of Louisiana was unconstitutional. J. Q. Adams commented: "Tazewell's name as the authority explains it all. . . . My only curiosity now would be to see the countenance of Mr. Madison if Rives should ever put the question to him as he promised." Adams to Plumer, March 22, 1828, J. Q. Adams Papers, LC.

[7] Marbois, *Histoire*, 307-311. Livingston and Monroe to Marbois, April 22, Monroe to Livingston, April, 1803, NYHS. Monroe, *Writings*, IV, 12-16.

[8] Haswell, 331. Hunter Miller, *Treaties*, etc., II, 498.

[9] Livingston to Madison, August 16, 1802, to Jefferson, May 2, TJ-LC, 1803. The Perdido claim was carefully protected in a request Livingston and Monroe addressed to Marbois, May 2, soliciting Napoleon's aid in negotiations with the king of Spain for "so much of his territories as lay to the east of the ceded territory." (EU 55, 416.) For the contention of Henry Adams that the ministers did not claim West Florida until later, see Adams,

II, 69, and Brant, "James Madison and His Times," *AHR*, LVII, note 38.

[10] Livingston to Madison, May 20, 1803. Monroe *Writings*, IV, 40.

[11] *Ibid*. Livingston to Monroe, May 23, 1803, TJ-LC.

[12] The Island of New Orleans is bounded by the Mississippi, the Iberville, Lakes Maurepas and Pontchartrain and the Gulf.

[13] Monroe, "Opinion," *Writings*, IV, 503-509. Livingston to Madison, June 3, 1803. Livingston and Monroe to Madison, June 7, 1803.

[14] Berthier to Talleyrand, September 11, 16, Urquijo to Berthier, September 16, 1800, and treaty *projet*, EU Supp. VII, 139-155. Adams, I, 363-370.

[15] Project of treaty, October 18, 1802, EU Supp. VII, 246. Talleyrand to Napoleon, November 1802, Adams, I, 401.

[16] Livingston to Madison, May 20, 1803. Marbois, *Histoire*, 312.

[17] Madison to C. Pinckney (NA), to Monroe, to Livingston, July 29, 1803. Jefferson to Madison, August 28, Madison to Coxe, November 11 (JM-LC), 1803.

[18] Josiah Quincy to Wolcott, September 5, Wolcott to ——, September 12 (CtHS), King to Gore, July 22, 1803.

[19] Duane to Madison, August 3, 1803, MHS *Proceedings*, 2d series, XX, 279. Madison to Jefferson, August 13, 21, 1803, TJ-LC.

[20] Madison to Jefferson, July 26, August 13, 1803, TJ-LC. J. Beckley to Madison, May 3, 16, Jas. Ker to Madison, August 13, W. Thornton to Madison, August 17, 1803, JM-LC.

[21] Yrujo to Madison, September 4, 1803, *ASP* II, 569. Madison to Jefferson, September 12, 1803, TJ-LC.

[22] Pichon to Talleyrand, October 4 (two), 1803, January 31, February 16, 1804. Yrujo to Madison, September 27, October 12, to Cevallos, August 3, September 12, 30, November 4, 5, 1803, Robertson, II, 69-121. Yrujo to McKean, November 20, 1803, PHS.

[23] Monroe to Madison, July 20, Livingston to Madison, September 18 (JM-LC), to E. Livingston, October 15 (NYHS), Madison to Monroe, September 29 (Rives Papers), 1803.

[24] Madison to Yrujo, October 4, Yrujo to Madison, October 12, 1803, *ASP*. Yrujo to Cevallos, November 4, 1803, June 12, 1804, Robertson. Madison to Livingston, October 6, 1803.

[25] Madison, notes on President's message, October 1, 1803, Jefferson *Writings*, (Ford) VIII, 266n. Gallatin, I, 160.

[26] Pichon to Madison, October 14, 1803, *ASP* II, 571.

[27] J. Q. Adams, *Diary*, October 28, 1803. Adams to A. Stevenson, July 11, 1832. G. Morris to R. Griswold, November 25, 1803, Yale.

[28] Pichon to Talleyrand, October 20 (21), 23, Madison to Pichon, Pichon to Madison, October 21, 1803, EU 56, 127, 154v, 155.

[29] Monroe to Madison, August 11, September 6, Marbois to Monroe, October 8, 1803, Rives Papers. Livingston to Monroe, undated (early August), September 9 (both in Monroe Papers), December 10 (NA), 1803. Monroe to Livingston, August 20, 1803.

[30] Pichon to Madison, October 27, November 1, Madison to Pichon,

November 4, 1803, EU 56, 176, 216. Madison to Talleyrand, to Marbois, November 4, 1803, EU Supp. VIII, and Madison *Writings*, VII, 75n.

[31] Jefferson to T. M. Randolph, December 19, Madison to Livingston, November 9, 1803. Pichon to Talleyrand, January 4, 10, 16, 30, 1804.

CHAPTER XII

(Pages 160 to 176)

[1] Thornton to Hawkesbury, May 30, King to Hawkesbury, May 7 (NYHS), 1803. Madison to DeWitt Clinton, December 23, 1803, Columbia. King to Madison, July 1803, *King*, IV, 259 (also III, 401).

[2] Madison to Thornton, August 5 (NA), Thornton to Hawkesbury, July 29, August 26, 1803. Madison to Jefferson, August 13, 20, 28, Jefferson to Madison, August 13, 25, 1803, TJ-LC.

[3] King to Madison, April 10, 30, 1802. Thornton to Hawkesbury, March 11, 1803. Monroe to Madison, September 18, 1803, Rives Papers.

[4] Foster to his mother, June 2, 1805, July 20, 1806, Foster Papers, LC. Canning to Bagot, October 31, 1808, *George Canning and His Friends* (ed. Bagot). Armstrong to Gates, December 30, 1803, NYPL.

[5] Merry to Hawkesbury, December 6, 1803. Madison to Monroe, January 19, 1804, Rives Papers. Adams, II, 367-372.

[6] Pichon to Talleyrand, February 4, 1804. Merry to Hammond, December 7, to Hawkesbury, December 31, 1803.

[7] Pickering to R. Peters, December 24 (MHS), King to Madison, December 22, TJ-LC, Madison to King, December 18 *(King)*, 1803.

[8] Pichon to Talleyrand, February 4, 1804. Smith, *First Forty Years,* 46. Jefferson to Martha Randolph, January 23, 1804.

[9] Madison to Monroe, December 26, 1803, January 19 (Rives Papers), February 16 (including Merry to Madison, February 9), 1804.

[10] Pichon to Talleyrand, February 16, 1804.

[11] Merry to Madison, May 11, 20, H. Suttle to Merry, May 10, 1804, NA. Madison to Merry, May 19, 22, Merry to Hawkesbury, June 1, 1804, FO. Foster to his mother, July 20, 1806, Foster Papers.

[12] Monroe to Madison, March 3, to Jefferson, March 15, 1804.

[13] Merry to Hawkesbury, December 6, 31, 1803, January 20, March 1, 1804. Madison to Monroe, February 14, 1804, Monroe Papers. Boundary convention and letters, *ASP*, II, 584-591. *King*, IV, 329-332.

[14] Merry to Hawkesbury, December 5, 31, 1803. Madison to Monroe, December 26, 1803.

[15] *Ibid.* Thornton to Hawkesbury, November 1, 1803, to Hammond, January 29, 1804. Merry to Hawkesbury, January 20, 30, 1804.

[16] Madison to Monroe, January 5, 1804, *Writings*, VII, 81-90.

[17] King to Grenville, October 7, 1799, *King*, III, 47, 115-121.

CHAPTER XIII

(Pages 177 to 187)

[1] Pichon to Talleyrand, October 5, 1803.

[2] Madison to Pichon, May 20, 1803, NA, Domestic 14. Rochambeau to Pichon, July 18, to Madison, August 22, Pichon to Talleyrand, November 2, 1803, EU 56, 200ff.

[3] Pichon to Talleyrand, March 19, 1804.

[4] Pichon to Madison, March 9, 1804, NA.

[5] Tazewell to Madison, April 28, 1804, JM-LC. Pichon to Talleyrand, March 18, June 5, 1804.

[6] Madison to Yrujo, March 1 and March —, to C. Pinckney, April 10, Yrujo to Madison, March 1, 1804, NA.

[7] Pichon to Talleyrand, March 18, 19, June 5, 7, to Madison, May 7, August 27, S. Smith to Madison, May 17, JM-LC, 1804.

[8] Pichon to Talleyrand, June 5, 14, August 27, 1804. Madison to Philadelphia merchants, August 30, 1804, JM-LC.

[9] Madison to Livingston, March 31, 1804. Livingston to Talleyrand, June 27, August 25, Talleyrand to Livingston, August 27, 1804, EU 57.

[10] Madison to Jefferson, September 8, 1804, TJ-LC. Madison to Pichon, September 3, 1804, EU 57, 291.

CHAPTER XIV

(Pages 188 to 199)

[1] *ASP*, II, 596-606. *Annals*, XII, 23, 270; XIII, 311.

[2] *ASP*, II, 605. *Annals*, XIII, 311, 313, 314. Adams, II, 259.

[3] Collected after lawsuits running until 1830.

[4] Madison to C. Pinckney, February 6, April 10, 1804.

[5] Madison to Livingston, January 31, 1804. Robertson, II, 51, 233n, 240, 245. *Territorial Papers* (C. E. Carter, editor), IX, 177-188.

[6] Robertson, II, 51, 234, 252, 268. *Territorial Papers*, IX, 201. Madison to Claiborne, February 20, 1804.

[7] Yrujo to Cevallos, February 21, 22, 1804, Robertson, II, 130-134. Pichon to Talleyrand, March 18, 1804.

[8] Madison to Livingston, January 31, March 31, 1804.

[9] *Annals*, XIII, 415, 1253. Pichon to Talleyrand, March 18, 1804.

[10] Trist died of yellow fever on August 29, 1804.

[11] Gallatin to H. B. Trist, February 27, 1804, *Territorial Papers*, IX, 192. Madison to Livingston, March 31, 1804.

[12] Yrujo pretended that a newspaper had libeled the American government by inventing Section 11.

[13] Yrujo to Madison, March 7, 1804, NA. Madison to Pinckney, April 10, to Livingston, March 31, 1804.

[14] Merry to Hawkesbury, March 13, 1804.

[15] Gallatin to Jefferson, March 15, to Trist, March 19 (NA), 1804.

[16] Ellicott's *Journal*, published in 1803, placed the limit of tides at Fort St. Stephens, forty air miles north of the boundary. Army engineers place it 106 miles by water above the city of Mobile.

[17] Madison to Yrujo, March 19, 1804, Monroe Papers.

[18] Yrujo to Madison, March 21, 1804, NA.

[19] Jefferson, proclamation, May 30, 1804, *ASP*, II, 583.

[20] If "lying within the United States" did not apply to Section 11, that section would nonsensically cover everything to the Atlantic Ocean. For a contrary interpretation see Adams, II, 263.

[21] Jefferson, message, November 8, 1804, draft in TJ-LC. Madison, memo, October 25, 1804, misdated in Jefferson, *Writings* (Ford), VIII, 384n. Gallatin to Jefferson, October 29, 1804.

[22] Especially Adams, II, 261-263.

CHAPTER XV

(Pages 200 to 212)

[1] Madison to Livingston, March 31, to Monroe, April 15, 1804. Claiborne to Madison, May 30, 1804, Monroe Papers.

[2] Madison to Monroe and Pinckney, July 8, 1804. E. Kerby to Jefferson, February 2, April 7, 20, 1804, TJ-LC.

[3] Isaac Joslyn Cox, *AHR*, XIX, 794. Wilkinson "Reflections" (wrongly identified), Robertson II, 325-347.

[4] Livingston to Madison, June 20, 1804, JM-LC. Madison's decipherment reads: "I have intimated to you that I had projected to 840 1179 847 . . ." The numbers stood for "re commis Talleyrand." Since 1173 meant "concile," the obvious reading is "reconcile Talleyrand."

[5] Livingston to Madison, June 20, 1804, JM-LC.

[6] Madison to John Armstrong, June 6, 1805.

[7] Madison to Jefferson, April 24, TJ-LC, Dolley Madison to Anna Cutts, April 26 (VaU), Yrujo to Madison, May 10, 15, 1804, NA.

[8] Madison to Jefferson, August 4, 7, 1804, TJ-LC.

[9] Madison to Monroe, July 21, 1804, Monroe Papers. Jefferson to Madison, August 7, 23, 1804.

[10] Monroe to Madison, May 5, Madison to Jefferson, August 14, TJ-LC, Jefferson to Madison, August 15, 1804.

[11] Jefferson to Madison, August 19, 23, to Gallatin, August 23, September 1, Madison to Jefferson, August 25, TJ-LC, to Claiborne, August 28, 30, Jefferson to Gallatin, August 23, September 1, 1804.

[12] Madison to Jefferson, April 9, August 28, 1804, TJ-LC. Cevallos to Pinckney, May 31 (NA), July 2, 8, Pinckney to Cevallos, June 22, July 5, 14, 1804, *ASP*.

[13] Yrujo to Jefferson, W. Jackson to Jefferson, September 7, 1804, TJ-LC. Merry to Harrowby, October 1, 1804.

[14] Jefferson to Yrujo, September 15, Pichon to Talleyrand, November 9, 1804. Yrujo to Madison, in *Intelligencer*, October 5, 1804.

[15] *Relf's Philadelphia Gazette*, September 14, 15, 17, 1804. Wagner to Madison, September 20, 23, 1804, JM-LC.

[16] Madison to Jefferson, October 2, 1804, TJ-LC. Madison to Monroe, October 26, 1804, NA.

[17] Monroe to Madison, October 7, 15, 1804, Rives, Monroe Papers.

[18] Madison to Yrujo, October 25, 1804, Monroe Papers.

CHAPTER XVI

(Pages 213 to 229)

[1] Livingston to Board (U. S. Commission of Claims), March 13, Board to Livingston, April 30, 1804, *ASP*, VI, 189, 193.

[2] Register, Claims Board, August 1803, February 1804, NA. Folder of *Nancy*, Allen, master (claim renewed by Clason and Livingston). Lists in *ASP*, VI, 569; Moore, V, 164, 255, 304 (No. 124).

[3] Livingston to Madison, October 31, 1803. Board to Madison, December 26, 1803, Moore, V, 222, 272.

[4] Claims were in livres because the franc was new.

[5] Conjectural note, *ASP*, VI, 170, Moore, V, 164, Haswell, 339.

[6] Board to Madison, December 26, 1803, to Livingston, March 22, 1804. W. Maclure, *To the People of the United States*, 29, 37. Livingston to Talleyrand, February 24, to Board, March 13, Marbois to Talleyrand, March 8, Monroe to Mercer, June 8, 1804, *ASP*, VI, 186-189.

[7] The Swan and Livingston claims can be traced in lists published in Maclure (1807) and Moore, V, 287-306, collated with Register and case papers of the Board and with *ASP*, VI, 569 (No. 195).

[8] *ASP*, VI, 186, 188.

[9] Claimants to Livingston, November 4, Livingston to Claimants, November 5, 1803, *ASP*, VI, Resolutions, November 7, 1803, NA, France, 8a. Livingston to Board, October 25, 30, 1803, Maclure 15, 16.

[10] R. to E. Livingston, December 1 (NYHS), to Madison, November 15 (NA), 1803. Madison to R. Livingston, November 9, 1803, *ASP*, VI.

[11] Livingston to Madison, January 1, 13, 30, 1804, NA. The last letter, in cipher, is misdated 1803.

[12] Livingston to Madison, January 1, 13, 1804, *ASP*, VI, 182, 183.

[13] Skipwith to Livingston, February 18, 25, Livingston to Skipwith, February 20, 1804, NA (annexed to No. 103). Madison to Jefferson, August 13, 1804, TJ-LC.

[14] Madison to Livingston, February 7, Livingston to Madison, February 8, 13 (cipher), 1804, NA; May 5, 1804, December 22, 1806, JM-LC.

[15] Marbois to Talleyrand, March 8, Board to Livingston, March 9, Livingston to Board, March 13, 1804, *ASP*, VI. J. Mercer to Monroe, June 17, August 23, 1804, Monroe Papers.

[16] Board to Livingston, March 9, 22, 26, April 30, Livingston to Board, March 13, 22, 26, 1804, Maclure (part in *ASP*, VI). Mercer to Monroe, June 17, 1804, Monroe Papers.

[17] Madison to Livingston, January 31, Livingston to Madison, May 3, 4, 1804, *ASP*, VI, 184, 196-198.

[18] Monroe to Madison, June 10, July 11, 1804, Rives Papers. London *Chronicle*, July 4, 1804 (quoting Paris *Moniteur*). Livingston to Talleyrand, June 27, to Madison, June 19, July 25, August 28, 29, September 14, 1804, Marbois to Livingston, July 1, Talleyrand to Livingston, September 6, 1804, *ASP*, VI.

[19] Merry to Hawkesbury, June 2, July 2, Mercer to Monroe, August 23 (Monroe Papers), Pichon to Talleyrand, June 11, 1804.

[20] Madison to Livingston, June 29 (NA), to Jefferson, August 4, 16, September 22, 1804, TJ-LC. Jefferson to Madison, August 18, 1804.

[21] Madison to Jefferson, August 18, September 22, 1804, TJ-LC.

[22] In Armstrong to Board, November 23, 1804, Moore, V, 269.

[23] Livingston to Madison, August 28, November 17, 1804, NA.

CHAPTER XVII

(Pages 230 to 240)

[1] T. Law to W. Eustis, September 10, 1802, Eustis Papers, LC. Jefferson to T. M. Randolph, July 5, 1803.

[2] *Anas,* January 26, 1804 (written later). J. Hopkinson to Wolcott, September 25, 1803, CtHS.

[3] DeSaussure to Pickering, February 26, 1804, MHS. Plumer to J. Smith, February 10, 28, 1804, Letterbook IV, LC. Randolph to Monroe, February 28, 1804, Monroe Papers.

[4] Randolph to Monroe, February 28, 1804, Monroe Papers.

[5] Catherine Mitchill to Margaret Miller, April 3, 1806, NYHS. *Life, Letters and Journals of George Ticknor,* I, 27.

[6] H. A. Garland, *Life of John Randolph,* I, 184. Plumer, Register, I, 83. Bruce, II, 487-499. Foster, Journal, December 22, 1811.

[7] Plumer to J. Mason, February 14, 28, 1804, Letterbook, IV, LC. Foster, Journal, December 22, 1811.

[8] Committee reports March 2, 1797, April 2, 1800, *ASP, PL,* I.

[9] Articles of cession, April 24, 1802, *ASP, PL,* I, 114.

[10] Madison, Gallatin and Lincoln, report to Congress, February 14, 1803, *ASP, PL,* I, 120. *Annals,* XII, 1342.

[11] J. Jackson to Gallatin, March 27, 1802, JM-LC. J. Ward to Eustis, November 14, 1803, Eustis Papers.

[12] *American Citizen,* March 12, 1808, quoting Richmond *Enquirer.* J. Q. Adams, *Diary,* February 1, 1805. Gallatin to Madison, July 21, 1802, JM-LC, indicating he drafted Yazoo letters for Madison.

[13] Act of March 3, 1803, *Annals,* XII, 1593-1601.

[14] *ASP, PL,* 145. Madison *et al.* to Hull *et al.,* May 1, 1802, PHS.

[15] *Annals* and *House Journal,* February, March 1804.

[16] J. Davenport to J. C. Smith, February 2, 1805, J. C. Smith Papers, LC. *Annals,* XIV, 1031-33, 1110-13, 1172-74.

CHAPTER XVIII

(Pages 241 to 253)

[1] Jefferson to Madison, April 13, to Gallatin, April 15, June 9, 12, Gallatin to Jefferson, February 21, April 5, June 11, 1804. Memoranda, Gallatin March 31, Madison April 20, 1804, TJ-LC.

[2] Wolcott to R. Griswold, January 14, March 3, Griswold to Wolcott, March 11, Yale. Mitchill to Madison, May 3 (JM-LC), Cutts to Madison, June 8 (NYPL), 1804. *King,* IV, 355-356.

[3] J. Smith to Plumer, January 28, Plumer to Smith, February 10, Plumer to J. Mason, February 15, 1804, Plumer Papers. W. North to Eustis, July 25, 1814, February 9, 1815, Eustis Papers. Peters to Pickering, January 9, 1804, MHS.

[4] Madison to Monroe, July 21, 1804, Monroe Papers.

[5] *Annals* and TP IX. G. Chinard, *Letters of Lafayette and Jefferson,* 188-194, 224-335. Lafayette to Madison, July 7, 1803, October 10, 1804, NYPL, April 22, 1805, PHS. L. Tousard to Madison, July 10, 1805, PHS. Peters to Madison, May 18, Madison to Duplantier, June 2, Gallatin to Madison, August 6, 1805, JM-LC. Madison to Monroe, March 1, April 20, 1803. Madison to Lafayette, May 1, 1809.

[6] Madison to Monroe, July 21, 1804, Monroe Papers. Gallatin to J. Nicholson, July 19, 1804, NYHS.

[7] Farrand, III, 397. T. Dwight to Wolcott, September 5, Wolcott to Dwight, September, 1803, CtHS.

[8] Noah Webster to Madison, August 20, Madison to Webster, October 12, 1804, *Writings,* VII, 162.

[9] Dallas to Gallatin, October 16 (NYHS), Plumer to J. Norris, November 6 (Letterbook), R. Griswold to ——, November 11 (CtHS), 1804.

[10] Pickering to King, March 4, 1804, *King,* IV, 365. W. A. Burwell, Memoir, 13, LC. J. Taylor to Jefferson, December 26, 1804, TJ-LC. Jefferson to Taylor, January 6, 1805.

[11] *Annals,* XIV, 664, 669. J. Q. Adams, *Diary,* March 1, 1805. Madison to ——, May 29, 1805, JM-LC. Adams, II, 238-244.

[12] Jefferson, "Notes on . . . second Inaugural Address," TJ-LC.

[13] Jefferson, draft, Gallatin memo, February 12, 1805, TJ-LC, 27135, 27147.

[14] T. Law to Madison, July 18, 1804, JM-LC. Madison, memo, rec'd February 5, 1805, Jefferson *Writings* (Ford), VIII, 342n.

[15] Foster to his mother, June 2, to his brother, July 1, 1805, Foster Papers.

[16] Merry to FO, August 6, 1804, March 29, April 29, August 4, November 25, 1805. Adams, II, 402. Nathan Schachner, *Aaron Burr,* 282-288.

CHAPTER XIX

(Pages 254 to 265)

[1] Merry to FO, July 2, 18, August 6, September 4, 1804. Madison to Merry, June 25, July 3, 7, 23 (FO), Merry to Madison, June 28, August 15, 1804, NA. D. Clinton to Madison, June 19, July 1, 1804, Columbia.

[2] Madison to Jefferson, August 18, 28, 1804, TJ-LC. Monroe to Madison, June 3, 23, September 8, 1804. Harrowby to Monroe, September 3, 1804, Monroe Letterbook, LC. Adams, III, 91-92.

[3] Jefferson to J. Randolph, November 19, Merry to Harrowby, December 26, 1804, March 4, 1805. Madison to Monroe, March 6, 1805.

[4] Madison to Merry, April 9 (FO), Merry to Madison, April 12 (NA), 1805. Harrowby to Merry, November 7, 1804, AHA *Report*, 1936, III. D. Clinton to Madison, May 1, 1805, JM-LC. Wagner, memo, Rives Papers.

[5] Merry to Madison, June 30, August 19, Gelston to Madison, August 8, November 7, 1805 (all with enclosures), JM-LC.

[6] Madison to Monroe, April 15, 1804. Monroe to Madison, September 8, 17 (NA), October 3, November 27 (NA), December 16, 1804, January 19 (NA), 1805. Livingston to Monroe, August 23, 1804, Rives Papers. Livingston to Talleyrand, August 23, 1804, EU 57, 172.

[7] Livingston to Madison, September 21, Armstrong to Madison, December 24, 1804, NA. Madison to Jefferson, March 1, Jefferson to Madison, March 29, 1805, TJ-LC. Monroe to Madison, December 16, 1804, January 27, 1805, Rives Papers. Madison to Armstrong, June 6, 1805.

[8] Madison to Jefferson, March 27, TJ-LC, to Armstrong, June 6 (NA), 1805. Armstrong to Monroe, March 12, 18, Madison to Monroe, May 23 (NA), to Livingston, July 5 (JM-LC), 1805.

[9] Armstrong to Monroe, May 4 (rec'd by Madison July 5), 1805, NA. C. Pinckney and Monroe to Madison, May 25, 1805, Rives Papers.

CHAPTER XX

(Pages 266 to 279)

[1] Armstrong to Madison, October 20, 1804, NA. Plumer, 345.

[2] Adams, II, 273-274.

[3] Petry to Talleyrand, September 20, to Turreau, December 6, 1804, March 29, 1805. J. Street to Madison, December 15, 1804, NA. Turreau told Americans that he sought the Washington post to escape his wife, who followed him. Petry's letters show that Turreau arranged for her voyage and was cheated on the passage money (EU).

[4] Dolley Madison to Anna Cutts, June 4, 1805, Cutts, *Memoir*, 51. Merry to Mulgrave, June 30, 1805. Foster, Journal.

[5] D. Madison to A. Cutts, July 8, 1805, VaU. Plumer, Register, I, 90, 104, 181. Plumer to his wife, January 26, 1806, Plumer Papers.

[6] Talleyrand to Turreau, November 21, 1804. Pichon to Talleyrand,

January 9, 20, 21, December 26, 1805, July 11, 1806. Pichon to Madison, April 11, 1805, JM-LC. Cleared of the Decrès charges, Pichon became a Foreign Office lawyer.

[7] Talleyrand to Napoleon, November 19, 1804. Turreau to Talleyrand, November 19, 1804, January 26, 1805, EU Supp. VIII, 103, 174.

[8] Turreau to Talleyrand, April 20, 1805. New York *Herald*, June 15, 1805. Napoleon to Talleyrand, August 10, 1805.

[9] Madison to Turreau, May 31, Turreau to Madison, June 2, 1805, EU 58, 172, 174. A. Foster, Journal, LC.

[10] Turreau to Madison, August 14, 1805, NA. Madison to Jefferson, August 20, September 1, 1805, TJ-LC. Jefferson to D. Clinton, October 6, 1804, to Madison, September 25, 1805. Wagner to Clinton, October 5, 1804, enclosing Livingston to Madison, June 22, 1804, Columbia. Turreau to Talleyrand, March 14, 1806. Plumer, 340.

[11] Henry Adams (III, 90) translated *"ne pourrait durer davantage"* as "must last no longer" and commented: "For the third time within six months Talleyrand used the word 'must' to the President." In reality he did not use it once. The second case cited was the Moreau *"ne doit point"* (ought not); the third was mere inference. *ASP*, II, 727.

[12] Talleyrand to Armstrong, August 9, 17, 1805, *ASP*. Turreau to Madison, October 14, 1805, January 3, 13, 1806, *ASP* and EU 59, 16.

[13] *ASP*, II, 725-727. Plumer, 414. S. Smith to ——, January 30 (Letterbook, LC), Plumer to W. Plumer Jr., February 21 (Plumer Papers), Madison to Armstrong, March 15, 1806. *Annals*, February 25, 1806.

[14] Turreau to Talleyrand, July 9, 1805.

[15] Burwell, Memoir, LC. *Annals*, XV, 1158. Jefferson to R. Smith, June 21, 26, Smith to Jefferson, June 23, 24, 27, 29, 1805, TJ-LC. The *Huntress* was captured by British cruisers, tried, restored to the United States. Monroe to Madison, December 11, 23, 1805.

CHAPTER XXI

(Pages 280 to 292)

[1] Madison to Monroe, September 24, 1805. Dolley Madison to Anna Cutts, July 8, 29, 31, August 19, 1805, VaU. Garbled in Cutts. Madison to Jefferson, August 2, 1805, TJ-LC.

[2] Wagner to Madison, July 28, JM-LC, to Jefferson, July 27, 29, Madison to Jefferson, August 2, 1805, TJ-LC.

[3] Madison to Jefferson, August 2, Adams III, 59; to Gallatin, August 2, 8, 1805, NYHS. Gallatin to Madison, August 6, 12, 1805, JM-LC.

[4] Jefferson to Madison, August 4, 7, 17, Madison to Jefferson, August 20, September 14, 1805, TJ-LC.

[5] Jefferson to Madison, August 27, September 16, Madison to Jefferson, September 1, 14, 1805, TJ-LC. Adams, III, 40.

[6] Jefferson to Madison, October 16, Madison to Jefferson, September 30, October 5, R. Smith to Jefferson, September 10, 1805, TJ-LC. Gallatin to Jefferson, September 12, 1805.

[7] Jefferson to Madison, October 11, 23, Madison to Jefferson, October 16, 1805, TJ-LC.

[8] Merry to Mulgrave, November 3, 1805, Adams, III, 98-100.

[9] Madison to Jefferson, October 5, 20, TJ-LC; J. Carroll to Madison, November 20, 1805, JM-LC. Dolley to James Madison, October 23 to November 1, 1805, Cutts, 56-61. James to Dolley, two undated letters, about November 5 (*Writings*, VIII, 76, misplaced) and 22 (MHS), 1805.

[10] Dolley to James Madison, November 15, 17, 1805, Cutts, 61-62. Jefferson to Dolley, November 1, 1805.

[11] W. Thornton to Madison, October 3, 1805, JM-LC.

[12] Armstrong to Madison, September 10, 1805, NA. Bowdoin to Jefferson, May 20, 1806, TJ-LC.

[13] Madison to Jefferson, September 14, October 16, TJ-LC; to Erving, November 1, 1805 (two letters), NA and *Writings*.

CHAPTER XXII

(Pages 293 to 304)

[1] Madison to Monroe, January 5, 1804, March 6, 1805. Madison, memo and draft of bill, October 23, 1804, TJ-LC.

[2] Madison to Monroe, April 12, September 24, Merry to Mulgrave, June 30, Madison to Coxe, June 11, JM-LC, 1805.

[3] Madison to Jefferson, September 14, October 5, TJ-LC; Madison to Monroe, September 24, 1805. Memos, Madison, Wagner, Rives Papers.

[4] Madison, *An Examination*, etc., *Writings*, VII, especially 207, 268-269, 320-321, 346. J. Stephen, *War in Disguise*, 199-201, 206, 207-208. Monroe to Madison, October 26 (Rives Papers), Madison to Monroe, September 24, 1805.

[5] Madison to Monroe, January 13, Monroe to Madison, March 11 (NA), 31, 1806. Plumer, 388, 389. King to Gore, January 26, U. Tracy to King, March 12, 1806, *King*, IV, 479, 499.

[6] Jefferson, draft, TJ-LC. Jefferson to Madison, November 22, 24, 1805, with Madison's reply, *Writings* (Ford), VIII, 385n.

[7] Plumer, 478, 481 (April 8, 11, 1806).

CHAPTER XXIII

(Pages 305 to 322)

[1] J. Bryan to Madison, February 3, 1806, JM-LC. Plumer to T. Lowndes, December 30, 1805, Letterbook. Plumer, 333-359. Madison to Jefferson, September 17, 1806, TJ-LC.

[2] Plumer, 347, 349, 362. Foster, "Notes," Plumer to Plumer Jr., Novem-

ber 20, 1804, to T. Lowndes, December 30, 1802, Letterbook and Papers. J. Q. Adams, *Diary*, November 25, 1805.

³ Plumer, 486. J. B. Harrison, notes of talks with Madison, November 27-30, 1827, Jesse Burton Harrison Papers, LC.

⁴ Madison to Jefferson, May 17, July 25, 28, August 1, September 4, 1806, TJ-LC. Jefferson to Madison, May 19, July 30, September 16, 1806. Wagner to Madison, September 26, 1806, JM-LC. D. Clinton to Madison, July 24, August 7, Madison to Clinton, July 24, 25, Lavaud affidavit, September 9, Madison, list of Tunisians, July 25, 1806, Clinton Papers, Columbia. Papers from Monroe in NA, GB, 13. Tunisian household, NA, Tunis 3.

⁵ Wagner to Madison, September 7, 1801, JM-LC. Jefferson to Eaton (not sent), February 8, 1804. Charles Prentiss, *Life of General Eaton*, 206, 235, 236, 238, 242, 259, 262. Plumer, 494-497.

⁶ *Intelligencer*, November 20, 1805. J. Q. Adams, *Diary*, April 1-12, 18, 1806. Plumer, 472.

⁷ Randolph to Gallatin, October 25, 1805, NYHS. Burwell, Memoir, LC. Richmond *Enquirer*, September 19, 1806.

⁸ Foster to his mother, March 10, 1806, Foster Papers.

⁹ *Annals* (Supplementary Journal), XV, 1117-1144.

¹⁰ S. Smith to Madison (February 1806), JM-LC, XXX, 15. J. Q. Adams, *Diary*, February 13, 25, 1806.

¹¹ Burwell, Memoir, LC. Tucker, Memoir, Rives Papers.

¹² Erving to Monroe, May 23, 1806, Monroe Papers.

¹³ *Annals*, XV, 771, 948. S. Smith to ——, April 18, 1806, Letterbook, LC. Monroe to Madison, October 18-25, 1805.

¹⁴ *Annals*, March 5, 6, 1806. S. Smith to —— March 5 (6), 1806, Letterbook, LC. J. Q. Adams, *Diary*, March 6, 1806.

¹⁵ *Annals*, XV, 573, 591, 775, 1259. S. Smith to —— March 14 (Letterbook), Jefferson to Monroe, March 18, J. Q. Adams, *Diary*, March 6, Pickering to King, March 24 (*King*, IV), Pickering to Peters, April 13 (Essex Institute), Merry to Fox, November 2, 1806.

¹⁶ Jefferson to Monroe, March 16, May 4, 1806, April 11, 1808. Madison to Monroe, May 15, 1806, Rives Papers. Randolph to Monroe, March 20, 1806, Monroe Papers.

¹⁷ *Annals*, April 4, 5, 7, 8, 1806. Pickering to King, March 24 (part later), 1806, *King*, IV, 509. Gallatin, I, 295-299.

¹⁸ Burwell, Memoir, LC. *Annals*, XV, 962. Randolph to Nicholson, endorsed "just before the report was made," Nicholson Papers.

¹⁹ *Annals*, XV, 604-605, 963-964, 988.

²⁰ "Decius" in Richmond *Enquirer*, August 15, 1806. Bruce, I, 223-232. W. Nicholas to Madison, July 7 (Rives Papers), Wagner to Madison, October 13, JM-LC, 1806. *Pickering*, IV, 461.

²¹ B. Lay to Madison, February 3, 1806, JM-LC. Madison to Monroe, March 10, 1806, Rives Papers. Smith, *First Forty Years*, 51.

²² Randolph to Monroe, September 16, 1806, Bruce, I, 337.

²³ Randolph to Ann Morris, October 31, 1814, Bruce, II, 274.

CHAPTER XXIV

(Pages 323 to 339)

[1] Yrujo to Madison, December 6, 1805, January 16, 19, Madison to Yrujo, January 15, Yrujo circular, January 21, 1806, in newspapers and partially in Adams, III, 186-188. Plumer, 383, 384.

[2] Plumer, 391. J. Q. Adams, *Diary*, February 13-20, 27, 1806.

[3] Hamilton to King, August 22, 1798, NYHS. B. Rush to Madison, December (*ca* 4), Miranda to Madison, December 10, 1805, JM-LC. Vansittart to King, August 14, King to Madison, November 25, Madison to King, December 4, 1805, *King*, IV, 519-523, 526. W. S. Robertson, *Life of Miranda*, I, 245-247, 291-295. King-Gore letters, *King*, IV. Merry to Mulgrave, November 25, 1805.

[4] *King*, IV, 577-586. Madison to Gelston, February 10, to N. Sanford, February 13, 17, NA; to Armstrong, March 15, 1806.

[5] Yrujo to Cevallos, February 12, 1806, EU 59, 194. W. S. Robertson, *Life of Miranda*, I, 297-299. King, memoir, *King*, IV, 581, 582. See Note 7.

[6] James Biggs, *History of ... Miranda's Attempt ...*, 4. Smith statement, Gelston testimony, in *The Trials of Wm. S. Smith and Samuel G. Ogden*. Miranda to Madison, January 22, 1806, JM-LC. Yrujo to Turreau, February 4, to Cevallos, February 12, 1806, with enclosures, EU 59.

[7] S. G. Ogden to Jonathan S. Smith, September 6, 1806, intercepted, *Intelligencer*, October 16, 1807.

[8] Biggs, *op. cit.*, 12, 287n. JM-LC, XXX, 21.

[9] Adams, III, 194. Madison to N. Sanford, February 7, 1806, NA, Domestic 15. Turreau to Yrujo, February 7, 8 (misdated 7), 1806, Arch. Hist. Nac. Madrid, Estado, Leg. 5544, Apar. 1, 85 and 38. The misdating makes it appear that Turreau's talk with Madison was on February 7, the day orders went to Sanford. It actually was on the eighth. On February 7, Turreau wrote to Yrujo that "I am going to take" the steps you desire. The second letter, also dated February 7, said he had left Madison "in order to write to him. I am doing so." ("*pour lui ecrire. Je m'en occupe.*") The letter thus referred to is dated February 8 and Madison's reply of the tenth repeats what "I had the honor, two days ago, of stating verbally." (EU 59, 118, 119.)

[10] Adams gave a literal rendering of "*J'ai cherché ses yeux, et . . . les ai rencontrés . . .*" The ensuing clause fitted only the idiomatic meaning, and was left out. He then mistook *abattement* (dejection) for the medical term *prostration* and exaggerated the error by insertions and transliterations. See *AHR*, LVII, 866.

[11] Turreau to Talleyrand, February 13, 1806, Adams Transcripts, LC, from EU 59, 38, to which Madison to Sanford is appended.

[12] Turreau to Madison, February 8, 11, 15, 26, 1806, Madison to Turreau, February 10, 12, 17, 1806, EU 59, 118-121v.

[13] Yrujo to Cevallos, December 31, 1805, February 12, 1806, EU 59, 189, 194. T. Stoughton to Yrujo, January 30, 31, February 2, 1806, AHN

Madrid, Estado, Leg. 5544. Baltimore *Federal Gazette,* January 24, 1806. *Aurora,* January 28, 29, 1806.

[14] W. S. Robertson, *Life of Miranda,* I, 300, 305, 325.

[15] Madison to Monroe, March 10 (Rives Papers), Gallatin to Jefferson, March 11, 1806. Turreau to Talleyrand, March 10, enclosing Turreau to Madison, March 14 and Madison's reply, 15, 1806.

[16] Sanford to Gallatin, April 14, Grand Jury Report, April 9, 1806, NYHS. A later and slightly better jury tried the cases.

[17] *Annals* (Senate), April 21 (House), April 21, 1806.

[18] Madison to Jefferson, May 28, TJ-LC, Sanford to Gallatin, June 9 (NYHS), Madison to Edwards, August 4, 1806 (JM-LC).

[19] *Trials of Smith and Ogden* (including Madison *et al.* to the court). Madison to Jefferson, July 28, 1806, TJ-LC. Sanford to Gallatin, July 15, 17, 19, 24, 30, 1806, NYHS. Mitchill to Madison, July 17 (two letters), Edwards to Madison, July 30, 31, 1806, JM-LC.

[20] Madison to Edwards, *op. cit.* Jefferson to Gallatin, August 15, 1806. Wagner to Madison, August 15, 1806, JM-LC.

[21] Coxe to Madison, June 28 (postmark), 1806, JM-LC. Miranda to King, December 30, 1805, King to Gore, March 9, 1806, King memoir on Miranda, *King,* IV, 526-527, 530, 584-586.

[22] Erving to Monroe, June 18, August 11, 1806, Monroe Papers.

CHAPTER XXV

(Pages 340 to 359)

[1] U. S. Gazette (country edition), August 2, 1805. Anonymous to Jefferson, rec'd December 1, 1805, TJ-LC. Merry to Mulgrave, August 5, November 25, 1805. McCaleb, 42-48.

[2] Yrujo to Cevallos, December 5, 1805, January 1, 1806, Estado, Leg. 5546. Adams, III, 233-240. McCaleb, 53-58.

[3] *Anas,* October 22, 1806. Eaton, deposition, *Intelligencer,* January 28, 1807. Truxton refused to act with Burr against Vera Cruz.

[4] *Annals,* XVII, 508. Blennerhassett, "Journal," Adams, III, 462.

[5] Jefferson to Hay, June 5, 1807. Narrative T. Hinde, September 26, 1829, Rives Papers. Taylor to Madison, October 13, 1806, JM-LC.

[6] J. H. Daveiss to Jefferson, January 10, February 10, 13, March 28, April 21, July 14, 1806, TJ-LC. Daveiss to Madison, August 24, November 16, 1806. Daveiss, *View of the President's Conduct,* etc.

[7] *Annals,* XVII, 405-407. N. Williams to Madison, September 5, 1806, JM-LC. Nevill and Roberts to Madison, October 7, 1806, Letters in Relation to Burr's Conspiracy, LC.

[8] J. Taylor to Madison, October 13, 1806, JM-LC. Wilkinson to Jefferson, October 20 (memo), 21 (two letters), 1806, Letters in Relation *op. cit.,* excerpts in McCaleb, 122-126.

[9] Burr to Wilkinson, July 29, 1807, McCaleb, 68. *Annals,* XVII, 524, 541, 630.

[10] McCaleb, 116, 120, 129-131, 135.

[11] Wilkinson to Yturrigaray (translation), November 17, 1806, Yturri-

garay to Wilkinson, January 21, to Godoy, March 12, 1807, AGI Sevilla, aud. de Mexico, 90-1-8.

[12] R. Smith to Jefferson, December 22, 1806, TJ-LC. Madison to Monroe, November 28, 1806, Rives Papers.

[13] *Annals*, XVI, 39, 1008-1016, XVII, 521-525, 563, 1396. Randolph to Nicholson, June 28, 1807, Nicholson Papers. Isaac Briggs, statement, Briggs Papers, 29-30, LC.

[14] Memo of Bollman's communication, January 23, 1807, Madison, *Letters*, II, 393-401. *Intelligencer*, January 26, 1807.

[15] *Intelligencer*, January 16, 28, February 4, 11, 1807. Key and Dorsey to Madison (January 26, 1807), JM-LC, XXXIII, 72.

[16] *Annals* (Senate), January 23 (House), 26, 1807. J. Q. Adams, *Diary*, January 23, 1807. Burwell, Memoir, 37-40. McCaleb, 181-186.

[17] *Intelligencer*, January 23, 28, February 13, 16, 25, 1807. Madison to R. R. Livingston, January 28, 1807, NYHS.

[18] Dolley Madison to Anna Cutts, March 27, 1807, VaU.

[19] Richmond *Enquirer*, March 27, *Intelligencer*, April 1, 1807.

[20] C. Rodney, W. Tatham to Jefferson, March 27, 1807, TJ-LC.

[21] Rodney to Madison, March 31 (misdated 21), April 1, 1807, JM-LC. Beveridge, III, 376, 395-396. J. B. Thayer, *Life of Marshall*, 80-81. "A descendant" of Marshall told Thayer that Marshall knew Burr was to be a guest. Beveridge called this "almost certainly a myth," told "more than a century after the incident occurred." This was incorrect. Thayer knew both Marshall and his children personally.

[22] Jefferson to Madison, April 14, 25, 1807. J. Graham to Madison, March 18, April 23, May 11, 1807, Letters in Relation.

[23] Jefferson to Madison, April 14, to Hay, June 12 to 23, 1807.

[24] J. G. Jackson to Madison, July 5, 1807, JM-LC.

[25] Dayton to Madison, August 5, 1807, Dayton-Madison films, LC. Madison to Jefferson, August 16, 19, 1807, TJ-LC. Jefferson to Dayton, August 17, to Madison, August 20, 1807. Madison to Dayton, August 18, 1807, JM-LC.

[26] Jefferson to Walker, April 13, 1803, Va. St. Library. Randolph to Nicholson, October 24, 1806, Nicholson Papers. H. Lee Jr. to R. T. Brown, August 24, 1833, Henry Lee Papers, LC. Subpoena of Madison, July 29, J. Nicholas to Madison, August 22, September 7, 1807, JM-LC. Granger to Jefferson, October 9, 1806, September 8, 1807, January 19, 1808, TJ-LC. Jefferson to Granger, January 22, 1808, to W. Nicholas (unreliable as to sequence), June 13, 1809. For an appraisal, see Dumas Malone, *Jefferson and His Time*, I, 153-155, 447-451.

[27] Testimony and court opinions in Burr trials, *Annals*, XVII, 385-778. J. J. Coombs, *The Trial of Aaron Burr*, etc. (1864).

[28] Rodney to Madison, September 16, 1807, JM-LC. Jefferson to G. Hay, September 7, 1807.

[29] Jefferson to Hay, September 4, to Wilkinson, September 20, to Rodney, October 28, 1807. *Annals*, XVII, 385, 589-633.

[30] Quoted by I. J. Cox, in *AHR*, XIX, 807.

[31] Anon. to Madison, December 10, 1811, NYPL. Roux to Champagny, March 1, 11, 19, July 27, 1810, EU 63 and Supp. VIII. Petry to Cham-

pagny, July 11, 1810, EU 64. Champagny to Napoleon, July 7 (EU Supp. II), July 29 (Arch. Nat. AF IV), 1810.

CHAPTER XXVI

(Pages 360 to 373)

[1] Merry to Mulgrave, January 3, February 2, 1806. Jefferson to Monroe, March 10, 1808. S. Smith to W. Nicholas, April 1, 1806, Adams, III, 169. J. Q. Adams, *Diary*, February 1, 1806.

[2] *Ibid.*, March 13, 1806. Turreau to Talleyrand, May 10, 1806. Nicholson to Monroe, May 5, 1806, Monroe Papers. Adams, III, 149-153.

[3] Madison to Jefferson, August 9, 1805, Armstrong to Jefferson, January 2 (TJ-LC), Plumer to Sheafe, January 13 (Letterbook), 1806. Turreau to Madison, May 1, 1808, NA. Plumer Repository, II, 131, 226.

[4] Jefferson to Madison, October 11, 1805, to Armstrong, February 14, to Mitchill, February 14, March 1, 1806. Madison to Monroe, March 10 (Rives Papers), to Jefferson, October 16, TJ-LC, 1806.

[5] Madison to Armstrong and Bowdoin, March 13, 1806, to Armstrong, March 14 (Rives Papers), Armstrong to Jefferson, February 17 (TJ-LC), Jefferson to Madison, April 11, May 11, 1806.

[6] Madison to Jefferson, May 26, TJ-LC, to Armstrong and Bowdoin, May 26, Armstrong to Madison, February 17, March 9, 1806, NA.

[7] Armstrong to Madison, April 26 (NA), May 4 (JM-LC), June 1 (NA), 1806. Bowdoin to Erving, November 28, 1805, MHS *Collections*, 7th series, VI, 263.

[8] Bowdoin to Erving, January 7, 15, February 3, 1806, MHS, *op. cit.* ("and West" omitted). Bowdoin to Jefferson, May 20, 1806, TJ-LC.

[9] Talleyrand to Napoleon, May 6 (EU Supp. VIII), to Armstrong, June 4 (NA), 1806. Turreau to Talleyrand, February 13, 1806.

[10] Skipwith to Bowdoin, June 12, 1806, MHS, *op. cit.* Bowdoin to Jefferson, October 20, 1806, TJ-LC.

[11] *Ibid.* Bowdoin to Erving, January 15, and June 12 through October 28, 1806, MHS *op. cit.*, Adams, III, 376-386.

[12] Madison to Monroe and Pinkney, May 17, 1806.

[13] Madison to Monroe, May 15 (Rives Papers), to Jefferson, May 26 (TJ-LC), 1806. Merry to Fox, May 4, 9, June 1, 1806.

[14] Merry to FO, March 19, May 4, Jefferson to T. M. Randolph, July 13, Armstrong to Monroe, July 9 (Monroe Papers), 1806.

[15] Mitchill to Madison, May 2, 1806, JM-LC. Madison to D. Clinton, May 1806, Columbia. King to Pickering, March 3, 1806, MHS. J. A. Sullivan to Monroe, May 9, 1806, Monroe, *Writings*, IV, 482n.

[16] George Joy to Fox, July 4, to Holland, August 25, 1806. Madison to Joy, May 22, 1807, JM-LC.

[17] Monroe and Pinkney to Madison, August 15, Merry to Madison, August 18 (NA), Merry to Fox, August 31, Madison to Jefferson, August 30, TJ-LC, Jefferson to Madison, September 2, 1806. W. Lyman to Madison, October 23, 1807, MHS, *op. cit.*, 435.

18 Madison to Monroe, November 28, 1806, Rives Papers. Foster to his mother, November 27, 1806, Foster Papers. Turreau to Yrujo, December 18, 1806, EU Supp. V. Madison to Erving, January 20, 1807, NA.

19 Monroe and Pinkney to Madison, September 11, Madison to Monroe and Pinkney, November 28, 1806. Erskine to FO, February 2, 1807.

20 *Ibid.* Monroe and Pinkney to Madison, November 11, 1806.

21 Madison to Monroe and Pinkney, February 3, 1807.

CHAPTER XXVII

(Pages 374 to 391)

1 J. Q. Adams, *Diary.* Plumer, 603. *ASP*, III, 289-290.

2 *ASP*, III, 141. Erskine to Howick, March 6, 1807.

3 Madison to Monroe and Pinkney, March 18, Erskine to Madison, March 12, Madison to Erskine, March 20, 29, 1807, *ASP.*

4 *U. S. Gazette*, February 23, March 9, 12, 1807. S. Smith to Madison, March 14, 1807, S. Smith Papers, LC.

5 Madison to various people, March 27, Coxe to Madison, April 1, 1807, JM-LC. S. Smith to Madison, April 3, 1807, Letterbook, LC.

6 Erskine to Howick, April 22, 1807. Madison to Joy, May 22 (JM-LC), to Peters, September 5 (PHS), 1807.

7 Madison to Jefferson, April 13, TJ-LC, to S. Smith, April 12, Smith to Madison, April 18, 1807, Letterbook, LC.

8 Monroe to Madison, February 28, 1808, Monroe and Pinkney to Madison, January 3, 1807.

9 Madison to Jefferson, April 13, 17, 20, 24, May 4, 1807, TJ-LC. Gallatin to Madison, April 13 (Rives Papers), Jefferson to Madison, April 21, 1807. Madison to Monroe and Pinkney, May 20, to R. Livingston, May 30 (NYHS), 1807.

10 T. Mathews to Madison, June 23, 1807, TJ-LC. Jefferson, draft of July 2 proclamation, TJ-LC. Madison's draft and Jefferson's final revision are in *Writings* (Ford), IX, 89, 99n.

11 Erskine to J. E. Douglas, July 8, 1807, FO 5, 52. Tazewell to Jefferson, July 6, 1807, TJ-LC. *ASP*, III, 6-23.

12 *Anas*, July 2, 4, 5, 7, 26, 27, 28, 1807. Dearborn to Madison, July 17 (JM-LC), Madison to Monroe, July 6, 1807.

13 Foster to his mother, July 16 (Foster Papers), Madison to Armstrong, May 22, to Armstrong and Bowdoin, July 15, to Bowdoin, July 17, Monroe to Madison, August 4, Jefferson to Madison, August 16, September 1, 1807.

14 Madison to Monroe, July 17, 1807.

15 Erskine to Canning, July 31, to Berkeley, August 20, 1807.

16 Madison to Monroe, July 29, JM-LC, October 21, 1807. Erskine to Madison, October 18, Madison to Erskine, October 28, 1807, FO.

17 *ASP*, III, 13-18. Madison to Erskine, September 13, 1807, FO.

18 Madison to Jefferson, August 15 (rec'd), September 3, Jefferson to Madison, August 16, 1807, TJ-LC. Foster to Madison, September 20, 1807, VaU. Madison to Monroe, May 15, 1806.

[19] Madison to Jefferson, September 20, TJ-LC, Monroe to Madison, August 4 (*ASP*), 1807. Erskine to Madison, September 8, to Canning, October 5, Madison to Erskine, August 21, October 9, 1807, FO.

[20] Madison to Jefferson, September 21, 1807, TJ-LC.

[21] *Intelligencer*, October 5, 7, 19, 1807. J. C. Campbell, *Lives of the Lord Chancellors* (1875), IX, 6n.

[22] Jefferson, draft, Gallatin and Rodney, memos, *Writings* (Ford), IX, 145-166. Erskine to Canning, November 5, December 2, 1807.

CHAPTER XXVIII

(Pages 392 to 403)

[1] Erskine to Canning, October 5, 1807. Joy to Madison, August 25-26, October 5, 1807, JM-LC.

[2] *Anas*, October 22, Jefferson to T. M. Randolph, October 26, Dearborn to J. Crowninshield, December 2 (Essex Institute), Madison to Armstrong, October 18 (NA), 1807.

[3] *Intelligencer*, November 16, 20, 1807. *ASP*, III, 25.

[4] Gallatin to Jefferson, December 2, 1807. Madison to Gerry, February 19, March 13, 1806, Joy to Madison, October 11, 1807, JM-LC. Monroe to Madison, October 8 (Rives Papers), 10, 1807. *Intelligencer*, December 18, 1807.

[5] Jefferson, Madison, drafts of message, TJ-LC, 30603, 30612.

[6] Gallatin to Jefferson, December 18, Erskine to Canning, December 23, 1807.

[7] Williams to Pickering, January 1, 1808, MHS. Randolph to Nicholson, December 24, 1807, Nicholson Papers. Turreau to Champagny, December 30, 1807. Madison to Livingston, January 23, 1808, NYHS. G. Tucker, Memoir, 66, Wheaton to Madison, July 3, 1824, Rives Papers.

[8] Joy to Madison, October 5, 1807, JM-LC. *ASP*, III, 29-31.

[9] Adams, IV, 82-100. *Intelligencer*, November 16, 1807.

[10] Madison to Gates, March 24, to Jefferson, 26, May 25, 1794.

[11] Jefferson to Granger, January 22, 1808. Pichon to Talleyrand, July 22, 1801. Madison to Jefferson, September 14, 1805, TJ-LC.

[12] *Intelligencer*, November 13, 18, 20, 1805. Josiah Quincy to Wolcott, November 30, 1805, CtHS.

[13] Erskine to Canning, December 23, 1807. London *Chronicle*, January 27, 1808. Joy to Holland, February 3, 1808, Rives Papers.

CHAPTER XXIX

(Pages 404 to 418)

[1] *Intelligencer*, January 1, 6, 13, 15, 1808. Canning to Rose, October 24, 1807, AHA *Report*, 1936, III, 235. Rose to Canning, and exhibits, January 7, 17, 1808, FO 5, v. 56.

[2] *Ibid.* Erskine to Canning, December 2, 1807, January 28, 1808. Pink-

ney to Madison, December 31, 1807, Rives Papers. Foster to Lady Elizabeth, November 2, 1807, Foster Papers. Adams, IV, 185.

[3] Madison, Negotiations with Rose, JM-LC, XXXIII, 100, 106, 107; XC, 53; *Letters*, II, 411-421; *Writings*, VIII, 1-11. The true dates of Madison's notes are found by collating the manuscript with Rose's dispatches. The published notes also have such errors as "continental" for "*continual*" disobedience, unexpected "time" instead of "turn" of the negotiations, "harmony" for "humanity."

[4] Philadelphia *Gazette*, January 15, Jefferson to C. Thomson, January 11, Rose to Canning, January 18, 1808.

[5] Rose to Canning, January 21, 27, February 6, 1808. Madison, notes, *Writings*, VIII, 10-11 (misdated).

[6] Rose to Canning, January 30, 1808. Jefferson to Wirt, May 3, 1811. Besides naming Madison 102 times and Smith three times, Rose identified them by their titles seventeen and four times respectively. Of these four, only one concerned the negotiations.

[7] Adams, IV, 190. Edward Channing, *History of the United States*, IV, 396.

[8] Rose to Madison, January 26, to Canning, January 27, 30, February 3, 5, 6, 1808. Madison, Notes, January 29 (misdated February 1), February 2, 3, 4, 5, 1808, *Writings*, VIII.

[9] *Ibid.*, February 6, 8, 9, Rose to Canning, February 6, 9, 1808.

[10] Madison, Notes, February 14, 16, 17, 22, 25, Rose to Canning, February 16, 17, 25, 27, March 19, 1808. Madison to Rose, March 5, Rose to Madison, March 17, 1808, *ASP*. For Ratford see *ASP*, II, 17.

[11] Adams, IV, 187-194. Rose to Canning, February 6, 16, 25, 1808.

[12] Madison to Pinkney, April 4, 1808.

CHAPTER XXX

(Pages 419 to 440)

[1] Plumer, 634. N. Voss to Madison, March 20, July 8, 1806, JM-LC. L. Smith to Monroe, June 7, 1805, NYPL. Gallatin to Jefferson, October 13, 1806.

[2] Joy to Madison, January 28, 1808, JM-LC. Randolph to Nicholson, June 3, 24, 1806, Nicholson Papers. Randolph to Monroe, March 20, September 16, 1806, Monroe Papers. Madison to Monroe, May 15, 1806, Rives Papers. Monroe to Madison, September 13, 1806, NA.

[3] Randolph to Monroe, May 30, Tazewell to Monroe, *ca.* May 30, 1807, Monroe Papers. Randolph to Nicholson, May 31, Macon to Nicholson, December 2, 1807, Nicholson Papers.

[4] R. Livingston to Madison, July 12, 1807, Rives Papers. N. Y. *American Citizen*, January 25, February 24, March 2, 3, 1808.

[5] Randolph to Monroe, December 24, 1807, Monroe Papers. Gardenier to King, January 16, 1808, *King*, V, 58. Pickering to C. W. Ware, January 16, 1808, MHS.

[6] Richmond *Enquirer,* June 14, 28, 1808. Burwell, Memoir, 47. J. Clopton to A. McRae, December 25, 1807, Monroe Papers.

[7] *Enquirer,* January 23, 26, *Intelligencer,* January 29, February 1, 1808.

[8] *Intelligencer,* January 25, March 16, *American Citizen,* January 27, August 26, N. Y. *Public Advertiser,* September 7, Masters to Genet, March 29 (Genet Papers, LC.), 1808. (The 150 do not include Darby, who was dying, nor the clouded Senator Smith from Ohio.)

[9] J. G. Jackson to Madison, October 18, 25, November 20, 27, December 10, 25, 1807, January 7, 15, July 17, 1808, JM-LC.

[10] *Intelligencer, op. cit.* Jefferson to T. Randolph, January 26, 1808.

[11] M. Clay to Monroe, February 29, Wirt to Monroe, February 8, J. Taylor to Monroe, February 22, W. Jones to Monroe, January 18, 1808, Monroe Papers. Masters to Genet, *op. cit.* Erskine to Canning, March 8, 1808.

[12] Monroe Papers, XVII. 2916. Jefferson to Monroe, February 18, 1808. J. Minor to Monroe, March 10, 1808, Monroe Papers.

[13] George to D. Clinton, February 18, April 10, 1808, Columbia. G. Clinton to Van Cortlandt, February 20, March 10, 1808, NYPL.

[14] Richmond *Enquirer,* June 28, 1808.

[15] J. Q. Adams, *Diary,* March 19, 1808. H. Lee to Madison, February 10, 1808, JM-LC. Pickering to Peters, February 12, 1808, Essex Institute. Peters to Pickering, February 26, March 15, 1808, MHS. Foster to his mother, December 1, 1805, Foster Papers.

[16] *Intelligencer,* March 7, 1808. Monroe to Randolph, June 16, Randolph to Monroe, September 16 (Monroe Papers), 1806. Macon to Nicholson, March 1, 7, 1808, Nicholson Papers.

[17] *Aurora,* March 4, 10, 18, 28, June 4, 1808. Richmond *Argus,* March 11, 1808. Truxton to Tingey, Truxton to Madison, March 17, 1808, JM-LC. T. Leiper to Jefferson, (rec'd) August 18, 1808, TJ-LC.

[18] J. Main to Madison, March 7, April 18, 1808, JM-LC. *Public Advertiser,* March 16, April 5, 13, 1808. "H" to Madison, February 12, 20, 1808, Anonymous Letters to Madison, NYPL.

[19] Madison to Jefferson, May 11, 15, 1808, TJ-LC. D. Madison to Anna Thornton, May 18, to Anna Cutts, May 5, June 3, 1808, VaU. I. Coles Diary, June 10, 1808, LC. *Va. Gazette,* May 25, June 12, 1808.

[20] *American Citizen,* August 15, 1808, quoting *Farmers' Register.*

CHAPTER XXXI

(Pages 441 to 454)

[1] *Annals,* February 20, 22, 1808. *Intelligencer,* March 4, *Public Advertiser,* March 2, Richmond *Enquirer,* March 29, 1808.

[2] W. Pinkney to Madison, November 23, Armstrong to Champagny, November 12, 1807, ASP. Madison to Jefferson, February 25, 1808, TJ-LC. J. Q. Adams, *Diary,* February 26, April 11, 1808.

[3] Pickering to James Sullivan, March 9, 1808, *Pickering,* IV, 190. *Aurora,* March 16, 1808.

[4] J. Sullivan to Madison, April 12, 1808, Rives Papers. J. Randolph to Nicholson, March 28, 1808, Nicholson Papers. ASP, III, 80-220, 243-247.

American Citizen, March 23, N. Y. *Evening Post,* April 1, 1808, quoting
U. S. Gazette.

[5] *Public Advertiser* (quoting *True American*), June 29, Richmond *Enquirer,* April 15, *American Citizen,* April 4, N. Y. *Evening Post,* April 6, 8, 1808. Burwell to Jefferson, May 21, 1808, TJ-LC.

[6] *Intelligencer,* March 30, Baltimore *North American,* April 6, 1808.

[7] Champagny to Armstrong, January 15, Erskine to Madison, February 23, 1808, *ASP.* Jefferson, message, March 30, 1808.

[8] Madison to Armstrong, February 8-18, May 2, 1808.

[9] *American Citizen,* June 9 (Gray's circular), 25, 1808. *Annals* (Senate), April 16, 1808. J. Q. Adams, *Diary,* April 6, 15, 1808. Jefferson to Madison, March 11, Madison to Pinkney, April 30, 1808.

[10] Madison to Pinkney, February 19, March 8, 22 (NA), April 30, 1808. Erskine to Canning, April 26, May 2, 1808. Rose to Pickering, May 8, 1808, in H. Adams, *New-England Federalism,* 371. Pinkney to Madison, December 29, 1807 (Maryland Historical Society), February 17 (NA), April 25 (JM-LC), 1808. Washington *Monitor,* July 14, *Intelligencer,* July 11, 1808.

[11] Gallatin to Madison, May 10, 1808, Rives Papers. Erskine to Canning, June 4, 1808.

[12] Washington *Monitor,* June 16, *Intelligencer,* July 6, 25, 1808. S. Smith to Eustis, June 7, 1808, Eustis Papers, LC. Turreau to Champagny, July 1808, EU Supp., V, 255

[13] *Ibid.* Turreau to Champagny, June 28, 1808, EU Supp. V, 238. Madison to Armstrong, May 2, July 22, 1808.

CHAPTER XXXII

(Pages 455 to 468)

[1] Madison to Armstrong, July 22, to Pinkney, July 18, to Livingston (NYHS), July 18, Erskine to Canning, July 14, 1808.

[2] Madison to Jefferson, August 7, 1808 (misdated 1807), TJ-LC. *American Citizen,* August 2 ("Samuel Adams"), 10 (Cragg), *Public Advertiser,* August 4, *Intelligencer,* August 29 (quoting Binns's paper), 1808.

[3] Lewis to Madison, September 7, 1808, Rives Papers. *American Citizen,* July 2 (quoting Albany *Register*), Baltimore *North American,* July 27, August 19, September 9, 17, *Intelligencer,* August 24, 1808.

[4] Madison to Roland, April 1793. Brant, *Madison,* III, 373.

[5] *Public Advertiser,* August 3, 13 (quoting Albany *Register*), September 16, 21, 1808. Lewis to Madison, September 7, 1808, Rives Papers, Barlow to Jefferson, September 12, 1808, TJ-LC.

[6] Madison to Jefferson, August 10, September 14, 1808, TJ-LC. Madison to Gallatin, August 19, 1808.

[7] Graham to Madison, August 29, September 6, 1808, Rives Papers. *Intelligencer,* August 28, 29, September 2, 7, 1808.

[8] Gallatin to Madison, September 9, 1808, Rives Papers. *American Citizen,* July 30, August 17, *Aurora,* November 21, 1808.

[9] T. Tillotson to Madison, November 15, Lewis to Madison, November

14, 1808, Rives Papers. Randolph to Garnett, August 31, 1808, Randolph-Garnett Letters, LC. Marshall to C. C. Pinckney, October 19, 1808, Pinckney Papers, LC. *Intelligencer*, October 28, 1808.

[10] Jefferson to Gallatin, Madison to Jefferson, October 30, 1808, TJ-LC. Message, first draft, TJ-LC, 32344, final 20251; revisions, Madison, 32470-75, Gallatin, 32715-58, 32332, 32335. Jefferson, *Writings* (Ford), IX, 213*ff*.

[11] *ASP*, III, 221-232. *Aurora*, November 14, 26, 1808. *American Citizen*, November 18, 1808. J. White Jr. to Joseph Story, December 28, 1808, Story Papers.

[12] *Intelligencer*, November, December 1808.

CHAPTER XXXIII

(Pages 469 to 482)

[1] *ASP*, III, 228-232. *Anas*, November 9, Pinkney to Madison, September 21, Madison to Pinkney, November 9, 1808.

[2] Jefferson to Lincoln, November 13, Gallatin to Jefferson, November 15, R. Smith to Madison, November 17 (Rives Papers), 1808.

[3] Campbell's report said the stiffening of the Berlin Decree "was not known in England when the Orders in Council were issued." Pinkney wrote privately to Madison, December 7, 1807: "It is perfectly certain that the British government had no knowledge of this paper when the orders of council were issued." (Rives Papers).

[4] *Annals*, November 22, 1808. Gallatin, I, 435.

[5] Adams, IV, 368-369, 386-387, 392. Erskine to Canning, November 26, December 3, 4, 1808.

[6] Jefferson to Logan, December 27, 1808, to Eustis, January 14, 1809. Madison, memo on reply to Eustis, January 13, 1809, TJ-LC. Gallatin to Nicholson, December 29, 1808, Gallatin, I, 449.

[7] Madison to Pinkney, January 3, Erskine to Canning, January 1, 3, 1809. Adams, *Life of Gallatin*, 372.

[8] *Intelligencer*, January 16, 18, 1809. Canning to Pinkney, September 23 (separate), Pinkney to Canning, October 10, 1808, *ASP*. Erskine to Canning, January 26, Madison to Pinkney, February 10 (NA), 1809.

[9] S. Smith to Madison, January 19, 1809, Rives Papers. E. Bacon to Story, August 22, November 4, 5, 1808, Story Papers. Madison, memo on Story, VaU. *Annals*, January 24, 30-February 3, 1809.

[10] Bacon to Story, February 5, 1809, Story Papers. W. Nicholas to Madison, February 6, 1809, Rives Papers.

[11] Jefferson to T. M. Randolph, February 7, 1809.

[12] W. Nicholas to Madison, February 14, 1809, Rives Papers. E. Bacon to Story, February 26, 1809, Story Papers. J. Montgomery to Houston *et al.*, February 28, 1809, Maryland Historical Society.

[13] Resolutions, JM-LC, XXXVI, 68, 82. Huntington to Madison, March 2, 1809, Rives Papers.

INDEX

Political factions, 12, 85-86
Polk, Charles Peale, 50
Port au Prince, Haiti, 177
Preachers in politics, 19
Preble, Edward, 342
Presidential electors, how chosen, 13-14, 20; method of voting, 13, 14; of 1804, 434
Prince of Peace, *see* Godoy, Manuel de
"Protesters, the," 433
Public Advertiser, 437

Quincy, Josiah, 151, 335, 399

Randolph, Edmund, 356
Randolph, John, Alston affair, 233-234; and Madison, 313, 314, 315, 317, 319, 320, 351, 420, 433, 441-442, 444, 446; antagonism to Jefferson, 303, 304, 313; bribery, 317; Burr conspiracy, 349, 350, 353; Chase impeachment, 249, 250; desire for post in England, 310, 311, 313; Embargo Act, 395; for Monroe, 419, 421, 463; Mobile Act, 192, 193; newspaper attack on Jefferson and Madison, 370-371; opposes nonimportation, 316; personal appearance, 85, 232-233; rising leader, 85, 86; slanders Dolley Madison and sister Anna, 243, 322; Yazoo compromise, 237, 238
Randolph, Martha Jefferson, 167, 210, 289
Ratford, Jenkins ("fourth seaman"), 388, 413
Rawle, William, 189
"Reflections," Wilkinson, 203
Relf's Philadelphia Gazette, 211
Religious tyranny in New England, 19
Report of January 1800, 12
Richmond *Argus*, 435

Richmond *Enquirer*, 237, 352, 429, 431, 442, 445
Rigaud, Gen. ——, 62
Rives, William C., 13
Rives Papers, 25
Roberts, Sam, 345
Robespierre, Maximilien, 457, 459
Rochambeau, Donatien M. J., 177, 178, 179
Rodgers, Capt. John, 75, 78, 79, 305
Rodney, Caesar, 29, 352, 353, 356
Roland, Jean Marie, 459
Rose, Frances, 38, 39
Rose, George, letter to Pickering, 450; mission in *Chesapeake* dispute, 394-395, 404, 409-418, 445, 461; talks to Madison, 405, 441
Rose, Robert H., 38
Ross, Senator James, 119, 122, 127
Roux, Ernest, 358, 359
Rule of 1756, British, 294-295, 296, 297, 298, 299, 300
Rush, Dr. Benjamin, 301, 326
Rush, Richard, 301
Rutledge, John, Jr., 18

Sabine River, 286, 347
Sadeu, 75
Sadler, Henry, 222
St. Augustine, Fla., 96
St. Cyr, Laurent, 152
St. Domingo, American ships to, 270; bearing on Louisiana, 65, 78; blockade of, 176, 177; civil rights, American, 184; commerce with, 62-64, 76; Congress forbids trade with, 274; French-Spanish attack American commerce, 180; influence on Louisiana, 140; military keystone (French), 64-65; revolt, 62, 64, 74, 76, 79, 82, 93, 102; slave insurrection, 64, 76, 274, 275; trade, 92, 179, 184, 186, 273, 334; trade agreement sought, 275